D1165748

AND YET, I AM HERE!

AND YET, I AM HERE!

Halina Nelken

Translated by Halina Nelken

with Alicia Nitecki

UNIVERSITY OF MASSACHUSETTS PRESS   *Amherst*

Copyright © 1986 by Halina Nelken
English translation © 1999 by Halina Nelken
All rights reserved
First Polish-language edition, published by the Polish-
Canadian Publishing Fund, Toronto, 1987
First German-language edition, published by
Bleicher Verlag, Gerlingen, 1996
First English-language edition, published by the
University of Massachusetts Press, Amherst, 1999

All rights reserved
Printed in the United States of America
Designed by Mary Mendell
Printed and bound by BookCrafters, Inc.

Library of Congress Cataloging-in-Publication Data
Nelken, Halina.
[Pamietnik z getta w Krakowie. English] And yet, I am here! /
Halina Nelken ; translated by Halina Nelken with Alicia
Nitecki. — 1st English-language ed.   p. cm.
ISBN 1-55849-156-2 (cloth : alk. paper) 1. Nelken,
Halina—Diaries. 2. Jews—Poland—Kraków—Diaries.
3. Holocaust, Jewish (1939–1945)—Poland—Personal
narratives. 4. Kraków (Poland)—Biography. I. Title.
DS135.P63N46 1999   943.8'6—dc21   98-30275 CIP
British Library Cataloguing in Publication data are available.

The past—for the future

To my grandson, Jason,
and to his parents,
Helen and Les Nelken

CONTENTS

FOREWORD

While researching the history of the Polish Aryans, I came across some important polemics between Catholics and Protestants regarding painting at the time of the Reformation and the Counter Reformation in Poland. The editor of these volumes was Halina Nelken, whose scholarly works published in Poland I knew long before I met her in person in front of Widener Library.

She was brought to Harvard University by one of the most eminent art historians, Professor Jakob Rosenberg, as his assistant at the Graphic Art collection. While she worked at the Fogg Art Museum, she cooperated with me in reading together the sixteenth- and seventeenth-century texts in Polish and Latin and interpreting them with her profound knowledge of Polish history, art, and literature. Such was the beginning of our long intellectual friendship.

Her energetic and cheerful nature hardly let one suspect what she had gone through during World War II. She was an effective and beloved teacher, a respected researcher and author—but above all, she was a mother.

I witnessed the difficult struggle of a woman alone in a foreign land, raising her little son—the only family she had in the world. No matter how difficult the task, she succeeded. She told me that nothing could compare to Auschwitz, her measure of all things, and she mentioned her diary. I urged her to transcribe it. While reading it, I realized what a treasure it was, not only as a historical document, but also as a testimony of the unconquerable human spirit.

It touches us all, young and old, how this resourceful woman, unscathed by cruel depravity, evil, and hatred, survived with spirit, courage, and integrity.

George Hunston Williams
Hollis Professor of Divinity, Emeritus
Harvard University
Cambridge, Massachusetts
October 15, 1997

INTRODUCTION

Hundreds and perhaps thousands of Jews in the cities, towns, ghettos, and camps wrote memoirs and kept diaries during World War II—"they were journalists, writers, teachers, social activists, young people, and even children." Quoting the Warsaw ghetto historian Emmanuel Ringelblum, Dr. Jozef Kermisz from Yad Vashem reports with profound sorrow that most of the diaries vanished or were destroyed during the deportations, first uprisings, and fires. He supplies a long list of writers, social and resistance activists, whose diaries shared the tragic fate of their authors.

After the war, some of the miraculously saved survivors continued the mission and published their memoirs. But memoirs are not the journals or diaries written immediately during the events as they happened. Memoirs re-create the past through the prism of many years, enriched by additional information unknown to the author before. They are true, but the truth is controlled by the knowledge of later events that might distort the authenticity of their account.

Diaries of writers, politicians, and scholars are different from those written by children or very young girls, like Anne Frank. The journals of famous activists or leaders tend to be written "for posterity"; as a conscious legacy to future generations, they describe this tragic era to be ever remembered. The authors do not emphasize their personal experience, but the historical, social, political, and economic elements.

A diary of a young girl who was locked up in the ghetto and removed from normal life before it even began for her—such a diary is her true confessor. She confides to her diary her personal experiences, thoughts, hopes, and disillusionments, which she would not even share with her mother or her best friend. The general events are described and seen through her own experiences. The strength of the diary lies in its utterly personal context; it is an authentic, unfeigned, and purely human document. If a young but intelligent and sensitive author is also blessed by literary talent, then her personal diary becomes a priceless document of an epoch—of a life in a certain milieu, of one social class and the dramatic changes brought about by historical events.

Such a document is Halina Nelken's diary (awarded a competition prize by the Kraków Association in Israel). Written in the first person when she was fifteen, sixteen, and seventeen years old, it begins about a year before the war and continues during the German occupation and the creation of the ghetto in Kraków. Eventually, Nelken gave her diary away to a Catholic friend for safekeeping. In the ensuing years she began to write in the third person "for security reasons" (what naivety!), but mostly in the form of poetry which she read to other prisoners in the concentration camps of Płaszów, Auschwitz, Ravensbrück, Malchow, and Leipzig.

Like *The Diary of Anne Frank*, this is an intimate diary, full of the "secrets" of a young girl who, though intellectually mature, lacked experience of the world. Dynamic and full of life, she was hampered by being locked in the ghetto and also by her proper upbringing at home and her own instinctive inhibitions. Her dramatic inner conflict—and her rancor at her fate—emerge during the gradual downfall of her upper-class family, who were members of the Jewish intelligentsia and steeped in the Polish patriotic tradition. This happy and loving family was driven into poverty and total ruin. Against such background emerges the general demoralization of the young people, seeking escape in alcohol, and the quiet despair of the older generation, trying desperately to maintain human dignity against all odds.

Utterly sincere, though sometimes naive, Halina's conversation with her diary is supplemented by her later mature reflections on the past, written in Cambridge, Massachusetts, in the 1980s. This volume enriches the diarist literature of the German occupation with a priceless document of rare value and importance. It allows the reader and the historian of that period to comprehend more clearly the psychological plight of the people locked in the ghetto, through the personal experience and thorough self-analysis of a young girl.

Gideon Hausner
Chief Prosecutor of the
Eichman Trial in Jerusalem
and author of *Justice
in Jerusalem*

A small white bed with a net. The sounds of many voices, among them, a child's. "Is that her?"

Here, the smiling parents, and there, the grandmother holding a little boy by the hand. He hides his blond head in the folds of his grandma's mauve dress. "She has such big eyes, I am frightened when she stares at me." Laughter. "All infants have such wide open eyes. This is your little sister, Feluś. Are you afraid of Halinka?"

Felek's fright was a favorite family story. So was the revelation that my first words were not the usual "mama-tata," but "Titina, oh, Titina," a tune, fashionable at that time, which my nanny sang.

About ten years later, Felek and I pored over the family album and came upon photos of ourselves as babies, lying on white fur.

"I was afraid of you, Liliok"—that's what my brother called me.

"I remember."

"Don't be ridiculous. You just think you do, because they talked about it so often."

"I do remember," I persisted. "Grandma had a mauve dress and you a velvet suit."

Grandma stopped embroidering: "Wait . . . the mauve dress . . . the one from Vienna, that's right! Would you believe it?" she said to my mother, and both of them looked at me in wonder.

Perhaps, these really were only echoes of oft-repeated stories, but they constitute my earliest memories of my family—those stories and the images of four pairs of eyes: the violet-blue of my mother, the grayish blue of Grandma, and the green-blue of my father and brother.

My parents' bedroom was filled with Viennese furniture decorated with inlays of light blond wood. Evenings, the hanging lamp threw an elaborate design on the high ceiling and a soft glow over the spacious and cheerfully cozy room. There stood my bed. A wide-open door led to the combination dining and living room. Half the wall space opposite the door was taken up by an enormous credenza which looked like a mighty castle flanked by two turrets and decorated with carvings and little galleries. In the niche between them stood a statue of a horned Moses in a wind-blown gown, walking down Mount Sinai and carrying the tablets of the Ten Commandments. I was afraid of this dark and formidable sculpture. One night, the light from the other room woke me and I suddenly imagined that Moses was about to hurl those tablets at me. I jumped out of bed screaming. My parents came running. Shaken, I cried hysterically, clutching my mother tightly and glancing furtively at the frightening figure. Following my glance, Mama guessed: "That is what has scared the child! Moses must be removed from his throne!" My very tall father did not have any trouble reaching "Mount Sinai." With the sculpture in his upturned arm, his shadow, a giant shadow stretching from floor to ceiling, scared me even more.

A glass china cabinet replaced the big credenza, which was moved to another room. During the Second World War, this beautiful antique went to the Stieglitz Gallery on Rynek Główny, Main Square, which had been renamed Adolf Hitler Platz. But in my childhood, it stood in our living room. A watercolor by Fałat of a blue-white snow-covered village and a charming pastel of flowers by Wyczołkowski hung above it, and above the door a large "Landscape Before the Storm" with wheat sheaves in stacks on a stubble field, looking golden under a graying sky. The painting had been given to my grandmother by the artist Kamocki himself, I don't remember on what occasion. On the other wall galloped horses by Wojciech Kossak, not as highly prized as those by his father, Julius, but, on the other hand, his included uhlans and a lovely girl with lips like cherries. Near the cream-tiled stove ornamented with flower reliefs hung a large hand-colored etching of a palace surrounded by a park; in front of the palace stood carriages and, on the tree-shaded paths paraded ladies in crinolines and riders with their hounds. I would climb on a chair and follow the path with my finger "going" to the palace, till my nanny, Józka, chased me away. "Don't smudge the glass!" I also liked the thin slender dogs on the small tapestry above the piano embroidered by my mother after a Dutch painting. Between the windows smiled the jolly "Mallows" by S. Filipkiewicz, while a small T. Grott watercolor hid itself modestly away from the light. This one picture survived, and now, in my living room in Cambridge, Massachusetts, it radiates the tranquil rural charm of my native Poland.

The turn of the century art of "Young Poland" was as popular in the homes of the Kraków intelligentsia as Oriental carpets, oleander plants, or delicate asparagus fern in decorative vases, and bric-a-brac. The back of the china cabinet mirrored tiny animals carved in coral and ivory, decorated with gold or silver; animals of agate, amber, and venetian glass; graceful figurines of Meissen porcelain, and a little Hansel and Gretel house—the witch's house really—ornamented with shells of all kinds of shapes.

On the middle shelf stood rows of slender wine glasses; in the center, heavy mugs surrounded a tall pitcher made of thick dark green glass and, on it, the crimson coat-of-arms of Poland and Lithuania. This pitcher was just level with my head when Grandma explained to me that the Crown, or the White Crowned Eagle, means Poland, while "Pursuit," the knight with a raised sword galloping on horseback, symbolizes Lithuania. I always associated the union of Poland and Lithuania not with the famous painting by Jan Matejko, but with this, my grandfather's antique pitcher.

A silver carriage filled with small crystal spice bottles ruled over the lower shelf. For family celebrations, or at holidays, the carriage appeared on the table in a glow of candles in a tall silver candelabra and in smaller crystal candlesticks. Adorned all around with pendants in the shape of prisms, they threw rainbow sparks on the Viennese porcelain dinner service for twenty-four. This extravaganza of cups, plates, sauceboats, serving dishes was a wedding present of my Mother's—taken out of the bottom of the china cabinet for such festivities. During the war, Józka took that service to her country home in Łagiewniki, and after our return from the camps, she served soup on those plates to my mother and me, but for now, the tureens, sugar and salad bowls stood on the bottom of the china cabinet.

Sometimes we were allowed to play with the treasures from the top shelf. I arranged them carefully on the Oriental carpet turned into the garden of a fairy tale palace. On another continent, first my little son, and then my little grandson, arranged on that same carpet—now the jungles of an as-yet un-discovered planet—their mechanical robots, space ships, and plastic astro-nauts known to them from TV. But then, in Kraków, in addition to my toys, Felek's armies of tin soldiers marched across the carpet, attacking my for-tresses of cards or dominoes defended by chess pieces.

Our favorite tent was under the round table covered with a fringed Turkish throw. When cousins or friends came to visit, we built a second tent out of overturned armchairs covered by another Oriental throw taken from the piano. Such games did not last long; soon all the mothers, or our nanny, Józka—and she the most effectively—returned order to the room.

Mama and Grandma had the best method for calming down rambunctious children, even if those children were only Felek and me: songs, poems, and reading out loud. We sang folksongs and carols together. Felek, who played by ear, immediately harmonized the accompaniment. We sang all kinds of mu-sic. When Grandma began her repertoire of German "Lieder" and "Sorrento," Mama would joke: "Oh-ho! Grandma is getting sentimental again!" But she, too, like us, "felt love in her heart again," and begged to "return to Sorrento!"

Reading usually took place on the green velvet sofa in Grandma's room. We looked at the illustrations as we listened to "The True Fairy Tales" of the Brothers Grimm and Andersen, and the Polish poem, "Mr. Kitty was ill and lay in bed." And then, after those, to "Kichuś Majstra Lepigliny" and Julian Tuwim's poems. When Kichuś wandered in from Kraków to Cambridge and she was the one who read now to my son, Mama reminisced about those times. Both Felek and I liked these books even after we had progressed to other readings—*Robinson Crusoe, David Copperfield*, Konopnicka, and Mickiewicz. We heard Mickiewicz so many times that we recited whole passages of it by heart.

Grandma's old illustrated weeklies and albums with views of cities and famous relics were the best amusement whenever we were not well, I especially. By contrast with my big brother, I was a sickly child. Felek was the picture of health, a smiling fatty, always happy with life. When he went to *Gimnazium*, high school, he suddenly thinned out, but for now, round and rosy as an apple, he was the pride and the joy and the sunshine of the entire family. He was well liked by the boys in school, with whom he skated and sledded, collected stamps, played chess and dominoes—everything entertained him, but most of all Felek liked to play piano, to read books, and to eat good food. Nothing bothered him, but almost everything bothered me, even the bows tied in my hair. Except for batiste, everything itched, and I could not even move in starched dresses. Every meal was a torture for me, every bite stuck in my throat and no medicine, no walks in the parks could improve my appetite. I was called "Little Green Frog," a fragile flower eternally confined to bed by different illnesses.

I remember scarlet fever, the dimmed night-light, my parents watching over my bed. Father carried me in his arms whenever I cried out in a high fever. I did not have the strength to lift my head, so my mother fed me lemonade through a straw and softly sang a folksong about a servant and animals. It was long enough to keep me quiet for half a night. During my convalescence, Felek made cutouts and played chess with me and didn't tease me as he usually did, knowing that "the child has to be pampered," but even more than that, because I gave him the sweets and the delicacies which had been brought to me as presents. I still could not even look at food.

In secret from my mother, Józka brought up Mrs. Heller, a neighbor from downstairs, and the two of them "warded off the evil eye" by floating a piece of bread and a burned-out match in a glass of water. They rubbed my forehead, my chest, and my wrists; Józka crossed herself and prayed to the Virgin Mary; Mrs. Heller gibbered something in Yiddish. They placed the glass of water under my bed for twenty-four hours. If the bread fell to the bottom, a man, if the match, a woman, had cast the evil eye on me, and, in either case, it would be gone by tomorrow. My father found this glass and was furious. To avoid "making a fool of the child," he poured the water out and we never did discover who had given me the evil eye.

The doctor who saw me through all my childhood illnesses was petite, elegant, high-heeled Dr. Blankstein. Her French heels tapping, she paid house calls; took the stethoscope out of her big doctor's bag; listened attentively to my lungs; prescribed iron and cod liver oil. I hated both. For checkups and shots I walked to her office in the health center nearby. The waiting room was full of small patients, crowded with crying children brought there by ladies in fur coats and fancy hats or by women bundled up in shawls.

After I had finally pulled through endless childhood sicknesses under the watchful eye of Dr. Blankstein, I graduated to the care of Dr. Alexander Bieberstein, who had cured our whole family of sore throats, coughs, or upset stomachs for years, and who knew us children from birth. Actually, no one was really seriously ill, not even that "older lady," Grandma, who took the waters in Karlsbad and mineral waters at home, and who suffered from "blood sugar" and "acids"—we were always surprised that the one did not cancel out the other. Sometimes she felt a twinge of arthritis, so, for one of her birthdays, Felek and I painted an elaborate scroll for her inscribed with a verse of our own composition:

Dear Grandma!
Don't ever again
moan in pain
from an arthritic arm!
Live to be a hundred
happy and calm!

Grandma put this scroll in the secretary in her room for safekeeping. This was a most beautiful piece of furniture, with inlays of colored wood and little drawers in which there were even more little drawers and secret compartments. Over the secretary hung a large portrait of Grandfather Fabian Barber wearing a frock coat and a fancy scarf tied under his high collar. It was from him that Uncle Ignacy, his son Mietek, and I inherited our copper blond hair and a light complexion which never tans.

"My deceased husband, a fighter in the January Uprising against Russia in 1863!"—Grandma would proudly announce to the uninitiated. "A delegation of veterans and their orchestra attended his funeral and played funeral marches and patriotic songs up to the gateway of the cemetery on Miodowa Street."

His pale marble gravestone was adorned with a Polish eagle. After Grandma died in 1935, I would visit the cemetery with Mama on the anniversary of her death, or on holidays, or just for the sake of it, bringing flowers. Under the viaduct of the railway which stood in front of the cemetery gates, Jewish beggars stretched out their hands and clamored for alms. I dreaded their pleas, *rach-*

munes, rachmunes. On the other side of the gates, it was peaceful. Shaded by old trees, the cemetery itself was not at all frightening. The gravestones along the alleys were engraved with names familiar to me from the nameplates of Kraków lawyers, doctors, stores, or institutions. My grandfather's slender monument was reflected, as in a dark mirror, in a huge block of polished black marble—the gravestone of Dr. Ozjasz Thon, congressman to the Polish Sejm.

The Germans overturned and destroyed the gravestones in Jewish cemeteries, but whoever survived the Second World War and returned to Poland searched for their families in the cemeteries—and we did, too. The white monument with the Polish eagle was gone. Marian, the janitor from our house, had replaced it with a modest granite block. The gilded inscription to my grandfather's heroic past had given way to a simple "Rozalia and Fabian Barber" and a list of names of the members of our immediate family from Kraków who had been victims of Hitler.

Only after the death of my mother, who had been buried in the foreign soil of America, did I realize the significance of the phrase, "place of eternal rest." It hurt me that she was not in Kraków with her own people where, perhaps, that eternal rest would have been less lonely. In an atavistic gesture, I gathered a handful of soil from her grave and brought it to the Kraków cemetery, and the soil that I had collected from around my grandparents' monument in Kraków, I scattered around my mother's grave in West Roxbury, Massachusetts.

The youngest of her siblings, my mother had been just a little child when her father died. She knew him mostly—as we did—from the stories our grandmother told. She would take the opportunity of such occasions to teach us, her grandchildren, to recite patriotic odes and to sing national songs.

Grandfather had studied in Vienna—when he wasn't busy fighting in some revolution or war. He even made his way into Turkey, from whence came our Oriental carpets and tapestries. He had distinguished himself in the January Uprising, and my grandmother, as his widow, received a lifelong pension from the Polish government.

Grandfather eventually settled down in Kraków, married, and managed the breweries of Baron Götz. He was obviously an open-minded man, free of old-fashioned prejudices, since he took care to educate and to find professions for all his children, daughters as well as sons—and he had quite a number of offspring, by several wives! The women gave birth and gave birth and gave birth—and then died. The children grew up, went off on their own, had their own families, immigrated to foreign lands—and Grandfather searched for another wife. He found her in a teenage orphan.

My grandmother Rozalia, born Herstein, must have been very beautiful. Even in her seventies, with her clear porcelain skin and pale blue eyes, she was still charming. Her immediate family had died during an epidemic of cholera-morbus, when—and we listened in fear—men, looking like ghosts in their protective clothing, used long hooks to pull the corpses out of homes and throw them into wagons filled with lime. The orphaned girl had relatives of some kind outside of Kraków, but she was bewildered and lost, so she certainly must have been grateful for the serious attentions of an elderly gentleman. No doubt he loved her. He also gave her status—he was worldly, well situated, and represented security. He cared for her like a father, but he was evidently still virile, since Grandma bore him seven children. Two of them died in infancy, but a boy and four girls grew up healthy to the great joy of their young mother, soon to become a widow.

I wondered why Grandma never got married again. "It was a different time," my mother explained. "Grandma received a large pension from Baron Götz after her husband died, and stipends for each child's education. The whole family was well provided for. A second marriage would have canceled out all these privileges. In those days only Croesus could have offered marriage to a woman burdened with five children!"

And so, as the respected widow of Fabian and the owner of real estate with a garden, Grandma had a secure, comfortable living. Each year she vacationed in spas abroad. In Kraków, she had a season ticket to the Słowacki Theater— in those times there was a new premiere each week. She educated all her children well and saw her daughters married to good husbands. Was hers just a narrow, circumscribed, small, middle-class world? Perhaps it was. But how much more peaceful it was than the unlimited personal freedom of our time. Grandma was not lonely. She had a circle of mostly female friends and a large and loving family. I knew them from old photographs in the fancy albums Grandma allowed me to look at whenever I was miserable in bed with one of my endless childhood illnesses.

My grandmother's only son, Ignacy, studied at the Polytechnics in Lwów/ Lemberg and Vienna and earned his engineering degree just as World War I broke out. As a military engineer, he blew up bridges on the first line of the Russian front. Badly wounded, he was taken prisoner and deported to somewhere near Kiev. As soon as he was able to walk again, he escaped and wandered back through "the flames of revolution" and across the vast Russian empire (which was just about to fall apart) to Poland and to his home in Kraków. There he founded his engineering firm and married lovely Aunt Dora. Their first two children died in infancy, but Mietek and Jurek grew up healthy—for Hitler. Mietek survived World War II only to die a few years later of complications from the severe beatings he suffered in a concentration camp.

The oldest daughter, Bronka, though otherwise good natured, had a quick temper, and Grandma thanked God that she married early and moved to Słovakia. Her Hungarian husband, Ferdinand Heda, owned a Viennese chocolate factory. For every holiday and birthday we received parcels of delicious candies, baskets of marzipan fruit, Santas and figurines in colorful tin foil. I remember a chocolate rooster so big and heavy that I, just a little girl then, could not hold it in my hands.

Aunt Bronka visited us often: a large vigorous woman, exuberant. She used to laugh herself to tears. She taught me some patriotic songs, but also—to Grandma's indignation—some naughty ones from the cabaret.

I must have been about four years old when I encountered her quick temper on our vacation visit to her villa in Słovakia. I remember that rosebushes bloomed in large pots on the patio and velvety pansies encircled tall trees in the garden where I loved to play. My aunt walked with me over to the gazebo at "high tea" time. I do not remember why I was cranky; perhaps it was too hot and my starched embroidered dress made me uncomfortable. But I sat down among the pansies and, looking at her with defiance, refused to move—by temperament we were obviously related. Aunt Bronka lost patience and spanked me.

I screamed to high heaven and ran to my mother who was sitting in the gazebo. Safe on her lap, like an evil witch from a cruel fairy tale by Grimm, I threatened my aunt between my sobs: "When I am big, I am going to climb with you up to the top of the tallest mountain, and then I am going to push you down, and when you have killed yourself, I am going to laugh!"

Instead, it was my aunt who laughed, so hard that tears flowed down her cheeks. My mother looked at me, disgusted: "Shame on you for being so cruel! Stop crying at once!" But I wept and wept, gaining myself the nickname, "Little Witch," until finally I felt sorry for my aunt and hugged and kissed her.

Bronka had three daughters, all pretty, but Lilly, the youngest, was a strikingly beautiful brunette with creamy skin. Young Ribbentrop, the son of Hitler's high dignitary, fell in love with her. Lilly's parents strongly opposed his romantic advances, but who knows? Perhaps this romance might have saved Lilly's life. The whole family perished a few years later in Theresienstadt. All, except the oldest daughter, Margit, who was in hiding in Słovakia with her son Peter.

Aunt Helen I knew only from her photograph and Grandma's accounts, which were always cut short by her deep sigh and suppressed sobs. My grandmother's most beloved daughter had been unusually talented. All the sisters attended the best girls' school, St. Scholastica, but only Helen's report card received awards every year. Her behavior was "laudable" and every subject "excellent." Her needlework, embroidery, and drawing were "neat and imaginative," her voice was "melodious." But above all, her mind was "precise and logical." At a time when women had great difficulty even gaining entry into the exclusively male professional world, Helen, a quiet, responsible young lady, soon excelled, becoming a leading employee in a renowned import-export firm. She was also beautiful, "like a cameo," as they used to say then. Young gentlemen sent her flowers; they serenaded her on summer evenings, they played violin and sang. Sitting on the balcony, Grandma would be moved to tears by their sentimental music, but Helen would just listen quietly to the Schumann or Schubert and caress her little black dog.

Bernard from Vienna fell madly in love with Helen. "He was very handsome, but he couldn't compare to a girl like Helen with her intellect and talent," Grandma would say with a disdainful shrug of her shoulders. "But it is true that he really adored her. He showered her with flowers, perfumes, and expensive gifts. He knelt in front of her and finally won her heart. He threw himself at my feet, begged me for her hand, swearing that he could not live without her, that he would wait on her hand and foot."

Helen married Bernard and moved to Vienna where he, the "Shoe King," provided her with every luxury. Nurses took care of their son, Fritz, and their daughter, Doddy, while Helen invited all her siblings and most often my Grandmother to visit.

"We boarded the express train in Kraków and a few hours later, dressed in elegant gowns and jewels, we went to the opera or the Burgtheater. Helen liked opera and drama but could sometimes be talked into an operetta." At this point, my grandmother and my mother would both begin to sing arias from *The Merry Widow* or *The Gypsy Baron.* Sometimes they attempted *Madame Butterfly* or *The Jewess,* while from the adjoining room my father would bellow the tragic final aria, "Rachel, now I myself lead you to the stake." Who would have thought that real flames would soon blaze for Jewish daughters and sons?

Tragedy struck earlier in Helen's happy family. Summoned by telegram to a private clinic in Vienna, my grandmother found her beloved daughter in agony. "Mama! Mama!" called poor Helen, not conscious that her mother was already there, combing her golden brown hair which hung in two braids down to the floor on each side of the bed. Bernard was kissing his wife's feet tenderly. Oblivious to his children, he wanted to commit suicide at the moment of her death. "No one will ever take her place," he swore, and indeed, he never married again. A housekeeper and a governess took care of his home and children.

Their son, Fritz, completed his medical degree just before Hitler's Anschluss of Austria and traveled through Czechoslovakia on his way to Belgium, where Bernard and Doddy were already living. He stayed with Aunt

Lola in the Sudetenland and began to practice medicine while waiting for his Belgian visa to arrive. Hitler, however, arrived first. In order to save her illegal Austrian nephew, Aunt Lola quickly rushed him to Prague and returned home to find her children, Gyury and Wally, gone. The Zionist Żabotyński had taken them to Palestine. Lola had not had the chance to say good-bye to them. She never saw them again, but their lives had been saved.

Fritz's visa never arrived. He perished in Theresienstadt.

Of all my mother's sisters, Aunt Lola was the one I knew and loved the best. She was also the sister closest to my mother, for there was only a three-year difference between them. Lola and my mother had to wear hand-me-downs from their older siblings, and Mama, being the youngest, was in the worst situation. When my mother was still marching to St. Scholastica in her navy blue uniform along Planty—a circular park where the medieval walls of the ancient center of Kraków had stood—Bronka and Helen were already married.

When the time came for Lola's first debutante ball, Mama was left at home, like Cinderella, because it was not appropriate for younger daughters to be seen in society before the older ones were at least engaged. My mother wept bitterly and waited at the window until early morning, when the carriage bearing the family returned home. Uncle Ignacy in a tailcoat and top hat, the escort of his mother and sister, jumped down first and gallantly helped them to the door. After having danced all night, Lola immediately kicked off her high-heeled pumps, and Grandma took off her corset with similar relief.

I knew all about those ball gowns, tulles, veils, ribbons, silk flowers, and elbow-long gloves from photographs. My grandmother kept their lace shawls, fans, and purses in a round box, together with the faded dance cards of her girls. "They were all very popular, not one of them was ever a wall flower, not for a single dance," my grandmother boasted, "and your mother was spotted high up in the balcony, when I gave in to her once and allowed her to watch the masquerade before she was a debutante!"

On that occasion, my mother had looked down from the balcony and admired the ballroom and Lola, whose healthy, fresh beauty and blond braids were perfect for her Cracovian peasant girl costume. The room swarmed with princesses and knights, odalisques, wizards, countesses in crinolines, fairies, nymphs, and gladiators. Grandma, in a black lace gown, had to sit out with the other matrons, keeping an eagle eye on who was dancing with whom, and at what distance, and making sure that no couple disappeared into a side room without a chaperone.

Just when the slow music of the last waltz changed into the fast rhythm of a white mazurka, Grandma, to her horror, spotted my mother cheerfully dancing in the arms of an unknown young man in an artist's cloak! He had noticed my mother on the balcony, rushed up there, and asked her for a dance. Mama explained in vain that she was just an onlooker in an everyday dress (a hand-me-down from Helen and Lola, at that). "I am not in costume, either. I am a student at the Academy of Fine Arts! Painter H.B.," he introduced himself and kidnapped her for the dance.

"You will never go with us again!" Grandma raged. "Wait your turn."

It did not take too long for Mama's turn to come. Another fiery Hungarian married Lola and took her to the Sudetenland. He owned an artistic portrait studio in Turoczent Marton. There he immortalized all four sisters sitting together at a table covered with a kilim. All of them have expressive eyes and elaborate coiffures, all wear chains with pendants. There is a clear family likeness among them, but individual differences, too. Lola is feminine and charming; Bronka, complacent in her authority and mature fullness; my girl-ish mother with smiling eyes, so slender that she is just half of Bronka; and Helen in a graceful pose, tranquil, yet serious.

I was scared of this studio with its large cameras covered by black sheets. The painted backdrops showed a park with a pond and swans, the terrace of some palace, a romantic stream in a forest, the interior of an elegant drawing room. The furniture was real: mahogany armchairs and overstuffed sofas, small tables with long slender legs and bouquets of artificial flowers. There were also platforms of every height; I remember sitting on one of them with a big ball on my knees, wearing a raspberry-colored silk dress with a white bow on my shoulder. The harsh glare of a reflector lamp dazzled my eyes. I was close to tears. Aunts tried to make me smile, yet when my uncle disappeared beneath the black sheet, I froze. My nanny had this photograph and showed it to me after the Second World War. There I am, desperately clutching a ball, with my hair smoothly combed into a pageboy, wearing forget-me-not ear-rings, and with my eyes wide open in terror and my mouth turned down.

A few years before the Second World War, Grandma jumped out of bed in the middle of the night and woke up my parents. "Something terrible has happened to Lola." From my bed, I saw Grandma wringing her hands and nervously pacing to and fro in her room. In the morning a telegram arrived from Lola informing us of the sudden heart attack and death of her husband. My father accompanied Grandma to the funeral.

It was not only Grandma who had had a premonition. Lola's husband had, unexpectedly, given their daughter Wally her birthday present a week early, handing her a little gold watch as he kissed her goodnight. A few hours later he was dead.

Latzi, Lola's oldest son, became the head of the family, taking care of his mother and younger siblings and providing for them. He is the one who had made the difficult decision to send his little brother and sister away to a kibbutz in Palestine, while he stayed behind with his mother. Aunt Lola wrote desperate letters to my mother saying that her precious little daughter was peeling potatoes in a kitchen like an ordinary servant. My parents sent the children parcels of goodies, because it was easier to do so from Poland than from Czechoslovakia, which Hitler had annexed to the German Reich. Afterwards, it was the other way around: Lola mailed parcels to us in the Kraków Ghetto from the Sudetenland. Latzi got married, but he did not leave his mother. Lola later perished in Theresienstadt, together with her devoted, noble son and his young wife.

When Bronka, Hela, and Lola were already happily married, my mother grew up and developed into a long-legged, slender stick—just at a time when feminine charm depended on wide hips and abundant breasts! After graduating from the St.Scholastica school, she attended private courses for young ladies. Every morning on her way through Planty, she would find, on a particular bench, a small bouquet of spring flowers, mostly violets "to match her eyes," said the note hidden among the flowers. On a neighboring bench, a young student looked up furtively from the book he was pretending to be reading to check whether his declarations of love were reaching the right girl. Their innocent romance ended with the young man's departure to a university abroad.

Mama never forgot this dark-eyed Henry, and fell sick with misery. Grandma took her to Marienbad, and after their return, she and Uncle Ignacy declared that they needed to find her a practical profession rather than to allow her to study history in courses for young ladies.

A doctor of dentistry whom they knew gladly took my mother on as an intern and put her into a small laboratory at the back of his office, where she would learn all the secrets of dental technique. And so, among false teeth and broken dentures, the girl with a broken heart nearly died of disgust. Unnaturally perfect teeth set in grinning red gums! Bridges shining with gold and silver! The sound of the drill and the moaning patients! Mama came home with a migraine, crying that she was going to commit suicide, that she would rather be an office worker, because at least in an office one had contact with people.

So what could they do? They sent her off to learn bookkeeping, correspondence, typing, and stenography. Within a year, she was promoted from assistant secretary to secretary to the board of directors. She enjoyed a certain financial independence. In keeping with custom, she turned her salary over to Grandma, who gave her a weekly allowance for "small expenses." Her expenses were not always small. My mother told me with pride how she bought herself a blouse adorned with lace, a navy blue velvet suit, and a "Rembrandtesque" beret with a white feather. "That Rena, what an elegant girl she is," boasted the matrons who sat with Grandma at the outside cafe, Maurizio's, while the young people strolled outside and an army orchestra played in the Rynek Główny, the Main Market Square. It was there that the beautiful beret was blessed by a Kraków pigeon flying overhead. My mother cried out in shame and annoyance. "It's nothing, it's just for good luck!" said an Austrian officer who was passing by, and, making a deep bow, he handed her a bouquet of roses from the flower stand on the corner. My mother's dislike of pigeons probably dated back to that episode, although she loved animals and birds, particularly dogs and sparrows.

Social promenades included Planty and Błonia outside the center of the city. Public exhibitions were held in special pavilions along the avenues there. My mother went there often as well. During one of these walks along the avenues, a friend escorting the young ladies stopped in front of a tall, dark-haired gentleman in a black suit.

"The eyes of girls in Vienna drown in tears when you, *Herr Baron*, are in Kraków! Beware, ladies! This is our wittiest, most dangerous flirt, Mr.Edmund Emanuel Nelken!"

"Baron?" asked my Mama, impressed.

"Of course not. The baron's name is spelled Nöllken." A slight smile revealed a dimple in his chin and another in his cheek. But soon the blue eyes in his pale face turned sad and serious again. He bowed politely and returned to the older couple on the bench.

"And this is supposed to be the funny, witty, joyful Nelken, the life of every party?" asked my mother in amazement. Her companion explained: "He's in mourning. He just lost his grandfather who raised him from childhood." On an impulse, my mother ran to the bench: "I am so sorry! Please, accept my deepest condolences."

The older lady in black looked my mother up and down, from her Rembrandt-beret to her fashionable high-heeled, buttoned shoes. She smiled in approval and tactfully decided to see the exhibition with her husband. "And you, Mundek, take a nice walk in the fresh air with Miss Barber."

This was my parents' first meeting, and the older lady was my dear Aunt Mala, who told me all about it.

My father was one of the "Galician Nelkens" from Lemberg and Brody. He had been an infant when his father was killed in a railroad accident. His mother died shortly afterwards. The two small orphaned boys, Leopold and Edmund Emanuel, were taken to Kraków to the home of their grandfather, a knowledgeable and respected man whose advice was sought by Jews and non-Jews alike. His picture hung in the bedroom over my father's night table. He always remembered him with great love and esteem. The grandfather sent young Edmund to business school in Vienna where, in time, my father was employed by the bank in Praterstern. Vienna was a great city in which to study and to work—and to play and flirt with lovely girls. After the death of his beloved grandfather, my father matured quickly. Instead of returning to the carefree life of a Viennese bachelor, he joined the Polish Legions organized by Marshal Józef Piłsudski and went to war against Russia. When the Polish Legionnaires were incorporated into the Austrian army in 1916, my father was sent to the Italian front. Badly wounded in the battle of the Isonzo River, he was transported to a hospital in Vienna. My mother went to see him whenever she visited her sister. Toward the end of the First World War, my father returned to Kraków ready to get married. Shortly before the wedding, at the Press Ball, their engagement was almost broken. In a photograph, they stand affectionately cheek to cheek, hand in hand, Mama in a fashionably short, shiny taffeta dress, father in tail coat and with a carnation in his lapel, both obviously very much in love. Smiling naughtily, my mother told us the story.

During a waltz, the couples changed partners, and Father—a famous ladies' man—was paired with an actress, a famous femme fatale. After a while, Mama lost interest in dancing and asked her partner to escort her to their table, while Father led the actress in a Charleston and a shimmy and a passionate tango. The music stopped at the announcement of a competition for the "Queen of the Flowers," and the dancing couples turned toward the podium. The actress graciously climbed up the stairs, followed by my father, while poor Mama grew more furious with every minute. The actress reached the podium and posed against the column, ready to be crowned, while my father, dashing toward her with a basket of roses, stumbled and fell down the stairs, scattering the flowers. My mother's loud, uncontrollable laughter disrupted the silence preceding the announcement of the queen of the ball. She could not stop laughing even when her fiancé, whose leg was broken, was helped into a carriage to go to the hospital.

"Cut it out! You're heartless!" Father was incensed. "I am!" said Mama, "but I am here with you, while your actress is shimmying with other men!" She was angry, but not for long, knowing that deep down this bon vivant was a kind, responsible, and devoted family man.

They got married and lived with Grandma in an apartment on one entire floor of the house Grandpa had built for her. My mother, and then, my brother Felek and I were born in this house with a garden. Neither of us inherited our father's dimples in our chins and our cheeks, but my grandson, Jason, did.

The fifteenth-century chronicler Jan Długosz unwittingly predestined me to become a historian. Home to me was Długosza 7, a short, cheerful street between Kalwary, jingling with blue trolley cars, and the stone chapel by the entrance to Serkowski Place in front of which, on evenings in May, little old women, maids, and children prayed, and sang the Loretta Litany and "Praise the Maytime Meadows." Nearby on Planty, chestnut trees and wild lilacs bloomed around the memorial on the little island. Children played there, and I, too, poured sand with a little yellow spade into a yellow pail decorated with flowers. I pushed my doll Kizia in her pram there, and everybody remarked how big she was and that her eyes shut. Grandma had brought her back from Karlsbad. I rolled my hoop, rode on my scooter, and jumped rope on that island, or else caught circles made out of colored willow onto a rod, also of willow. As we played, we sang, "The circle goes round and always comes back," and other songs.

My nanny sat on the bench with the other nannies and they told each other horror stories: that someone threw acid into someone's eyes out of revenge; that someone poisoned himself with iodine; that this was the island of suicides, because a young couple had committed suicide here with shots from a revolver. The oldest of the children, Janka, explained to us what that meant, and after that I never wanted to play on Planty.

I used to go with my nanny to Podgórski Park or to Krzemionki, and so that I wouldn't get bored she used to take my friends from Długosza Street along, Anda, Stefa, and her older sister, Janka. Those heights gave onto a beautiful view of Kraków. We ran on the rocks and gathered flowers and wove them into wreaths, while my nanny darned socks and sang all the verses of an interminable song about a mountaineer and his girl. Whenever Felek and his friends came with us, we played with a ball or looked for small, empty snail shells. On the way home, Nanny would stop by the Church of the Redeemer on Krzemionki. Once, when I was still just a little girl and we both went into the darkened interior of the main nave, bells rang, the organ boomed, Nanny knelt down, and I nearly fainted, I was so overwhelmed. No other church except that one ever filled me with fear: not the enormous Mariacki Church, not the high Romanesque church of St. Andrew on Grodzka Street, and never, never, the parish church on Podgórski Market Square, which we stepped into if we went home the other way by the park. The entrance was at the top of many steps because that slender Neo-Gothic structure had been built on uneven ground with its back to the Krzemionki Heights.

If there were decorated droshkies at the front, spectators often waited on the steps for the wedding procession, curious to see whether the bride was crying. Normally, however, both my nanny and I blew our noses with emotion when the organs blared out, "Veni Creator Spiritus," and at the altar, the bride in white and a veil rose from her knees. The bride and groom would then walk over to the *Secesja* photography establishment nearby at the Rynek Podgórski, the Podgórski Market Square, which had immortalized entire generations of babies on white fur, in first communion dress, in wedding attire, and on identification cards.

Going home from the Market Square on the sunny, right-hand side of Kalwary Street, we first passed by Pan Lewkowicz's ironmongery, where there were always lots of peasants who had come from the neighboring villages in their farm wagons. Nails and padlocks were sold here, and keys were cut. Tolek Lewkowicz was in the same class as Felek, and his sister Runka in the same one as I. They both had pale complexions, dark hair, and gray-blue eyes. We played together, ice-skated in the park, and once on vacation in Muszyna. Tolek played in the school orchestra on an enormous helicon, to the despair of his parents and neighbors. When he graduated from the gimnazium he went to Palestine and then became an electrical engineer on a freighter. Of the whole family only his mother survived, and after the war I gave her a photograph of Runka cut out of a group picture of our elementary school class.

Next came Jadowski's, the large grocery and spice store. Grandma liked to choose coffee and tea here rather than riding to Szarski's in the Rynek Główny, as my mother did. Marian Jadowski was also a schoolmate of Felek's. The wares in the grocery store were not interesting, but the ones in the next shop were worth admiring—fluffy woolens, shiny silks, a mannequin in gold lamé at Mardi gras time, velvets, laces, brocades. Right next door was Medan, with a magnificent display of footwear. We looked with great interest at the pumps with French heels, especially the gold and silver evening shoes decorated with sequins, similar to ones Papa brought home from Vienna as presents for Mama. Unfortunately, they rubbed, so with some difficulty our maid, Janka, squeezed them onto her own wide feet and hobbled around on them all afternoon so that Mama could dance in them at the ball that night.

And finally, Cyzer's drugstore on the corner. I liked to come here with my mother or my grandmother to buy soap, toothpaste, Chypre, California Poppy, or Nivea cream. It smelled nice in there, and I'd be given fragrant little boxes and sometimes a tiny little soap.

On the other side of the street, opposite the military barracks, stood the large building containing butchers' shops, and I couldn't look at the never-ending rows of bloody flitches of something that had once been a cow, a pig, or a calf.

The farther away from the Market Square, the more modest the shops, not only in terms of goods but also of premises. "Southern fruit" was sold by "Grunerka," who wore a wig. She knew her customers and would run out of the shop calling out to my mother or my grandmother, "Pani Barberowa, Pani Nelkenowa, I've got oranges as beautiful as Venus today!" The little shop was crammed with crates full of fragrant bananas, lemons, grapes, and yellow and dark red California apples. "See how crisp and juicy they are," she'd say, holding one out for us to try and at the same time putting the ones that had started to spoil into a basket at "half-price." "When does a Jew eat oranges? When the orange rots, or the Jew does." She maneuvered briskly around the tight space, weighing, packing, wiping the snotty noses of her small sons in yarmulkes and with sidelocks.

Next door up the steps was the yard goods shop. A young bearded merchant in a caftan measured lengths of cretonne with a yardstick, and his—it seemed eternally—pregnant wife sold threads, buttons, ribbons, hooks and eyes, and shirt studs. Up the steps, too, was Geizhal's stationery. I knew that shop well because it was where we bought school supplies: number 2 Hardmuth pencils, pens and nibs, rulers and rectangles, marbled paper for covering books, and notebooks with ruled or squared or margined pages. Neśka's grown-up daughter waited on customers, and when she talked to my mother she marveled at how clever Felek was and what a good girl that "Green Frog" Halinka was.

And lo! Fate brought us together in Ravensbrück after the evacuation of Auschwitz in January 1945. About six hundred people were crammed into a barracks for one hundred. We squatted on top of one another on the bare ground, and the air was foul, but at least we were not far from the entrance from which came gusts of frigid wind. I was burning with typhus fever and with thirst. Summoning all my energy, I dragged myself on all fours to the door leading out of the barracks for a handful of dirty snow. In the meantime, people had spread out. "There isn't any room here, you didn't have to move, now you can sleep outside," said my sister-in-law, for whom that evening I had obtained a bowl of soup by carrying planks. Neśka's calm voice reached me through the humming in my ears: "Room has to be made for her, come here, Halinka." I fell in a faint on a pile of bodies and found myself, I don't know how, next to Neśka and her younger sisters. We met for a second time in Wrocław two months after the war and marked the occasion with a photograph.

Behind Geizhal's stationery was Birn's bakery. My nanny went there for fresh whole-wheat bread with caraway. It was that bread of Birn's that would come to me later, during my hallucinations from hunger, and in my Auschwitz poem of 1944.

Do you know what HUNGER is?
Hunger
that twists your gut
sweeps thought out of your brain
knifes your belly?
Breath fails
the heart stops beating

In the end all thought halts
all the maddened desire
to eat! Eat! EAT!

Hours drag slowly
Parched lips crave spit
The sick imagination is tormented
by a nightmare
of a loaf of bread.

If only it would fall suddenly from heaven
fresh
warm, fragrant,
sprinkled with caraway on top . . .
runs through your crazed brain.

Oh, to tear with your teeth
chew greedly
swallow chunks
feel at last on your tongue
and feel in your mouth
and in your throat
and in your belly
that
satiety.
Eat! Eat! Eat!

Darkness before my eyes.

God! Have pity on me.
Send me down a piece of bread!

Look—how little I need today
God
Were you ever hungry?

Going farther down Kalwary Street in the direction of Długosza, we some-times crossed the street to call on Pani Mania Neuwelt, an older friend of my mother's who had a Christmas ornament factory there. I watched with fas-cination as the workmen blew glass balls out of pipes heated to redness over a gas burner. One specialist lightly touched the tummy of a ball with a stick and immediately a starry indentation appeared. Another blew enormous balls and lengthened the end into a spike to crown a Christmas tree. Still another performed miracles over the gas flame: pine cones, gnomes, Santa

Clauses, roosters, baskets—all of them as transparent as soap bubbles. In the depths of the hall, workers wearing rubber gloves deftly dipped the balls into basins of molten gold and silver and rainbow colors. Mama once told us a story about a glass ball that was jealous because she was just red and she wanted to be golden, and she nudged the gold one so sharply that she fell off the branch herself and landed in shatters under the tree. "It served her right," Felek and I agreed, because the moral was clear—envy was an ugly quality. The balls of a single color were beautiful enough, never mind the ones that the women at the last table decorated with curlicues and snowflakes! Packers put the finished glass balls into boxes with dividers, and those, in turn, into still bigger boxes—and in that way Pani Mania's Christmas decorations went out into the world, even overseas. The Christmas tree in our house was the most beautiful one, of course, especially since those balls drew attention away from the sometimes clumsy chains of colored paper and straw which the children had made.

From Pani Mania's, Stroma Street led from Kalwary to Zamoyska in the direction of our house. The lending library was located there. Felek used to go in there on the way home from gimnazium and borrow the books of Karol May. Once he borrowed *The Połaniecki Family*, by Sienkiewicz. "Isn't he too young for Miss Maryna's passions?" my parents wondered at suppertime, while Felek turned beet-red—he was thirteen years old at the time.

Pan Zeimer's pharmacy was on the corner of Stroma Street. His daughter Irka sometimes came to Felek's dances and played Sinding's *Frühlingsrauschen* on the piano. She went to a private gimnazium and was two classes ahead of me. I didn't know her very well, but she was always nice to me, friendly and serious. I ran into her once during the war in some camp—I no longer remember which one—but I am certain that she survived and is living in New York.

From this pharmacy, we crossed back onto the other side of Kalwary. There were very odd shops here. I particularly liked the one containing sacks of flour, kasha, and sugar loaves, because I could stroke the two huge, fat and fluffy cats there. One white, the other gray, they saw to it that mice didn't get into the stores. Next door, the tiny shoemakers' supply shop, where Pan Heller bought hobnails and soles, smelled nicely of leather. After that, candies— at the back was the candy factory, and in front, jars of hard boiled candies tempted children with their colors alone. Grandma bought us lollipops and pineapple candy there, betraying as she did so her friend Pani Erlich, whom we called the Chocolate Grandma, because she had a chocolate factory and bestowed orange creams on us, unaware that our family in Czechoslovakia showered us with "Milka," "Velma," and "Bitra."

And finally, the nasty, dismal, crowded "Gas, Oil and Grease." I went there once with Janka to buy sandpaper for cleaning the kitchen stove and for floor polish. The fat shop woman sat in front of the store in a wig and with a greasy apron on over her coat. Rubinstein's, the grocer next door, had a tabby cat. On Sunday you could get to the store across the courtyard, so the Rubinstein daughters went from apartment to store to wait on customers, keeping a sharp eye out for policemen by the gate, because business was prohibited on Sundays.

Right next to that stood the spotless but tiny dairy belonging to the Landerer sisters. Young women in white overalls and with permed hair weighed Danish butter, cream cheese with chives, Dutch and Swiss cheeses in large wheels on the shelves. Pan Słomak's pork butcher's shop abutted them. The butcher was huge, redfaced, bullnecked, and had an enormous belly. Diminutive, quiet Pani Słomak carved thin slices of wonderful ham, Kraków kiel-basa, and liver sausage. Her son Władek was Felek's schoolmate, a quiet, very nice blond boy with warm brown eyes. Pani Słomak came to the party for the graduating class wearing a dark dress and a thick coral necklace. "My Władek is almost grown-up! How quickly these children grew up, Pani Nelken!" she said to my mother, while Pani Płatek on the other side just nodded her bleached-blond head.

Władek went to the military academy in Lwów with Felek and Zbyszek Płatek. When the war broke out, he found himself in a prisoner-of-war camp. Pani Słomak cried over him with my mother, even though Felek was also in a POW camp. No one knew, no one ever suspected, that Pani Słomak was in the least bit Jewish. Her own husband didn't even try to save her. They imprisoned her first in Montellupich and then took her to Auschwitz, where she perished. Władek came home after the war. He listened to what had happened, spat in his father's face, and left Kraków for good.

The hairdresser's was owned by Pan Siwek. When the short hairdresser wielded a razor and scissors over the heads of his clients, his hunchback wasn't too noticeable beneath his white overall, and he tried to make terrified children laugh by tickling them under the ear. Like all the engaged girls in the neighborhood, our Janka went to Siwek's on her wedding day to have her curls set on hot irons so that they would hold better under her veil.

The only shop with a big display window on that stretch of Kalwary Street was Zamczyk's men's outfitters. Here we looked at ties and pins; shirts; pullovers and hats; silk socks; umbrellas; and, discretely off to one side, a small sign, "Olla-gum?" The question mark intrigued me, but even when Stefa explained that these were condoms so that you wouldn't have children, I still didn't understand.

On the corner of Kalwary and Długosza, the taproom was redolent of beer and tobacco. "I'll just pop over to Haber's for cigarettes," Mitka the tiler from our house would say, and that would be the last of him. His wife would chase after him with a broom—"He'll spend it all on drink!"—and bemoan her fate. Janka sometimes "popped over to Haber's" for delicious rollmops or pickled herring. She took me with her there once and the sight of Pan Haber reaching for a piece of smelly cheese as a chaser for beer caused nausea to sweep over me. Janka sometimes liked to pop into Feder's on the other corner of our street from Serkowski Square because this small food store carried pickled cucumbers, cabbages, and pickled apples in barrels, "contraband, soap, and jams," and even stale cream cakes crawling with flies from the horse market on Serkowski Square.

There was only one shop on Długosza street—Płatek's bakery. Wagons of flour came through the courtyard to the back of Number 3. At the front, elegant Pani Płatek and the shop lady sold delicious baked goods: crusty water rolls and caraway rolls; graham flour buns; kaiser and crescent rolls; salted breadsticks; braided breads and squat poppyseed rolls; wheat and rye peasant bread and dark pumpernickel.

The Płatek's lived on the second floor, above the shop. Zbyszek knew Felek. They had played together since first grade, collected stamps, swapped books, and gone out on escapades from which younger children were excluded. Hala, his twin sister, graduated from gimnazium and got engaged to a young pilot. Zbyszek and Felek went off to the military academy in Lwów.

Marysia, the Płatek's younger daughter, died of tuberculosis in the last days of August 1939. One of the rooms was made over into a chapel. Marysia lay in her coffin in her white first communion dress and veil, surrounded by flowers. Pan Płatek, who had already been called-up for military service, walked tall and straight in his reserve officer's uniform behind the bier leading his wife draped in deep mourning. That must have been on the last day before the war broke out. Pan Płatek was killed in Katyń.

In September, Zbyszek came home and took over the bakery. Hala's pilot found himself in England—Hala married someone else. She was in despair when her pilot came back to her after the war and she had another family. Zbyszek was always very nice to me; he never teased me because I was younger, wrote me a friendly card from summer camp, and asked me to dance at school functions or tea-dances at home, along with the grown-up girls. When I came back to Długosza Street after the war and no one from my family was left there, I met Zbyszek in the bakery. He was very pleased to see me, and noticing that I had nothing and nobody, he offered me ten loaves of bread for next-to-nothing so I could make some money. He wouldn't charge me anything at first, and then we'd see. Marian, our doorman, packed them into a suitcase and carried them over to 78 Starowiślna Street in Kraków, to the fifth-floor of a large tenement building where I was then staying with Genia.

We should have sold the breads right then and there on the spot, but Genia said no, she'd be embarrassed. So I took my wares and "distributed" them with difficulty. A month earlier we had been keeling over with hunger, people had killed each other for a piece of bread, and now they were turning their noses up!

I feel deep gratitude for those people who took me in with such whole-hearted devotion after the war. Zbyszek wanted to help me financially without making me beholden to him. Strangers were living in our apartment, but our doorman, Marian Jedrygas, who occupied a single room with his wife and three children, gave his bed up for "the young miss" and spent the night on the floor. I sat and cried, and our tenants cried with me that nice Pan Nelken had been gassed—I had already known for a year that he had perished in Auschwitz in May 1944. They told me that lame Pan Karol Chmiel—"You know, Miss, the one with tuberculosis who lived in the basement apartment"—the one who listened to the underground radio with my father in my grandmother's old room, also perished in agony. The Gestapo came in the night, dragged him out of bed in his underwear to the shack at Montellupich, and shot him on the hill in the camp at Płaszów. Ancient Granny Sewialkowa, who remembered my mother's birth, came back from vespers and wrung her hands. "Oh, Jesus! Where's the young master? And where's the younger lady?" while her red-haired daughter-in-law quickly interjected, "Don't worry, Miss, your mother will come back, and so will the young master," and she lifted her skirt to show the large scar on her leg and to remind us all how my mother and Felek had cured her by applying ointments and changing her dressings. "That wound had been toxic for half a year, and the younger lady cured it in two weeks!"

At the time, I thought that such a reception was perfectly understandable; after all, we had been close to each other here. People lived here from generation to generation. Tiler Mitka, from the room on the first floor facing the courtyard, had lived with his beautiful daughters, Staszka, a prostitute, and Bronka, who worked in a button factory, and their illegitimate children, the apples of their eyes. The Germans took Staszka to Montellupich and murdered her, too. Baker Sewialek on the ground floor worked nights and by day chased his son Stefan's pigeons. Stefan married our maid, Janka's predecessor. Pan Heller, the cobbler, repaired shoes at the window of his room; his wife cleaned tripe brought to her from the butcher's. Their daughters Etka and Baśka sewed in tailors' establishments in Kraków—and they all lived together in a single, spotlessly clean room. I used to like to watch Pan Heller sole shoes. Nothing tasted nice to me at home, and here I ate up the whole bowl of soup with a wooden spoon—the silver ones were for the Sabbath, sparkling like beautifully cleaned candelabra on a white tablecloth. Pani Heller baked challah and cakes with ginger or anise. Etka and Baśka, fashionably dressed, used to come upstairs to borrow books and to gossip. Pani Heller, also dressed in her best, used to bring "arbys," peas cooked with pepper. Grandma used to tell us that the Hellers had had a son who suffered from the "English disease," rickets, and couldn't walk. His parents carried him in a shawl on their backs, even when he was big. They looked after him. He lay on a clean bed, while they toiled up to their elbows for their only son. Eventually he contracted some other disease on top of rickets and he died. Etka and Baśka, on the other hand, grew up healthy, swarthy, with dark eyes which sometimes looked sad, sometimes sunny, like their mother's. Except for holidays, Pani Heller was always doing something, bustling about her work, humming under her breath. She never complained, quite the opposite. Even during the war she would say to my mother, "Kraków is a blessed city. The war will be over, and everything will be fine." The war passed, and not one of the Hellers remained. Our janitor, Marian, moved up from his basement into their apartment.

The Hellers' neighbors were fat Pani Balon, the wife of a rope maker, and her three daughters. The oldest one, Franka, used to lie exhausted by the window; sometimes they took her out into the yard for some sun. Pani Balon used to complain that here was Franka, so sick with tuberculosis, while the youngest one, Maryśka, was just interested in boys, and only the middle one, Hanka, had an honest job. Franka died. Maryśka was deported to Germany for forced labor and met her husband, a Belgian, there. After the war she went with him to one of the colonies in Africa.

The Madej family lived in the basement at the front. Red geraniums stood in their below street-level windows. Their two rooms were quite light and cheerful, not like the rooms that faced the courtyard on the other side of the corridor and smelled of stale cabbage.

On the right-hand side of the entrance lived the old greengrocer, Pani Łukas, who had a vegetable stall in the market. Grandma sometimes took me to the market with Janka behind us carrying the baskets. I also had a small woven basket, and Pani Łukas gave me young carrots and radishes to put in it. I liked to walk around the fruit stalls with my grandmother, but best of all, I liked to go where the peasant women sat in a row with their baskets full of pots of butter. The imaginative patterns they had made with a spoon on the butter were hidden by cabbage leaves. Metal churns held milk and cream; straw punnets contained wild strawberries and raspberries; eggs lay on straw. A bit farther on, live fowl—unfortunate hens and roosters with bound feet. Janka lifted them up off the ground, out of the peasant woman's hands, and blew on the feathers under their tails to see if they were plump. Energetic white geese wriggled out of her hands with loud shrieks. In the fall, swarms of bees would rise from golden pears and from piles of prunes out of which Grandma made jam.

Pani Łukas sometimes had early sour cherries, and she would hang them from my ears like earrings. In her layers of skirts, her misshapen ankle boots, her headscarf which came down so low that you could barely see her big nose and toothless mouth, Pani Łukas always seemed to me like a witch, although a good one. Every month she'd climb heavily up the stairs to give Grandma the rent. They'd sit down at the table and Pani Łukas would slurp tea out of a glass and reminisce about how Poland had "exploded" at the end of the First World War. Houses had to be decorated in the national colors, and there was no linen to be had! Pani Łukas had rummaged through her trunk and brought up a pair of red pantaloons made out of fustian for the landlady. Grandma had cut up a white underskirt, and, in a trice, sewed a flag which did not lose its colors in the rains of November. "Fustian was sturdy, my dear lady, it didn't fade. You can't find material like that anymore." I didn't have the nerve to say that the flag we had now, which flowed down from the roof to the first floor on all the national holidays, also stood up to downpours without fading.

Pani Łukas complained that her bones ached, her joints throbbed, she'd probably pack up her stall and go to her son's. He was an enormous man, a porter who carried huge sacks of flour in a warehouse on Kalwary, and as a result, his back was bent and his hands stretched down to his knees.

Pani Łukas's small room was next to the cellar where coal and potatoes were kept. The window gave out onto the courtyard and garden, but because it was screened by the porch on the ground floor above, it let in little light. After Pani Łukas left, lame Pan Chmiel, his wife, and young children moved in there. I don't know why he didn't finish gimnazium, or why he lived in such poverty, but I do know that he was a socialist, an intelligent man, and a remarkably honest one. When gangs of thugs broke into abandoned apartments at the beginning of the war, Chmiel guarded ours as though it were his own. "Chmiel, Chmiel my friend!" My father greeted him emotionally when we returned from our wanderings during the evacuation. Chmiel hobbled up the stairs more and more frequently for long discussions with my father in Grandma's room, the two strategists bent over the map of Europe in the large atlas. Various "contacts" slipped into our apartment for a night's lodging, while Chmiel stood casually by the gate puffing cigarettes and keeping guard. I remember his words when he said good-bye to my father as we were leaving our home to go into the ghetto: "Only fools think that they're better than Jews, that they'll be spared. They'll go after the Poles, just you see! We are all in the same boat, Pan Nelken, and we all have the same enemy."

They embraced—my tall father murdered because he was a Jew, and small, crippled Karol Chmiel murdered because he was a Pole.

Opposite Pani Łukas, in the basement to the right, lived Old Pani Franciszek, the janitor. Her son, Kuba, was already out on his own, but he came over to help his mother scrub the stairs and the oak floors in the hallways and to chip the ice and clear the snow from the sidewalk in front of the house. In the winter, Old Pani Franciszek put rags out as extra doormats by the entrance. "We don't want to trek everything in—it's very messy, and when it freezes we'll have one unholy disaster!" At Pentecost, Kuba decorated the gates with fresh green branches, and in spring he dug the garden with us. Old Pani Franciszek planted pansies, nasturtiums, and daisies in the flowerbeds, and marigolds between the rows of vegetables, "because their stink will scare off the pests." Sunflowers seeded themselves to make a tall forest, but they ripened while we were on vacation so anyone could help themselves. We played beneath the bush of wild lilac here with children of the third generation of tenants in our house, with Władka and Mietek Madej, Józka Sewialek, Celinka and Hala Mitka, and with Felek's friends. The little girls dressed their dolls in colorful scraps of fabric provided by Etka and Báska. We sewed dresses for our dolls while the boys kicked a ball around the courtyard. "Just don't break any windows and keep out of the shed," Old Pani Franciszek would remind the children.

Old Pani Franciszek came up to help with major cleanings and in particular with the household laundry. First she and Janka counted out and sorted the "colors." Then they dragged a huge wooden tub out of the cellar and into the courtyard and filled it with water so that the dried-out planks wouldn't leak all over the kitchen. The children floated paper boats in this tub. Upstairs, the laundry was left to soak for twenty-four hours, and then Old Pani Franciszek bent over the scrubbing board and did the "first" wash with such determination that the braid she wore rolled into a bun came undone and dangled there, thin and gray, like a rat's tail. The whites were boiled in a huge copper pot. She and Janka stirred them with a long cane amid clouds of steam, and then washed them for a second time. After the last rinsing in water and bleach, the laundry was ready for its beautifying bath. Old Pani Franciszek dissolved "gray" dye, and the tub filled with cornflower blue—"white goes yellow if you don't gray it." Meanwhile, cooking on the stove was a thick starch made out of flour, which would be used to stiffen the tablecloths, bed linens, and men's shirts which had gone limp from all the murderous washing. The two washerwomen didn't leave the kitchen for two days, eating in shifts to help speed the process and "drinking like wet nurses because water takes it out of you!" Old Pani Franciszek preferred to sit on a small stool rather than at the table, where she would attack a great mug of milky coffee and a doorstep of bread and dripping. Food always made me gag, but I willingly ate the crusts that Old Pani Franciszek cut off when they were too hard for her few teeth. Finally, the clean washing was folded into a big basket, and the two of them carried it up to the attic and hung it out, taking good care not to break the line and not to get dust on it.

The attic was mysterious, but not as much as the cellar, where it was dead quiet and dark despite the light from a candle. Only after a minute was it possible to distinguish the black nuggets of coal and the sacks of potatoes in the corner. Marian laid his hands on our Janka here once and "made her big with child," or, as she put it, "stuck it in and took it out." The cellar was damp and gloomy, but the attic was spacious, and the beams that came together under the roof made it look a bit like a church. A skylight opened onto a broad view: first, the steep red roof tiles with swallows nests among them; then the garden, which looked very small from this height; and finally, a swarm of houses as far away as Dębniki, Ludwinów, and Zakrzówek.

The washing, which had blown dry in the wind, was rolled up and taken to the mangle-iron on Kalwary Street. Janka and Old Pani Franciszek carried a laden basket and unfolded the washing under an enormous roller which clattered as its handle was turned by the mangler. Maids from the neighboring houses stood around it and gossiped.

Ironing followed a different ritual. Old Pani Franciszek liked the heavy heating iron, Janka preferred the lighter, charcoal-filled one. One of them held the heater in the fire until it grew red hot, and the other one blew into the iron and shook it energetically in the hallway until the cinders glowed. At first, the two of them would be singing and trilling away, but then, as the carbon rose out of the iron, they would both get cross. Janka would very shortly be dipping slices of raw potato into vinegar and water and applying them to her forehead to ease her headache. The two of them, bundled up to the eyeballs in wet scarves, would object when Grandma opened the door and the window wide because they were afraid of drafts. And out of their suffering would rise a mountain of sweet-smelling laundry, smoothly ironed and without a single wrinkle.

Old Pani Franciszek was gentle, quiet, and tiny. She went around in wide skirts and a big shawl, like most of the older women on Długosza Street. Her gentle eyes, blue as forget-me-nots, peeped out from the kerchief knotted under her chin. She suddenly failed. Both Grandma and my mother went down to the basement with soup and homemade remedies. Old Pani Franciszek could barely be seen beneath the large down comforter. Her sunken cheeks were red-hot, her eyes bright with fever. A light burned beneath a picture of Saint Mary in her spotless little room. Kuba sat anxiously by her bed. "We'll send for Dr. Abend, right away," my mother said, and Kuba went out into the courtyard with us, stuttering more than usual with worry. "We have to s-s-send f-f-for the priest, Mother's dying."

Every time the priest visited someone who was sick, the entire street went with him, everyone in the building ran out, everyone knelt down and prayed aloud for forgiveness of sins, easy death, everlasting peace. Perhaps death in your own bed and amid your own was easier than death amid the medical technology of modern hospitals. Maybe in the light of a consecrated candle and carried by communal prayer and lamentation, the soul left for the after-life more easily. Ten men would come to pray over dying Jews, as they did for Old Redlich from Długosza 13. Obituaries giving the date of the funeral ap-peared on the gates. Notices with a cross announced: "The dearly departed of sacred memory has fallen asleep in the Lord, after receiving the Last Rites and Sacraments, and after long [or short,] suffering, leaving behind his grieving family." The Jewish dead were of "blessed memory," didn't fall asleep in the "Lord," but simply died, also leaving behind a grieving family. Old Pani Fran-ciszek, like Franka Balon before her, was laid out in her coffin by the neighbor women, and the whole street saw her to the cemetery. Religious Jews were taken between four planks of wood, signifying that everyone, rich or poor, was equal in the face of death. The box, covered with a mourning cloak, was carried by men, who also walked at the head of the funeral procession, and behind them walked weeping women. There was no music and no wreaths, only the rattle of tins with coins into which passersby threw donations for the Society of Final Assistance for the poor and rich alike.

When Old Pani Franciszek died, Marian Jedrygas moved into the janitor's room, thanks to the good offices of his wife, Maryna, who had once worked for us. They were both young, and their daughter had just been born. Marian worked as a mason, while tall and pretty Maryna "janitored it." Our Janka was nothing compared to Maryna! What on earth got into Marian to touch Janka in that cellar? Janka was carrying the children's afternoon snack on a tray and suddenly fainted in the middle of the room. My mother ran in to help her, and Janka cried and admitted, "I hope that bastard gets it!" Mother wrung her hands. "For goodness' sake! You've already got one illegitimate one in the country at your parents!" Maryna rushed upstairs in a rage, yelling, "You pig! You shameless tart! You do it with a stranger! I'll tear your hair out, I'll smash your face in, you whore!" Women milled around nosily; Marian got himself drunk and raged to high heaven in the courtyard. The entire building decided that for the sake of peace and quiet Janka had to "fix it" with the midwife, but my mother interfered. "If it comes to that," she said, "she's going to the doctor's." She accompanied Janka to Dr. B's, and the tempest quieted down.

Shortly, though, another one erupted. A more serious one. In 1936, strikes sprang up everywhere. We took food to the strikers, we collected donations for their families. Crowds of workmen marched to demonstrate in front of the county offices on Basztowa—shots were fired, eight people were killed, among them our Marian's brother. Later on, a small memorial was erected on Planty bearing the names of the victims of these riots, Jan Jędrygas among them.

And so the "winds of history" blew across Długosza 7. Up to that point "history" had meant hanging out white-and-red flags on national holidays.

In May 1935, two flags mingled—the national one and the flag of mourning. Marshal Piłsudski had died. Papa arranged with the veterans' club to allow us to watch the leader's funeral from its attic window. All the windows, roofs, balconies, and streets were filled with people. Mama and I had a difficult time pushing our way through the crowds early in the morning to take up our positions and to wait endlessly until the ceremonial funeral procession appeared. The great royal Bell of Zygmunt rang from the Wawel. The gun carriage bearing the coffin moved slowly. Behind it the family in black and delegations from other nations walked. I noticed an enormous fat man in uniform and carrying a mace—Hermann Göring. Perhaps he was already thinking that instead of the Polish flags, flags with swastikas would flutter over Market Square, renamed Adolf Hitler Platz. Perhaps he was already deciding which works of art he would take for himself out of Kraków's museums.

Influenced by national mourning, I wrote a poem—not for the first time in my life—but the first one to be published. The poem was long and probably dreadful, and mercifully I have forgotten all but the first verse.

My teacher sent the poem to the paper, *Tempo Dnia*. All of Długosza Street snatched up the papers. I thought that the boys in the opposite house were just teasing me, but then I really did see in print, "Halina Nelken, a pupil at the Dąbrowki Elementary School." The editorial offices called the school to tell me to come to collect the fee for my poem. Papa took me to the Pałac Prasy, the Press Palace, where the editor congratulated me. They gave me chocolate and five and a half złoty, the first money I had ever earned in my life. My publishing debut amused my parents, but Grandma, who was very proud of me, sent the newspaper clipping to all her acquaintances.

I was her youngest, her most obedient, and probably her most beloved granddaughter—in her will she divided her real estate and garden among all her children but reserved five hundred American dollars in gold "for Halinka when she comes of age." The deed has been preserved, but the house and garden remain to this day in state hands. The law, not foreseeing Hitler's annihilations, demanded witness depositions and testimonies from the heirs, but all had perished without a trace. The impossibility of arriving at an understanding from overseas and the inflated bureaucratic procedures turned out to beyond our means and our strength. The house, garden, and my golden dollar inheritance are still in the hands of the City of Kraków.

That year we went to the pension Lalka in Rabka for the whole summer.

Papa was very busy and came up only on Sundays, and Grandma didn't want to trek up to a large villa full of young people and children. She preferred to stay peacefully at home with Janka to look after her. Pani Mania's mother was also not leaving Kraków, so Grandma had company. "Perhaps I'll finally finish that sweater I'm knitting," she promised herself. "I've still got to make a sleeve." "Admit it, Mama, it's a question of keeping an eye on your son-in-law," my father teased her. "It never hurts to keep an eye on a grass widower, even though I've been lucky with all my sons-in-law, even you, you rotter."

I wrote telling Grandma that I had no one to play with because all the girls were older. I sent her a photo taken on the verandah—we were all sitting there like sparrows: Blanka graceful in her pajamas, Liwia with braids, Rysia and I—and another photo of Maryla and me under the apple tree. She's showing her teeth and I'm standing there gloomily, thin as a stick, wearing a wreath of chamomile flowers.

My mother became sick toward the end of August, and that delayed our return to Kraków. At night she had a vision of Grandma lying on the floor in her room covered with black linen. I was terrified and ran across the corridor to Felek's room. My mother was thrashing around in the throes of a high fever, and meanwhile my grandmother really did die. My uncle had taken her to the hospital. Papa went to see her in the evening, and that night she died of a heart attack. Papa telephoned the Pension Lalka, but the doctor would not allow them to tell Mama because she wasn't even well enough to get out of bed. The telegrams to Aunt Bronka and Aunt Lola got delayed, so neither one of them got to the funeral on time. None of the sisters was able to forgive Uncle that he hadn't waited for them before he buried Grandma. My mother, mad with grief, was completely inconsolable—"She had so many children, and she died all alone, without any family member near to close her eyes!"

I remembered her despair and never, if I could help it, left my mother alone. I was with her on 19 March 1963 when, for the first time in her life, she went into the hospital. Her stay lasted less than an hour and turned out to be her last. We talked to each other and looked at the beautiful setting sun. The sun set, and a heart attack killed her. I kissed her sapphire eyes, torn apart by pain and frozen with terror, but I was grateful that it was my hand, and not that of a stranger, that had closed her eyes forever.

Grandma's room remained unchanged. My mother continued to be "the younger lady" as far as the whole of Długosza Street was concerned. The tenants came to her, now, with their rent and their problems. They might argue among themselves in their families, or gossip about their neighbors, but none of the tenants in our building fought with each other. Uncle Ignacy saw to repairs and dealt with problems—for example, if a water pipe broke and leaked, or a chimney got blocked and caused a stove to smoke. Janka especially liked problems with the stoves because she could run over to Pan Pałka's and come back with the chimney sweep.

After Grandma died, Mama lost all interest in social engagements. She still liked the theater, the café, and the cinema, but not parties. Papa couldn't drag her out dancing, and he probably missed that. My mother had grown more serious, but Papa still liked to enjoy himself, so he'd sometimes go out with Aunt Fela, or, what was worse, by himself! He'd come back contrite, with a present for Mama, and she'd just look at him without saying a word. I didn't like these silences between my parents, but Janka would comfort me, saying, "In the name of the Father and of the Son, it has begun. And of the Holy Spirit, don't read anything into it. They'll make up in a minute and things will be as they were!"

"As they were"—that means well. Weren't people different then? Weren't they bound by strong bonds of emotion, a mutually strong sense of responsibility, respect and love for the family which they placed above all else? Clouds were drawing in all around, but the deep warmth of our house made me feel secure and became a model and a standard of marriage and family for me.

The rhythms of life were marked by the seasons: going on vacation in summer; picking chestnuts and colored leaves in the fall; skating, skiing, and sledding in winter; outings in May. The droshke would arrive and take us to the forests and the fields. Our parents took us to concerts—my father loved music and never missed a single one. He had a wonderful collection of Chaliapin records, but when he wound up the gramophone and the deep bass filled the whole house, Amik, Mitka's spitz, would begin to howl. Our own white mutt, Bobby, put up more patiently even with my five-finger exercises on the piano and our family operas, which even drew Janka in. Our parents would take us to *The Marriage of Figaro*, and at breakfast the following morning, Felek would take his coffee back to the kitchen singing, "There's skin on my cream here, there's skin on my cream there," and Janka would trill back, "Get out of my hair."

We put on impromptu performances at home. Our playmates from Długosza Street would sit in a row in the darkened dining room, a sheet hung in the doorway, while behind the sheet in a lighted room, Felek and his friend Marian would act out Laurel and Hardy routines and cast their shadows on the makeshift screen. Józka did magic and card tricks. We also performed an operetta of "The Prodigal Son" with text and music by Felek and a guest performance by Janka in a double role. As chorus girl in top hat and man's jacket, Janka kicked her legs, a Marlene Dietrich of the Seven Sorrows, and then, donning a pair of men's trousers, took on the role of the troubled father and lamented,

> What shall I do with my son?
> All he wants to do is have fun.
> He doesn't know Latin, he won't learn German,
> I'll have to apprentice him to a shoe repairman.
>
> He has a tutor
> It doesn't help
> The teachers hit, my son can't sit
> I'll have to apprentice him to a shoe repairman.

Felek had a tutor for math, but no one hit him. He went over his Latin with Mama, who also worked with him on other subjects because Felek was lazy. In fact, he only studied those things that interested him, and in those cases, they just seemed to come to him without his having to work. It was easier for me, because like all children with older siblings, I acquired a lot of information just by hearing it. I learned to read at the same time as Felek, three years before I went to first grade. I didn't get the point about the shoe repairman in his song because it was much more complicated to sole a pair of boots like Pan Heller did than it was to learn lessons. Despite that, I applauded Felek's operetta along with the other children and was proud of him.

At the real children's theater, I embarrassed my mother. They were performing *The Frog Prince*, my mother and I were sitting next to the stage, and I was waiting anxiously for the frog to turn into a prince. For the moment, he was sitting on the edge of the well watching the nymphs dance around barefoot. "Those ladies have got dirty feet," I said aloud, to the joy of our small neighbors and the shame of my mother.

When I was in school, I sometimes went to the Słowacki Theater without my parents. The afternoon performances filled the enormous theater to capacity with children in uniforms. You couldn't have asked for a more appreciative audience or better applause. We sat wherever we could—in the stalls, the balcony, the boxes. We saw *The Blue Bird* by Maeterlinck; comedies by Fredro; Dickens's *A Christmas Carol*.

I didn't go to the movies very often, because there weren't many children's films and it was better not to risk the ones for adults only. Janka went and would tell me little about the film but instead about what had gone on in the cinema. She was at the Atlantic cinema and that couple from the sweater shop was making out. The lights went on and the terrified pair couldn't disengage themselves from each other! An ambulance arrived—and the arrival was a sensation in and of itself—and the unfortunate lovers ended up in the hospital!

Shirley Temple films didn't appeal to me as much as Disney's *Snow White*, but I collected film programs and photographs. Janka and I would tell each other the plots on our way to my music lessons at Aunt Fela's, to which Janka accompanied me so that I wouldn't be coming back alone in the late afternoon. After the lesson, Aunt Mala would give me shortbreads and a cup of tea with a drop of milk, and Janka would gossip with their maid in the kitchen. Instead of waiting while I was at gymnastics or ballet classes, Janka would go and look at the window displays in the shops in town or to church for vespers. Miss Stella of the Jewish Society for Gymnastics taught girls eurythmics, and we even danced in an exhibition once. That was the first time that I had been in a group of exclusively Jewish youth, except, of course, on holidays.

We went to Temple on Miodowa Street for Rosh Hashanah, Kol Nidre, and Yom Kippur. Sometimes Yom Kippur would fall on my birthday because I had been born when my mother was coming back from Kol Nidre. Felek liked to tease me that I had probably dropped straight out of hell, because on Yom Kippur heaven and hell stand open, but Pani Heller, who worshipped at the synagogue in Podgórze, said that having such a birthday was a great blessing. Rosh Hashanah was jolly. Yom Kippur very serious, especially Kol Nidre.

I didn't understand the prayers, but the music moved me to tears. In the balcony, elegantly dressed ladies wearing new hats and furs and dripping with jewels also sniffed into their handkerchiefs. My mother, wearing diamond earrings and a new suit, would slip the fox fur off her shoulders and stand for the formal prayers, reading the Polish translation in her prayer book. She explained to me that on Yom Kippur God judged who had done what to whom and decided who would live in happiness, health, and riches, who in suffering and poverty, and who was to die from water or from fire. That was why, she said, people prayed, so that God would forgive them their sins and inscribe them into the book of life and plenty, the Gates of Heaven would stand open, the prayers of those who atoned and fasted on this day would flow straight to the Lord God. After the setting of the sun, the Lord God has already made His judgment, inscribed and sealed the books, and when the Shofar sounds the Gates of Heaven close until the following year.

We brought Mama an apple studded with fragrant cloves—holy day smelling salts. Friends and acquaintances wished each other health in the new year and an easy fast. Those who survived until the end of the war had behind them quite a different fast!

We did not observe the feast of Succoth, but in the neighboring house and across the courtyard a tabernacle was set up. The children watched with interest as branches were placed on the wooden roof of the hut, tables and benches were set up, and food was brought in for the men. Songs and murmurings reached us from inside, while the women sat apart on the porch and shelled nuts with a nutcracker. At Hanukkah, Papa lit candles at the window, one more candle each evening, while Felek played Hanukkah melodies. Grandma told us about the rising of the Maccabees and showed us Gustave Doré's pictures in the big Bible. All national uprisings were her domain.

We got sweets and gifts for Hanukkah, but also for St. Nicholas's Day and under the tree on Christmas Eve.

In spring, Easter brought a neighborly exchange of decorated eggs, ham, and Easter cookies, poppyseed cakes, coconut cakes, and matzo. Janka cursed the matzo because it made crumbs and left a mess everywhere.

Our Seder was conducted very festively at a beautifully laid table with the wine served out of the antique green glass pitcher. Felek posed questions, beginning with "Why is this night different from all other nights?" Papa read the text in Hebrew, but I looked at my mother's or at my grandmother's Haggadah because it had pictures and a Polish translation. Felek didn't understand Hebrew either, although a Jewish teacher had prepared him for his bar mitzvah.

The teacher came from a neighboring house. He was thin and had a beard, sidelocks, a caftan, and a felt hat beneath which he wore a yarmulke. He didn't eat anything because we didn't keep kosher, but he drank tea with lemon and honey. Felek repeated after him in a monotone, "aleph, bet, gimmel, daled," and the teacher swayed on his chair and encouraged him, also in a monotone and ever more quietly, "Ny, Felek, ny, ny." My brother would slip secretly out of the room with his finger to his lips ("He's asleep!"), ready to go out into the courtyard to play. That poor, tired man, however, did teach Felek something, because he was bar-mitzvahed. A noisy party followed at our house. Cakes and wine were set out for the teacher and his "Hassidim" on a table in Grandma's room. I don't know who brought the records of "Rebecca," "Shtetl Belz," and "My Yiddishe Mama," sad ones, all of them, but the saddest of all was the one about the ungrateful son, Srul, who refused to acknowledge his own father. Aunt Mala didn't even want to listen to it. "No one could possibly be as evil as that, and no one could possibly be saintly enough to forgive such behavior! Change that record at once!"

And yet . . . many years later, and on a different continent, Srul's story repeated itself to the letter in our own family.

The ritual morning prayers with the wrapping of hands took up too much time for Felek's taste. But I liked the prayers and insisted that I wanted to do them as well, so Papa taught me a version for girls:

I raise my hands to you, Oh, Lord,
And pray for Papa's and Mama's health
(and Grandma's and Felek's and everyone's).
And keep me, too, from harm, I pray,
Angels guard my every step.

"Why can't I be confirmed? Józka and Cela and Władka are going through First Communion and they're all dressed up like Aunt Mila when she was getting married in the Temple and I carried her veil. So why can't I?"

Aunt Mila Friedman was a distant relative of Grandma's. She lived in the last big house by Piekarska Street and had a soap and candle factory in the courtyard. Her sister, Aunt Rega, who was older, took the place of her mother. Mila married a judge from Tarnobrzeg, Dr. Zygmunt Wisznicer. I went to them on vacation during the great floods of 1934.

Aunt Rega used to make sure that the soap was being cooked strictly according to the recipe. I couldn't get over how big the kettle was. The soap, which had been cooled on big sheets and then cut into blocks, was put through a press and came out in even pieces, each one stamped "Crown Soap." The recipe for the soap was kept in the desk, and Auntie always took it back home with her. Walking across the courtyard, we used to pet her watchdog, Hitler. The huge mastiff deserved his name because he always attacked Jews in caftans. Uncle Bien, an engineer who came from near Lwów, used to lock the recipe up in the safe, and Auntie would take me into little Rysio's and his baby sister's room. Both Mila and Rega perished when the ghetto was liquidated. Uncle Bien took the children and little Henio, Mila's baby son, to Julag, where they were shortly afterwards shot in front of his eyes. Only the men in that family survived: Zygmunt Wisznicer in London; Bien in the camps. Zygmunt stayed in England. Bien got rid of the factory and went to Sweden.

And so, out of all of us, I was the first to set off for my beloved home as soon as I could walk after I had been liberated outside of Dresden. Długosza 7 was known from my poems and stories to all the prisoners of Block 5 in Malchow camp near Mecklenburg. No wonder, then, that anyone from that block who had survived and gone back to Kraków could find me if they wanted to.

And yet that return home could have been quite other than mine was. In the first days, when I was staying in turn now with one, now with another friendly tenant, Tiny, found me. She was wearing a black armband of mourning. Her name was Ruśka Knobler, she was as stocky as a peasant girl and had a thick golden braid. She was the daughter of a music teacher from Słomniki and was musical and sensitive herself. She had worked with me at the airfield and that's how we had become friends, even though people used to laugh that we looked like a string of spaghetti and a fat pea. Nurturing our broken icons of music and poetry, we went through all the camps together: Płaszów; Birkenau; Auschwitz; Ravensbrück; Malchow, and Leipzig. My Mama stood in place of her family. The Germans had murdered her little sister; her mother and other sister had been taken to the camp in Skarżysko; her father perished in Mauthausen. And then, right at the end of the war, literally by miracle, Tiny found her mother and sister Dorka in the munitions factory in Leipzig. The three of them went back to Kraków. The girls remained behind with the Jewish Committee there while their mother went to Słomniki to get their house ready. That same evening, she was axed to death, no one knew whether by roving bands of NSZ partisans or by local peasants. A week after the funeral, Tiny, who was so much in love with Polish poetry and folksong, quickly left her native land and settled, irony of ironies, in Munich.

Podgórze was not Słomniki. It was different here. That section of Kraków had been developed after the January Uprising. In the suburbs—Ludwinów, Zakrzówek, Dębniki—little houses encircled orchards. Among broad meadows by the Wilga and Rudawa Rivers stretched plantations of potatoes, wheat, and vegetables owned by small farms, like the one belonging to our Józka, with one or two cows, a few geese, and chickens. In Podgórze there were no large factories billowing out smoke, there were small manufacturers here who employed perhaps ten, perhaps a couple of dozen people. Large companies, quarries, for example, were rare here. Socially, Podgórze was rather mixed: the working intelligentsia, free trades, small businesses, and craftsmen. Podgórze was democratic and progressive, proud of its gimnazium, of the splendid church in the Market Square, of the Mining School on Krzemionki, and of its beautiful park. Podgórze was basically honest—sometimes one heard that some drunks had had a fight, that someone had beaten a woman with a belt and someone else had broken a man's head with a pot, that someone had cheated someone, but larger robberies and crimes were unheard of.

Students in Kraków brandishing sticks boycotted and smashed shops in Kazimierz—but in prewar Podgórze, where there were so many Jewish businesses, no one boycotted, no one smashed, no one robbed. Merchants usually lived above, or behind, their shops. They were neighbors one had known for years, for generations; one didn't do things like that to "one's Jews." And if each Pole had "his" Jew, each Jew had at least one Pole who was "his."

War and terror broke the natural bonds that existed between people. Those whom death spared, fate swept away across the globe. Both Poles and Jews.

After a quarter of a century, I came from another continent wanting to show my son Długosza 7. First I went there by myself, and my heart ached at the sight of the completely ruined building. I couldn't bring Leszek here. The mold-covered stucco was peeling off in strips, the red roof was broken, the carved oak gates were cracked, the white stone step at the entrance was chipped in two. I couldn't bring myself to cross the wounded threshold of my family home.

A building hurt by bombs, fire, or an earthquake dies an honorable death. Even ruins have majesty. But this was the collapse of an abandoned house. The whole street was abandoned, orphaned, even though it was crammed full of new tenants. None of them had roots here, or traditions.

1 DIARY FROM THE GHETTO IN KRAKÓW

Cambridge, Massachusetts, 1981–1986

It seems that I always kept a diary.

My beloved great-aunt Mala, who carried herself like a great lady and expressed shocking opinions in a most proper way, visited me often when I was sick as a child. I loved to listen to her hilarious stories from the banks of the Blue Danube, and when she pressed her hands to her heart in a mock-heroic way, raised her eyes sentimentally up to the ceiling, and sang with ecstasy "Wien, Wien, Nur Du Allein," we would both burst out laughing. Aunt Mala read children's books aloud to me, many of which along with other things, she had given to me herself.

Her gifts were always different from anyone else's: miniature animals of Venetian glass; embroidered hankies arranged in a fragrant violet-soap box; a doll's house in the form of a book which, when you opened it, contained a drawing room with ladies sipping tea, children in the nursery with a governess, a kitchen with a cook. My aunt never failed to point out to me the frock-coated man-of-the-house and the mustachioed youth with the cigar who were both looking furtively from the study next door at the coquettish maid dusting the bedroom!

One day, my aunt presented me with a diary and solemnly recited to me the motto which she had written in beautiful calligraphy on the first page:

Blessed be the age of youth!
you golden dream among flowers!
ideals of faith and virtue,
and love and freedom!
(Bohdan Zaleski, "Przesilenia")

Less solemnly, she added, "Be a heroine of the everyday (Eine Heroine des Alltags). Write your own novel. This is the place for your dreams and complaints. A lady may complain only in writing and to herself."

I commenced at once and still remember my scrawls on the first forget-

me-not-decorated page: "Aunt Mala gave me this diary. I am sick in bed. Felek ate the chocolates Pani Mania gave me. Papa played chess with me and I lost. Mama read a story about a gray kitten to me and I want one." It was not easy to write in bed, dipping my pen in the inkwell on the night table. The ink spilled onto the lace pillowcase and onto my pajamas and put an end to the diary writing for a while.

Neither this very first one, nor the many other diaries that followed, survived. What did survive are a few pages from before the war, one thick diary written through March 1942, and four unfinished notebooks which my Polish friend, Hanna Łętowska, took for safekeeping in December 1943, together with a few books and family photographs, and saved from destruction.

One could not keep a diary in the German concentration camps. My "dreams and complaints" took the concise form of poems written in tiny script in a notebook small enough to be hidden in the palm of my hand. It survived Auschwitz, Ravensbrück, Malchow, and Leipzig. I rescued nothing— just this inconspicuous little notebook with the proud heritage of Polish Romantic poetry as a motto on the first page:

> *". . . lift your spirit so high*
> *that evil cannot reach you!"*

Harbutowice, July 1937

I do not know why I brought my diary since there is no time to write. For the first time, I am on vacation without my parents. It is pretty here and pleasant and there is always something different to do. I like it here because I always longed to be in boarding school, like the one described in Lydia Czarska's books, although it appalled me how cruel the pupils could be to new girls and that they didn't just come down sick with tuberculosis but sometimes even died.

No one is "new" in Harbutowice; we are all from our two state gimnaziums in Kraków, the exclusive schools for girls, and there are a lot of girls from our class here. The head of this summer camp is one of our teachers. No one dies of tuberculosis, and if the girls get sick it is from eating unripe apples. We went on a trip to Lanckorona, we go for walks in the woods, we swim in the river, or row on a pond full of frogs. In the evening, when the lights are out, we tell each other stories from books or films, or we fool around pretending we see ghosts.

Hermina M. swapped film programs with me and gave me photos of the film stars, and I got one of Joan Crawford. "Just look at her blue suit with a tuberose on the left lapel!" she said. I wonder how she knows it's a tuberose, but obviously it must be, because Joan Crawford would not pin just anything on herself. Hermina does not like her, she says that she's an ugly old woman with a big mouth. I think elegant modern women, ones who have nice figures and are intelligent, should look like Joan, they don't have to have angelic faces. In any event, I know Joan only from photos and not from her films, to which we are not admitted.

We went canoeing: Joasia at the prow, Maryśka at the stern, and Hermina and I in the middle. Today it was my turn to tell a story. Once our maid Janka had taken me to the movies without my parents' knowledge, so I told the story of a Polish film, *Heather*. I described the farewell scene at the railroad station with great emotion. The desperate heroine looked at her lover in silence, then closed her eyes and grew pale . . . and Hermina yelled, "It's a black and white film, so how do you know she grew pale?" "She had to," I insisted, fully convinced. How could she not grow pale, parting forever from her beloved, standing alone on a platform right next to the "No exit" sign making it clear that there was no way out? I lost all desire to tell them any more of the story. We started to paddle like mad, and at a sharp turn I leaned over stupidly and fell into the water fully dressed. I could have died! Not from drowning but from disgust at all those frogs! Joasia held out a paddle, I clambered out onto the bank, and all the girls roared with laughter. I did, too, when I saw myself in the mirror in our bathroom. I was sent to bed, just in case. I am writing out of boredom.

18 July 1937

I can't bear to hear "You are my lucky star," or "Blue Roses," or "I'm in Heaven, Seventh Heaven," or "Harbor Lights" anymore! The older girls are dancing to these few miserable records to the point of boredom. If there were a piano here, I would rather play for them.

Yesterday Hermina had supper duty, so Zośka sat next to me. As usual, after the meal, we sang the patriotic "Rota"—"We won't give away the land where we were born"—and the religious, "All our daily deeds take you, oh Righteous Lord," and, "When we lie down to rest, let our sleep praise you!," and immediately that horrible Zośka nudged me and hissed: "Stop singing! You're Jewish, you're not allowed to sing our songs."

I wanted to tell her that those songs are not just directed at Christ, and that the Righteous Lord is the same one for all people, and that I, too, want Him to know about my daily deeds. But I didn't say anything to her, I just went on singing. Zośka is always having some kind of heart attack and that is probably what makes her so mean. The other girls are not nasty like that either to me or to Maryśka, who is also Jewish. Still, when I thought about it at night, I wept.

Krakow, 17 January 1938

When Papa took me to the private Kollataj gimnazium and saw how frightened I was, he kissed me and smiled: "Don't worry, Little Green Frog, don't worry!"

"Don't worry, Little Green Frog!" repeated Pani Kusiakowa's voice as she entered the room. She is our homeroom and Polish literature teacher. I liked her at once, a big, stout, young woman with a friendly smile. Behind her stood Runka Schüssler, a tall girl with a thin, sharp nose and equally thin pigtails.

"Take Halinka to the classroom, you will sit together, but no talking during lessons!"

On the way down the dark corridor, Runka reassured me, "No one is going to eat you. I don't bite, either, though I have gold in my mouth." She twisted her left cheek up in a comical way and flashed a tooth at me, so we were both giggling as we walked into the classroom.

On that first day after winter vacation, everyone was talking loudly and scuttled back to their seats when the teacher came into the room after the bell rang. The boys sat on the right, the girls on the left, except for the last rows, which were just for boys. Runka and I were in the third row of desks. I sat by the aisle. I did not dare to look to the right, even though, because of my older brother, Felek, I am used to boys, our house is full of them all the time. Nobody tried to torment "the new one"; no one was even particularly interested in me, and those who were, were rather nice. Hanka Łętowska, who sat next to Runka, muttered something mildly malicious, but funny; Hela Bojman and Dola Hoffman, who sit in front, turned around and waved to welcome me; at recess, Zosia in back batted her long eyelashes and asked whether I was seeing anyone and whom? Ala Orlowska, a thin and pale ashblond with a narrow little face, nudged her with her elbow and winked knowingly at me; plump Irka Wozniakowska, the principal's daughter, wanted to change places with me, because Adam Arsenicz, the boy of her dreams, sits in the same row on the other side of the aisle—alas, the teacher did not allow any changes. I walked home with a girl called Janka and a boy, Bronek, who, it turns out, lives not far from me. Jurek walked with us, too, but only as far as Planty because he is living with his uncle, the famous Bolesław Drobner, the leader of the Polish Socialist Party.

I am starting to get to know some of my classmates, particularly the big ones in the back row. One of them is Jurek Bisanz, whose family owns one of Kraków's best cafés and the Cichy Kącik, the Quiet Corner, in Błonie near the Wolski Wood, where we go for new potatos with kefir and wild strawberries with whipped cream.

I have come to like this new school and brag about it to my friends from the State gimnazium. I was always in fear of the lady professors, there, especially one spinster witch who taught natural science and another one who taught math. The one really nice teacher was an older gentleman, Professor Niespodziański, who taught Latin.

Here, the professors are so friendly that no one is nervous. Every lesson is fun and we learn without even realizing it! Even the building itself, close to Planty, is much jollier than the old sullen edifice of the state gimnazium.

Cambridge, Mass.

The immediate reason for my transfer to the other school was an anti-Semitic incident, although it was one which did not involve me personally. In our class of about forty-eight students, there were just six of us who were Jewish: Maryśka, Ewa, Irka, Zośka, Żanka and I. Maryśka, Żaneta, and I were friendly with everybody in the class. Ewa and Irka kept to themselves and were close only with each other, while Zośka kept entirely to herself and had no friends, neither Jewish nor Catholic. She was incredibly clever and studied with intensity, as though it were a matter of life and death. By contrast, Żaneta could not care less about good grades. She had to repeat the same year twice and so she found herself in our class. Zośka was the only one of us whose parents were merchants and religious orthodox Jews. The rest of us came from families fully assimilated into Polish society, families of the "working intelligentsia" or from liberal professions. Ewa's mother was a sculptress. I liked Ewa, a quiet blond girl with soft brown eyes, and a quiet wit. I would probably have been as friendly with her as I was with Maryśka if Irka had been less possessive.

The six of us were together only during Catholic religion lessons, when we left the classroom and had a free period, and during our own religion classes. These were held in the afternoon and included Jewish girls from other schools. I dragged around with me the History of the Jews *by Bałaban, which I had borrowed from Felek. The volume was as heavy as the rabbi who taught us. I don't know why I could hardly remember anything of these lessons except for the word "Sanhedryn." I think that perhaps if I had not been required to go to them, especially if I had not had to return to town by streetcar and go home again at dusk in winter, I might have been less tired and more ready to learn. None of us evinced any enthusiasm for these Jewish lessons, not the girls from my school nor those from any other school, and we knew more about the Punic Wars than we did about King David. Zośka was the only one who recited every lesson by heart perfectly and like a machine gun. And it was this Zośka—as I learned long after the war—who survived, immigrated to Switzerland, studied medicine, and converted to Catholi-*

cism! I couldn't believe it, and I think this might have been some other girl with the same name. Irka survived the war in Russia and returned with the Polish army. My friend Maryśka perished despite her false papers and her platinum-blond dyed hair. I do not know the fate of Żanka and Ewa. Did they perish or did they lose themselves somewhere in the world? When I visited Kraków in 1967 and went to the Jewish Museum in the restored Old Synagogue, I was deeply shaken by the statue of a little girl in the center of the large and empty Gothic hall. Ewa. Not one of her family survived the Holocaust. The only trace left of them is this Ewa, immortalized by her mother as a life-sized five-year-old child.

But for now, we were attending gimnazium, and together with our entire class we went to a particular store where the regulation uniforms and coats had been ordered for us. The next day we all arrived in school in our new outfits, and it was only when we were ready to go home after classes that we discovered a terrible thing. Irka, Zośka, and Ewa's new coats had had big holes in the shape of the Star of David cut into the backs with a razor. The fact that three of us had been spared was as painful to us as the vandalism suffered by our three Jewish classmates.

The next day, my father, who was very active in the parents' committee, came with me to the office of the principal, Dr. Maria Dobrowolska. All of us students were afraid of "Donia." She was short and spoke in a quiet voice, but she had the eyes and the smile of a lizard.

She got up cheerfully from her desk, as if nothing had happened. "Welcome, Mr. Nelken! You, child, go to your class." But I waited in the hallway and heard snatches of their conversation.

"Why do you want to transfer her? You will deprive your daughter of the advantages which only a state gimnazium can provide. Besides, she was not a victim in this unfortunate incident."

"Because her coat was not cut to pieces? But she already feels threatened! Is this a proper atmosphere in a school? My child is not going to grow up harassed and humiliated, I won't allow it."

My Papa. If he had only known what kind of humiliation was soon to be my future!

"She shouldn't stay one day longer in this school. But if you insist . . . Only till Christmas."

Finally they both emerged. My father, tall and elegant, "Donia" wrapped in a shawl, finishing a sentence: "It really is a pity . . . and tomorrow we have a committee meeting. Please, don't forget about it, Mr. Nelken!"

My father shook his head and smiled, suddenly amused, "Am I so much in demand?"

"Of course! We need you. We will miss you."

Father bowed, kissed her hand, and we both went to the Department of Education to ask for a transfer from the state to the private gimnazium.

On Felek's birthday in November, the entire "Sanhedryn," as he called it, of family and friends arrived. He and I presented a small concerto for four hands on the piano, then Felek disappeared with the girls and boys into another room and closed the door in my face. So I went into the dining room, where the guests sitting around the big table were discussing my leaving the highly selective and desirable state gimnazium. Mama's blue eyes sparkled with indignation. "Her school years are supposed to be the best, most care-free period of her whole life. The great honor of attending the state school is not worth such humiliation. Such a thing could not have happened in a private school."

"Perhaps. But we all have to swallow some pretty bitter pills in life."

"She has plenty of time for bitter pills. Right now she has parents to ensure that she has a peaceful and cheerful childhood."

I remember this conversation well, and the moment at which our maid, Janka, came in with a walnut and coffee cream birthday cake. The girls and boys reappeared quickly from the other room. I did not want to join them now. I sat on the side of Papa's armchair, embraced by him like a chick under a wing.

After the war, all the schools were run by the state. I registered at my old school because it was the one closest to our apartment on Starowiślna, now called the Street of the Heroes of Stalingrad. I was now a grownup, had gone through the gehenna of the ghetto, the horrors of Płaszów, Auschwitz, and Ravensbrück, and yet for a moment in "Donia's" office I felt a tremor of fear, a remnant of the old fear of the little schoolgirl.

"Nelken!" She recognized me immediately. She looked over my reports from the underground courses I had taken during the wartime and assigned me to Class 1 of the Humanities Lyceum. "Donia" informed me that because of the lack of space our lessons would be held in the afternoons in a classroom on the second floor. Of the former teachers, only the Germanist, Pani Lus-niakowa, the physicist, Pan Węgrzynowicz, and our "Grandpa," the Latin teacher, Niespodziański, were left. Finally, she got up from behind her desk.

"And how is Mr. Nelken?"

"He's not longer alive. He perished in Auschwitz."

"I am so sorry! I remember your father very well. He was a handsome man, cheerful and irreplaceable in committee work. I am so very sorry. Please go to class, the first bell has rung."

Kraków, 14 October 1938

There is little time to write my diary. A lot to study, to read—for school as well as for myself—the piano to be played and the park to be walked in. Sometimes I meet Felek's girls who used to come to dances at our house and who now cannot wait for the boys to return from Cadet School in Lwów. Last month, they left for a year. It seems such a long time!

It is quiet at home, although a few of the boys who stayed in Kraków keep coming to visit. Czilek even brought me greetings from Andrzej C. Six months ago I would have been overjoyed, but now that it is over, I can write about it.

The teachers' seminar invited a band from Felek's gimnazium to play at the dance. Felek took me along to turn the music for him instead of being, as he put it, "a wallflower." Czilek with his sax, Romek with his violin, and some other student with a drum waited by the podium for Felek to sit down at the piano. "Percussion, not drum, don't put me to shame," grumbled Felek and introduced me. Czilek had brought Andrzej to turn his music, but these musicians were so experienced that there was nothing for us to do except dance.

We danced all evening long. During one tango, I actually felt amorous, but when Andrzej tried to hug me close, I drew away stiffly to a decent and elegant distance. It was the last dance.

We went home along Planty, Andrzej and I ahead of Czilek and Felek. Andrzej wanted us to see each other again. I wanted to as well, but I said, "No. If someone were to see us they would think I was easy to get." Andrzej couldn't care less—he is about to take *matura*, the final exams—but I could be thrown out of school. We all said good-bye and shook hands. On the way home, Felek admitted that I still had plenty of time to go out with boys, but that, on the whole, I am stupid.

I never met Andrzej again, but he must still remember me. I am going to play that tango for myself. This is a nice ending to this notebook; it is the last page.

Cambridge, Mass.

My next notebook diary did not survive. It covered the period when the childish girl I was developed physically and intellectually in the cheerful atmosphere of her home and school. It was the happiest time of my life. The loving environment and my caring family gave me a sense of absolute stability and security, such as I would never again feel at any point in my life.

I was sure of my place in the world; I knew what was expected of me, and therefore it was not worth rebelling against home or school discipline. My occasional melancholy was brought on by music, poetry, or literature, or because Felek was in Lwów and there was no one to banter with except in letters. Each day was full of intense joie de vivre, especially in the spring.

I remember going home from school in May 1939 and running into my mother and two of her friends along Planty. They had just been to some committee meeting. My mother was wearing a beige silk suit with violets on the lapel, Pani L. a colorful tunic and a Wallis Simpson hairdo, and Pani Mania something navy blue, as became an older lady with grown-up sons, the younger of whom, a physician, was already married. We all stopped at the Maurrizio patisserie to pick up pastries for dessert.

At home—and I always associate this with the idea of home—there was a fragrance of narcissuses and freshly waxed parquet; a spring breeze coming in through the open windows gently stirred the batiste curtains.

I remember this dinner with Pani Mania: the taste of the spring soup of young carrots and green peas, of sauteed chicken with new potatoes, cucumber salad with sour cream and dill, and the cream pastries for dessert. It was Friday. We planned a lunch outing to Lasek Wolski for the next day. But in the morning, my parents went with me to Kościuszko Kopiec, Kościuszko Mound. The fresh breeze brought with it the sweet scent of lilacs and chestnut trees which bloomed around the villas. From the top of the mound, we had a panoramic view of the city—the cloister of Norbertanki, the Vistula arching around the Wawel, the houses and the church towers—which moved as in a kaleidoscope when I grabbed my parents and danced with them in a circle.

Mama in her high-heeled pumps walked down along the street, while Papa ran with me across the grassy hill and straight to the Cichy Kącik, the Quiet Corner, to enjoy new potatoes with kefir. My parents' friends arrived shortly and we all went to Lasek Wolski, all except Papa, who preferred to watch Cracovia play Wisła at soccer.

A month later, all the Kraków gimnaziums took part in a sports exhibition at the main stadium. The boys performed athletics, the girls did folk dancing. In a large circle with a standard-bearer at the head of each group, we moved to the rhythm of a polonaise. Our school was presenting the Kujawiak. We were dressed in original Łowicki costumes borrowed from the theater. I was paired with Myszka. We held hands and whirled fast in front of the judges, when suddenly Myszka squealed, "Dear Lord! The elastic has broken. I am losing my pants!" Without breaking the rhythm, or taking leave of common sense, she quickly disentangled herself from her pink underwear, waved it high in the air, and hid it under her cloak. Hela B., who was dancing next to us, almost choked with laughter.

The following day, still in our costumes, we marched over to the photogra-

pher who took pictures of each group. The girls signed my photo, "In memory of the Kujawiak with p. . . ." Decency prevented them from spelling out "panties."

Each class had its picture taken with the bearded principal and the faculty. What marvelous young people were in our class! Children of rich and poor parents, of professionals and craftsmen, workers and merchants, army officers and well-to-do peasants from nearby villages. Diversified socially by upbringing and religion, we were a friendly group, without any animosity.

The subsequent fates of my colleagues were not happy. Hardworking, honest Bronek was arrested by the Germans in 1940 and perished in Auschwitz at a time when not a single Jew was incarcerated there. Leszek J. from Pomerania was drafted into the German army, as was Jurek Bisanz, an Austrian. I met his cousin in 1959 in the art history department of the University of Vienna—he soon became director of the Museum of Decorative Art. "Jurek was killed in battle," his cousin sighed sadly. We spoke Polish. Herr Bisanz worried that his children knew hardly a word of Polish, even though he had hired a Polish governess for them. What a strange world! I had a German governess in Kraków, and he, in Vienna, wanted his children to learn Polish! Kaiser Franz Joseph, forgotten neither in Kraków nor in Vienna, would be happy to know how far the traditions of the cultural commonwealth of his monarchy had reached.

Or, perhaps it was Kraków and its specific atmosphere that made everyone assimilate quickly. Consider Franek, another boy from our school, son of an organist from Silesia. No one would have suspected the strength of character of this light blond, quiet adolescent. Once we both met in front of the school while we were waiting for our parents to return from their teacher conferences. Franek was worried, not so much about his own possibly mediocre grades, but for the absolutely certain failing grades of Zosia K. "Cow-eyed Hera," the girls called her, though Homer's epithet for the wife of Zeus was his way of saying that her eyes were big, dark, and limpid. Pretty Zosia did not have close girlfriends. She was only interested in boys. She flirted with serious Franek, and, sure of his absolute devotion, with many others as well. However, it was Franek who saved her life during the war by hiding her from the Germans. And Zosia? Right after the war, she left him and Poland.

After the war, Franek played with a band in one of Kraków's elegant cafés, and I met him there once at a dance. During a break, we reminisced about our class. Jurek W. had returned in the uniform of an officer in the Polish army, having fought everywhere from Lenino, in Russia, to Berlin. He was still living with his uncle from the PPS. We had been close friends until Jurek left to study science in Moscow. Józek S. had been deported by the Russians to the Samarkand; he and his family had survived, and back in Kraków he went into his father's profession, studying law at the university. Gregarious and witty, Józek spent more time in cafés telling jokes than he did at lectures and seminars. Mietek G. survived the war as an O.D. (Ordnungsdienst), a Jewish policeman, and because of that he quickly left Poland afterwards. Three other of our Jewish colleagues perished, no one knows where nor when, sharing the fate of most of our "non-Aryan" girls.

Cesia V., an orphan raised by her father, perished like Hela, Runka, and Dola Hoffman, despite her false, "Aryan" papers. The oldest girl in our class, Lena Sz., an unusual beauty who looked like a precious Chinese doll, was with me in the same camp of Malchow in March 1945. Starved and emaciated, Lena died at her mother's knees shortly before the end of the war. Her mother survived her only child by many years.

Our class brought to a close my carefree school years. It was, indeed, the happiest time in my life, orderly and secure. I knew misfortune, tragedy, and evil only from literature, theater, and opera, though their merciless power was soon to crush all our lives. But before that happened, there was still vacation.

Czatkowice, 22 July 1939

We went across the fields to the town of Krzeszowice with Henek to look at Duke Potocki's palace. Diana was chewing grains of wheat and choked. I was walking ahead, because I don't have the patience to meander along so slowly, and was picking poppies and cornflowers, when Rila yelled: "Wait, tall-stemmed Hala! Diana is suffocating!"

Diana wasn't suffocating at all. She was just leaning against Henek, who was fanning her with his handkerchief. His sisters are not well, so he is supposed to know what to do when someone feels dizzy. Hela rebuked her little sister, telling her that there was nothing the matter other than her feeling giddy from the fragrance of potato flowers or clover or from overeating, and that she was to get up at once so that we all could get going. Diana is the youngest one of us and she wants to attract Henek's attention.

Yesterday we all went to Czerna through the forest, which was so full of blueberries that our faces and hands turned bluish black. Our ladies went to the restaurant for a cup of coffee, while we ran over to the Elijah Spring, enclosed in a heart shape. Its water is supposed to be miraculous; whoever drinks from this spring will have good luck in love. I don't know what to wish for for myself, nor with which boy, but I drink this spring water, which tastes better than lemonade.

8 August 1939

A crowd of guests has arrived. The day before yesterday, on the anniversary of the *Wymarsz Kadrówki,* the departure of the Piłsudski Legion for the First World War, everyone came to our house for a bonfire and to listen to the radio transmission from Kraków. The long and boring speeches were interrupted by applause and enthusiastic shouts: *silni, zwarci, gotowi* (strong! united! ready!), followed by a roll call of the fallen soldiers. Battle after battle and a long list of names: "Rokitna—cavalry captain Józef Szperber, artistic pride of the family, was wounded there," and so on.

Uncle Ignacy mentioned how the Cossacks had almost killed him on the bridgehead after he had blown it up. "The military engineer wanted to serve in the sappers," taunted Aunt Dora, and we all sang a funny little jingle, "*Najdzielniejsze* to sappery," the sappers are the bravest. . . . My tall, thin uncle survived his wounds, and then later escaped from a POW camp and forced his way in disguise through "the flames of revolution" in Russia, as Grandma used to say.

War was terrible, but it brought freedom to Poland, and was fought by the Legionnaires.

And by my Papa, too. The radio sounded out "The First Brigade," the Legionnaires' anthem, and we all joined in chorus. My parents exchanged glances. I know that they had already been engaged when Papa had to go to war. Suddenly, I blurted out, "I could not stand it if my beloved had to leave with the army, without a word as to his whereabouts."

"Without a word, indeed! Their romance almost ended because of his letter!" Aunt Mala pointed at Mama and they both burst out laughing, Papa, too. In her elegantly mischievous way, my innocent-faced aunt introduced the Nelken family's secrets to us.

My father had lived with his Aunt Mala, and it was from her house that he left for the front. His aunt packed his knapsack with care, adding stationary and addressed envelopes. How indignant my mother was when, instead of a love letter, she read: "My Dear, send me my warm long johns because my balls are freezing off and I won't be able to father. And add some stomach drops. Cabbage and beans cause gas and the whole detachment is exploding like cannon."

"Who, in those days, would have dared to mention men's underwear to a young lady, never mind flatulence, for Heaven's sake!" Aunt Mala rolled her eyes dramatically. Everyone laughed, including my parents. "I was certain that the war had affected his mind, especially since, in another letter, he made a declaration of unlawful love to his own aunt, 'My dearest little one.'"

"We believe you! We believe you! You don't need to quote chapter and verse," interrupted my father. Pani Mania started to sing something in a very high key. The radio sounded some other music, and we sang a boy scout song by the bonfire. "The fire is burning and the forest murmurs."

"Nothing is murmuring here," stated Henek, who had just arrived and talked me and Hela into taking a walk. A fragrant and warm summer evening. The mild shine of the moon over the stubble fields and silvery oats. The small windows of the peasants' huts on the hill blinked with lights. It was so peaceful, so quiet. A shooting star caused me to exclaim, "Happiness! Let there be no war!" At least one wish has to be fulfilled. Suddenly, I grew very sad. In a week, we leave for home.

Kraków, 20 August 1939

Julka gave us big bouquets of phlox for good-bye, they perfume our whole apartment. The fragrance of asters and phlox means the end of vacation. That last day in Czatkowice was sad. Stefan loaded our luggage on the buggy while we walked through the empty rooms. Rigo, the small black and white mutt, followed my mother, as he had done all summer. Rigo was the privileged pet, running freely everywhere, not tied up on a rope like big Burek. Then, suddenly, Rigo jumped up onto an empty bed already stripped of its pillows and blankets, lay flat on his side, put a paw over his head like a human covering his eyes, and gave a long howl.

"O, Jezus!" Our landlady crossed herself. "Holy Virgin protect us from fire, pestilence, and war. Why are you howling, you ungodly creature? It gives me the creeps!"

Me too. I kissed the dog on his sad, smooth little snout. Stefan, also a little dispirited, saw us off on the train and shook my hand through the window. "See you next year, if there is no war. But there will be. Go home in good health!"

Krzeszowice, the Potocki palace, and the hill with the spring disappeared quickly, and before we had even read the humorous weekly, there was Kraków.

Our house is freshly painted and beautifully renovated. Janka had waxed the parquet, which shines like a mirror, and she ordered us to walk on it only in slippers. She is the "Tyrant of the Home Hearth," as Felek calls her. I have grown a lot over the vacation, my dresses do not reach my knees. I got a new navy blue dress with white polka dots and a white lace collar. I am a little tanned and have a few freckles on my nose, but who cares? No one pays any attention to me anyway. I am looking forward to school and am browsing through the textbooks for the new year and playing the piano a bit. Everything would be great, if only my parents were not so upset. They are worried about Felek. He should be home soon, on 15 September, when he finishes his one year of military service, and he is supposed to start medical studies—unless no Jews are going to be admitted to the university because of *numerus nullus.* What a curse this anti-Semitism is.

Yesterday, in my new dress, I went with Hela and Rila to meet my classmate Jaśka who lives on Wawel and whose father works at the cathedral. As we waited for her, we looked down at the city, it was so beautiful. On the way home, a street photographer took our picture by the monument to Kościuszko on his horse. Hela brought the picture today. The girls signed it, "Tall-stemmed Hala flanked by two dwarfs."

I am going with Mama to the café on Planty now where my father and Mr. W. and his wife are expecting us. Why do grownups love sitting in cafés so much? At least there will be interesting magazines and foreign journals to look at, and of course pastries and ice cream.

Good Heavens, what is going on? Kraków is now full of people from the "West," from Katowice, Sosnowiec, and Bielsko. The stores are besieged all of a sudden, people are buying everything. Our Janka returned home overloaded with provisions and complained that prices had gone up. All over the city, yellow posters inform us about anti-aircraft defense. The glass in the windows—and ours were cleaned so beautifully by Janka—has to be pasted over with strips of paper. We are preparing black shades and Marian is readying a shelter in the basement.

On Planty and in the parks, people are digging zigzags for anti-aircraft ditches. As usual, when the city is in danger everyone, young and old, rich or poor, works together. I am digging these ditches, too. People joked and laughed, but I suddenly felt terrible—as if we were digging a funny little grave for ourselves. I washed my hands at the street hydrant and ran to look for Mama in the Café Cristal. She was sitting, very sad, at a table with Pani Mania and Aunt Dora. They hardly spoke and I was bored to death. Papa arrived and took me for a walk along Planty to the pond. The smooth greenish gray water resembled the large mirror in Grandma's room, but the lighted fountain shone with colorful drops. My poor mother worries for five years ahead. At least Papa is always optimistic, and even now, when I admitted that I was frightened, he tried to joke, "Come on, you're a big girl, almost as tall as I am. Don't worry, you're home with your parents!" I snuggled up to him. I know that nothing bad can happen to me at home, because the family home is untouchable. It is the safest place in the world. And yet. . . .

Large white posters with MOBILIZATION! splashed across them in big red letters appear all around the city. Heavy tanks thunder through the streets, while private cars dart swiftly by toward Warsaw or Lwów. In front of every building, people talk and gesticulate nervously. The voices of our janitor, Marian, and Mr. Heller, the shoemaker, can be heard in our room screaming to high heaven and blustering threats against the Germans. Out of his first-floor window, Sewiałek, the baker, who works at night in the bakery on the corner, yells that they are disturbing his sleep. My mother and I had just arrived at the front door and so they asked us about "the young master," Felek. We only know from the telegram that he has left Lwów with his regiment—but where to?

"A soldier never knows where he is going, that's a military secret, but we know. They're going to Berlin!" shouted Marian in an upbeat mood, but Sewiałek just waved his hand: "If they don't stop Hitler, that is the end for all of us. Nothing will be ours anymore, neither our life, nor our possessions, nor the nail in the wall, nor the pegs for Heller's soles. That's the law of war."

"Stop griping, son. The Lord Jesus won't allow such a misfortune, our priest said so in church. I'm just coming back from vespers. Don't you worry about Felek, young lady." This very old lady, Pani Sewialkowa, remembers when my mother was born. My grandmother has been dead for several years, yet for our tenants my mother is still "the young lady." I ran over to the army barracks with Józka, the baker's daughter, with cigarettes for the soldiers. Weighed down with knapsacks, ready to march out, they were singing, every detachment singing something different and off-key.

I can't stand this chaos. In the evening, I sat on the balcony, completely alone. The start of the school year has been postponed, and here I thought that I would be going there the day after tomorrow. I don't want this kind of vacation.

Maybe things will quiet down after all, perhaps there won't be any war? How I long for that to happen! And yet, I already sense that it's impossible. A shooting star, a common enough phenomenon in August, has scared me, a harbinger of misfortune. It reminded me of the aurora borealis that streaked the evening sky with blood-red rays in February. Shuddering, I ran from the balcony to Janka in the kitchen. She said she's glad not to have a boyfriend because she does not need to cry for him now. What does she mean, she doesn't have one? What about the chimney sweep who used to visit her? And the bombardier from the artillery detachment, to whom I wrote love letters for her? And, besides, does one cry only for a boyfriend?

Hela and Jurek and I ran ourselves ragged through the town all day searching every drugstore for annogen powder for the anti-gas filters—there was none left. Things are very sad at home. Felek sent a card written during the march out of Lwów. My poor brother, an eighteen-year-old soldier! I cannot even imagine that tall adolescent marching like a camel with his knapsack and blanket. Mama despairs, "Where is my son? Dear Lord, have mercy on my son!" Papa keeps silent. I became restless and went shopping with Hela. We came back in the evening with nothing. Hela badly wanted to go to the cinema to see a new Deanna Durbin film. (She talked me into parting my hair in the middle like Deanna, as if this could help make me pretty!) I would rather see *The Testimony of a Spy* because one should know the methods of spying. Jurek saw me home, and standing in front of my house, we made arrangements to go tomorrow. All of a sudden, Jurek said in a gloomy voice, "A lot can happen by tomorrow." "Don't frighten me!" I returned. "I'm scared enough as it is on this blacked-out street."

Even our own little street seems strange and unpleasant, the cars' headlights covered with blue paper give a ghostly light. I ran home, jumping three stairs at a time. Papa checked the blackout shades in the windows, Mama cried in corners.

Oh, God! What is going to happen?

1 September 1939

I awoke suddenly, my heart pounding. I did not know where I was. The dense inky blackness of the room choked me like cotton. A horrifying silence clogged my ears—as if the whole world were holding its breath. I jumped out of bed and opened the window wide, realizing with relief and joy that it was already dawn. In the dim light of early morning the furniture seemed old and ugly to me. The sleepy street was lifeless, only the bright and clear, cloudless sky stretched high above the city like a bright dome. Standing at the window in my pajamas, I inhaled the crisp September air deeply, when suddenly a quiet and strange noise reached me. I leaned out, listening, and then all at once an ear-splitting shriek of sirens blared from all the factories accompanied by the sound of a poker beating wildly on a skillet—our janitor Marian was letting us know about the air-raid alert.

"Air raid!" I screamed and burst into my parents' bedroom. I was terribly shaken, but I was trying to stay calm. "It must be some kind of air-raid drill. Polish aircraft." I pointed to the sky. At that moment came the deep growl of heavy bombers and a strong detonation, the dry rattle of machine guns and a deafening boom.

"*Jezus, Maria,* they are bombing us! Go down to the cellar!" yelled Janka hysterically, while I, wishing to convince others as well as myself, desperately repeated that this was impossible, that this was an air-raid drill. The radio began broadcasting some completely incomprehensible codes, isolated words and numbers: *Karolek . . . kawa . . . 203 . . . czekolada . . .* (Charles . . . coffee . . . 203 . . . chocolate . . .).

A frenzied tumult followed the air raid. Through the streets rumbled heavy tanks, soldiers marched bestrewn with flowers. Janka and I went downstairs and distributed cigarettes and candies, then empty-handed, ran to the corner where a large strangely silent crowd stood in front of a yellow poster. The letters jumped before my eyes when I read:

"POLES! LAST NIGHT OUR PERPETUAL ENEMY INVADED OUR BORDERS."

Someone shouted: "War has been declared! The railroad station has been bombed!"

I wanted to ask something, but a new wail of sirens dispersed the people. Immediately the street emptied, only tanks moved heavily down the middle. We ran back home, fast. My heart pounded unevenly. I staggered against the wall in our entranceway. The mirror reflected a strange, unfamiliar, gray face, frightened eyes, and trembling lips. War . . . war . . . so far an empty word for me, acquired now a terrifying and dangerous meaning. War . . . there really is a war.

I am writing this in a small first-aid station where, in case of an emergency, we are supposed to help victims and call for the ambulance. Mama went home for a while, and I am in charge. Today is the third day of war. England and France both took pity on us and declared war against Germany. Perhaps this really will be over soon! After all, the Germans have only a few real tanks and the rest are made of plywood, while we have a strong army and France and England are world powers. But why do troops march to the front by day, and why do horse-drawn wagons with refugees shuffle along in an unbroken line in the opposite direction by night? Why do people run away? Why are they so horrorstruck? Oh, God, there is an air raid again and I am here alone and I am afraid and I do not have any heroism in me!

November 1939

I wrote that in September—now it is the middle of November. Just two months have passed, yet they seem like centuries. On the fourth day of the war, Kraków went mad. The reservists and the young men were ordered to flee to the East, and everyone else followed them like sheep. I cannot adequately describe our escape from the Germans: the bombing of the train and the long trek east in an enormous crowd of troops and refugees blocking all roads. I cannot describe the glorious Polish autumn which turned on us and helped the enemy. The nights spent under the open sky, or, rather, under millions of stars. The days full of scorching sun and fear of the constant air raids. The battle at Żabno, when suddenly we found ourselves in a field under artillery fire and where, for the first time in my life, I saw the truly horrifying glow of fire against the night sky. A village was in flames, people and cattle were fleeing in random directions. The Germans do not have tanks made of plywood. They have the same kind of tanks we do, but they have many, many more of them.

We scarcely had time to pick ourselves up from a field of cabbage after one air raid when a German patrol on motorcycles hurried along the road. "They look like Gods of War! I am impressed," said a lady with whom, among others, we dragged ourselves onto a horse-drawn wagon. Papa snorted angrily, "Gods of War, indeed!" and said would she please damn well stop using such lofty expressions. Really, that's how he expressed himself, "damn well." If Mama had been here, she would have quelled him with a glance, as Felek would say, for using such language. But Mama was not here. One day during an air raid we lost each other in the confusion, and Papa and I searched for her desperately, in vain. We even returned to Oleszyce, and then, assuming that she had gone ahead, we reached the small town of Bełz just on 20 September, my birthday.

For the first time, I came in contact with a real Jewish community, quite different from Kazimierz in Kraków. Dignified old Jews with long beards paced majestically in measured steps around the house of their famous rabbi. Apparently, he had told them that nothing threatened them, and Jews believe their rabbi. But, is it possible that while the whole world has been turned upside down, here it is as though nothing has happened, daily life continues as it was, with the little shops and booths and geese waddling on the small market square? Resting in someone's front yard, I looked around at this idyllic scene in disbelief. All at once, a joyful voice called my name. I rushed to my feet and here, behind the fence, was Julek on his bike! He was headed toward Warsaw, but our capital had already probably fallen. I wrung my hands, "This is the end!"

Felek and I had always ridiculed dramatic gestures, but now life itself called for one! Julek spat out, "Stop sniffling," and started to prove on the basis of literature and history that the war had only just started and that we had conspiracy, uprisings, and underground battles ahead of us. He seemed to look forward to conspiracy! He sounded different from the way he had sounded in Kraków. Julek was, in my opinion, the most handsome of all of Felek's friends. A tall, golden blond boy with greenish eyes. I had met him sometimes at the skating rink and often at tea dances in our home, but he had never paid any attention to me. No one paid any attention to me! No one treated me the way they did Blanka or Lena and other girls older than me. I was only Felek's little sister, and I stopped caring when they discovered my dolls and—those mean boys—hanged them all from the chandelier in the dining room. All of them! Sleepy, Kitty, Basia, the paper one, Wicunia, and the black doll, Maksio. I did not play with dolls like other little girls, I just told them the stories I would write someday. Who else could I tell these stories to when only Janka Z. listened to me, and that only because she also wants to be a writer?

And here he was, that unattainable Julek on whom half of my class had a crush—the other half had a crush on Romek, but Romek was nowhere nearly as handsome—that same Julek it was who sat next to me, munched an unripe green apple, and suddenly remembered, "You were the best one to dance a waltz with!"

Of course! Of course, I was the best one, because a waltz requires distance between the partners, but as soon there was a tango, he ran to Blanka and danced with her cheek-to-cheek and Papa took pity on me and pulled me out of the corner behind the piano. I told Julek the whole truth. He burst into loud laughter, until someone chastised us, saying there's a war on and our heads are full of nonsense!

At noon the whole town was thrown into turmoil when a new wave of refugees rushing east arrived from Warsaw. We moved out at once, and by the next air raid we had lost Julek.

I remember Lwów and Żółkiew as if through a fog because I came down with the flu. In Żółkiew we stayed in the marketplace with the nice family of a Jewish merchant. Papa insisted that I attend gimnazium and I did, but not for long. The math teacher complained that the students from Kraków had not been taught anything, but the Latin teacher singled me out as an example of how well the Kraków students were educated in Latin because I translated a few paragraphs of *"Pro Archia poeta oratio ad iudices"* faultlessly. It was lucky he didn't examine me on *gerundivum* or *consecutio temporum*. A lonely stranger, I walked around in a long black coat with Persian lamb fur which Mama had thrown over me on that cold morning before the air raid. I missed Mama and our home terribly. I was very unhappy, a stranger and lonely, and I used to go to the park to seek solace among the golden maples and chestnut trees along the quiet and deserted avenues.

Papa went to Lwów for a few days, and at the "Café de la Paix," a center for refugees, he heard from someone who had just arrived there from Kraków that Mama was at home and searching for us! We decided to leave at once and go back to Kraków. Everything here in the East was alien to me, particularly the Red Army in their ungainly long coats. I was afraid of Soviet soldiers, although they sang beautifully. We waited for hours on the border bridge at Przemyśl. People cursed the Russians, but quietly, and sighed, "Oh, if we were only on the other side already." One Russian officer looked at us as if we were mad to be returning to the Germans; but we were going home! As soon as we crossed the bridge, the Germans locked us all up in the barracks to sleep on straw full of fleas! No one knew what the Germans planned for us, and when after a few days they put us in locked boxcars, we did not know where we were going or why. Finally we arrived in Kraków and were again locked up in some fort outside the city. When after a few days they began to let us go, Mama arrived bringing fresh clothing to replace our worn-out rags, and we went home together by streetcar. I was deliriously happy and could not see enough of Mama and my native city. But so many foreign soldiers are stamping their boots along the streets of Kraków. We have lost the war. The red flag with the swastika flowing from the ancient walls of the Royal Castle Wawel symbolized the enormity of our defeat. It brought tears to my eyes, and I turned to Mama, sobbing. People in the streetcar stared at me sadly.

Our apartment, faithfully watched by Janka and, indeed, by all the tenants in our house who, wiser than us, had stayed at home, is cozy, but unusually quiet. No news from Felek, though his colleagues Zbyszek, Marian, and Józek returned home in the first weeks of the war. I roam around the rooms, do not dare to get close to the piano. As soon as Mama left, I began playing Chopin softly, and, after that, the "Marseillaise," but then I stopped abruptly. It is a sacrilege to play this anthem so quietly. It has to roar with emotion, not whimper like a sick melody.

I put on my school uniform, just for the sake of it, because I cannot attend my school anymore. School is forbidden to Jews, unless it is the Hebrew school. Papa has already enrolled me, but I don't know how I will manage there because so many subjects are strange to me. I don't know Hebrew and Hebrew literature, and I hardly remember the history of the Jews.

It's all over with the Hebrew gimnazium. The Germans have closed it. There were searches in Kazimierz, they beat the Jews, plundered the Temple and the synagogues. The Torah and books were thrown out into the mud and trampled, the old Jews were pulled by their beards and shaved. They are rounding up the Jews on the streets for the most humiliating work—so how could they allow us to get an education? Well anyway, I do not miss this school, I felt alien there. It was not my gimnazium,.

I wrote a little poem about my school years, mentioning all the "sins" the students usually committed, though I hardly ever did, except for a few. Apart from a few hated math problems, I never copied anyone else's homework. I always did my homework at home. Actually, I enjoyed studying. I never played hookey, and I haven't been out with anyone yet, though some of the girls in my class go out with boys. On the other hand, not all of them have an older brother like I do and a house full of his friends. Boys—big deal! They pulled my pigtails, and only when Felek wasn't around would Zbyszek or Marian or Tolek start a reasonable conversation with me and not tease.

It is war now. Who knows where my brother is? The few boys who came back are nowhere to be seen, as if ashamed that others fell or went abroad with the Polish army, like Andrzej. How I adored him! But when he asked me to go out with him, I turned him down. I was too shy. Instead, I agreed to go out with Roman, on whom all the girls in my class had a crush. But I was the only one who knew him personally and I did not care for him. Anyway, Mama did not let me go, because I was too young. Deep down I was glad that nothing came of this rendezvous. Anyway, who cares about going out, it is war now and one does not know what to do with oneself.

November 1939

I am attending clandestine courses held in different private houses, but it's not the same as school. There are about eight of us girls, two of them from my class, Runka S., who used to sit next to me, and Dola Hoffman, a pianist, who played Schubert's "Impromptu" in *Sala Saska.* Our Felek performed in two concerts there a year ago to the wild enthusiasm of the audience, half of whom, of course, were his classmates from gimnazium, proud of his artistic endeavors. During the concert I experienced stage fright, but not Felek. He came up to the podium in a leisurely way, bowed, winked at his friends, and, scarcely concealing his laughter, sat down at the piano. Even when his finger slipped off a key once in the fastest movement of the "Perpetuum mobile," he went on undisturbed without skipping a beat—I would have fainted with shame, for sure. During the second part of the concert, I stopped worrying because Felek played brilliantly and flawlessly. He's very gifted, that brother of mine, and I am very proud of him.

Dola's family, her father and her seven siblings, are all musicians. They have a large apartment on Dietla Street near the Vistula River, and we meet there for classes most of the time. It is an education, all right, but it is not a school. Neither our professors nor we can concentrate on learning. We are all tense and anxious and frightened that something terrible may happen at any moment.

We read Aesop's fable *"Lupus et Agnus."* He was clever, that schoolmaster, to give us such a timely Roman parable:

Haec propter illos scripta est homines fabula
Qui fictis causis innocentes opprimun

I translated this in a form of a prose poem:

This is a fable for people with the nature of a wolf
who oppress innocent victims for imaginary reason.

I have to stop my writing in order to wash the dishes. I hate to do it, but our Janka has gone back to her village, my parents are working, and I am in charge of housekeeping. Janka used to talk to the dishes, "Come, you dirty plate, soon you will be pretty again. And you, smoke-smeared pot, don't look so unhappy, see how shiny you are now? Smile!" There are so many things we do without anything to show for it; at least washing dishes brings immediate results.

Staszka, my new friend, is coming this afternoon. Her mother works with mine. Staszka is a better housekeeper than I am—she knows how to cook. She is an intelligent and amiable and very graceful girl, but not very pretty because she has a red birthmark on her neck and cheek. By now I don't even notice it. I like her a lot, for we both like to read. She is serious and funny at the same time, and talking with her is a pleasure.

At last! At last! News from Felek! He was wounded in his hand in the battle of Warsaw and is a prisoner of war in Pomerania. How lucky that he is alive and his wound not serious enough to affect his piano playing! We are delirious with joy. Each of us wrote a letter to him, and I ran to the main post office with a parcel as well and waited in line a long time at the "*Kriegsgefangenen-post*" window. This parcel was from our whole family. Yesterday I went to Aunt Amalia's, my beloved aunt in Kraków. Her daughter, Felicia, works in an office, so my aunt was home alone, wrapping her freshly baked marble cake in elegant white tissue, sighing dramatically, her eyes raised to the heavens. "Dear Lord! I can't even imagine that poor Felek, hungry and cold and alone, without Mama, without Papa, without Aunt Amalia! . . ." I had to laugh, even though nothing was really funny.

Then I went to Aunt Dora's at Słowackiego Avenue. I hardly recognized her in her apron and with a kerchief over her black hair. They also do not have a maid anymore, and my aunt, blue-eyed and tall, moved around swiftly cleaning the large apartment and singing a folksong, with her tame yellow canary flying behind her. My cousins, Mietek and Jureczek, were out with Uncle Ignacy at his engineering firm. Finally we sat down in the kitchen, waiting for the poppyseed cake for Felek to be baked. Aunt Dora served us tea and grew pensive, her beautiful eyes filled with sadness. "Mietek is eleven years old and he is not allowed to go to school. Jureczek will soon be six years old, he is still a young child, yet he knows what is going on. He keeps asking, 'What is a Jew? I don't want to be a Jew!'"

Strange, where did he pick that up? In their part of the city, as in ours, there aren't many Jews, and no bearded, Orthodox Jews at all. Aunt Dora is worried that the Germans may requisition their apartment because it is in the most modern, most recently developed section of Kraków. Apparently the main headquarters of the Gestapo are to be in the Aleje. We both grew sad and sat in silence. Only Kuba, the canary, trilled his silvery coloratura from the top of the credenza in front of the open doors of his cage.

8 December 1939

The Germans have issued a most hideous ordinance. From now on, all Jews have to wear a white band with a blue Star of David on the right arm. David was the greatest king of the Jews, and the Star of Zion was once a sign of triumph—today it is to be a sign of contempt.

And how could anyone concentrate on Newton's law of gravity? One of the girls in our group, Anka, said she is ashamed, that she is never going to wear this armband, that she does not look Jewish. I, also, do not look Jewish, for according to the German definition in their newspaper, *Stürmer*, racially pure Jews have scraggly black hair, long, hooked noses, and flat feet. There is nothing black about me except—in Felek's opinion—my character, but even if this were true, character doesn't show on the surface, so to the eye I'm not in the least like a Jew. However, I'll probably wear the armband. If everyone has to, everyone must.

We talked about it at home. Mama fried potato pancakes for supper. Papa said that there's no point turning our noses up at the fact that we are the Chosen People, it is not up to us where and as whom we are born. The Germans are the ones who should be ashamed of the armband, and not us. He's going to wear the Star of David with pride. At this, Mama smiled a bit ironically. "Since when did you become such a devoted Jew?" But Papa was not joking. "If being of Jewish origin is a sentence of death, I will die as a Jew. I do not want a different fate from the rest of my people."

He got up and left the room. Shivers went down my spine. Mama also felt uneasy. We cleared the table in silence and I wanted to sit down to my homework. But how could I concentrate on Newton's laws of gravity in the face of German laws?

January 1940

A small iron stove connected by a pipe to the large tiled oven stands in the middle of the dining room. Here we cook, and in order to save coal, all the other rooms are closed off. Supposedly it is healthy to sleep in a cold room, but I hate to lie down in an icy bed. So we all sit around this small iron stove, except when crippled Pan Chmiel from the basement comes limping over to visit Papa, and then Mama and I go over to the neighbors. Sometimes we all tell fortunes using a book and a big key. The book turns to the right or to the left and points to a number and that says when the war will be over. I don't believe in it, but it's better to prophesy that at some point in time things will be all right. I remember that in May, when the graduating class had their final exams and the younger classes were off, Hanka Łętowska and I went for a walk along Planty to the Słowacki Theater. A Gypsy woman sidled up to us and read my palm: "Your name is Helina. You won't finish school. There are clouds above your head, but the sun will shine. Give me a few groszy."

From then on, Hanka called me Helina. The Gypsy's words terrified me, but Hanka, ever logical, explained that when you see schoolgirls on Planty at a time when they are supposed to be sitting in class, it seems obvious that nothing good is going to come of them. I was a good student and there was nothing to fear. But now I wonder whether that Gypsy really did read something in my palm. Clouds above my head?

April 1940

For several days I have been working at the pharmacy on Wolnica Plaza. It is very pleasant so far. My boss is nice. Anyway, I already knew him from before. Apart from him there is his relative, Józek, a handsome, young man, and Pan Staszek, whom the boss promoted from errand boy to assistant. On the first day I got acquainted with the small laboratory behind the front store and with the storage room, all smelling of perfume and medical remedies. Large barrels with vaseline and bottles of some strange liquid crowded the passageways, the tables are full of jars, funnels, small and large test tubes and measuring cups. Sizable cardboard boxes with herbs clutter the shelves. *Flores chamomille vulgaris*—the chamomile fragrance reminds me of a meadow. I compared the inscriptions with the pharmaceutical dictionary: *Radix althae*—wild mallow root. *Flores tiliae*—linden flowers. *Species laxantes*—who would imagine that such melodious words mean herbs used for a loathsome decoction against upset stomach! Apothecary books are piled up around the large *Pharmacopea* with added pages of handwritten prescriptions for ointments, emulsions, lotions, and creams.

I packed herbs into small paper bags and weighed them carefully on a small scale. Later I weighed the ingredients for the zinc ointment, which I ground into a paste in a large mortar. It was not easy—my hand ached, and yet there were still plenty of zinc lumps. Józek came and showed me how to do it. He skillfully ground the ointment, and then we set ourselves to work on powders against headache.

Late afternoon I went to my class. The girls laughed at me—I smell like the pharmacy, though I wear a smock there, like everybody else. It is as if I had become a worse person, because I *have to* work.

"Most hateful of all words is the word DUTY"—whoever said it, and I don't know who, was absolutely right. What is more terrible than having a duty, an obligation, whether one likes it or not!

Before the war, whenever the weather was bad I did not go to school because I immediately came down with a sore throat. And now we have such a severe winter, frost and biting wind, and I have to tramp back and forth over the Vistula River four times a day. An enormous German soldier is standing sentry on the bridge. Perhaps he is not such a giant as he looks in his large sheepskin coat and double wooden boots. Stamping his feet for warmth, he holds his big rifle at the ready. I pass him by looking straight ahead, but I don't run as though I were afraid of him. How bitterly cold and long this first winter of the war is! For the last few days my dearest Papa has been bringing me soup from home to the pharmacy, so I only cross the bridge twice a day. I am not used to being on my feet all day, and my back aches. I am overtired and have no desire to do anything in the evening. Mama pampers me on Sunday, lets me sleep late and serves me breakfast in bed, as if I were a princess.

I was reading something in bed and was half asleep when Marian P., a former student at the School of Fine Arts, came to visit my parents. I heard part of their conversation: "Just in case—would you take our pictures for safekeeping?" What is my father talking about?

April–May 1940

Spring has come at last! I could hardly bear to sit by artificial light in the dark lab. I sprinkle a piece of cotton with pine essence, bend over an open box of chamomile, and, closing my eyes, make believe I am in the country. Dola and Hanka, already chocolate brown, are sunbathing on the Vistula with their boyfriends. They take their Jewish armbands off when they go there, of course. On Sunday, I went with Maryśka and Staszka to see my old nanny, Józka, who lives in the suburban village across the Wilga stream. Józka knows how to read cards and tell fortunes; she said that Felek will return home in summer, but not for long, because he will get married soon.

I play piano softly by the wide-open windows which let in a fragrant breeze from the nearby park. Evenings are peaceful, but the nights are disquieting because of suspicious marches by the military. A strange, monotonous sound woke me up yesterday. I jumped out of bed, and through the curtains Papa and I watched an endless procession of trucks loaded with fully armed soldiers, helmets and rifles and all, and bayonets bristling. Their lights dimmed, they rode and rode in the pale moonlight, like evil ghosts. "A regrouping of the armed forces," whispered Papa. "They are moving westward. Offensives always start in spring." I trembled and sighed. "Stop playing Napoleon and don't frighten her with your military strategy!" said Mama. "Go back to sleep, both of you!"

I do not understand politics, but I sense that something terrible is going to happen again.

May–June 1940

It has already happened. Belgium and Holland have fallen. The Germans used the same trick they used in World War I. Everyone is talking about it and I remember it from history lessons. Papa explained it to me in detail on the map in the large atlas. Couldn't they build the Maginot Line over the Belgian border? I look at the map of Europe divided by the colorful countries: green Russia, pink Poland, brownish Germany, red France, bluish England . . . It seems as though brownish Germany overflows like pus from a burst abscess and devours its colorful neighbors. Germany must be a great military power if so many countries are surrendering almost without a fight. And we had been told that the Germans have tanks made out of cardboard! Or . . . is it treason? How can one betray one's own country?

What is most important now is that France hold her own!

Hela came to visit me. She looks very pretty and very grown-up, uses lipstick and nail polish. She kept talking about her new acquaintances and invited me to go for a walk in the Dietla park and later to a party at her home. I did not find it at all amusing. Small talk is boring. The girls dance, pretending to be vamps, the boys are arrogant and try to be funny. They make grim jokes about the requisitionings and the roundups for forced labor. Some joke! But in fact, what else can they do? Without school and without any chance of reasonable entertainment because the theaters and cinema are forbidden to us, what else is left other than to gallivant around on the only permissible patch of Planty between Dietla and St. Gertrud! I felt like a stranger among my once close friends, and perhaps I spoiled their good time. I certainly scared the boys away. But why should I dance cheek-to-cheek with some pimply boy I could not care less about? Hela said, "Why not?" and told me that I am too demure. I do like to have fun and to laugh when there really is something to laugh about!

Hela has changed a lot since the beginning of the war, when we discussed books (Cronin, Zola, and the "lighter one" by Vicki Baum) for hours, or recited Polish Romantic poetry. Hela and I have grown apart. Luckily, Staszka and I can talk together—and keep silent together.

Hela came to the pharmacy today to pick me up after work, but I excused myself and went home. It is a beautiful May evening, and I sit alone and sorrowful at the piano. To cheer myself up, I play my entire "Romantic repertoire"—Beethoven, Tchaikovsky, Schubert, and Chopin, all the sad, encompassing music of great longing and eternal loneliness. I am ashamed of my tears, because I am already grown-up, but I feel lost and unhappy, and I cannot change as quickly as Hela and the others. But who knows? Perhaps they also feel immature and lost like me?

17 June 1940

I was pouring perfume into small flacons when I heard the electrifying scream of the newspaper boy: "Verdun has fallen! The Germans are in Paris! France has surrendered!" A flacon of "Le Chat Noir" fell out of my hands, spilling perfume onto the floor; that subtle fragrance will always remind me of something terrible. We threw ourselves into the newspaper, which carried a terrifying triumphal headline in red print. It is over. France did not hold out even as long as we did, our poor Poland, the first to be invaded by the full force of Hitler's army! Before the war, there was a film, *France is Watching*, which showed the Franco-German border with children playing in the meadows and cornfields. Underground, however, there were cannons, heavy aerial bombs, big gun barrels, shells, and machine-gun cartridges. Among them, in these subterranean vaults, the sentinels on the Maginot Line moved like ghosts. There were squadrons of military planes and innumerable divisions of soldiers singing "Madelon." Children could safely play because their fatherland, France, was on guard! Ha! I saw this movie with my parents, and at home in the evening we talked about it. Papa was rather silent, drinking that awful "herba-rum" tea. Finally, he said quietly, "Patriotic fervor alone cannot withstand military superiority—and betrayal."

Betrayal of one's own country! Whatever became of fidelity? Heroism? Chivalry? Are they all in the past, or only in our Romantic poetry? Is no one ready for sacrifice and fight? But one has to fight for ideals and for freedom! What if the Germans alone fought—and won? Would it mean that they were indeed right? No, never! Their crimes in Austria and Czechoslovakia after the annexation cannot be justified. Or . . . if they can, it is not worth going on living. No, there must be something noble and beautiful in the world—unless all the books were just lying, unless parents and teachers were also lying when they told us about goodness and human ideals. How can one obliterate and forget what makes us human?

July 1940

This summer drags on hopelessly. All day, the pharmacy until 5:00 P.M., then courses, or my music lesson, in the evening a walk with Staszka and Maryśka. The pharmacy is not interesting anymore. Making ointments, pills, powders, and lotions is hardly inspiring. Sales "in front" is also not very amusing. Our clients are mostly men and they ask me to go for a walk or to the movies with them. I don't care. Only one of them is nice, tall blond Włodek from Lwów, who reminds me of Felek's friends. Sometimes Włodek goes along to my piano lessons, gallantly carrying my music case. He waits patiently until I finish playing Grieg and Czerny and walks me home. Unfortunately, I am not as well prepared for my lessons as I used to be, because there is hardly any time left for practice.

My current piano teacher lives on Przemyska street, across from the former dormitory for Jewish university students. And what is there now? A brothel for German soldiers who, as my teacher complains, yell and scream all night, giving her constant headaches. She needs to take several pills daily against her migraine, so I bring her big boxes from the pharmacy for a cheaper price. Anyway, because of this brothel, Włodek wants to protect me, and so he, an "Aryan," and I, with my Jewish armband pinned to the short sleeve of my summer dress, walk together talking in a friendly manner. Włodek is a Ukrainian. I do not know from where, or why, he came to Kraków, perhaps in order to do some business and profit from the war. I prefer not to ask and not to know. He attended a Polish gimnazium and knows our literature well. He is really nice, yet I am a bit uneasy about seeing him because he is still an enemy. I have to wonder how I arrived at such a judgment. A person's nationality, or religion, or social status was not important to me before; what counted was whether a person was decent or not. I have learned to find these things important now, because suddenly we are considered Jews, and Jews are supposedly the lowest of the low. Streetcars are divided across the middle by a rope, the Jews in the back and the "Aryans" in front. There are signs saying "Purely Aryan" on many buildings, apartments, and stores. One Sunday Włodek came with us to my nanny's. We all bathed in the Wilga stream. Maryśka and he fell in love—good luck to them. Everyone is attached to someone, except Staszka and me—the two high-minded old maids!

Cambridge, Mass.

During this time I refrained from mentioning anything about Felek in my diary. Quite often strange guests appeared in our home, haggard-looking men arriving just before curfew at night. They would sit down to supper at the table and discuss something quietly with my parents, while I made up beds for the guests in Grandma's room. During the day they did not go out of the house, unless they were leaving the next day. They smuggled in letters from Felek and small gifts: rings made of horsehair braided around a "stone" cut from the handle of a toothbrush, or small figurines from clay or bread.

Felek was working in a field hospital for POWs, full by now of wounded Belgian, Dutch, and French soldiers. Polish prisoners freshly released from the hospital used the confusion to escape from the camp. Our home was their first contact; here they received civilian clothes, letters from their families, and further directions related to the underground organization.

One day in July, there was an unusual commotion on the street and a loud scream: "People, look what soldier is marching here!" We ran to the windows, hardly believing our eyes: next to the Wehrmacht soldier carrying a rifle walked a young Polish POW with the Red Cross armband of a hospital orderly. We ran to the hall to greet Felek who, bounding up the stairs five at a time, did not even wait for the German. They were both followed by all our tenants, neighbors, and Felek's friends, who crowded into our large dining room. Mama emptied our miserable pantry to feed Felek and the German. Papa talked with him and found out the reason for this incredible visit—one of the prisoners had suffered a nervous breakdown and had to be transported to the mental institution near Kraków. Felek, being an orderly, accompanied the patient, and the German guarded both of them. On the way back to camp in Pomerania, the guard agreed to stop at our house, but he watched Felek like a hawk, even getting up from the table to stand with his rifle in front of the toilet. Little did he know that the toilet window faced the balcony where Mama was standing, and so she learned where to send Felek's civilian clothes. We parted with heavy heart: "Not for long" Felek waved to us and marched to the railroad station with the German.

Our "crazy" soldier soon escaped to the Underground. Next, we were informed that the camp was going to be transported to Germany. But whether or not it was, Felek did return home soon, to the great joy of the whole family.

However . . . perhaps if he had stayed in the POW camp he would have been spared a lot of suffering and humiliation during the years in the ghetto and in the concentration camps of Płaszów and Dachau.

July–August 1940

Felek has returned home! We are madly happy. Mama is herself again, for Felek is her darling. Papa has regained his humor, and the house is alive again with Felek's friends welcoming him back all day long. Felek plays piano furiously, with a satanic passion, because for so long he has had only a harmonica, a prisoner's only musical instrument. I do not dare to touch the piano. Felek will work at the Jewish hospital in surgery as the orderly-assistant to Dr. Nüssenfeld. He is supposed to live in the hospital, but for now he is home. Thank God that all four of us are together again!

October 1940

Maryśka has moved with her parents and her sister to live with relatives in Wiśnicz. Some people consider Kraków to be the safest city because it is the capital of the General Government, but others leave and go to the provincial towns and villages. Maryśka had experienced some sweet moments of happiness and is now in despair over her separation from Włodek.

Staszka, like Runka, could not give a damn about romantic affairs. She has been working as a forced labor cowherd, and a young agronomist is very impressed by her—and by her disdain for his wooing. And I? There was Lonek, of course. But this was not love, not even a flirtation, only a fleeting infatuation, perhaps, and a desire to know, for once, what the big deal about a kiss was. As it happens, nothing, absolutely nothing, moved me, and I am embarrassed that this was my first "experience," for that's what they call the first kiss, isn't it? It was a meaningless episode, and it is too bad that it was, because now I will be bitter and cynical forever.

4 December 1940

Felek, my beloved brother, why are you sometimes the closest person to me, and sometimes a stranger? Why are you arrogant and brusque? Why are you rather selfish? Is it all because of your war and prison experiences? I don't want to judge your behavior, or even to reflect upon it, because it might make me feel bad about you, so I try not to see the flaws in the way you act. As a young girl, I can understand that you prefer a carefree life, but as a daughter and sister, I cannot condone it.

Cambridge, Mass.

For the first time in my diary there appeared a trace of the discord which, after several years, turned into the central drama of our family. My brother had left home as a seventeen-year-old adolescent at that formative time in his life, the period of transition from child to man. Cadet School in another city replaced family and home as the dominant influence in a boy's life. A handful of friends from his school was mixed with hundreds of other young soldiers from all over Poland, and Felek was, at that time, probably the only Jewish cadet among them. Our family was Jewish more by ethnic tradition than by depth of religious feeling. For Passover we had matzo and a Seder, but also Polish hand-painted eggs. At Hanukkah we lighted the Menorah, but we also had a Christmas tree and sang melodious carols. Felek was the musical star of his gimnazium and played the organ in church at Sunday

Mass. I do not know exactly what happened, but shortly after the pledging ceremony at the Cadet School, my parents returned from Lwów deeply worried. No rabbi had been in attendance at the pledging of the one Jew (who never prayed in a synagogue), and, as a result, the authorities subsequently found that Felek had not been entitled to swear the Pledge of Loyalty with the other cadets. They stripped Felek of his rank and insignia in front of his whole regiment, shaved his head, and demoted him to the rank of conscript until he had completed one year of service in the Nineteenth Infantry Regiment of the Defense of Lwów. The Polish military authorities had committed an enormous wrong.

Without telling me what had happened, my parents informed me that letters to Felek should now be mailed to a new address. My father wept over his son's humiliation and quickly left the room. My brother reacted with animosity toward the Jews as eternal victims of persecution. He reacted with aversion toward any religion and with cynicism and irony toward everything except music and medicine. After his first joyous outburst on his return home, Felek suppressed every emotional impulse with a brusque joke.

Our parents excused such rude behavior because of his experience in the Cadet School, at the front in Warsaw, and in the POW camp. Whenever he dropped in for a while from the hospital, they gave him affectionate care, literally denying themselves for his sake, especially our mother. I met Felek more often because the pharmacy was close to the hospital and he would invite me to the pastry shop nearby. To me, he was a model of all virtues and talents, until I realized that, in fact, he ought to feel obliged to assume some responsibility for our parents, instead of just taking their daily sacrifices for granted. We never talked at home about love between parents and children, for it went without saying. Once, however, I asked Felek whether he really did not care about us! He bridled, "Of course I care! Don't talk nonsense."

"Why, then, do you behave so strangely?" He shrugged his shoulders, turned to the piano, and began to play Beethoven's "Moonlight" Sonata, Papa's favorite. Music was my brother's language.

About twenty years later, in Boston, Massachusetts, Mama died suddenly of a heart attack. Her very beloved prodigal son arrived from Texas immediately and looked around for a piano in the funeral home. "I want to play for Mama and there is no instrument!"

Large tears ran down his cheeks.

28 January 1941

I am slowly recovering my inner balance, perhaps because of my temporary "vacation" from work, from the unpleasant environment and its problems. I am resting in bed, reading and answering letters. I miss Maryśka; correspondence is a poor substitute for a person. Maryśka had a positive influence on me, while Staszka depresses me. Staszka gets more and more introverted and gloomy. Her wit has turned into a biting irony and into sarcastic remarks about my clinging to the shreds of optimism. True, there is hardly anything to be cheerful about, but how else can one exist?

Maryśka, you had better write me something uplifting and encouraging, because I do not want to lapse into pessimism and misery!

30 January 1941

Our new next door neighbor is from Bohemia. She came to visit and told us about her daughter, still in Prague, who works at the cosmetics institute. She showed us photographs from their travels to Paris, Italy, Greece, and Palestine. After the war, they will join their family in America. The daughter is a few years older than I am, but she has already experienced wonderful adventures and has such a great future! Meanwhile we, school dropouts against our will, toil as unskilled laborers, like Stacha, or waste away in some forgotten little place, like Maryśka, or prepare laxatives, like me, earning 29.04 zlotys monthly. This big salary equals exactly the price of two loaves of bread. Why is our fate so lousy, with no prospects of a change for the better? Mama consoles me that someday we will be happy. Someday! In fact, it looks as if things may get even worse. The world has gone mad, but for now only we, the Jews of Poland, are being forbidden all cultural pleasures—education, libraries, theaters, and movies!

Cambridge, Mass.

The Bohemian woman's daughter soon arrived from Prague and died of tuberculosis in the ghetto. Her mother disappeared in one of the deportations of 1942.

6 February 1941

For several days we have been eating only potatoes. There is no money for anything else. Coal is scarce, and that goddamned frost never ends. At the pharmacy it is also freezing most of the time because the stove burns only in the afternoon when Miss Muszka, daughter of the *Volksdeutsch* commissioner, arrives. Considering me "socially acceptable," she likes to chat when she is in a good mood. Today she kept talking about a fabulous party and reception with liqueurs and champagne and "out of this world" food. What fun! They threw hors d'oeuvres and pastries out of the window at a target! She laughed. Suddenly she noticed that I had been eating a cold potato pancake for lunch, and she sent Józek to buy pastries for all of us. I refused to take any, but she practically forced me to. With the taste of a cream cake in my mouth, I slouched into a corner of the ice-cold storage and wept. How weak I was. I had lost my strength of character in accepting that pastry. That Muszka herself is sometimes friendly is beside the point. Our enemies destroy our existence, then buy us a cake and everything is fine. My poor parents, too, eat only potatoes now, and no one buys them cakes; and we are all so miserable and under such stress that we start fights about anything. Well, we have reason enough to feel angry: lack of money, freezing weather, that abominable pharmacy, and hunger. Hatred toward life and myself is growing in me because I am so powerless! All I can do is curse—though only in my diary—damn it all!

8 February 1941

Money rules the world! Does this cynical maxim indeed represent the basic truth in life? Money can do wonders, even if it were only that meaningless thirty zlotys raise in my salary beginning March 1, which, like magic, has changed my mood. Too bad, however, that this raise has happened, because Józek did not receive permission to stay and work in Kraków and has to move to another town.

The commissioner should have protected Józek and said that he was needed in the pharmacy but instead he fired him. The laboratory was mostly Józek's responsibility, and now I have much more work. Still, I prefer to make the ointments and face creams than to do the most boring and the hardest work which the men tried to shift onto me.

15 February 1941

At last, the end of this damned week of surprises! Did it indeed pay to rejoice at my raise! A call from the commissioner was cut off by the post office, but because it was I who answered the telephone, he thinks that I, "that arrogant girl in the lab," dared to hang up on him. He threatened to fire me in two weeks, or at best to retain me on the old terms, without the raise. Never mind the money; it is almost only a token, anyway. It is more the injustice of it all that hurts. I did not do anything wrong! My boss commiserates with me and worries, "That old fox wants to get rid of all of us. He began with Józek and will finish with me."

There is a new wave of deportations of Jews who did not receive the *Kennkarte*, which authorizes staying in Kraków. My parents, Felek, and I received such I.D.'s on Thursday. Really, it would be great if it were not for that damned commissioner. I am worried sick, cannot sleep, and have had a headache all day. Miss Muszka suggested that I go to "Daddy" to apologize and ask for forgiveness. I won't! What do I have to apologize for?

At home, both parents looked worried when I went to bed weeping. "What do I have to apologize for? Humiliate myself for nothing!" "Goodness, the poor child is so unhappy," Mama pitied me. Papa came to kiss me good night. "You have to go see the commissioner. You must. But it is not your humiliation."

20 *February 1941*

Never before have I had so many worries at once. I am going to go crazy or kill myself. Maryśka and Staszka and I talked about suicide once. One, two, three and it is over. Peace. But suicide is not for me. At least not now.

I must be a coward to still cling to life, even to such a miserable one. But today was a gorgeous sunny day, spring will arrive soon, and how can one die in the spring? I have had to make the leap much too soon from being a school-girl to being an adult, with troubles and responsibilities which I cannot bear. I ask myself the same thing a hundred times: Why? Why am I so tired and so worn out, like an old person? I, who not long ago was still a child? Why am I a victim of such injustice? I cannot change anything, no matter how hard I try. Why do I sit here alone in my helplessness on such a serene evening and shed bitter tears, instead of dreaming about love and happiness?

23 *February 1941*

I turn to my diary in the most difficult moments. How come I do not write when—on those very rare occasions—something nice happens, and I am in a good mood? Today, I write and cry and cry and my stomach is growling and I am hungry, hungry, HUNGRY! Every page is like every other one in my vain revolt against this existence which deprives me of youth's illusions. My aunt Mala used to quote Krasinski:

> Blessed be the age of youth!
> you golden dream among flowers!
> ideals of faith and virtue
> and love and freedom!

My great teenage years, indeed! Damn!

25 *February 1941*

I just came home from a day of forced labor. The Jewish *Kennkarte* obliges us to remove snow and clean streets. The pharmacy is required to release me for this work. I have gone twice already and came home dead tired. Before the war, I received a fancy ski suit for my excellent grades in school; who would have thought that I would be sweeping the streets in it? But today was somewhat easier. Our group consisted of mostly young and nice people. The boys chipped the ice and we threw it on the sides. A short older man of twenty-six, Janek Müller, well mannered and serious, reminded me of Lolek and treated me in a similar way. After an hour, I hardly felt my frozen feet. Our supervisor from City Hall, a professional street sweeper, told me to go inside a building and warm myself in the hallway. Toward evening, a drunken Wehrmacht soldier ordered all the girls to go home because "This is not a job for ladies." What a merciful gentleman! We know very well what would happen if we did, indeed, stop working. In the evening, we marched down the middle of the dark muddy streets and Janek offered to carry my shovel, but I refused, suddenly feeling sorry for him. He kept tripping beside me, an impoverished law student in a worn-out coat, shivering like the rest of us. When he looked up at me, his intelligent eyes sparkled and a gentle smile lit up his plain features. We avoided the subject of our present misery and talked instead about Polish poetry and literature, undisturbed by the scornful, or embarrassed, glances of the "Aryan" passersby who walked along the pavement. Were we really undisturbed? Perhaps we were only pretending, because what else could we do?

1 March 1941

A sudden and totally unexpected blow has hit me. I am crushed. Staszka, is it possible that we shall never meet again? The deportations out of Kraków are raging, there are raids and roundups on the streets. We know neither when or to where Aunt Mala and her daughter Felicia have disappeared. Staszka also received an order of expulsion from Kraków, although her mother and sister already had left for the suburbs. Staszka, who was now an illegal person, stayed with us overnight and met her mother and sister downtown the next afternoon, planning to travel with them back to Rabka. But there was a roundup, and all three of them were captured straight off the street, locked up in the temporary camp on Mogilska, and sent in a transport to Lublin or Rzeszów today. I have returned home from snow removal duty dead tired. I am desperate, unable to write. Where are you now, Stasiu? Are you cold? Are you hungry? What are you thinking about? Or are you just smiling ironically, a corner of your mouth lifted, in that way you have? I am alone now. No one, not even Hanka, Maryśka, or Runka meant as much to me as Staszka. And I cannot even cry.

5 March 1941

Bad news arrives suddenly and in quick succession. The departure of Staszka, the dissolution of the Jewish hospital, and today, finally, the rule about the creation of the ghetto in Podgórze. Bewildered as I am, I feel empty. In all these troubles and worries, the forced labor of removing snow is a kind of— Dear Lord!—pitiful diversion. At first, I found marching with a shovel across the city humiliating. Today I don't even care.

We worked on the muddy boulevards over the Vistula, and at dusk we softly sang forgotten boy scouts songs. The silvery moon and the orange shine of the street lamps were reflected in the gray Vistula, together with the heaps of melting snow along its banks. Lyrical serenity lets us forget our troubles for a moment, but now I am very sad again.

8 March 1941

In a few days, we have to vacate our own apartment in our own house and move into the ghetto. I was born here, so was Felek, and so was our mother. I look around our nice and cozy rooms with sadness, realizing that I am leaving behind my happy childhood and the carefree teenage years forever.

10 March 1941

It is amazing how easy it is to impress young men, whether or not one wants to. They follow me without any encouragement, the tall chemist, Józek Hollländer, and the short Janek, both of them "older men." Józek was about to get his chemist's degree last semester, but the university was closed. He walks me home in the evening, but I act as if I do not notice his interest in me and keep him at a distance. Janek did not receive a *Kennkarte* and, being illegally in Kraków, he cannot go out on the street. Will he stay in his room until the end of the war?

He wrote a letter to me at the pharmacy, asking me to visit him. With Mama's approval, I will go tomorrow, for today I still have my snow duty. I have learned something from my "older admirers" and have noticed a change in myself. I have become wiser, still open toward people, but without completely trusting everyone.

Cambridge, Mass.

Such was my wish, unfulfilled until now. My approach toward people was, and is, spontaneous and unreserved. I could never recognize sly and cunning scoundrels, and I paid dearly for it. This reasonable and careful person who did not allow herself to be hurt by others was not a tribute to me, but to those young decent men who were sensitive in dealing with a young, inexperienced teenager.

10 March 1941 cont'd.

I went to visit Janek wearing my navy blue dress with a lace collar held down by a pinned-on bunch of violets. Felek teased me: "You look like a mixture of Ophelia and a chambermaid who has stolen 'Soir de Paris' perfume. Who would dare to seduce such Holy Innocence?" And he struck up "The Virgin Prayer" on the piano.

Janek, who now lives like a hermit in his studio lined up to the ceiling with books, was overjoyed by my visit. We had a long conversation about things other than our everyday existence. Still, the uncertainty of our situation hangs over us, clouding every moment. Janek read parts of his war diary to me, which made me uneasy, because he wrote about me with fond affection. It's too bad that he has to resettle in the suburb Borek Fałęcki and that we will be left only with letters. At least he will be in the sunny, green countryside which I, in the ghetto, will miss.

12 March 1941

I am in my most furious mood again! Papa is working in the *Judenrat* at night, helping with plans for the translocation to the ghetto, and Mama is helping our aunts from the Crown-Soap factory who, because of their small children, cannot deal with packing up a large household. Late in the evening, Mama brings supper home from them. Our place is in disarray, and it seems that nobody cares. What a lousy life! To hell with it!

18 March 1941

My mood today presents itself as a splendid mixture of all the humors.

20 March 1941

That note from a couple of days ago describes how confused I was the day we moved into the ghetto. I fought sadness and tears and at the same time joked grimly with Felek at the sight of the migration of people. On one side of the street there were huge trucks, wagons, and wheelbarrows loaded with furniture, trunks, carpets, washtubs, pots and pans, odds and ends; on the other side of the street, Poles moved in the opposite direction, because the Poles living in this poor quarter of Podgórze have had to make space for us. To think that all of a sudden Kazimierz, that traditionally Jewish section of Kraków, is going to be full of Aryans! The chaos of the translocation brought gales of laughter to Felek and me. In the afternoon I had to go to work at the pharmacy, and when I was coming back in the evening I instinctively turned toward our home and Długosza Street, instead of to the ghetto. As I turned back, I saw the arch of the bridge over the Vistula and the cluster of trees from our park nearby looming in the foggy dusk, and tears of sadness filled my eyes. I don't want to see the new place without our furniture, just as I won't go to our former home which is stripped of it. We could not take all the furniture anyway, because in the ghetto we have been allotted only a single room with a kitchen. Besides, the antique china cabinet and Grandma's mahogany furniture were sold long ago, while our china, silverware, carpets, books, some pictures, and so on are at my nanny Józka's. The one consolation is that now that the hospital has been moved to the ghetto, the piano is back.

They are supposed to close the ghetto today. I don't know whether I will be able to work anymore. If not, I will have wasted one year. I play Chopin's "Prelude" with one finger and fight back tears.

25 March 1941

I don't want it. I don't want it. I don't want my empty stomach to growl, our room to be freezing cold, and my father to be so tired, to be so terribly skinny after the last few days that his skin hangs on his bones. I don't want Mama looking gaunt, and all of us constantly hungry, cold, disheartened, and bitter. God, what can I do about it? There really is no way out of our situation. There is no way out. We are without money, without provisions, without hope of getting any appropriate paying job. And what good can my miserable salary do? It barely covers my small needs, and how could that laughably small wage of mine cover the mass of small debts and help us to live?

So far Mama is isolating Felek from our family problems, but I think she is wrong. He is selfish. And why does he, a man, have to be spared the truth? Why should it be only me who has to bear the burden of family responsibility, and, like my parents, struggle to find a way out of this terrible situation from which, alas, there is no escape? What to do? What to do? How to help? It's enough to drive me mad.

Tonight, my heart ached as I looked at the worn, tired faces of my parents, who are still not old. On a sudden impulse, I wanted to hug the graying head of my poor Papa, I wanted to rush and kiss my Mama's roughened, hands, once so white and smooth. Instead, I hurled hard and angry words at them, though my throat choked with tears and deep down I was furious with myself. I am helpless. I am mean. It is no excuse that the war has demoralized me. I am wretched.

Cambridge, Mass.

Before life in the ghetto became more or less "normal," my family was quite simply starving.

The outbreak of the war brought an end to my father's position and to our savings in the Polish Bank. It brought an end, also, to income from our own house. Our Christian and Jewish tenants were equally impoverished. Out of necessity, my parents took insignificant little jobs at the Judenrat, dealing with the orphanage. Both had been interested for years in the care of poor Jewish children and youth. During the relocation to the ghetto, my father was sorting the files in the Judenrat building when the Gestapo trucks arrived to round up everybody there and take them outside the city to witness a public execution. Polish convicts were hanged by Jewish policemen. My father came home shocked, his face gray. Without a word he fell on the bed, frightening me by his despair. A messenger summoned him to a meeting regarding a position at the Judenrat—my father silently turned his face to the wall. But a few days later he reported to the Judenrat asking for a modest job as a sanitation supervisor, which had nothing to do with the preparation of lists for contributions or deportations. Taking care of sanitation works in the ghetto, my father felt the satisfaction of social usefulness and of having clean hands, untainted by doing wrong to anyone.

26 March 1941

Surely, someday, things will be good again! Surely, someday, the war will end and life will return to normal. And then . . . I will tear myself away from here and share an apartment with Staszka in Warszawa, Lwów, or Gdynia. I will study and work, and she will keep house, or do whatever she likes. As a matter of fact, I have no idea what she would like to do, what kind of person she will grow into. I can't even hazard a guess, she has such a reserved nature. Perhaps we will share a flat with Runka and Maryśka, perhaps we will form a whole clan of young women who take life seriously. I am not sure if Maryśka could stay long in such a female household. She will marry fast. I miss Staszka a lot—our walks, our talks—no one can take her place. Ah, if only Staszka knew how sad I am without her. No matter whom I am with, deep down I think about her. I am getting sad again and I don't want to.

Today, they walled in the ghetto. So far we are still allowed to go out, but what will happen after April 1? I try to cheer myself up by singing "I know that there will come a lucky day, . . ." though I know that whatever happens I won't be able to leave our home, and for a long, long time I will share in a miserable, gray, impoverished existence. . . .

28 March 1941

Only now is the significance of my first "experience"—my first real rendezvous, my first boyfriend, and my first kiss—slowly becoming clear. I stopped thinking about Lonek long ago, and even forgot about him completely. Today we met by accident. To me, he is just an acquaintance; but he claims I am his fondest memory. He made reference to last fall, and admitted that he had read my letter to Hela before he dropped it in the mailbox and thought he had me in the palm of his hand! Ha! In fact, I exaggerated my romance to Hela because I was annoyed by her notion of me as an eternal innocent, even though I was terribly embarrassed by a kiss on the cheek, let alone on the lips. Half a year has gone by and I have not grown any wiser despite the experience of a boy's kissing me. But I did not love Lonek. I distanced myself from him at the first sign of his vacillating between Lusia and Gusta, both vacuous, uneducated girls, but rich ones. Only black-marketeers have money these days. On top of that, Gusta, who has very short, fat legs, wears knee-high boots which don't suit her at all. It is I who should be wearing knee-high boots because I am a beanpole, but there is no money even to repair my old shoes, never mind to buy boots!

3 April 1941

On the first floor, below our apartment, lives the family of Dr. Lustgarten, the attorney. They have a son, Rysiek, and a daughter, Hala. She is "little Hala" and I am "big Hala." Rysiek is a classical pianist and thumps out Beethoven and Chopin's "Revolutionary Etude" and "Impromptu" from early morning on. Then "little Hala" practices a Chopin waltz over and over again. What a relief when Rysiek returns to the piano! On the third floor in our courtyard someone plays "Legend" by Wieniawski on the violin. Today I played for a long time, too, first Mozart, then songs by Franz Schubert and our Polish Moniuszko. Both these composers are full of charm. Both write songs about nature, filled with lyrical emotions and very dear to my heart.

6 April 1941

Of all the boys I know, Mietek and Ksylek are closest to me. Józek, the chemist, whom Mietek calls "Netherländer," remains distant, too grown-up, and I am also put off by the knowledge that he finds me attractive. I feel nothing for him, even though he is intelligent and good natured. Yesterday I behaved really badly toward him because I left him to visit Mietek who has had some small operation and is in the hospital under Felek's care. I fled from Józek in full knowledge that I was leaving someone who gets genuine pleasure out of taking a walk with me just to see someone who simply likes me. I made up for it today by telephoning Józek and arranging to go with him to the café in the ghetto where Felek works evenings, playing the piano, to make money. I left the pharmacy a bit earlier today to visit the hospital. I had a long talk with Mietek about school, how carefree our life had been in peacetime, when studying was our only responsibility. "Don't forget the rules about wearing uniforms in and out of school," Mietek said, adding, "and not being caught with a cigarette, or on a date in the park!" He must have had quite a past as a student! We laughed and had a good time. I was sorry to leave.

Edek Birn, whom I like very much, came to say good-bye, because he is going to another city. He walked me along the hallway. "It's too bad that it is almost impossible to keep as close in touch as one would like! Take care, Halinka, you are great to talk with." Great to talk with! I am always the intellectual friend and never the femme fatale, the women for whom men burn with desire. True, there are Janek and Józek, the Netherländer, both of them kind and gentle men who revere me. But where is the man to seduce me? Irka, Felek's friend at the hospital, was supposed to have come to admire Felek playing in the café, but it was her turn on duty so I walked back by myself down the boulevards to the ghetto. I went along the Vistula River, the mild spring air caressing my face tenderly. I had no desire to go to the noisy café, except that I can't always behave like a barbarian.

The boys from the hospital made room for me. I sat at a table with Lonek and Ksylek and soon Netherländer joined us. They joked around, ate, and gave the impression of having a great time. And I! I did not like this café, the only one in the ghetto. A few dreary rooms—is this what would be called a dive? The cafés frequented by my parents were totally different. The orchestra made up of Felek, some violinist, and a percussionist played very well. The beauty of the music and this ugly place—what a contrast! The singer, Heniek, presented his song "Funia Neuman." Great applause. And then dance music. Hala L. sang words to a tango, "Forget it, it was only a joke, you believed in his sham." Lonek turned to me with a triumphant smile. I shrugged my shoulders and looked at him with disdain, while Hala rolled her eyes and continued, "Forget it, he was not worth it." Suddenly Lonek took a photograph from his wallet which he himself had taken in the summer and showed her my dedication:

... and after a few years,
stacked into the very corner
of the wallet,
sighs a small forgotten
picture of One among many. . . .

Furious and indignant, I grabbed the photo and crushed it in my hand. How could I ever be friendly with someone who was unable to respect the painful irony of this dedication! I hated everyone at this table. With a flushed face and stifling a loud sob, I jumped up and ran home, gritting my teeth to avoid bursting into loud tears.

9 April 1941

Once again, as in the fall, whatever I think of is unpleasant. Today that girl Gusta came to visit Mietek. She's the one who used to pursue Felek, but he is after the pretty Hungarian Fela who walks around without a Jewish armband now. Actually, Gusta is pretty, too, although she's such a small and stupid girl. We sat by Mietek's bed and talked about nothing, and I felt somewhat sad. How do they do it, these girls, while I am eaten by sorrow, unable to talk, or write, or even to cry? Downstairs, someone is drumming away at Schumann's "Traumerei," most probably "little Hala." It gets on my nerves, that playing. My head aches.

12 April 1941

Papa's birthday. From one extreme to another, from being overjoyed to being profoundly sad. I am like the weather. It snows and snows and suddenly the sun brightens the world for a moment. On the way from work I met Lonek. He walked me home and apologized profusely. Yesterday was Passover. All four of us celebrated the holiday in a serene and loving atmosphere. Papa read the Haggadah. We are again slaves, like our ancestors once were in Egypt. Who will "bring us forth with a mighty hand and an outstretched arm"? From now on, the ghetto is closed. I was denied a pass to the city and won't be able to work. There is only one pharmacy, that of Tadeusz Pankiewicz, the only Christian business in the ghetto, with its own staff and no need for another employee. The year and a half of my apprenticeship and hard work was in vain.

Regardless of the need to earn money as I did at the pharmacy, I cannot even imagine living within the limits of the ghetto, within its few congested little streets without any free green space. Just the very thought of it chokes me.

14 April 1941

There is nothing to do when I have no pass. I went with Netherländer and Hala to hear Felek play at the Café Polonia. This time, it did not seem such an ugly place to me. I drew caricatures of some funny-looking fat men seated in the corner and talking German, refugees from Vienna. I also made caricatures of us, and Józek laughed and looked at me with love and admiration because, in his words, he adores "this hilarious girl!" Does he realize that I like him only as a friend? And that behind my humor there is great sadness?

20 April 1941

Day after day it rains. It is dark and cold and our room is even colder than outside. No sun. No spring. No school. No work. No money. How are we to live? I grumble to myself, but soon, with a polite smile, I will set the table for lunch and wash the dishes afterwards. Mama is sick, so I am taking care of our housekeeping. I hate our unheated grave of an apartment with its view of the courtyard, and of garbage, and of just a tiny geometric segment of gloomy sky between the roofs, high above. God is supposed to be somewhere, high above. Why does he let people shed so many tears that the sun, saddened, hides behind the clouds and cries with us?

22 April 1941

I am scribbling in bed by candlelight. At nine o'clock suddenly, a blackout! Is there a possibility of an air raid? I am upset, and let's face it, scared. Yes scared! A few neighbors came over to discuss the situation and sipped tea, or rather hot water, with some rum substitute and saccharine. "In the present configuration of powers, the outbreak of a new war could be decisive to Poland and to us Jews," said Papa, and everybody agreed. Who cares about the political conflicts of foreign states? A human being is completely lost in big politics and killed in action or in the air raids. I don't want to perish like that! Pan Chmiel from the basement apartment in our home, who had been coming to Papa for their secret talks, said that the world awaits this war that will change Poland's border to the Oder River in the West. Our janitor, Marian, visited us here in the ghetto and told us that Pan Chmiel was arrested at night and shot by the Gestapo. He was a hero and I am a coward, I said to Mama. "Just do not let the fright overcome you," she advises me. "First, terror makes you lose your common sense, then your human dignity, and when this happens, you are doomed. Don't worry in advance. Just keep going from day to day in a decent way, chin up, shoulders straight."

This is exactly what my parents do, but I feel lost and insignificant "in the storm of history," as Felek would say with ironic pathos. Does it matter whether one dies at the hands of enemies or allies? For over twenty centuries people have racked their brains in order to conquer the air and fly. What for? To murder one another in such a cruel way?

2 May 1941

May? As cold and rainy as November. I cannot cope with the household. Now I see how hard it is to carry coal up from the basement, to light a fire in the stove, to do the laundry by hand. I cleaned the house yesterday from top to bottom, and today every muscle aches. Mama is pale and weak. She coughs at night and we worry terribly.

I joined *Centos* as a volunteer, a hygienist. The work consists of checking the housing and health of the children. The Germans chose the most neglected and poor quarter of the city for the ghetto. Roaches crawl around the dirty basement rooms of the wretched Aryans into which the equally wretched Jews have now moved. It is heartbreaking to see small anemic children with hollow cheeks huddling around their sick mothers. Back home I looked at my own mother and wanted to fall at her knees. Instead, I fight with Felek and help her sulkily with the housework. Suddenly, I cannot show tenderness to those whom I love most. Why?

4 May 1941

Hatred and fury have stifled my tears. What is happening to me? "Apprentice to the hat maker" is my new assignment from the *Arbeitsamt*, which is going to turn me into a slave! I won't! Never! NEVER! "The work protects you from deportation," said Papa. "I don't care! Not this job! I won't go there! No!" My desperate raving surprised my parents. "You have to save her from this assignment," Mama said. Papa took my *Kennkarte* and left without a word, while I could not breathe, choked by tears.

9 May 1941

The boys came to the party late, Mietek, Ksylek, Netherländer, and three others. There were only four of us girls. Even Lonek dragged himself along and took pictures with his Kodak camera. There was a lot of orange vodka. I sipped some, but it does not taste good, and I felt dizzy instead of cheerful. A scratched record played "La Habanera." Some danced the tango, while all the others lay on the sofa tightly next to, and on top of, one another. Not knowing what to do with myself, I sat down in the kitchen, my head spinning, and closed my eyes. Suddenly, someone kissed me—Mietek. Hala tumbled off the sofa, and we both stepped out on the balcony. "Is this supposed to be a party?" I asked her. "I am burning with shame!" Hala answered emphatically. "Such a drunken orgy in our home. What would my parents say? Enough!"

There were couples in every corner. Mietek and Lonek lay spread out on the bed snoring. Edek mumbled obscenities in the middle of the room. I slapped his face and threw everybody out. Some party! Not for me.

28 May 1941

A day of weakness and stupidity.

29 May 1941

Yesterday I had enough of fights at home (even with Mama). Nothing mattered to me any more. I didn't care about anything, except, perhaps, that I wouldn't see Staszka anymore and she would miss me. I wrote a letter to her and to Felek and poured whatever I could find in our medicine box into a glass of water: six luminal pills, three aspirins, and a pill against headache, and, ready to drink my poison, I lay down on the sofa. Suddenly, Felek came into the room. Even if I had not wanted to commit suicide as I had intended to, now I had to out of embarrassment. Crying loudly, I had hardly taken a sip when Felek tore the glass out of my hand, and, surprisingly, instead of teasing, hugged and kissed me and grunted: "What are you up to, you stupid Ophelia with salty cheeks!" Before I could say anything, he added, "Don't worry, I won't tell our parents. But you had better calm down and play Saint-Saens' 'Skeleton's Dance' with me on this occasion, you would-be corpse!" I did. We went for a little walk and Felek's witty remarks made me laugh. What a good brother he is in his funny mischievous way! "Let's go to the bakery. Let's spend my last hard-earned penny on my little sister!" We shared a Napoleon pastry.

Felek is tall and slender and so handsome that people turn their heads to watch him go by. No wonder that Felicia is so much in love with him. Who isn't? We like her, that pretty girl with long black hair, shiny brown eyes, and cheeks like peaches. She is tall as well, and they look stunning together. Tonight was Felek's evening off and he had a date with her. He walked me home, waved from the street, and smiled, "Life is great, no matter what! Remember!" In the evening, no one remembered my noontime fight.

Papa brought home a large bouquet of lilacs today. I buried my face in the fragrant blossoms. It is great to be alive, no matter what!

9–17 June 1941

One day is like another. I read our great Romantic poet, Krasiński. Instead of recording daily trivia, I wrote little poems which represent my feelings much better.

Sunday Afternoon in the Ghetto, or,
    A Dream of a Villa in Italy:

My wish is to own a modern villa
beneath the blue Italian sky—
and to stuff myself with pastries
as mortals do with bread!

My wish is to own a small swift car
and a wardrobe full of dresses,
soft furs and precious diamonds
sapphire rings and chains of gold.

My wish is to rock in my sailboat
on the sea in the sun every day,
and every night I wish
to laugh, to dance, to play.

My wish is to live to the fullest,
to travel wide and far,
My worries left behind.
Me—a Grande Dame! A star!

In vain I try with my wish
of a villa under a blue sky
to kill my hunger and my wish
for a piece of gray wartime bread.

Could I really be such a great lady? I am just daydreaming as I browse
through prewar society magazines. Doing nothing but playing must be boring, too. What is the meaning of life, anyway? It's too bad that none of my
wise men—Janek, Lolek, or Edek Birn—are here, because I don't think I can
come up with an answer to that, not even with Staszka. I don't want to bother
Papa with my questions, he is overworked and dispirited enough himself. He
only livens up in the evening when we all gather at the Lustgartens to listen
to music. My poor father. I complain about not having a normal girl's life and
he doesn't complain at all, he just endures and goes to his sanitation department, softly whistling symphonies by Mozart or Beethoven. The first bars of
the Fifth Symphony have become a signal to our family. I read some of the
books which we brought with us from home to the ghetto. I keep reading one
French book after another, and have just read A. Carrell's *The Human: An
Unknown Being*. I found some of the chapters boring, perhaps because the

text is full of unfamiliar terminology and I got lost. Well, what can you expect? I am only a half-educated ignoramus.

Sunday, 22 June 1941

A new war, with Russia. Everyone is pleased, even pessimists like our neighbors. People say this is our only salvation because either Russia will break them, or—and God forbid!—they will conquer Russia, and in either case the war will end more quickly, and that is our only hope. As yet no one has ever conquered Russia, not even Napoleon, so perhaps the Germans will finally get what they deserve.

Today, the ghetto was like a proper city. There was a charity concert in the large hall of the orphanage. Rosner performed in the café where Felek plays. A street collection for the orphanage was organized in which Henka and I took part. Actually, these collections take place every Sunday, so we were not so much collecting donations as taxes. There was a great burst of energy in the ghetto's few little streets. I was full of spirit and courage, too. In the afternoon at Eva's, I fooled and clowned around like a little kid, but in the evening . . . in the evening! How depressing the darkened streets are during the blackout. The former entrance door to our building was walled-in because it had opened onto the street outside the ghetto, and they made an entrance through a labyrinth of courtyards on the Dąbrówki Street side. There is no curfew here, and people gathered and stayed up talking until late. The lighted windows created a pleasant and cozy atmosphere. It is pitch black tonight, but still in the courtyards and on the balconies the various residents were engaged in lively discussion, Papa, too, of course—he even pulled out a mandolin and played "Oczy Czarne!" After everyone else had gone home, he remained on the balcony, whistling Beethoven's Ninth Symphony. He is whistling full of hope, and I am scared. Nineteen thirty-nine is still fresh in my mind, the bombardments, the burning villages, and our defeat. It is strange that in the most dangerous moments I tried to think about carefree trivia. Once during an air raid, I lay in a field and noticed an ant trying to walk across a leaf of grass. The ant was carrying something and struggled first to go over the blade, then underneath it, and finally, around it. The bombs were falling, the world was on fire, but that ant going about her own business was very soothing.

An acacia tree blooming outside the ghetto sent up its sweet fragrance. I joined Papa on the balcony, and looking at the first silvery shining star in the evening sky, I thought: that clear sky, ideal for air raids, brings annihilation. I wanted to scream up to high heaven: I don't care about the conflicts of history! I am young. I want to live and enjoy a warm night without worrying about air raids! Is this selfishness? Or is it a primal survival instinct? History! In school, it was nicely arranged according to dates and periods, and now we are creating history. Even I? That's ridiculous. Anyway, I would prefer to be living in another era.

23 June 1941

I am working again and distancing myself from my friends. First I started as a student nurse at the hospital for infectious diseases. The patients here suffer from typhoid fever, hepatitis, scarlet fever, measles, all kinds of inflammations. Among the many children, there is one severely retarded five-year-old boy who is like a small, helpless animal, unable to speak, sit up, use his hands to eat. He just lies there without making a sound, even when he has wet himself. I fed him, with aversion at first, but when he politely swallowed the food and looked at me with such trust in his big eyes, I felt tenderness for this beautiful, unfortunate child and caressed his smooth cheek.

The quiet and orderly atmosphere of the hospital suited me well, as did the white cap and uniform, and "Sister Halina" sounded so important! Unfortunately, not only did I work for no pay, but also there was no vaccine available to protect me. I had to resign and go back to the bosom of my family and become a governess to an eight-year-old girl, Rita. I am very fond of children, but I was nervous going there because Rita is an energetic child and I was not so sure of my own authority. I had to guess what she likes to do and suggest it ahead of time, otherwise she certainly would not have listened to me. Perhaps my "method" was not pedagogically correct, but it worked. Luckily, Rita is a sensible child and doesn't crave foolish things. By now she likes me, and without any tricks on my part, we read books together nicely and play "educational" games.

Rita is not one of those poor anemic children in tatters who plays noisily in courtyards full of rubbish. But even the other children, including those whose parents, like Rita's, are not so poor, are also deprived. There is no school, and "small group instruction" can not take the place of school. There are no toys, there are no books. Rita's father is "on the Russian side" in Lwów; her mother, a big woman with dyed blond hair, is somewhere in the city. Rita is being raised in the ghetto by her grandparents, and she doesn't even have any nice books. So I dragged out my own trusty, worn volume of children's stories, typed out several poems, and drew and colored some amusing illustrations to give to Rita and also to the other children in our house.

My new role absorbs me completely. I am busy all day and hardly have time for evening walks with Netherländer or Lonek and their proclamations of love and devotion to me. I don't believe them, anyway. I don't mind being alone. I am scribbling now by the light of a candle on the kitchen table, while young people talk and laugh in the courtyards and behind doors, just as our maids once did with soldiers.

28 June 1941

By chance, I met Henka's Fred. He is her neighbor. She has a crush on him and is possessive about him. Fred is very tall and athletic and he towered over everyone on the street, and when he saw me he called out in his deep voice, "Greetings! Admirations! Oh beautiful governess! Has no prince asked for your hand yet? If not, come for an ice cream with me!"—he was alluding to a silly novel about high society life. "Admirations for *your* knowledge of literature!" I replied. "No princes, I'm afraid, but an overabundance of lowlifes! I'll come for an ice cream, and then I'll take me to a nunnery." We walked to the pastry store, laughing.

We sat at a corner table, and Fred began a discourse in praise of his own invaluable virtue as a cheerer-upper of lonely women—me, in particular. He is amusing and amiable, but how can I flirt with him when Henka is so jealous? Let her have him! Fred walked me to the door, because the curfew was approaching, and asked, "So, shall we meet tomorrow?"

"What for?"

"My, you are strange. Don't look at me so innocently. So, what time and where?"

"No time. I don't want to see you so often!"

"Look, you complain about being alone, and you are turning down a magnificent man! Why are you rejecting me? Well, I won't force you. Good night!" He kissed my hand.

He was angry. But out of loyalty to Henka, what else could I do?

1 July 1941

I dug out poems by Asnyk and Syrokomla from among our books. "Grinding" poetry at school and reading it for one's own pleasure—what a difference! I chose Syrokomla:

What do you miss? Waves from past years
clouds passing by in the sky?
forget old dreams—save your tears
you need them for tomorrow.

From Asnyk, I chose "Vain Regrets." But how is one "to go forward with the living and reach out for new life"? What new life? I know that even here in the ghetto some people work for the future, but there is no way to reach them. When I think about them, I am ashamed of brooding about my own little world and scribbling silly poems to the Unknown:

I wanted so much to see you
I wanted you to come to me today.
Today, I was so tired
and so very sad.

I wanted you to sit next to me,
hug me softly to your side,
gently stroke my hair.
I missed you!

I wanted to share my silence
with someone close to me.
You did not come.
Today, I hoped that you would lend me
courage with your hug.

Instead of my Unknown, the endless columns of the German army move through the gates of the ghetto toward the East. The soldiers sing stupid anti-Semitic songs, and small children run behind them, echoing:

Die Juden hin und her
sie ziehn ans Rote Meer
die Wellen schlagen zu
die Welt hat Ruh!
(From here and from there, the Jews draw toward the Red Sea, the waves close above them, and the world has peace!)

They advance along the whole of the enormous front, and no one stops them. Poland was the first to be invaded, without any warning, and yet we held out much longer than anyone else. Even Finland helps them. They have forgotten that two German divisions fought with the Russians against them in 1939–40, the first year of the war. Politics is a rotten business. The Germans have Europe now, and everybody is afraid of them. They march freely across Bulgaria, Romania, Hungary, Yugoslavia, and Greece. Every few days they declare another victory; every victory is followed by the mournful echo of terrible pogroms of the Jews in Przemyśl, Lwów, Wilno, Kiev. . . . The rabbi of Bełż told his Jews in 1939 that nothing bad would happen to them. And now?

2 July 1941

I cannot and I do not want to think about it. Like the ostrich who hides his head in the sand, I hide mine in the past, a past no longer my own, searching for a time when there was no war. Perhaps only on the cusp of the nineteenth and twentieth centuries did a single generation in Poland not have an immediate experience of war. I peruse the yellowed pages of the *Tygodnik Ilustrowany*, the *Weekly Illustrated*, which belonged to my grandmother.

You held your hands neatly clasped
Your lips primly pursed.
Your waist was like a wasp's
Your hips were like a barrel.

You wore a stiffened corset
Drawers which were ruffled
Underskirts of linen
Trimmed with lace that rustled.

You attended, as was proper,
A boarding school for girls
And then you went to balls
Which entertained you greatly.

And any care or worry
Ceased being your concern
The day that you got married
In order to procreate.

You stitched at the side of the fire
By the light an oil lamp cast
And your husband read aloud to you
Novels out of serials.

You didn't know tramways,
Cars, the radio or the cinema,
You, a virtuous wife,
A virginal young girl.

Sometimes you pondered over things
Secretly, deep inside your heart.
Confining though it was—
Yours was an easier life.

Netherländer gave a tea party—in fact, a drinking bash. He has a large room with space enough for dancing. The only record, "La Habanera," played over and over again. I did not drink a drop. Why should I force myself to when I can't stand it? Never again will I attend any such party. Actually, I feel a bit sorry for the others because I think they are all only pretending to enjoy themselves. They are good people who have gone astray because of the war. I sat down in a corner and wrote a poem.

And so we live today
without a radio, streetcar and movies

Do we live just to knock back
a glass of vodka or wine?

With no school, no things to do
no goal in life—no will to live.

So few hold their heads high
so many give up with hands down!

Death waits for us young every day
not natural death, though the same.

Do not wonder at us. We drink
to drown our sorrow in wine,

to drown this lousy life with no tomorrow
in a full glass of vodka or wine!
While somewhere out in the world there exist
schools, radios, streetcars, and cinemas.

4 July 1941

I am busy with children all day, because in the afternoons I now take care of a six-year-old boy. Marek has light blond hair, blue eyes, and is well behaved. All day with the children I am *Panna Halina*, Miss Halina, a governess and a teacher, a serious grownup. My personal life disappears. In the evenings I go for a walk with Mama or with some acquaintances, and write letters to my friends. Our correspondence costs a lot of money, but this is my only real pleasure. I miss Staszka the most, and read her letter in bed sobbing, while downstairs Rysiek plays Beethoven's "Apassionata." The dense blackness of our room chokes me with desperate sadness. I am very tired in body and in spirit and don't want to think at all, just sleep like an idiot.

Sunday, 13 July 1941

I am dizzy and feel terrible once again. Somehow the ghetto's social life centers on our house, and we all planned to meet here. The usual collection on the streets was held today to benefit the hospital for infectious diseases. Afterwards, Eva and Netherländer arrived earlier than everyone else. We waited until half past six and were about to leave when the others showed up with the vodka. They all got drunk and yelled; only Netherländer behaved nicely, as always. Suddenly, Papa appeared. Surprised by all the drinking, he strode out onto the balcony with a terrible expression on his face and summoned me. "What's going on here? You ought to be ashamed of yourself!" he thundered, and I cried. My drunken guests left quickly. In the courtyard they got entangled in a scuffle with Fred, who punched them, yelling, "What kind of bastards are you, leaving an innocent girl (me!) by herself to face her father's anger?" Hearing the screams, Fred's mother raced downstairs to the entranceway to take him home. What are she and our neighbors going to think of us? Netherländer is the only one who can be relied on. He appeased the fighting boys, sent them out into the street, and went back home with me to apologize to my parents. Mama was already at home and convinced Papa that he had made a mountain out of a molehill, and so the event is over—for my parents, but not for me. I don't like this kind of party and I never will.

23 July 1941

A year ago Felek returned home, and exactly on the anniversary a year later, something broke apart between us. We used to quarrel, he used to tease me— but this?

He almost killed me. Ever since he stopped going out with Felicia, who has left for Hungary, Felek has fallen into the hands of common, plain girls whom no one would have even looked at before. These girls have money now because their parents know how to make it—only the intelligentsia is impoverished. Lonek and Felek paraded near Krzemionki with two of those girls, all decked out in their finery, while I was sitting there like a maid, with a book in my hand, minding the children. They barely acknowledged my presence.

I brought Marek home for his midafternoon snack, and shortly afterwards all four of them arrived. They had a vial of chlorethyl, used in anesthesia, and decided to try it on someone. "On Hala! Try it on Hala!" said Genia, making eyes sweetly at Felek. Without saying a word, I walked out onto the balcony to play with Marek, but they grabbed me, pushed me onto the sofa, and, holding my hands and feet, put a mask with the chloroform onto my nose.

Through a loud buzzing in my ears, I could hear Genia's and Cesia's laughter. The room whirled around and disappeared in darkness. With my last ounce of strength, I tore off the mask, stumbled into the kitchen crying, and collapsed on the bed, overcome by nausea. Not one of them bothered to help me. "She's just pretending to be half dead. Nothing is going to happen to her," Genia decided as they were leaving.

Marek, that good child, played quietly with cards. When Mama arrived, I was ashamed to tell her what had happened, but I asked her to take Marek home because I felt sick.

30 July 1941

I had an unexpected vacation because Rita went to Wieliczka for a week to see her mother, that tall Rubenesque woman who works outside the ghetto (for the Gestapo?) and who is certainly a good mother and daughter. She cares for her elderly parents and for Rita and provides them with food and money so they can live comfortably. I like Rita's grandmother. She reminds me of my beloved Aunt Mala because, like her, she recites Polish and German poetry very dramatically, but with an ironic twinkle. During this free week, I went in the mornings to Krzemionki to look down at my Kraków.

I suddenly felt well and optimistic, unlike Hela, who wrote to me complaining that we are rancid virgins without any fun in our lives. So what? We can wait. For her, beginning to live means sex. If we started at sixteen, life would have no secrets, nothing to expect at twenty. What's the rush? When the time comes, would it not be better to admit in the arms of a beloved that it was worth waiting for? But, perhaps, I'm a frigid woman unsuited to love?

2 August 1941

I walked to Krzemionki with the children. On the ghetto side, the hill slopes steeply, and at the top there is a newly constructed wall with rounded arches. Felek praises the Germans' discerning artistic sense, because they have built the ghetto wall in the style of rabbinical tombstones! The wall is still unfinished, and from there one can see onto the Aryan side. I like to sit on it and look down at the swarm of streets, buildings, tall church spires, and at the shining ribbon of the Vistula River. On the other side of the wall, there is a wide open space, green meadows and fields, and an old fort. German soldiers are stationed there. They play soccer, sunbathe, and often glance curiously at the ghetto wall. Young men in swimming trunks do not look like an enemy army. In the late afternoon, one of the soldiers hoisted himself up onto the wall. I sat there without moving, even when he smiled broadly—the picture of youth, health, and manly vigor. We looked at each other without a word. I thought, what harm would there be if he took my hand and ran with me through the fields to the hill and back? There he was, an unknown adolescent, friendly because not in uniform. He was certainly not thinking at that moment about war, race, and religion, those barriers which people place between each other. After a while he jumped down and slowly walked away, still turning back and looking at me. I had not expected anything else, and yet I felt strangely sad as his silhouette melted into the green field gilded by the mild rays of the setting sun.

At home I played a tango and wrote my own text.

6 August 1941

Papa has come down with dysentery. The apothecary in the ghetto didn't have the medicine, so I received a pass to Kraków in order to search for it in the city pharmacy. For the first time in five months, I left the ghetto and hurried toward our real home. What an ugly quarter of Kraków the Germans selected for the Jewish ghetto! As I walked toward the bridge and looked at the fresh green foliage along the boulevards, at the streets swept clean by a summer shower, and saw again all the places I know so well, I could hardly control my tears.

I visited our street, our house, our old neighbors, and finally our own apartment. What memories and what changes! Choked by tears, I could not talk as I remembered the past, and that last summer. I was very happy then, if one can be happy during a war. I had my family, my work, my closest friends, and even the illusion of love. Inanimate objects are cruel in their unchanging existence. The street, the house, the garden, some of the furniture we left behind, are all exactly the same—only I am behind bars like a dog.

Last year I was also somewhat lost, but that was the result of shock at the sudden rupture the war had caused in my life's routine. And Lonek ... his love had also let me down. Tears don't help, and I know that I cannot adjust to a life such as the one I am living, and I never will.

16 August 1941

Home has turned into a hospital. As soon as Papa got better, Mama came down with a high fever. Felek watched her by night, and I by day. Mama told me how to cook barley for her and potato soup for us; noodles with a marmalade made of beets is the main course. I am a housemaid, a nurse, and a cook. And then, at night Felek got stomach cramps and fever—I ran from bed to bed with pails and basins and water. Four nights and days of running around the house, and to the doctor for medicines, ended with my being sick, too. It must be an epidemic, for our neighbors were also ill in bed. I have a vacation again, unpaid, alas! Rita went to another ghetto to visit her aunt. I read books and worry that I am wasting precious time. After the war, I will have to be independent and work and help my family. It wouldn't be fair to ask my parents for help with our further education. We will have to do it ourselves and take care of them. Mama consoles me that it is still not too late for me. We read the biography of Maria Curie-Skłodowska together, how she worked for six years before she saved money for Paris and the Sorbonne. Perhaps, after the war, mature students won't be ridiculed, because there will be so many of us.

However, everyday reality crushes my hopes. I constantly hear, "There is no money . . . there is no bread left . . . we are in debt again at the bakery . . . I haven't the strength to get up." To buy food, my parents have already sold most of the jewelry they were keeping at my nanny's. They hold on to their wedding rings, as I do to my forget-me-not earrings and the gold ring with my initials which Papa gave me for my birthday in 1938. If I only knew how, I would sell the ring to buy food for Mama, who is so weak.

Lately we have been getting our meals from the so-called Kitchen for the Intelligentsia. Despite the pompous name, the food there is certainly worse than it was before the war at the Brothers Albert shelter for the homeless. Every day the menu consists of rutabaga and half-rotten potatoes with mustard gravy. But what can we do! I have to wait and to believe that there will come a time for everything: for learning, for work, for joy, and perhaps for love.

For love . . . ever since I went to Kraków on my pass, I have been under the spell of those days a year ago. I remember words which are meaningless now, but which were extremely important then. I remember the fragrance of the grass and the trees after the rain, the fresh breeze from the Vistula River, the crisp mornings of early fall, our songs. . . . I want to record those silly moments of our "idyll":

"Staszka, Felek is back!" I yelled to my friend who had come to visit me at the pharmacy as usual. I had not seen my dearest brother for two years, and I was so happy at his return. Our home was filled with the sound of music again and with the joyful voices of Felek's colleagues and friends who gathered to socialize and to dance. Among them, Marian P. often visited us. A twenty-year-old student at the Academy of Fine Arts, he had taken no notice of me before the war, while I secretly adored him. Now Marian enjoyed having long conversations with me on our balcony in the evening and revealed his feelings for me with a red rose, my first. As he sadly admitted, it was one week too late. He should have known better.

Felek worked at the hospital but lived at home. One evening, he arrived with a new friend, Lonek, a clerk at the *Judenrat* and son of the hospital's chief administrator. As usual, Felek played piano and piccolo-chromonica, while Lonek tried to follow Felek but only made silly noises. He was handsome and slender and had a triangular tawny face, wavy chestnut hair, and dark brown eyes which seemed dreamy to me. His long-fingered hands were what I noticed first. Mama called me in for supper, and before I even went to the dining room, Lonek turned to Felek: "How come you didn't tell me you had a sister like that, you rotter?"

The following evening, Marian brought his latest drawings over and spread them out on the table. Lonek came over, too, sat next to me, and, ignoring the artistic discourse, showed me his brand-new Lusina watch, "Pretty, isn't it?" "It is, but your hand is prettier!" I blurted out, scarcely believing my own ears, though I meant it just as a statement of fact, nothing else. Lonek took it a different way and immediately tried to speak . . . to my knee under the table! I left the room at once. He used the curfew as an excuse to follow me. I was seeing him to the door when he put his arm around me in the dark hall and tried to kiss my hand, but I wouldn't let him. I am not an older lady, and I quickly returned to the drawing room, where Felek ridiculed me and my admirer, who apparently wants to know everything about me. "If you give me your new flashlight and ten cream cakes, I will say only nice things about you," he said. "If not, watch out!" "Only a bad bird messes its own nest," I said, trying to appeal to his conscience.

Lonek kept coming over every day, prolonging our good-night chats more and more. Marian began to suspect "a vile deceit."

It was the end of summer and it rained the whole time. On the first nice evening, Lonek asked my Papa for permission to take me for a walk and for me to visit him at home the next day. "Are you going to show me your rare china or your stamp collection?" "Don't joke. Do come over, please, with Felek." Staszka, who did not like Lonek, glanced at him ironically.

The next day I put on a white silk blouse and sprayed myself with lavender perfume. Lonek waited for us at the hospital gate, and humming the wedding march from *Lohengrin*, led us triumphantly along the corridors to the drawing room of his family's apartment. He put on Ravel's "Bolero" and "Fire Dance," and after that some dance music. After tea and cookies, we danced. Felek smiled tolerantly at first, but later, having nothing to do, he complained that our lyrical mood was too much for him. Lonek walked us to the corner, kissed my temple and hair under the umbrella. The smell of moist leaves and my lavender was in the air. I did not tell Staszka about the kiss, because I sensed her disapproval, and also because I was curious to see how far one could go astray.

Lonek was in love. One day, while making antimigraine powders, our boss, who called them "Halinka" after me, drew my attention to a man standing in front of the store window in the pouring rain—Lonek. His important message to me was, would I finally believe that his feelings for me were real? I still did not have the courage for a kiss and always thwarted his efforts, until one Saturday he came unexpectedly while I was at home alone and locked me in his arms. I thought, "Fine. One has to start some time. Halina Nelken, close your eyes, this is the first kiss of your life. What? Already? Is this all?" I wondered. "Where is the fire, the throbbing, the wild passion?"

We were inseparable. Every morning Lonek waited for me on the bridge and walked me to the pharmacy; at noontime he accompanied me to the kitchen at the *Judenrat*; in the afternoon he took me to the corner bakery for a cream cake, and at six o'clock we went home or to the hospital garden or to Felek's room where I played piano and Lonek smoked cigarettes. But he had not succeeded in turning me into a wild sex-kitten. One day, when we both met Maryśka, Staszka and some other girl on the street and chatted for a while, Lonek suddenly took that other girl's arm and went off with her! Next day, he waited for me at the pharmacy. Ah! Our dramatic walk along the Vistula, the park bench, Lonek accusing me of not being good to him. When he explained what "being good to him meant," I jumped off the bench and left. He ran after me, and we patched it up, but I avoided being alone with him after that. He had to put up with Maryśka and Staszka, and Marian, too, especially at my birthday party. Marian gave me a red rose, Lonek came with an expensive enameled powder box, as if I ever used cosmetics! We all had a great time, but after my birthday something went wrong. The hospital organized a course in nursing and because so many pretty girls were taking it, our boys attended eagerly. One afternoon, Lonek walked me home and made arrangements for our evening date at the hospital shortly before the beginning of class. I was writing letters home and did not feel like going anywhere. Lonek got offended and did not show up all week. Marian took advantage of this in his gentle-manly way, declared his feelings, and demanded my "yes" or "no." At this point, I had had enough of men, their deadlines and decisions. Next day, Lonek came in the evening to clarify things. I spoke my mind calling him an immature, irresponsible brat and went on and on until he interrupted me: "Enough. Further discussions of this sort can have only one result, and I would prefer the earth to open beneath my feet."

I knew that the earth was not going to open beneath his feet, but I drew in my horns. We finally reconciled on our bench. For Lonek, a happy ending meant kisses, but I could not care less about them.

We did not see each other as often. I still practiced Grieg in Felek's room. On a gloomy November evening, as I was crossing the hospital gate, I passed Lonek with a fifteen-year-old girl! He raised his hat politely and walked away with her, arm in arm. If my successor had at least been some intelligent girl! My downtrodden pride hurt more than my broken heart. It was over.

Fortunately, I caught a cold and my stuffed nose could not detect any memorable fragrances. Together with my cold came Bronek. He is the one who played Wieniawski's "Legend" on the violin. He is soft-spoken, tactful, and caring. There was a concert at the *Ordnungsdienst* attended by almost everybody. Our tenement was deserted, and I was sick in bed alone. And then Bronek and Artek brought a gramophone, candies, and cakes to amuse me. Bronek took his nursing duty seriously, serving aspirin and tea and looking at me with disarming tenderness. He is my youngest admirer, and shorter than I am, while Artek is over six feet tall. They both live on the third floor in our courtyard and have watched me closely from their window. Who would have known! I never noticed them until we met at the Lustgartens' where "the cultural elite" converge. We begin with a political discussion; then Rysiek plays, first solo, then with Bronek; then I play. The classical repertoire is followed by the light and the lightest in music, songs, and conversation. We dance, play games, and sometimes discuss good literature. Bronek's remarks are surprisingly mature. At these gregarious evenings I laugh again, enjoying the witty talk and making up funny songs. We all try to forget our daily worries for a while. One does not live by philosophy alone.

20 September 1941

My seventeenth birthday! I said this to myself this morning, and so what? On my last birthday there was no ghetto. We rush through the days as if tomorrow had something better to offer, and so the empty weeks and months and years pass by, one after another. My most beautiful teenage years are lost for nothing. Yesterday Mama baked cakes for my birthday. In the morning both parents wished me *Sto Lat*, A Hundred Years.

After a few gloomy days, this morning was sunny and crisp. I went to Rita's in a cheerful mood. The door opened. An O.D. Rita ran up to me in her pajamas yelling, "Panno Halu, Mommy did something on the black market and the police are searching for her, so she has escaped together with my Aunt Ena, and they arrested my Grandpa and we are all under house arrest and the *Ordnungsdienst* lets everybody in but nobody out, and now you also have to stay with us!" She said it in one breath, then jumped to the window and called to the children in the street: "My Grandpa is in jail and yours is not, see?"

I looked at her grandmother in disbelief. She nodded silently. As it turned out, all of this was true, except the reason for the search: not the black market, but for being an agent, an agent moreover, for them [the Germans]. Sometimes they finish off their own secret agents. It serves them right, although I feel sorry for Rita and her grandparents, especially her nice grandmother.

Having nothing to do with this affair myself, I was sure they would let me go. In the meantime, I helped Rita get dressed and we read my children's book together. Then we played with building blocks, colored my drawings of funny animals with crayons, and since we could not go for a walk, we enjoyed the fresh air by sitting in the sun at the open window. The news about the trap soon electrified the ghetto. My acquaintances passed by, wishing me to get out safely. Another accidental prisoner was an elderly quarrelsome gentleman who complained out of the window, demanding to be let free at once. The representative of the authorities here, our O.D., lost his patience and closed the window. Now we were, indeed, locked in a prison.

Papa appeared on the other side of the street. He signaled nervously to me, from which I understood that he had intervened on my behalf with the *Judenrat* and the *Ordnungsdienst*. Hours passed. Rita was still delighted by the uncommon happening, but I sat in a corner, dispirited. Some birthday! At last, late in the evening just before curfew, the commandant of the O.D. released us. I sprinted home. All the windows were open in our three tenements, which are connected by courtyards; people welcomed me, like a miraculously saved heroine. It had, indeed, been a miracle!

My birthday presents were displayed on the table: a crimson red carnation and a silver pin from Bronek; pink asters and a chocolate from Artek; a silk flower from Dziunia, Bronek's little sister; lily-of-the-valley eau-de-cologne from Pan Benek and his wife; and a huge cake from the residents of our house. I had been unaware of my popularity, let alone the affection they all have for me. Felek gave me a phosphorescent pin of two small dogs, not only cute, but also very useful for preventing people from bumping into one another in the evening on the blacked-out streets. We sat until late, my guests having a good time. I felt as if I were also an ordinary guest, and not the "guest of honor."

My joyful mood vanished in the next few days. Rita left the ghetto, little Marek too. I have no work. The weather is nice, so I walk to Krzemionki, which is now completely enclosed by the finished wall. I read affectionate letters with birthday wishes from my friends and look around at the world: above, at the luminous, azure, autumn sky; below, at the city with its black railroad tracks and at the woods on the horizon. Steel trucks shine like silver in the sun. From time to time a train rolls along. The sound of the whistle brings tears to my eyes. The wagons roll across the free, wide-open space and off into the world. Into the free world, where there is life, life flowing free, that life which bypasses this damned walled-in prison! I look at the airplanes landing at Rakowice, at the railroad trains puffing smoke, at the blue streetcars ringing shrilly, at the fast cars passing down the streets, and something screams in me, "I am seventeen! I want to live and not just look at the world," and I weep helplessly, locked in this cramped cage, destined for certain destruction!

Cambridge, Mass.

I remember with absolute clarity my outburst of revolt while sitting alone on Krzemionki hill in my mother's flowered silk dress which had been altered for me. Dziunia joined me, and we both looked at Kraków in silence. She was just a kid; her world was the here and now and she wondered what it was that I missed in the ghetto. She did not question why we were here, although neither did I. It was obvious. We were Jews and had to be segregated—for our own protection from the anti-Semitic Poles, according to the Germans. I kind of realized that being Jewish left me open to harassment, and indeed there was relatively less of that in the ghetto. So why complain? Today it is clear to me that I revolted against being limited in my living space, a condition which, so I thought, might result in the narrowing of my intellectual horizons. Little did I anticipate that our Lebensraum would soon gradually shrink to a camp, a barracks, a bunk, a place to squat. I refused to give up my natural right as a young human being to live free.

And perhaps such stubborn resolve guarded our human dignity and saved us from spiritual and intellectual destruction, right up to the final moment of our physical annihilation.

4 October 1941

I defended myself desperately against working as a laborer at the factory. I cannot work at the factory because the war could linger on perhaps for another two years—Oh, Lord! That's terrible—and then I will be two years older as well, old and a complete zero! I won't be able to be just beginning after the war, because I won't have either the money or the energy, not to mention the time. So I cannot allow myself to waste time now, I have to learn and prepare myself for the future now. The pharmacy was that kind of preparation, even though I was not too enthusiastic about that profession either. Anyhow, it is over. This is also why I did not want to work at the hat factory, or at the wire shop, like little Hala. Not that I disdain physical labor, but I could be more useful as a "brain"; to quote Janek, I am an intellectual. A thinker. Times have been turning from bad to worse. It is dangerous not to be officially employed. Whether I like it or not, I have to take any work. A co-op producing brushes and brooms operates in the ghetto. This work is supposedly quite profitable, and people can also obtain the materials and work at home. Papa found out that I could get an official assignment to the co-op, and rushed back home. "Quick, give me your *Kennkarte*, tomorrow you will go to the *Arbeitsamt* to get the confirmation!" What joy! I am saved from forced labor.

The following morning I felt terrible, as I usually do these days. I was dizzy and tired when I crossed the threshold of the factory situated in a large hallway rebuilt into a workshop. Before the war, Blanka S. lived in this corner house on the Market Square. She was the object of everybody's desire, particularly Julek's. The tea parties at her house were famous because their spacious apartment spread, as ours did, over the entire second floor, and even the office of her father, the attorney, was available for dancing and plays. Not so much for me, that "real fun," I was only politely tolerated as Felek's kid sister. And today Julek is somewhere in Russia, Blanka is in the Tarnow Ghetto, and the attorney's elegant apartment overflows with tenants.

The office was in a tiny cubicle separated from the workshop by a few wooden boards. At the entrance, the bristle dust blew at me, irritating my throat. The loud voices of the noisy workers buzzed in my ears. The director, a short, skinny, withered old man, signed my assignment, and while he searched for a seal with which to stamp it, I wanted to stop his bony hand; through my mind ran the thought, "There is still time to prevent this, I don't want to be here, I don't!" When the red seal pressed down on the paper, I felt crushed, as if I had been hit over the head. "Too late. It's over. I am lost," I thought, while he told me to report for work on Wednesday from eight until half past one and from three until eight in the evening. Ten hours! I left benumbed, with lowered head and buzzing ears, and made my way to our house through the labyrinth of courtyards, unable to collect my thoughts or to see through my tears the uneven pavement beneath my feet. Ten hours! There won't be any time to learn, to read, or to go for a walk! All day in the dirty dust of bristle; all day without a ray of sun, a breath of fresh air. . . .

I don't want this! I am young! What is all this? What am I doing here? Where is my seat at school, or, at least, at the pharmacy? I raged in a helpless despair, helpless because it was too late, my fate was already sealed, stamped, and delivered.

8 October 1941

When I did not stop crying for the four days before the start of my new career, people consoled me that one could make a fortune producing brushes; that there would be no need, really, to work for ten hours; that all would turn out well. They said I was oversensitive, hysterical, crazy. Today, indifferent and apathetic, I went to work. The brush shop had been moved to a new place, so we had to report there at three o'clock in the afternoon. My co-workers intimidated me. Their sloppy dresses could be explained by the poverty in the ghetto; but we, too, are now poor, and yet not one of us wears dirty clothes. I understood the reason for this appearance soon enough, when after a few hours in the workshop my own neat dress looked as soiled as everybody else's. The young girls talked very loudly and all at the same time. They seemed to be very aggressive and pushy, and so it was with great joy that I noticed Janka W., a pretty and nice girl, also waiting for the afternoon shift. She used to attend the other state gimnazium in Kraków and was Felek's friend from his work at the hospital.

A terrible tragedy has happened to Janka recently; her father was captured and executed at the Montellupich prison. She and her mother are both in mourning, dressed in black with long veils attached to their hats. They must be as impoverished as we are if they have decided to work in this brush shop. Looking at our comrades in misery, we exchanged knowing glances and laughed a bit, all three of us perfect strangers in this group with whom we waited and waited, our feet freezing. We were not fully aware what to expect, but soon we lost whatever illusion we had, because the closed door hid disappointment.

The new place happened to be a dark hall with a dirty floor and a few benches which were immediately occupied by the most energetic women. There were not enough chairs for the workers; we have to provide this luxury for ourselves. The workbench consists of a board, or shaky table, with a screw and a wire for attaching bristles to the holes in a piece of wood which eventually will turn into a broom. The work is dirty, burdensome, boring, disorganized, and the conditions are terribly unhygienic. The drilling machine buzzes loudly, and there is the incessant noise of forty screeching women yelling to be heard. From time to time a man appears in the middle of the hall with a handful of wooden laths—the skeletons of a broom. He is immediately mobbed by screaming women, so he throws the laths into the jungle of their outstretched hands. Some workers grabbed more than ten—Janka and I managed to catch only one each. Now off to battle for the balls of bristle which another man brought in a sack and threw to whoever could reach him. We only managed to pick up some tufts from the floor, twice as filthy. Earnings depend on the number of brushes or brooms produced, fifty groszy apiece. The best, most experienced workers produce up to thirty brooms daily, about fifteen złotys, hardly the price of a loaf of bread. The supply of materials is inadequate, and the earnings not so great. The work is hard and dirty, and there is a constant noisy gibbering of forty women.

We became more and more disheartened, but we still tried to keep up appearances. With the abominable, sticky bristle on our laps, we started to learn our new profession, cursing like drunken sailors. Yes, *CURSING.* Mama was not here, and Janka's mother decided not to hear anything. Our neighbors watched us with puzzlement, yet also with a certain disdain. It was noticeable that we are from a different social class, and in the ghetto the intelligentsia is declassé, out. Still, they would not, perhaps, dare to swear as we did. Common people use bad language when they are quarreling or drunk, but not casually or nonchalantly. But after a while they did not pay any attention to us both cursing, and cursing loudly, because no one could hear a normal voice. The wire cut my fingers, which were dirty and sticky from the loathsome bristles. With utter abhorrence, I awkwardly attached tuft after tuft to the lath. The holes were not properly drilled, so we had to pierce them through again and again.

"Janka, do you have a pin? The goddamned hole is clogged!"

"One pin? You means pins! I do. A lot of pins in my ass! I cannot sit here any longer!"

"Just lend me a pin and leave me alone with your pin-cushioned ass!"

"Here, take it and go to hell with your clogged hole!" We laughed.

"Damn! Will we ever finish these brooms?"

"It's me who will be finished, first." "Help me to pull this shitty wire through; it's all tangled up!"

After an hour I finally produced my first broom, which looked like the head of a squalid witch. Whoever tries to sweep with it will be sorry. And another, and, this time, the losing battle for lath and bristle exhausted me completely. Extremely upset, my temples pounding and my cheeks flushed, I grabbed my coat and ran out. As soon as the door closed behind me, I staggered into the dim corridor and burst into tears, defeated and heartbroken.

"Can this be for real?" I groaned aloud. "I cannot endure this nightmare." I clenched my fists, which were coated with sticky dirt, and bit my lips in helpless rage. In my despair I walked home through the darkened streets and wept uncontrollably. For the first time in my life, I wept and wept bitterly for myself.

16 October 1941

The rectangular room with two windows is quite large and painted an ugly terra cotta. The paint is peeling off the walls, revealing holes filled with bedbugs. Mama fumigates them and fills them in with plaster. This is our new home. We exchanged a big room and a kitchen with balcony on Traugutta for this one room with a kitchen stove. It is cramped, but all our own and filled with sunlight. All this because people who earlier had not received the *Kennkarte,* and had settled in the suburbs of Kraków, are now being forced into our ghetto. While we were locked up behind the wall, these people had enjoyed relative freedom among the fields and meadows in the country. Now they are being rounded up, over sixteen thousand of them, but the Germans refuse to enlarge the ghetto by even one additional street. The housing office in the Gmina, the Jewish Council, invented an ingenious solution by counting all windows in the ghetto and allocating four people to each one! According to this rule, we would have had to share our old apartment with nine strangers. That's absurd. We are all equally hapless, so who is a "stranger"? Still, people prefer to be by themselves, or with close relatives. So we had to exchange our larger apartment for this one room, sharing it with our nightly guests, Uncle Ignacy and little Jurek. Aunt Dora and the older Mietek are staying with her sisters nearby—in the ghetto everywhere is "nearby." While they were in the country, Uncle Ignacy could still work at his engineering firm in Kraków, though not as the owner, but as an engineer. Now it is over.

Mama and I scrubbed and washed and waxed the floor and worked very hard before things more or less found their places. Because of lack of space, we had to get rid of a lot of furniture, chattel, and junk. Even so, at night the place looks like a hospital ward, one bed next to another, next to another. But during the day the room is cheerful, and my corner is the nicest. To make space for the large mahogany wardrobe, my sofa stands on the diagonal. Behind it on a small silver table are a lamp and a fern, and above it is a black Chinese lacquer corner shelf with some bric-a-brac from our glass cabinet, which is now at Mr. Stieglitz's antique store in the Adolf Hitler Platz. I miss our neighbors at the Traugutta and my childish admirers, Bronek and Artek. Actually, our evenings at Lustgartens have also come to an end because they, too, moved a few streets over. People gathered at our place, trying to cheer each other up. I barely took part in the conversation because I am so terribly unhappy about the brush shop.

25 October 1941

I know that you'll come to me some day,
Answer my summons with a smile,
Bring into my life, on a gray ordinary day,
The radiant glow of the sun—you, only you.

Sadness and loneliness will vanish then,
and the yearning for years over you.
When, at last, without words
We find each other again
and the world smiles its happiness on us.

Rysiek composed a song to which I wrote the words. I did it at Mr. Dembitzer's electrotechnical store, Lux, where a few days ago I began my new career as a cashier-clerk and salesgirl rolled into one. One wonders how many times during this war I will change my profession. I could not stand it any longer in the abominable brush shop. Papa was very sorry for me and arranged my employment at Lux for a ridiculous, symbolic salary of sixty złoty per month. It is not hard work and it saves me from forced labor, but still . . . The hours are from nine in the morning until one in the afternoon, and then from three until seven at night, including Sundays. The store is gloomy, dark, and very cold. The signs on the walls read: "Private talk and visits only at home"; "Do your business and farewell"; "Credit is dead." We are not allowed to read while waiting for customers, and since there are only a few, we just tramp along from one corner to the other. One customer per hour, but every trifle has to be meticulously inscribed in three books. Our boss is the embodiment of Dickens's Scrooge, nervous and so tense that when he rushes into the store and yells we start dropping things. In the evening we go through the ritual of closing the store: we goose-step behind our boss, who then celebrates the securing of the iron shutters, and only after he gives a nod of the head are we allowed to march out. "We" are Miss Lusia, in her late twenties; our errand boy, Janek, the fourteen-year-old son of a lawyer; and a handsome, adolescent mechanic from a village near Kraków. Lusia is a pretty brunette who wears blood-red lipstick, the mechanic is dull, while Janek is hellishly intelligent and arrogant.

Thank God our boss is seldom at the store. I inscribe sold merchandise into a ledger, give the receipt to the cashier, Lusia, and out of boredom I sing or draw. Could I apply some of my knowledge of the physics I studied at school here? Or perhaps learn bookkeeping? I know this is all wishful thinking. What I do here all day is freeze.

In the evening my "honor guard," Mietek and Rysiek, walk me home and stay for a while. Three times a week I help Bronek with history and Latin. It is nice to remember everything so well, and Bronek is a good student, but I am afraid that his enthusiasm has less to do with a thirst for knowledge than with his crush on me. And now I am not even good looking! Thanks to our diet, a million meals of potatoes, I have gained weight. It is not so obvious because of my height, but I feel heavy, also in part because I am constantly cold, regardless of the many jackets and sweaters which Mama puts on me. The sweaters are worn out, I cannot move around, and I am still cold. Only in the evening do I come to life.

Uncle Ignacy sleeps here now with Mietek. Jurek is with his mother. We all try to forget the "outside world"; an unwritten rule prevents us from talking about our daily humiliation and distress. It takes us almost two hours to move the furniture around in order to arrange and make the beds. We joke with Mietek and laugh as the pyramid of chairs on the table reaches the ceiling. Sailing among the sea of pillows and blankets, we go behind the screen one by one to wash up. We are all tall and the screen is low, but we tactfully ignore it, except for Mietek, who sometimes indiscreetly peeks where he should not. I like being alone at home. I like the silence and solitude. It is raining outside, but our room is warm and cozy. Soon Mietek and Edek and some girls will arrive, since they all like to visit "the Nelkens."

Actually, it should be good to have a regular job. And yet . . . am I too demanding, still feeling restless and miserable? Yesterday evening on my way home in a rainstorm, I thought: "water is leaking into my worn-out shoes; I don't have gloves or warm stockings; for supper we have potatoes again . . . ugh, that's what it has to be." But suddenly I realized that no, it should not be. What now seems a normal state of affairs one cannot accept ever! I turned my collar up, and squeezing my fists inside my coat pockets, I ran home furiously, soaked, cold, and depressed. Soon I warmed myself by the fire of the small iron stove, but mostly in the affectionate glances of my parents and friends.

29 October 1941

Whatever has happened to us since the beginning of the war left me, at first, astonished and dazed. It had been, perhaps, more perplexing than terrifying. The ghetto seemed something temporary, like a stay in the country during the vacations. Some beautiful summer resort, the ghetto! Today, I have reconciled myself to it, maybe only superficially, but I have. All the atrocities, orders, and prohibitions; the actions, roundups, and the sudden disappearance of people seem to me—how horrible!—almost natural. I do not dare to recall that once life was different. My life before the war seems to me as unreal as a buttered roll, a glass of real tea with lemon and sugar, or the roasted thigh of a goose. Even this comparison itself proves how long it has been since I was really well fed. But it isn't just food I yearn for. Because right there, beyond the wall, is a different world. War or not, that world is free in its way. Children attend schools, grownups work or go for a walk in the parks, or window-shop, or listen to the *hejnał* from the Our Lady's church tower. These people ride in a streetcar through the ghetto and look at us with curiosity and contempt—they, the free people, the Aryans, rush by in trains along the railroad embankment just next to the wall and to our little courtyard balcony, and they do not know that here, in this cramped, walled-in cage, someone is suffocating and is unable to understand why it is forbidden to walk around the city in which one was born and which one loves so much.

According to a recent decree, leaving the ghetto illegally is punishable by death. I cannot believe that although I am in Kraków, I will not see the Vistula River or Wawel Castle; that to the end of the war I must walk like an idiot on only these few little streets in the ghetto. Because we are Jewish people, the achievements of culture and civilization are forbidden to us. But I am also a human being! I have hands and legs, a mind and a loving heart. I want to live, for heaven's sake! Live and study and work and love! Something in me screams when I am ice-cold and hopelessly sad and I look out through Lux's window at Limanowski, the main street. I watch with disgust as the "new aristocracy" go into the café opposite us, well-fed and well-dressed wheeler-dealers, informers, ill-mannered boors, all of them dishonest, newly rich scum who, having unseated the intelligentsia, have assumed the lead in the ghetto today.

I look at the haggard and worn-out people on the street, at the overworked and harried young people already going astray without guidance from parents or school. Suddenly, with a terrifying feeling of abandonment, I realize that the world has forgotten us, while *they* [the Germans] are pushing us down into degradation and moral and physical destruction. Black with dirty oil comes Janek Miller, who just two years ago was a university student. All his knowledge is good enough for his hard, menial work of loading heavy machines. His eyes are black—from a beating, surely. Here my tall teenage cousin, Mietek, shuffles along, stooped and apathetic. He is still a frail child of fourteen, and yet he has to load coal all day in German barracks. In addition to forced labor, he has been beaten. He returns to the ghetto tattered and humiliated, his face swollen and dirty, wearily dragging his feet along those same city streets on which, nicely dressed, he once promenaded with his parents or ran to school. I stand at the window in sorrow and terrible, helpless despair. How much longer will this nightmare last?

1 November 1941

I have a cold again and am in bed. My three colleagues from the gimnazium came to visit: Janka Wieluńska who has also left the brush shop, Zosia K., and Marysia, who smokes cigarettes. Their school career ended in the wire factory. What are women talking about among themselves? Love, of course. I wonder whether they really are so experienced, or whether, like me, only making believe that the world holds no secrets anymore. Zośka stated with authority that only three things are important in life: 1. love, 2. health, 3. money. I would rather change the sequence: first health, then money, and then love. As a matter of fact, all three together at the same time are the best, but this would be too good to be true. Without love, life is empty, but it could be fulfilling provided one were healthy and had money. If I were rich, I would constantly travel. The world is so interesting and beautiful, and money opens all doors—this much I know already. It would be impossible for someone who did not have to struggle for everyday survival not to be happy! And love—"the one and only true love"—any love is true, or it is not love. Perhaps only one love is deep and lasting, but eventually one can console oneself; there is art, music, literature, learning! And interesting people! And the beauties of nature! How I want to travel around the world, see the wonders of nature and science and technology! And I am afraid there won't be enough time. When this war ends, it will take some time before I become a "somebody" enough to be independent and ready to travel. I know so little. . . .

May my life not be spent behind the window of some inferior firm like Lux, or at a typewriter as one of the gray army of clerks! Somehow I hope that *something* will happen and my life will change for the better.

The girls have left, and alone at home with my sore throat, I comfort myself with such dreams. They cannot hurt.

9 November 1941

I wrote a little poem for the Centos Charity Orphanage and Vocational Hostel for older orphans. Dziunia and Bronek organized a lottery at home for the orphanage. It was combined with a party and an artistic program for which I provided a poem as opening. I arrived late because my boss did not allow me to leave even a moment earlier, as though the store were packed with customers! We seldom get more than ten in one day, sometimes not even that many. Who comes to Lux mostly? My friends. Today Grześ Krakauer came again—a redhead with freckles, keen witted, bright Bronek's friend. He presented me with the "rhymed minutes" of the lottery. Grześ couldn't care less when my boss tells him rudely to get out; five minutes later he returns and innocently inquires about some electrical appliance, as though he were a serious customer. And then he banters with me! I like him a lot, but who would take seriously a boy one year younger than I am? Lately, all Bronek's friends consider themselves my admirers. Of all these funny brats, I like velvet-eyed Bronek most (he is somewhat more mature than the others), and then I like Grześ, because of his sparkling intelligence and wit.

14 November 1941

Monday evening, as usual, all five of us prepared for bed, moving furniture around the room and bantering with Mietek about the upcoming inspection of the *Kennkarten*. Soon we lay down complacently, each of us on our own bed of misery, ready to sleep. All of a sudden I woke up. Thick window shades had been ordered against the air raids, and the absolute blackness in the room always frightens me terribly. A premonition of danger clutched at my heart. After a while I heard rumbling at the entrance door downstairs and heavy steps on the staircase. I froze. I knew it could only be that announced inspection, not a big deal, and yet . . . "What is going to happen?" I whispered into the blackness. No one answered. We waited, tense. When would our turn come? Finally, they knocked at our door. Mietek's bed is next to it, so he was the one who had to open it. Trying to turn the light on, he knocked against the pyramid of chairs piled up on the table and it came crashing down. The *Ordnungsdienst* checked our *Kennekarten* and left. We sighed with relief, but Mietek swore, "Damn these chairs! I tried to hide my unemployment card on the table so that the O.D. would not notice it and catch me tomorrow for forced labor. I got an attack of painful jitters from fright, and just look at this, a furniture warehouse on my bed!"

We all burst out laughing, releasing the tension, and relaxed enough to go peacefully back to sleep.

On Tuesday Mama decided to prepare provisions for winter, so we celebrated the making of sauerkraut. She took command; Mietek and I shredded cabbage with a passion worthy of a better cause, while Papa, looking like an expert, crushed the cabbage with a club in a large pot. Suddenly, a knock at the door, an O.D. with an order from the president of the *Judenrat.* Papa was to go with him to some urgent night's work. My poor father is managing some idiotic computations regarding the removal of garbage from the ghetto. He calls himself "a super-garbage man," and sometimes he is, in fact, on night call. We did not suspect anything was wrong and went to bed. Next morning, however, we were amazed that Papa was still not home. Worried, we began to speculate: had Papa been taken hostage with other distinguished people, as has happened before in the ghetto? On that occasion, they were detained in order to ensure monetary contributions from the Jews. But now, in his miserable capacity as the sanitation supervisor, Papa is, thank God, not a prominent person.

Suddenly, people in the hallway were screaming that an "Action," a roundup, had taken place at night and that a transport was already on its way. Now we were certain that Father had been taken away. Things kept dropping out of Mama's trembling hands. I couldn't find a scarf or my gloves; at last all three of us ran out of the house and dashed over to the *Judenrat.* Mama ran in front, I followed her, and Uncle Ignacy brought up the rear. The streets were almost empty. Here and there stood groups of anguished people weeping.

"They dragged him out of bed at night, in his shirt, they did not let him take anything else. They rushed him to the rallying place, and at dawn the soldiers rounded them up, pushed them into the trucks and—search the field for the wind!—I could not even kiss my son good-bye," despaired an older lady, wringing her hands. "Dear Lord, I wanted to bring him a sweater and a scarf." And with that scarf she wiped her tears. The O.D. rounded up people according to the list supposedly prepared after the *Kennkarten* inspection yesterday. No one knows whom they were after, because both those with, and those without, I.D.s were taken away, as well as working parents without their children and children without their parents.

Worried sick about Father, we reached the *Judenrat*, pushing through the crowd of distressed people who were trying to intervene on behalf of their families. Finally, in one of the offices, I noticed Papa and threw myself on him, crying. He was completely exhausted and remained silent all the way home. Once there, he sat heavily down on the bed, his head in his hands. I had never seen him so unhappy and felt terribly sorry for him. Instead of answering our questions, he just looked at us helplessly: "With whom do these people expect to intervene? The relocation list was prepared a long time ago. The Gestapo signed it, the O.D. collected the innocent victims—it is done. Oh, God! Them today, us tomorrow." Suddenly, an innocent word, *Aussiedlung*, relocation, assumed an ominous meaning.

"These people were sent to the East to work, weren't they?" I asked trembling, because I could not take in the fact that cheerful Bella, or the fat seamstress next door, could simply disappear without a trace. For the first time my father waved me away, irritated, but soon he smiled slightly, and with a sigh, stroked my head. His hand was dry and hot, he had a fever.

Neighbors gathered around Papa's bed on Thursday evening. We were worrying about a rumor of another "**Action.**" Papa was not well, but he tried to calm us down. A few days ago I had promised to paint a poster for a charity concert at the orphanage, so I sat myself down to work. After the curfew at 9:00 P.M., an O.D. knocked at the door to call my father to the office again. "He has a fever, he is sick!" Mama objected. The O.D. spread his hands in a helpless gesture. "This is an order with no appeal. Someone has to type the list and there are not too many who know how. Please, don't be difficult."

I glanced at him with dislike. He did not look any better than Papa. His face was ashen from lack of sleep, but I did not feel sorry for him, not a bit. No one had forced him to be an accomplice in crimes against his brethren. But my Papa has nothing to do with this, except that he is working as a sanitation clerk and knows office work, so why don't they leave him in peace?

Frightened neighbors rushed over to us and shared their nervous, naive plans with Mama: "It is happening again . . . Whom are they hunting tonight? Shouldn't we sleep at your place, and you at ours, so they won't find anyone . . . ?"

With all my willpower I took ahold of myself and concentrated on my poster, as if drawing careful music notes were the most important task in the world. No one went to bed—we just strained our ears—and when after midnight someone clamored at the entrance gate downstairs, our hearts sank in terror. Heavy boots thudded up toward the third floor above our flat. "They passed us over," whispered Mietek. Soon we heard loud screaming and weeping. A young woman who was being taken away from her husband and children scuffled desperately with the O.D. men, who pushed her into the street. Why her? The family had arrived here from a small town near Kraków just a few weeks ago. Why, out of the entire family, were they taking only her? I jumped up from the table and threw the poster into the wastebasket. We looked at each other in silence. Mietek decided "to sleep tight while we can" and pulled the blanket up over his head. We heard the tumult on the street, the clamoring at the front doors, the loud screams and the crying. I began to paint a new poster, which I finished after midnight. Then I fell into a feverish sleep and woke up eight hours later. The murderous transport of deported people had already been sent off.

I cannot take in what is happening. Why, in the night and without any warning, are people torn away from their families and work and in a single moment reduced to penniless beggars? The man with the two small children on the third floor, how is he going to manage without his wife? Those hapless people . . . what were they thinking as they were being driven away on this autumn night toward the *unknown*, which is certain to be horrible. I don't ask myself anymore when all this will end, but how long can one put up with such suffering?

21 November 1941

In the evening, Uncle Ignacy brought us the 16 November 1941 issue of the German newspaper, *Das Reich*, and he and Papa read the news together, as well as an article, *Juden sind schuld*, "The Jews are Guilty." We are being blamed for all evil in the world! The neighbors came to visit, very depressed about our Jewish misfortune. There is no hope—or maybe only on false Aryan papers. Let's hide in a mouse hole, or let's hang ourselves. We retired for night in gloomy silence.

By candlelight in my corner, I scribbled:

It's not an art to moan and complain,
How awful it is in this world.
It's not an art to cry and despair
That the Germans keep us locked in a ghetto.

It's not an art to harbor envy,
To wring hands over shoes outworn,
To dodge our torturers
By cheating and lying on "papers."

But it is an art—to walk around
Smiling in spite of it all,
Though their humiliations hurt
And the conditions here appall,

And though our stomachs growl
And we have hovels instead of flats.
It is an art—to rise with a smile
Above hunger, poverty, boredom, and sorrows.

Above garbage pails, above walls,
To the sun, to a better world!
To conquer evil by having faith in a future—
That is a great art in life!

Cambridge, Mass.

For the first time in my diary there appears, despite reality, a new attitude toward the world. It is not wishful thinking anymore when I say that "some day it must be better"; it is clearly the awakening of psychological resistance. As if suddenly I had realized that, however justifiable, constant whining leads only to apathy and bitterness. As if I had discovered that our own inner world is independent of the environment, is dependent only on us alone, and that we alone can protect or destroy it; that doubting is dangerous, and that if it is only a miracle that can deliver us, then we have to believe in such a miracle with all our might and smile and hold our heads up high above human evil and inhuman crime.

In the first version of the last stanza I repeated "keep smiling," but changed it by calling for "faith in a future." Both taken together, a cheerful disposition and hope, became the basis of an instinctive skill at overcoming undeserved wrong as well as several tragedies in my life.

23 November 1941

I haven't written for two days. It is incomprehensible that after the tragic shock of the *Aussiedlung*, and in such a relatively short time, life in the ghetto is returning to its normal routine. In a single moment our world is turned upside down, and the next day we brush our teeth, eat breakfast, go to work, and perform a thousand daily activities. Life goes on as though nothing had happened.

Even the weekly charity concerts at the orphanage have resumed. Rysiek performed at the recent chamber music concert, and today is Bronek's turn. He invited me personally and solemnly presented me with a ticket, his velvet brown eyes filled with quiet request. I promised to come, especially now that—surprise!—I have a presentable outfit in which to show myself in public.

The entire family noticed that I looked too shabby for a girl as young as I am, and everyone offered his share. Mama had her gray woolen coat from Aunt Lola altered into a nice suit for me; Aunt Dora contributed her sealskin muff to make the fur collar on the jacket; making a magnanimous sacrifice, Felek parted with his gray "Borsalino" hat, which he had received after graduating from the gimnazium, and as a result I acquired my first adult head covering, a very elegant one.

I was looking forward happily to Sunday, and what happened? My boss, the old tyrant, forbade me to leave an hour early! "Out of the question! You had Saturday free, you should have gone then!" That may well be. But there was no concert yesterday. Mr. Eichenholz arrived to intervene, doubly prominent as both himself and also as the father of the performing violinist. The boss promised to let me go fifteen minutes earlier! Big deal! Home at noon, I put on the white silk blouse, the suit, Mama's pumps, and my hunter's hat with a bushy feather. The shiny blackness of the fur made my skin and eyes clear and lucid and gave my hair a golden glow. Looking quite nice in all this regal splendor, I went to the ice-cold store and left with a blue face and a purplish nose. My feet were so stiff and frozen that I could scarcely run to the concert. Bronek, with Rysiek accompanying him, played Wiemiawski's "Legend" and "Chanson," nicely and softly. Then, Mendelssohn's Violin Concerto, beloved by Papa and me, was played by an engineer, or doctor, with our Felek at the piano. Gruner, the only O.D. whom people like, sang Yiddish folksongs in his sonorous baritone. Not knowing the language, I could hardly understand "Avriemel" and "Rajzele" by Gebirtig. Gebirtig is our neighbor, and he promised to teach me. Then Gruner's brother and sister sang together. She wore a gorgeous black evening gown, decorated with gauze, gold lamé, and a bunch of cyclamen. A six-year-old ballerina performed some delightful dances. I had a great time. Perhaps because things seem to be all right, at least on the surface, or perhaps because I am scribbling in bed and from every corner comes grumbling that I should blow the candle out, I cannot write anything "profound." So, good night!

27 November 1941

Yesterday was Felek's twenty-first birthday. Mama baked a cheesecake out of potatoes and a bit of cottage cheese and served coffee and candies. His first birthday certainly was celebrated quite differently from this one, the first day of his maturity! Felek's new girl, that brat Genia, came over with her friend Cesia. Cesia giggles, at least, but it is impossible to have any conversation with Genia, who says only "yes" or "no" or just nods her head. Is she that shy? She communicates somehow with Felek, unless she only listens to him—which is the best way to avoid arguments. "A stupid girl, or else a case of still waters running deep—or both—but either way, Felek will be trapped," said Aunt Dora.

Felek's medical friend Irka, Ksylek, Mietek, and Edek were also among the guests. All of them gathered at five o'clock. Only I, poor slave, dragged myself in after seven because my tyrant-boss would rather die than allow his personnel to leave a minute before closing time—even in this bitter cold, when not a single customer comes to the store. Our boss, whose main business is in Kraków, returned from the city today more furious than ever. He threw electric heaters at us, called us scoundrels, scum, hoodlums, and shit, and jumped around like a madman or a puppet on a string. My sense of humor, or my lack of dignity, saves me, because while Lusia was crying about the humiliation, I could hardly control myself from laughing out loud. Closing the iron shutter, the boss barked in my direction, "Insolent, bald-faced bastard!" but I simply dropped a curtsey and said in a tone of enormous politeness, "Good night, Sir! Sweet dreams to our revered boss!" My overly polite "little tone," as Felek calls it, could best convey to him the kind of night I was wishing him.

It was nice to sit around the table at home and talk. Felek proudly put on his new tie from Genia. Papa kept telling anecdotes and teased us wittily—I have not seen him so exhilarated and in such good spirits for a long time. I looked at him with great affection, and even Genia glued her eyes to Papa in the same adoring way that she looks at Felek. My brother suddenly began talking about his war experiences, which he has hardly ever done before now. He told the stories with his typical humor and in a lively, self-effacing way. One would think he was very modest indeed! He mentioned his schoolmates, whom he meets sometimes when he goes out of the ghetto. I listened with a heavy heart, remembering our real home and all those people who passed through our "salons." We admired Marian P., who was poor and of low birth and yet was so well mannered and the best student in the gimnazium. We laughed at cross-eyed Milek R., called the father of the class because he was the oldest of all the boys. But no one looked more magnificent than he did as drum major marching at the head of the school band, with Felek blowing the clarinet and Tolek L. wrapped in an enormous trombone. We used to tease Jurek S., who was known as "Świca." Tolek left for Palestine shortly before the war, Jurek is somewhere in Russia. The other boys, like everyone else, had their weaknesses and vices, but compared to us they are now first-class citizens. Surely they also suffer because of the war, but not so terribly as we do; we, who cannot get out and breathe a bit of fresh air—fresh air, not the gloomy air of the ghetto. Have I already forgotten how to be happy and how to laugh? I sat at the table like an old crow, feeling depressed, bitter, and sad. My thousands of dreams have turned into one great longing, which eats at my heart, and a sense of inner rebellion which is about to explode in me. Why has everything I need been taken away from me? School, books, interesting work, piano, long walks, green spaces. What is there left? Exasperation and hopeless, desperate rebellion.

Cambridge, Mass.

Did any of the four of us realize that we were gathered together for a family celebration for the last time? The next year I was in the barracks at the Arbeitslager Fliegerhorst-Kraków, while my parents, Felek, and his wife, Genia, were still in the ghetto, now reduced to a quarter of its original small size. In 1943, my family was in Konzentrationslager in Kraków-Płaszów and I, as before, at the Air base. In November 1944, Felek was among the inmates left behind liquidating Płaszów, while my mother, Genia, and I were deported to Auschwitz, where my father had already been killed in the gas chamber on 13 May 1944. In November 1945, Felek celebrated his birthday in Munich, Germany, while my Mother and I were in Kraków.

Even less could we have suspected that a viper more deadly than the Germans, whose attempt to destroy us physically had not quite succeeded, had already insinuated itself into the midst of our family. Like the eternal evil which always endures to poison whatever is left, Genia endured, too. She slid into the comfortable nest we provided and silently continued to poison the second and the third generation. Who would have believed that the final tragedy in our family would occur a few decades later and on another continent?

1 December 1941

I had a long talk with Pani Mania Neuwelt about all my worries. Loving and wise as she is, she misunderstood me. "All you need is to go out and enjoy yourself," she said, and invited me to a party at her nephew's, Dr. Mundek

Engelstein. I had met him when he visited all of us in the country on our last vacation before the war. Once he even gathered up all of us young kids when we were swimming in the river and drove us by car in our wet swimsuits to Kraków and back. And so tonight I went to his truly elegant party. As usual I had to fight with my boss, who chose today, Sunday, to keep the store open much longer than usual and threatened to fire anyone who dared to leave at 7:00 P.M. There is no coal, Lusia explained to him in a long tearful speech, and we have been freezing all day. I did not say a word, but at 7:00 P.M. sharp I left for home. I put on my eternal navy blue, princess-line dress with lacy collar and pinned on the cyclamen-colored carnation from Dziunia, instead of the innocent violets. Mama sprayed me with the last drops of her French perfume, "Heather," and I went off with Pani Mania.

Mundek lives on Wita Stwosza Street in the only modern building in the ghetto. He hardly recognized me when he opened the door. "My, you are taller than I am!" he said, helping me out of my coat. Dance music sounded from the room, and all at once I felt like a great lady. However, as soon as Pani Mania had left and Mundek introduced me to the guests, I was intimidated and froze. There were doctors in their thirties with their wives or their girl-friends, all of them urbane, some slightly balding and comfortably potbellied. The apartment is spacious and elegant, especially the doctor's office done in blue. Medical reflectors filtered a dim light, which was darkened still further by silvery gray cigarette smoke. A record player provided soft music, a few people danced. As a specialist in venereal diseases, Mundek had successfully treated a high Gestapo official for this hideous affliction. He is still treating other German patients, and that is why he has received such a large apartment. Tonight his office served as the dance floor and buffet. Delicacies were piled on the table just like before the war: canapés of sardines and ham and cheese on French bread; pastries; cheesecake; cookies and fruit; vodka, co-gnac, and brandy. I felt contempt for myself because it was the food on the buffet table that interested me the most. It was a bit like those times when I was among Felek's friends and as the youngest, and the silliest, and in any case no beauty, I had no partner to dance and have fun with. All the ladies here were sophisticated women in long, elegant evening gowns, and they were not disconcerted by a kiss on the hand after a dance or by the offer of a gentle-man's arm to lead them to the buffet.

I danced with Mundek and his roommate, a very handsome, but alas mar-ried, man whose Catholic wife lives in Kraków. The mood of the evening was nice, and yet it occurred to me that we were all sad, each in our own way. Dr. Schell, an ophthalmologist, confirmed my observation. He arrived late, drank whatever was still left, and stated that he was intoxicated with sorrow. I agreed. From time to time someone asked me to dance. Unfortunately, every partner complained that I am so tall! Dr. Schell did not dance. He sat on the sofa with his arms around his knees, watched people, and talked to me. We exchanged some profoundly philosophical remarks about people and life itself, remarks so general that they were actually meaningless. He has serious gray eyes, thinning hair, strong features, and a nice smile. The nicest thing of all about him is his name—Michał, like the hero of Maria Kuncewicz's book. Mundek is quite different. Stocky, fat, and balding, his good-natured face is round, his eyes behind their thick, large-framed glasses are smiling and friendly—a banker-papa out of an American film! This party also seemed unreal, like something out of a film. It's too bad that there was no fairy-tale prince there for me.

The return from movies to reality can be painful, and so was my return from that spacious apartment on Wita Stwosza Street to our one room on Janowa Wola filled with furniture worn out by too many moves and with people who are equally worn. Felek slept at home tonight instead of in the hospital, so I had to share my sofa with Mama. I snuggled down on my side of the sofa and with a heavy heart sadly sniffed the delicate fragrance of Mama's perfume.

Pani Mania meant well, but she was wrong. I do not need parties. I do not need love, either, but if nothing else is left . . . ? Maybe I should talk myself into this Dr. Michał Schell, it would be better to sigh to him than into empty space. Should love not come by itself and burst like a flame? Why should I talk myself into anything? Good night.

2 December 1941

> You will be moved in a book, in a film, on a stage
> by someone's sentimental, melancholic mood,
> but in life—fate will arrange it
> that you will walk by it, indifferent . . .

Of course! Besides, he won't be moved by books, because he certainly does not read cheap novels. Movies—we do not have movies or theater in the ghetto. Well, it's the end of the song and to hell with it!

9 December 1941

Lately, I've had luck with becomingly balding, rich, and slightly paunchy older men. For a long time engineer Weissberg has had an outstanding bill with us for fittings—by "us" I mean, of course, Lux. He works in town all day for some German company and we can never find him at home. On Sunday our dear boss decided to "clear this up once and for all," and early that morning delegated me to settle the account. I went off for the money filled with hostile thoughts, because on Sundays "the old man" himself deigns to officiate in the shop, and on that one day the stove is lit. It's nicer to sit in the warm, even in the presence of our crazed boss, than to schlep through mud and cold rain and snow.

In the ghetto there are decrepid old buildings, disgusting, stuccoed tenements with wells in the courtyards. The one and only modern building is the one where Mundek Engelstein lives and where, one flight up, as I discovered by looking for the apartment number on the list of tenants by the gate, forty-year-old engineer Weissberg resides.

For once the engineer was home. He had, apparently, caught a cold and was lying in bed. Some other guy was milling around and lighting a fire in the stove. I received the money immediately, of course, but I didn't have the correct change. I left mulling over in my mind the image of the plump engineer. He has nice teeth, a handsome face, and regular features, is probably well developed and tall since he took up the whole length of the sofa. In any case, judging by the apartment, the down comforter, and the bluish-green pajamas, he's an elegant gentleman.

I came back quickly with his change, but he said it was only a trifle, not worth the trouble of returning. I should have kept it, he told me.

"I don't accept tips," I returned, "I am not a messenger, that's not what my job is."

"Oh? And what is your job?"

An amusing conversation ensued, because he is Viennese and speaks poor Polish, so we mixed the two languages in our drawing room conversation. He excused himself for his indecent appearance in pajamas (bluish green!) during a surprise visit of a young lady, and in haste he covered himself up to his chin. It was just for fun; obviously, he was not embarrassed a bit—I was. Dripping with snow, I towered like a pikestaff, because how could I sit myself down when I was there on business?

The engineer asked the young man to look into the drawer for chocolates "especially for pretty girls." Now I was certain that he wanted to compensate me for what was my duty. Why should I humiliate myself by taking a tip? So, against his loud protests I left immediately.

Two hours later the engineer appeared in the store "to purchase a lamp." He looked very elegant in a woolen tweed coat with fur lining. Our boss, all smiles, danced around him, knowing that he was "somebody." Among many lamps in the store there was, of course, none that he "actually had in mind." The boss went to the storage area searching for some more, while the engineer turned to me: "we found the chocolates!"

"Zu spät! Too late!" I laughed. He took a small package out of his pocket, placed it in front of me on the counter, and, blowing a kiss, left with a friendly "Bye!"

Hanka Łętowska came over yesterday evening completely unexpectedly with her boss, Mr. Ziembaczewski, a pleasant and cheerful man. They took me to the café for cakes, coffee, and chocolate (!). We strutted through the ghetto like peacocks and even went over to the *Ordnungsdienst*, where Mr. Ziembaczewski arranged a pass into town for me for Saturday. I am impressed by Hanka's behavior. She acts as though the war, the ghetto, the evil laws don't exist, and we are still two girls who share the same desk at the gimnazium.

And yet before we got to know one another better I used to be afraid of her ironic remarks, because she didn't try to cover up her anti-Semitism, even though these remarks were directed at the empty air, never at Runka or me. Hanka wasn't friendly with anyone in the class, except for the two of us. Her mother worked at the Pałac Prasy, the Press Palace, and as a result Hanka knew Jalu Kurek, a real writer. There was some tragedy in her family. I don't know where her father was, or why her older sister had poisoned herself. Hanka used to say that no one knew the reason, perhaps not even she, herself. Shortly before the *matura*, the graduating exam, when everyone thought she was studying in the other room, she took poison.

Hanka works in the City Hall and helps wherever she can. Her unexpected visit to our "zoo" lifted my spirits no end. And so, after all, the ghetto walls cannot completely separate people!

10 December 1941

For two days a new war is being waged: America and England against Japan, Romania, Hungary, and Bulgaria. War is taking the whole world. Is there a peaceful place anywhere on earth?

16 December 1941

I keep feeling that I am going to burst into tears. I feel bad, heavy hearted, and sad, and that rebellious feeling is rising in me again. Maybe it would be better if I hadn't had that pass for two days in town.

I went to Hanka's. I was so happy and so excited that everyone, from the policeman on the gate to people I know and strangers I don't, could see it and smiled at me. As I walked quickly across the bridge through the wind which blew my hair and wafted over my face, I could feel the blood racing through my veins and finally felt young! I took "my way" along Stradom by Wawel and over Dębnicki bridge to Barska. I came back down Zwierzyniecka, and in the evening I was in a good mood, pleasantly tired and filled with impressions.

In Hanka's office, a nice atmosphere and nice colleagues; in her home, a quiet room and the old, untuned, but pleasant-sounding piano on which I used to play so often after we had finished our homework. Hanka asked for those prewar melodies, and we conducted a friendly conversation to the rhythm of the music. Afterwards we took a long walk. Hanka bravely linked her arm through mine, the one without the armband. Our walk took us through the darkened and gloomy town, but it was my beloved Kraków. I've been cut off from the town for close to a year, and I had naively imagined that a normal life existed on the other side of the gates. But that freedom beyond the ghetto walls must surely be very problematic.

On the following day, I went to Hanka's again, but we couldn't chat completely freely because she had friends over, and in the evening there was an embarrassing situation with Mr. Ziembaczewski. Drunk as a skunk, he declared his enormous love for Hanka. That mature, serious forty-eight-year-old man has fallen in love like an adolescent. He does not dare to confront her himself, he is shy and helpless, and he appeals to me for help. When I started to tell Hanka yesterday how nice he is, she cut me off in her own inimitable way.

"Yes, of course, he is. He is also married. I am Catholic."

"He is, too, isn't he?"

"It's out of the question!"

Today, Mr. Ziembaczewski visited me in the ghetto and took me off to a café for coffee and cakes. He really is a nice and sincere man. He has to have loyal and friendly people around him. He's good and demands goodness. Unfortunately, I don't think Hanka loves him. Such strong and pure, such great, passionate feelings impress me enormously, and I feel sorry for him. But I also feel a bit awkward that he turns to me with his love problems. After all, I don't have much experience in these matters.

After these excursions into town, the ghetto seems even more unbearable to me. Actually, I'm sad for a different reason. Today I was reading a book I got from Hanka, *It Will Be Sunny Tomorrow*, about the life of some gimnazium girls from Warsaw. I remembered our skiing lessons, the school dances for "Mikolaja." And what's more, the tallest of the heroines writes poems, is called Hala, and is my mirror image. Really, if I had been writing about myself I couldn't have hit the nail on the head any better. Like me, she's sensitive and stubborn, but sincere and direct; like me, she is not very practical, impulsive and inexperienced, clever and a bit lazy, and, just as I had wanted to, she's studying literature. I actually would have preferred art history had it not been for the fact that everyone considered such a field the height of uselessness.

Hala also seemed closest to me of all the girls in the book because she, too, had days filled with sorrow and apathy. The "only" difference between us is that everything works out for her in the end. On the last page she gets engaged to a man she loves and attains her goal, while I can't attain anything, will never be anything but a dilettante, and am wasting the years of my youth.

I read the book under the counter at work, and trudging through the mud in the rain and fog in the evening, I cried and cried and cried.

20 December 1941

All Jews ages fourteen to twenty-five are obliged to go for an anthropological examination to the former Geographical Institute on Grodzka street. There are strange rumors: men are castrated, women are given injections to make them barren. Hard to believe such monstrous gossip.

My group went twice for nothing, because the doctor was too busy with others. Going for the third time, I was not even worried at all, but on the way something unpleasant happened. We were walking into the city not on the sidewalk but among the cars in the middle of the road. In my group, the girls happened to be rather short and dark haired, and one urchin called out to me, "Hey, Jewish auntie, stay away from those Jews!"

The doctor from the German health department, Jost Halbaum, looked like a butcher, fat and red in neck and face. He looked at us carefully, called us in one by one, leaving me to the very end. Without a word, he pointed to the screen where I was to disrobe. I came out in a slip. He weighed me and measured my height, my head, and my face, then looked at me at length and finally wrote something in a large book. Out of the corner of my eye I read: height 1,72 m; weight 54 kg; skull oblong—and some numbers; skin white; eyes blue; hair blond; nose straight. Then he took off my slip and I stood there naked. What could I do? I thought, he is a doctor. His examination, in total silence, was strange and loathsome. He moved something like a toothbrush over my nipples, felt me all over gasping heavily like a locomotive. Finally he pointed to a sofa on which I had to lie down. With a small hammer he checked my reflexes, measured my legs and looked in between, and suddenly I heard his voice which sounded muffled as if coming from an empty barrel: "A virgin! No Aryans in the family?"

How do I know if someone in my family ever committed a cardinal sin with an Aryan? There were and are mixed marriages with Catholics and Lutherans in our family, but not in my immediate one. And it is out of the question even to imagine my grandmother or mother having an extramarital affair. He continued with his "examination." The touch of his thick ugly fingers made me almost throw up. I bit my lips. He was getting some instruments when our O.D. knocked at the door and humbly reminded him about the curfew, because it was already late. The doctor muttered something, while I jumped behind the screen and got dressed quickly, crying. Even now I shudder from revulsion remembering the sleazy touch of his shaking hands.

Two days later I received a note again summoning me for an examination. I started lamenting that I could not face this butcher again. Papa went to the O.D. and asked the commandant to list me as an *"ausgesiedelte"*—a relocated person. No one exactly knows the names of the people involved in yesterday's "Action" in the ghetto streets, so the Gestapo doctor cannot find out the truth!

Cambridge, Mass.

It is unbelievable that the Germans could fool themselves about the "Aryan" or "Jewish look"! And how this racist ideology stuck in the German mind!

In 1976 I organized at Harvard University an exhibition called "Humboldtiana at Harvard" and wrote the text for the catalog. For this project I received an award and an invitation from the Alexander von Humboldt Foundation to lecture in Berlin and Bonn on "Alexander von Humboldt and Art." The distinguished academic audience evidently did not suspect who I really am, although I was introduced as an art historian born in Kraków. At the party afterwards, one woman recollected having been in Poland during the war: "I was in Warsaw. Were you there at this time?"

I did not feel like getting into such discussion during the reception in my honor, but I nodded, yes, I was in Poland.

"Really? Where?"

"In Auschwitz."

"Come on, you were not old enough to be employed at the camp!" Ha! She thought I had been an Aufseherin! *A Nazi female guard! I was flabbergasted, but before I could answer, another person joined in.*

"That you are Polish is hard to believe. I knew Poles, they were working on our estate, Poles are stocky with broad faces and dark hair, while you are tall, blue eyed, blond, a perfect example of the Nordic race. Were your ancestors the Normans or the Vikings?"

"They were Polish Jews. And I was in Auschwitz, indeed, but on the other side of the barbed wire. I was your Häftling, *sorry about that," I added with an ironic smile, and I turned away to the American consul who stood nearby.*

23 December 1941

I met Józek Holländer, Netherländer, unexpectedly, and he walked me to Lux. While Lusia went out on some errand, we were able to speak freely. He talked at length about ancient and modern Hebrew literature and about Palestine.

These are totally unfamiliar subjects to me, except that I know the name of a poet, Bialik. I have never joined any Zionist organization and cannot identify with the "chalutzim's" passionate feelings for the Promised Land. Józek explained to me that every Hebrew song, every holiday, is another link in a chain of tradition which unites and welds the Jews together and gives us strength to overcome thousands of years of persecution. I had never thought about it. Poland is my country. Our family has been fully assimilated for more than a century. No one ever ignited the "sacred fire of love for the ancient fatherland" in me, although we used to celebrate the traditional High Holidays, which are almost all very sad. The Jews remember their adversities forever. It seems to me that Jews are united mostly because of their common suffering. Why are we always being persecuted by other nations? Why are we constantly being pushed around and ridiculed?

Józek asked whether I believed that we should fight for our dignity, for the right to live, or at least to die, without utter degradation, to die like a human being and not like a rat in some gutter. Of course! But how? Civilians were always protected if they obeyed the law, but we are outside the law. Collective responsibility is paralyzing us. And it is impossible to act as individuals. "Not necessarily," remarked Józek. "One does not fight alone." Suddenly I understood. "Józek, you belong to an organization, please, take me with you!" But at this, Józek fell silent, perhaps because Lusia had just returned to the store.

Today I walked by his house and stopped in. His door was locked. What a pity!

25 December 1941

Christmas in the ghetto. How different, not at all Christmassy! Yesterday a rain storm came up, and weather like that does not create a mood for Christmas carols. Today, however, a strong snowstorm came at noon, and at last everything is white. I feel great, for a change!

Engineer Weissberg shows up at the store every Sunday. When our boss is around he pretends that he needs a light bulb or something else to fix the lights in his apartment, but otherwise he just comes in for a nice chat. Lately he mentioned that he is going on business to Lublin, Lwów, and Międzyrzecze. My beloved Aunt Mala and her daughter Felicia are there. They were deported from Kraków at the same time as my friend Staszka. The beautiful Felicia, our first piano teacher, stayed single because she loved a man who married someone else, a rich girl. I didn't say anything about Aunt Felicia's broken heart, but mentioned that they are both in Międzyrzecze. The engineer has the nice ability to make things easy. Naturally, he said he would visit them gladly. I wondered how he dares to travel with a Jewish armband. He laughed. "Easily. The armband travels in my pocket, and I travel in a compartment *Nur für Deutsche,* for Germans only." We all laughed. He added that he would gladly deliver a small parcel to my aunt if I could bring it to him early in the morning, before he leaves for work in the city.

Today, at the crack of dawn, that is at eight o'clock, I was at his door with our modest gift of carrot-potato cake and a letter. Our casual meetings at his place, the first when I came with the bill from Lux and now this one, are more grotesque than romantic. The engineer opened the door half-asleep, naturally, pulling a robe over his pajamas and smoothing his hair in embarrassment. He tried in vain to make me stay for a longer talk. "You are always in a hurry, you never have time, *Mädchen!* Do I have to catch you only in the store, as a customer? Please come to the café across the street from your Lux at seven tonight."

"Fine, I will be there," I agreed from the hallway as I stepped down the stairs. I had never been in a café alone, and never in the evening, and worried about how I would find him in the crowd. Luckily, he came to the store at closing time, and instead of going to the smoke-filled café we went for a walk in the streets, which were covered with fresh snow. I had to look up when I talked to him because he is a tall man. We arrived at the steep side of the Krzemionki hill and fell laughing into the fluffy, white snowdrifts. One might have thought we were in the Tatra mountains and Zakopane. We reached the top, right under the ghetto wall.

He linked his arm through mine and asked, "What is your name, anyway?" "Halina." "Halinka. In Russian it would be Galiczka. I am Alexander. Just look at this pretty, peaceful world!" The view was indeed beautiful. Silvery white tranquility under a starry sky. Down in the distance, the silhouettes of slender church towers loomed in blacked-out Kraków.

"Have you ever been here at this time before, Halinka? Never? That's at least one pleasant moment which you have to thank me for. We have conquered this summit in order to be closer to heaven. See, there's Orion," he pointed up to the shining stars. Remembering the High Tatra where the stars are as big as fists, I sang in a soft voice:

How good it is to wander at night
along the pale ribbon of the roads
watching the sky gilded with the stars
and waiting for what fate has for us.

"Was singst Du wieder, Mädchen! What are you singing?" he asked in his melodious Viennese dialect, which does not sound harsh the way proper German does. But his words abruptly pulled me away from my memories of

summer vacation before the war to the ghetto wall here. I shuddered. I translated my song and he sighed, "Well, so far, fate has not brought you anything particularly nice, but these walls are not forever. One day they'll fall and the good life will begin. Do you have any idea what you would like to do then?"

He asked this very matter-of-factly, as if the war were going to end tomorrow. I don't know why I revealed my secret wish to him so frankly, that I wanted to study and to write about art. He looked at me in amusement, and with a sudden interest said, "Finally! Something new and different. So far, all the girls your age that I have met want to be film stars! And you aspire to the heights of knowledge!"

"Where else but the heights? We have to accommodate ourselves to the situation we're in. We've already arrived at one height, haven't we?"

"It is not so easy to reach the top, *Mädchen*."

"We managed somehow. But how are we going to get down?" I looked with apprehension at the steep slope of the rocky hill.

"How? It's simple!" He sat down in the deep snow, I did the same, and we slid down laughing.

"Snowmen, that's what we are!" he joked, shaking the snow from our coats. I felt great!

We went to the evening concert at the café, and sipping a cup of ersatz coffee talked in German about literature. I could not express myself as freely as usual and blushed stupidly when he looked at me. He watched me with a slight smile. Thinking that he was laughing at me, I interrupted my discourse on Oscar Wilde's *Picture of Dorian Gray* in half-sentence, and he said, "I've got it! You remind me of the girl whom Dorian met under the flowering apple tree, the fresh and innocent girl, the only one he hadn't wronged."

I blushed even more and shook my head. Still, it was nice to hear this—after all, I am only a woman! He walked me home and kissed my hand good night.

What a nice gentleman. A handsome, mature, strong man with whom one feels safe walking arm in arm along the snowy streets.

26 December 1941

I miss him!

29 December 1941

Saturday morning—an unusual commotion in the ghetto. The Germans are driving around and calling over the loudspeakers for the surrender of all furs, warm boots, overshoes, and gloves, even children's winter clothing. All furs must be turned in by four o'clock in the afternoon on penalty of death.

Papa carried his and Mama's fur coats, our muffs, hats, and ripped-off collars to the collection center. Naturally, the Germans don't give any receipts, just a number for us to remember in the event of an inspection. Had we sold the fur coats outside the ghetto, we would have had a lot of food. I hated to ruin my new suit, which now shows interfacing instead of a fur collar. Trying to save it, I threw the sealskin into the coal bin. The loss of our only warm clothing in the middle of winter is a tragedy, yet the people in the streets were full of grim humor.

Grześ came to visit me at Lux and presented me with his song on the subject:

> I had a beautiful fur coat
> of camgarn lined with fitchwews.
> How strange that by tomorrow
> I shall have to be without it!
>
> Swarms of Jews today
> Went to give away their furs.
> I gave mine up, too,
> Along with all its lice.
>
> Jewish daughters brought their nutrias,
> Pretty minks and Persian lambs,
> Silver foxes, each gave gladly
> To keep German soldiers warm.
>
> But soon the hour will come
> When I shall rip
> The skin off a son-of-a-bitch
> And then I'll have two furs.

Cambridge, Mass.

Grześ's hour of triumph never came. I do not know how or where he perished, my charming, freckled, ever-loving Grześ. His song alludes to the large German posters which read "Jews, Lice, Typhoid Fever" and on which appeared a caricature of an ugly old Jew and a fat hairy louse. Vesta Iudaica Non Olet!

29 December 1941 cont'd.

The announced inspection did not materialize, but a surprise came on the following day: the janitors received an order not to let anyone out of the buildings before noon. Every household had to be prepared for an inspection, and every piece of unsurrendered fur spelled death. Even evidence of the removal of fur, a linen collar where fur once had been was also punishable. No trace of the confiscation was to remain.

People who had resisted the day before now dropped their furs secretly on the deserted and deadly silent streets, and the heavy snow that fell that day soon covered up those once-cherished possessions.

I burned my sealskin collar and muff, and we made use of the fire to boil up potato soup. As I waited for the inspection, I hid my diary in the thick album of *Sang und Klang* on the piano and placed Schumann and Beethoven on top. We looked out through half-frosted windows onto our little street which lay so serene beneath its thick blanket of heavy snow.

Not all the houses were searched, evidently, because no one came to ours. Where they did search, though, they requisitioned not only furs and sweaters but also typewriters, phonographs, sugar, flour, and other provisions. No inspection this, but plunder. To terrorize us even more, they shot five people on the street. To lose one's life for a stupid fur! The inspection was considered unusually lenient, and yet five people lost their lives.

In the afternoon I went for a walk in my shabby collarless coat which offered no protection against the wind. I looked like a beggar. In fact, everybody is walking around looking like plucked chickens. I went to the Polonia Café to make Felek's excuses, because he had a terrible cold and was unable to play there in the evening. He said his brain was dripping out of his nose. It certainly must be! He is such a lively fellow, how can he stand this Genia who sits by his bed with nothing to say for herself except "yes," and "no." Even Papa can get only a sour smile out of her. She waits for us all to leave so she can neck with Felek. She dropped out of the Jewish trade school in Kazimierz where her parents have a mattress stuffing business. Genia does cook fabulous chopped meat schnitzels for her family, though. But I don't know how to cook, so we have nothing to talk about with each other.

I marched along the snowy streets feeling exhilarated for no reason at all, except that I was walking in light frost and sunshine. I found myself thinking about the engineer, and I was not surprised when, at that very moment, I spotted him. The ghetto is so small that it isn't hard to see the same people several times a day. Weissberg and I nearly bumped into each other. He was also wearing a coat without its beaver lining. Smiling in a friendly way, he said something nice, and we stayed and talked for a little while. He had a woman with him, and he cordially invited me to join them for pastries. Feeling like the fifth wheel, I declined. I was cross with myself for being intimidated by her and by her mature, easy manner. I did not have any money and I did not want him to have to buy me pastry, and so, miserably awkward, I said good-bye and returned home sadly, though I would have liked to go with them.

Silent Genia was still by Felek's bed. She has succeeded in making Felek boring, too. I wonder whether boredom is a powerful female weapon? How else can Felek stand that little nothing after beautiful Hungarian Fela who was so full of life and energy and humor?

Why do I feel uneasy around the engineer? I felt that way this morning when he stopped by Lux to use the telephone. When he finished he turned to me as though he had something meaningful to say, and I spoiled it by hiding behind silly small talk. He glanced at me, shrugged, and left.

During these last few stormy days, Hanka and Mr. Ziembaczewski telephoned the O.D. to see if we were all right. They are worried about me! On an impulse of gratitude, I called Mr. Ziembaczewski "Angelus," and now this nickname has stuck. He promised to arrange for an official certificate for me to show that I am employed by the City Hall as a street sweeper. It should prevent me from being caught for forced removal of snow in the city. The "catchers" have been busy since early morning today.

Poor Papa in his shabby old jacket is shivering from the cold. Mama had to give away a fur collar which she had made herself from a Persian lamb coat that was too long. My gray suit originated thanks to gifts from the entire family, and all this has gone for nought!

Alexander has already ordered a new warm overcoat at the ghetto tailor's, so he certainly won't freeze for long. Why am I thinking about him so much, anyway? He seems to be a symbol of peace and security. It is not because he has money. He must have his troubles too, who doesn't, but he always appears to be in a good mood, level headed and calm, the only point of stability in this mad universe.

30 December 1941

It has been snowing all morning. Dry flakes softly cover buildings and streets, and even our abominable ghetto seems innocently clean in its splendid winter garb. Before the war such snow was sheer delight for skiing, sledding, and making snowmen, but now! People are being seized for snow shoveling all the time in the ghetto. What an ugly, degrading scene when helmeted soldiers, or our O.D.s, round us up like dogs and we, human beings, run away like frightened rabbits. I don't run away and I feel ashamed that others do. I prefer to face the danger instead of having the enemy at my back. On the other hand, perhaps people are right when they run away, unwilling to waste their energy on forced labor that is more chicanery than real work.

Evidently, I was lucky when I walked leisurely to Lux in the middle of this chase and was not caught. The mood in the ghetto is very tense. Two people were shot again for hiding furs. Yesterday someone left three fur-lined coats and a Persian lamb cape in the hallway of our building. All the tenants decided to burn the furs in the oven immediately.

In the meantime, the days and the months pass by relentlessly. Tomorrow is New Year's Eve. At this end of the year I should figure out "the balance," like a bookkeeper. There is nothing to write on the credit side. Nothing but monotonous days and weeks, and my wishes are ever so modest. I am depressed and miss the engineer. What the devil possesses me, that I always make the same mistake? He stopped by Lux today. I wanted to say something nice, to ask him when he is leaving. But instead I babbled on in a silly way, as if I purposely wanted to avoid a personal conversation. And then our boss arrived and Alexander left. Will I ever enjoy an inner tranquility the way I did on the snow-covered Krzemionki hill on that silvery white evening with Alexander?

31 December 1941

New Year's Eve. The old year is coming to a close and a new one beginning. What will it bring me? New sorrows and disillusionments? New bitterness? Tomorrow at 7:00 A.M. we all have to gather in front of the *Arbeitsamt*, no one knows why. The German employment office is in my old public school. I wonder what my beloved teachers, or the principal, would have said if they knew that those classrooms now house the Jewish files for forced labor?

The strange rumors have made all of us even more tense than we were before. And tonight is New Year's Eve.

I changed into a nice dress and went to Mundek. Music from the record player, little sandwiches, pastries, and wine, as usual. Among the guests, Alexander, of course. We danced and drank and laughed, and with this loud laughter I tried to stifle my pervasive sadness. We whirled around to a Viennese waltz. I floated in his arms, hardly touching the floor. At midnight the lights went out, we raised our glasses, and we toasted the New Year. Alexander hugged me and gently kissed my face, his smiling eyes looking at me affectionately. At dawn I cuddled next to him on a sofa, and secure and happy, I fell asleep.

Not true! Not true at all! I never went anywhere, neither did I drink any wine, nor did I cuddle with Alexander! It was only a fantasy, though it came so close to becoming reality. It did not happen because of my pride, or rather, my stupidity. Alexander invited me to come to a small social gathering at his place. On account of the curfew, I would have had to stay all night, and to me—what an idiot!—this was unthinkable. I turned down the invitation, and instead went to Dziunia's birthday party, a "Kinderball." God, how sorry I am, how very sorry.

It is now ten o'clock in the evening. Facing the wall, I scribble in bed, crying while five people in my family, including Uncle Ignacy and my two cousins, who sleep in the same small room, are complaining that I should blow out the candle and let them sleep because tomorrow we have to get up at dawn, who knows what for—forced labor, or transport. Work! Transport! Damn! Nothing but deportation or forced labor—what kind of life is this? New Year's Eve! Somewhere, in America or Switzerland, people are enjoying themselves; somewhere people are suffering the last moments of their lives, like our neighbor who is dying of a heart ailment; somewhere hungry children are crying, and starving people shivering in the cold—they are among us, in the ghetto. Somewhere people are being killed in air raids or on the battlefield.

The New Year comes with bombs, jazz, human suffering. Will this New Year 1942 dry our tears, heal wounds, stop bloodshed and the suffering of every innocent, persecuted human being? Will it bring a moment of joy and happiness to me, too? Will I be able to laugh again, instead of smiling through my tears? My family is asleep now and I do not have to hide my weeping. I am not praying like a little child, I am begging you, New Year 1942—have mercy upon us!

Cambridge, Mass.

Nineteen forty-two showed no mercy. That year, and the next two, were the most deadly years of the "Final Solution" and the Holocaust. As for my dream about the waltz, it was fulfilled—eighteen years later at the Opera Ball in Vienna. I danced in a white evening gown with a tall, distinguished gentleman, many years older than I, who loved me. I was not romantically involved, but happy, floating in his arms and in the warm glance of his mocha-colored eyes. It was not love—it was the sense of affectionate security and protection which I had always longed for, but which I had experienced only for fleeting moments in my life.

1 January 1942

Papa woke me out of pleasant dream at six o'clock in the morning, and we rushed to the *Arbeitsamt*. The streets were pitch black. People walked quickly past the houses, heads hunched into shoulders. The entrance gate to the ghetto with its bluish purple lantern, the policeman in a big sheepskin, and the soldiers in helmets looked like a stage set for a medieval drama. In front of the *Arbeitsamt* thousands of people waited, stamping their feet for warmth. Gradually groups marched off to work. We waited and waited in the bitter cold for five hours for nothing. Finally, our group was sent to clean the next street. I was frozen to the bone, my face, my hands, and my feet were numb. An older woman took pity on me and sent me home. Buried under covers and blankets, I thawed out.

In the evening it started snowing again. The snow, our enemy! I went to the wire factory to chat with "little Hala" and Zosia. They told their stories, I listened, but could not tell them mine, for I hardly know what is bothering me. We sang a little and tried to make jokes about our worries. On the way home with Zosia, I walked in silence, wondering why, with all the friends I have, I still feel alone and lonely.

3 *January 1942*

I miss Alexander. Perhaps not him so much as the conversation and the particular atmosphere of our sporadic meetings. I don't know. It hurts to be out of touch. And there are other worries: Lux might go out of business. Everybody has to work, or else. Who can help me find a job? "Angelus" is powerless in the ghetto in this respect. What am I going to do? It's all too much for me! Too much!

Yesterday, while waiting on the street for Lux to open, I suddenly met Alexander, and my heart jumped happily. During a casual talk I collected my courage and, averting my eyes, whispered, "I have to see you."

"When and where?" he asked simply. Well, where? I always feel at a loss when I have to decide something like this. Looking up, I noticed his friendly smile. Sometimes I suspect that he enjoys seeing me confused before he comes out with a solution: "Look, *Mädchen*, I know your apartment is very small and my visit might be inconvenient. It is too cold for a long walk, and besides, where is there to walk here? Around and around? Why not my place tomorrow morning?"

He convinced me easily. One smile, a few kind words, an affectionate glance, and at once my mood turned rosy! I am hoarse and coughing as a result of the long wait in freezing cold in front of the *Arbeitsamt* on New Year's Day. Mama stuffed me with aspirin and sent me to bed. I could hardly wait until tomorrow and quickly went to sleep.

Next morning I woke up in great spirits, got dressed in a minute, and strode briskly toward his house. The closer I came, the slower my pace. Frankly, I felt uneasy. What if he misunderstood my visit? After all, a young lady does not usually come to a bachelor's flat to discuss literature, as I sincerely hoped we would do. What, in fact, was I to expect? My heart trembling, I knocked at his door. Silence. After a while the cleaning woman opened the door and told me the engineer had just left.

I was flabbergasted. At first. Then furious and indignant. I tore a page out of my notebook and scribbled, "A *gentleman* never forgets." Going back down the stairs, I was not sure whether to laugh or to cry. Nothing made sense, except for the fact that in my life the simplest thing becomes unbelievably complicated. How am I going to tell Mama about this? What a disgrace! I was ashamed of myself, ashamed that a gentleman had dared to ignore me! Not knowing what to do with the rest of a free Saturday, I went toward Krzemionki hill, my feet sloshing through heavy, melting snow. The rocks and the ghetto wall were still powdered white, like a frosted pastry. I glanced at them with sudden disgust and returned home. Surprise! *Herr Ingenieur* had come looking for me here, explaining to my mother that he had just gone out for a minute to use his neighbor's telephone, asking the maid to let me in and call him immediately. Since we had, unfortunately, missed each other, he would permit himself to pick me up in the afternoon.

Good grief! Hanka Łętowska announced that she was coming over from Kraków to see me today. Everything comes at once—or nothing comes at all. Obviously there is no smooth sailing for my ever-so-innocent romance.

He arrived soon after lunch. Naturally the entire "Sanhedryn" of aunts and my parents' friends was at our place, so we left the gathering and walked to his house. His room was bright, clean, and smelled of floor wax. A low, tiled stove blazed forth a pleasant warmth. Alexander served chocolates and chatted. I never know whether he is serious or joking.

"That's the whole point!" he laughed, stroking my hair. "Well, what is on your mind?" I had had so much to tell him, and now I could not utter a word. Silence. He embraced me gently and tried to kiss me, but I lowered my head and said, "You are mistaken if you think that I came here for *that*."

Alexander suppressed a loud laugh and shook his head slightly in amazement. Looking at me with his warm smile, he said, "What a funny little miss! *kleines Fräulein, keine Angst.* Do not worry. No one is going to hurt you, you mixture of innocence and intellect! You are wearing blue forget-me-not earrings, your mother knows with whom you are going out, you can talk about literature and art and play piano as an educated girl should. But there is something else to you besides your somewhat old-fashioned principles, a genuine innocence which makes you different, distinguishes you from other young girls of your generation." "It's not me, who is different, it's you," I said. "You are an unusual man." "Indeed? you know s-o-o-o much about men that you can tell who is usual or not?" he laughed.

"Perhaps not, but I sense that you are a man of strong character. And you know so much, you are interested in so many things, not just in your physics, of which I do not understand a thing. Most people in the ghetto think about food all the time and about what used to be called 'business,' but you don't. I like listening to you; whatever you say is convincing and witty. I want to learn a lot from you, to talk with you for hours, but when we are together I am unable to, and whatever I say is wrong."

"But why?"

"I don't know why."

He got up, held me gently to himself, and softly kissed my cheek. I turned my head away, not knowing what to do.

"You are still a child, a sweet baby. Have you ever been in love?"

"I don't think so. I would not call this love."

"So, how do you live? What do you do with yourself, sitting all day in that store, what do you think about?"

I sighed and almost admitted that I mainly thought about him. Eventually our conversation turned to a more neutral topic, but I was still nervous; if Mama knew that he was about to kiss me . . . and perhaps Hanka had already arrived from Kraków and was waiting for me. I had to leave right away. Alexander did not pay any attention to my sudden haste, but leisurely browsed through some books on his desk, one of which he handed to me.

"If I'm going to be your mentor, be prepared for serious business. You like poetry, but I am sure that of German literature you know only 'Erlkonig' and 'Heidenrösslein.' " "Not only!" I interrupted. "I adore Heine's *Buch der Lieder*, I know boring Uhland, and Schiller's *Der Handschuh* and Goethe's *Edel sei der Mensch*." While I talked and talked, not shy anymore, he raised his hands in a gesture of exaggerated admiration. "It is difficult not to adore Heine. The Germans have many things to be ashamed of, especially of calling him 'an unknown poet.' Uhland is not as boring as you think. But you clearly do not know Rilke. Oh, what a poet! Here it is, *Buch der Bilder*. Read it, suffer, and next time tell me all about it. And now—listen!"

In his melodious deep voice, which I associated with gently falling snow-flakes, he recited "*Herbstag,*" a poem about falling leaves. I listened enchanted, suddenly forgetting the war, transferred into the world of eternal human feeling and sorrow. I did not want to leave at all now, but it was improper to stay.

He helped me on with my coat and suddenly lifted me high up. "See how tall you are, my little one!" He kissed me. I wrenched myself out of his embrace and muttered something, annoyed with my stupid, undignified position. We walked in silence through the melting snow. On the empty street in front of my house, he took my face in his hands and said, "You are not angry at me, are you?"

"No. I am angry at myself," my voice shook. "What? Why?" "Perhaps because what's just a meaningless episode for you is a very important one for me," I said. "Regardless of the war, I don't want to be just one of your many girls. Is it too much to wish for? Am I just being naive, sentimental, and foolish?"

"No, you're not. Naive—yes, but that's rather nice at your age. About being 'one of many,' let's talk tomorrow." His voice sounded serious. "You don't know much now, but soon you might find out a lot. Here you are, blushing again, I can see it even in this dim light! I have not been so impressed by anyone in a long time as I have been since I dropped by the store unexpectedly and you blushed like a rose. It makes a man proud. *Auf Wiedersehen*, my innocent *Frühlingsblümchen*." He kissed my hand, and I ran upstairs into my house. If he only knew what wild confusion and chaos there is in his "spring-blossom's" head!

19 January 1942

Alexander came to Lux while I was out for the day and then didn't show up again all week long. I missed him terribly. His planned journey has been canceled, so I sent our errand boy to recover the small parcel for my aunt. Alexander arrived in person at once, but the gloomy store with people listening to our every word is no place for personal conversation. Next day, I had to extend my *Kennkarte* at the *Arbeitsamt*, and he came to look for me twice at Lux. He came back in the afternoon, and we greeted each other happily. He asked how one could best protect one's ears in all this frost. "By keeping them in one's pocket," I advised. We all laughed, but just at this moment the boss arrived and sent me to the storage room for something. He considers Alexander an important and respected person, but after all he is the boss and I am only a "humble nobody" who should not be talking with the clients.

Another long week of waiting, and again Alexander comes precisely when I am out for a few minutes. He uses our telephone or buys an electric bulb—at least my "love affair" is good for business, if not for me.

The frost is reaching the minus twenty-five degrees Celsius, minus thirteen Fahrenheit, mark. I have never experienced such a cruel winter. And the snow! Every block in the ghetto is obliged to clean the streets for eight hours a day. On Saturday, my free day, I worked in my old ski suit with a blue scarf around my face which was shiny with vaseline to protect me from frostbite. We received our equipment and went nearby to clean Optima, which had been a chocolate manufacturer before the war. These days, Optima is the best place for the *Himmelfahrt Kommando*, the trip to heaven, as they say in the ghetto. It is a rallying point for transports for deportations. All this snow removal is in vain, for it is snowing and snowing and snowing.

The groups working in the city were already freezing on the way there, but those of us who were inside the ghetto took turns taking quick trips home to get warm. People were standing around leaning on their shovels, unwilling to waste energy. Out of boredom and also to keep warm, I brandished my shovel furiously until noon. On the march with the group back to the storage area to return our shovels, I met Fred Wahl. He dropped his briefcase on the sidewalk in mock astonishment at the sight of me in my new capacity as snow "street-walker" and exclaimed: "Glory be to hard labor! Let's have a pastry, you and your shovel!" And lifting me and my shovel, he carried us both to the pastry store.

Fred is tall and has green eyes. Like Józek, Netherländer, he was one of the oldest in our group. We recalled the crazy party in my house on Traugutta, when he beat up the boys who got drunk, and how my father came home and raised hell. He walked with me to the storage area and then home. We threw snowballs in the street like little kids. Fred decided to kiss my pink cheek, vaseline or not, and he did. I, too, kissed his cleanly shaved cheek, at the same time wondering why I cannot behave as naturally with Alexander in this respect. I came home as if I were returning from an outing. A year ago my Staszka and I walked around like this. I miss her so much! If only Alexander traveled to Rzeszow and could take me with him to visit her! . . . if, if . . .

I think a lot about Alexander, though a bit differently than I did at the beginning. It's hard to define this intangible "something" between us. I do not love him, I am not jealous, I would not be hurt if I saw him with someone else. Or would I be? Who knows how many women he has in Kraków? Nevertheless, he is in my thoughts all the time. If it is not love, then what is it?

20 January 1942

I feel so good at home. I am in a family mood again. I like our pleasant small room which is clean and sunny and where Mama always waits ready to listen and advise and criticize, too. I know that her nagging and grumbling are caused by her worrying about me. My work at Lux does not overexert me, and in fact I am dying of boredom, but Mama understands that it is hard for me to be in the bitter cold all day long with nothing interesting to do. Even if there are no clients all day I am not allowed to read a book or to knit. I do both, but in constant fear that the boss will come and scream at me. Mama sees to it that I have clean hankies and freshly washed blouses and sometimes even darns my only pair of silk stockings. Slender, quick, and lively, Mama is extraordinarily energetic and resourceful. My parents do not complain, they just go on. She and Mrs. Mania Neuwelt, Bella, and Aunt Dora and their friends must miss their good life much more than I miss my school, and yet they seem to take it all in stride. They know that wars come to an end and everything falls back into place again, as it did in the First World War. Is this war any different?

I love our family and Mama very much, even if she sometimes gives despotic orders. I argue and argue for nothing, because in the end I obey her anyway. She knows best, and so far she has always been right.

It is late evening. Mama's bed is standing next to mine for the night. She reads a book wearing my Papa's large-framed reading glasses, which they have taken to sharing lately. I look at her with great affection; these big glasses almost cover her face, and she has such fine features. In the morning her relaxed face is as glowing and smooth as a girl's. She has no wrinkles, but her pretty and slender hands are worn out. She chops coal with a small hammer, she lights the stove, cooks, cleans, darns and mends our clothes—and in her clear, calligraphic script does the bookkeeping in the orphanage for additional income. Mama also binds brushes with hard wire at home. We all help somewhat with the brushes and with housework. It is Mama's presence and work that makes this place a home, cozy and safe. In our hostile ghetto existence, her hands make our life easier and more comfortable. My mother's hands! Her dear, beloved "little paws!"

Alexander came to the shop today. He looks at me with concern and affection. I returned those beautiful poems by Rilke to him. I tried to translate "Die Einsamkeit," "Loneliness," but it is very difficult. At any rate, I tried to retain the rhythm and the mood.

I'm sorry that he's leaving. If he were to go to Rzeszów and take me with him to Staszka's . . . That would be too good to be true. Nice Alexander, serious Alexander . . . Oh, I'm just being stupid!

22 January 1942

Lusia is sick and I am in the shop by myself. I have to do her work and my own. I run the deliveries, the telephone, the files, and the cash register— wonder of wonders, everything tallies, which doesn't happen very often with Lusia. To tell the truth, we have fewer and fewer customers. Of necessity, people are very ingeniously fixing their own lamps and electric stoves.

Józek, the Netherländer, is engaged! This information was brought to me by a married friend of his who holds me responsible for the fiancée: she is ugly, simple, and poor. "You knew how much he loved you, why did you turn him down?" It's true. I did know. We used to discuss this personal matter as we took our summer evening walks in Krzemionki. We were quite honest with each other about the situation, and here this friend, who doesn't know anything about it, calls Józek's engagement "a leap of desperation into a void." I congratulated Józek over the phone, and on Sunday he appeared at the shop. Fortunately, the old man wasn't in.

"Halina! It's ages since we saw each other!" he said, looking radiant. Maybe it wasn't right to do so, but I had to, I *had* to ask, "Józek, tell me, are you happy?"

He thought about it for a minute. " 'Happy?' 'Important' is more like it. And, anyway, it's only you I love." He raised his thick bushy eyebrows in a comical way. I laughed. "It's too late! You're lost to the world, and if I tell your fiancée, you'll catch it!"

He bribed me with sweets. "No one could blame me. A beautiful and wise girl like you."

"Wise women are pleasant to talk to, but . . . ," I started to say, and bit my tongue. Instead I engaged him in conversation about the "ideological matters" which we had been discussing lately. He grew serious and affirmed that he was going to be leaving shortly.

"Does your chosen one have any connection with these things?"

"No. I don't want to expose her to danger."

"You're exposing her to danger in any event. When 'something' happens, the whole family, the whole house, the whole street goes. In any case, who is safe here? And what about me?"

"Leave it. It's not for children."

"Well, really. Don't fob me off with rubbish. I want to help, get involved, do something. Don't you trust me?"

But they are all tremendously conspiratorial. There's no use even dreaming about joining them, they pick you themselves. They're right. There are a lot of informers in the ghetto, particularly among the resettled German Jews like that rich one, Förster. What kind of creatures are they? Why do they do that? For money, and to save themselves at our expense. They have money, but they are surrounded by a wasteland. Everybody here avoids them, and the Germans probably despite people like that too.

"So, don't you trust me?"

"Of course I trust you. But you are completely unsuited for this work for a variety of reasons. We'll talk when I get back."

"Remember, I want to be of use as well, to have some work to do."

"You already do," he smiled at me from the door. "You already do, and how! You'll survive and immortalize us all!"

Cambridge, Mass.

How I would like to if I only could!

If only I could protect all of us from forgetfulness, individually, as we were, we living people! Our image has been falsified and distorted by the "profes-

sional Holocaustniks," the experts who were not there and who have grown rich on our martyrdom; by those who have institutionalized our suffering by turning it into their profession. Once again we are being turned into nameless, faceless, dehumanized theories and statistics.

I wish I could protect the memory of us all, young and old: not one of us thought of ourselves as hero or victim—and yet we were both.

I never met Józek again. I remember him as he stood in the Lux door, tall and still well dressed, smiling and waving good-bye. After the war I met his wife and liked her immediately. She was a decent, sensible woman, and it was good that for the short time left to him he had her as his companion.

22 January 1942 cont'd.

In the evening, as I was locking the cash register, the engineer arrived. He bought a light bulb because the old man was in the shop—he must have a collection of light bulbs at home by now—and said that he would wait for me in Wohlfeiler's café. I locked the register nervously, and, frozen after a whole day at the shop, walked into the café. He was sitting at the first table eating supper. Seeing that I was shivering with cold, he brought me coffee and cake. We were having a casual conversation amid the din of the smokey little café when a soldier wearing a helmet walked in to inspect the *Kennkarte*. Fear that this might be a roundup flew across the small room. When he walked out, voices were raised in even greater agitation. We stayed there a while longer, although the thick cloud of cigarette smoke was making me feel ill. It's a good thing that Alexander doesn't smoke. A crowd of my parents' acquaintances watched me in surprise walking out with him. Outside on the street Alexander grew more tender, and taking my hand, put it in the pocket of his coat to warm my numb and frozen fingers.

"*Na, wie geht es dir*, Halina? *Bist du noch traurig und allein und anders . . .* So how are you, Halina? Still sad and alone and different from all the other young girls? Why don't you find yourself *einen jungen Mann*, a young man?"

"Do you think that a young man is a cure for everything?" I responded, admitting deep down that everything else would take second place to a "beloved."

His room was warm and cozy. He lit a small side lamp and sat down comfortably in an armchair next to me. I was trying to get warm by the stove, unable to stop trembling with cold.

"How quiet it is in here—I can hear your teeth chattering!" He smiled.

Not the faintest sound reaches this modern room hidden from view. From the corridor the stairs seem to lead up to an attic, but they actually lead to a beautiful studio.

"The only peaceful place is this hermitage."

"I'm no hermit. I'm hardly ever home alone, I'd rather be with people. You're no loner, either. So Halina, you're still waiting for that one great, true love? For that great experience?"

"No. I'm just waiting for a man I could love," I said right out, knowing full well how banal that sounded even though it was quite honest.

"He doesn't exist in the ghetto? No one here appeals to you? Do you think people are different in other places?"

"Oh, yes. After all, conditions make people, influence their characters and their habits."

"The conditions here haven't lasted long enough to have influenced someone's character," he interrupted. "If the conditions have already brought about a change in someone, that means that they had absolutely no character to begin with. There are quite a few intelligent young people here. What turns you off about them?"

"It's actually not their fault that I'm repulsed by just about anything: stupid, arrogant behavior; dirty talk, especially when it's not even witty, because, if it is, at least it's tolerable; thick-skinned reactions—I don't know how to behave myself sometimes, but I don't cover up my shyness with vulgarities. I'm disgusted by dirty fingernails, sloppiness, slovenliness. A gentleman should be elegant and smell clean. When those boys walk around in muddy boots and torn shirts they start to behave like street urchins. I'm repelled by their behavior, especially when they are in a large group. They are rough, badly brought up, and tactless!"

"Ah! And what is your Prince Charming supposed to be like?"

I laughed. "He doesn't have to be a Prince Charming, just nice, intelligent, cheerful, and subtle," and in my heart I added: and someone I could love.

He gave me a searching look. "I thought you were going to say: My ideal is Alexander Weissberg!"

He really does possess all the virtues I had named, plus many more. Of course, I should have answered like that, if only I knew how to be a little flirtatious! I became a bit embarrassed, which clearly amused him, but after a while he directed the conversation to a different subject: What did I actually understand by intelligence? Was it not a slightly overused term? How did I like Rilke? Which of his poems had I copied out? Why those in particular, the reflective, sad ones?

I find it impossible to reproduce our very interesting conversation, scribbling here in bed by candlelight. I have to focus on personal things. At one point, Alexander grew thoughtful and said, "I don't like it when I sit here alone, but right now I feel good. It would be good, too, if some night I were sitting here at the desk, studying my physics, for example, and turning around I would see you in the corner smiling . . . But let's stop dreaming and eat some chocolate. No? People who don't like sweets have bad characters!"

"If you would like to, feel free to work!" For the first time I felt really comfortable there, and just watching him work wouldn't have bothered me.

"*Dummköpfchen.* Silly girl. Those were plans for the future. Right now you're a young lady who is paying me a visit and it wouldn't be proper."

"And the fact that I am here is proper?" I smiled.

"Why? What are you imagining now?"

I don't know myself, but I feel bad when I go to him and acquaintances might see me there and gossip. People have evil tongues, and it's easy to say "I don't care"—but I do care.

"*Baby, mein süsses Baby,*" he came up to me and hugged me lightly. Not quite knowing how to react, I pulled away and joked: "I'm no sweet 'Baby,' I'm too big."

"Your façade can mislead someone, but not for long. Do you remember the first time you came here with your bill? A tall girl, energetic and very official. But inside? A defenseless little creature. The first personal word reveals what a dreamer you are. And stubborn. It's impossible to get the lofty ideals out of your head. You cling to them despite all evidence to the contrary, despite common sense."

It was unbelievable, what he said. I had never thought about myself in this way before, and I wasn't sure how to swallow his criticism.

"Why the distressed expression? *Hör zu,* we were all raised on '*Edel sei der Mensch,*' honoring and respecting human worth, courage, ideal love, and ideals. The fundamental ethical principles are inviolate, but the romantic notions? They are only the fringes of existence, beautiful, but marginal. And meanwhile, you want life to conform to literature and to all those lofty notions it taught you, instead of assuming that literature ought to conform to life."

"How can you be so sure?"

"*Ganz einfach.* Quite simple. Because people are supposed to fall in love '*im wunderschönen Monat Mai, als alle Knospen sprangen,* in the beautiful month of May when all the buds are bursting,' you can't imagine romantic feelings without that background. Any place that lacks moonlight and lilacs isn't worthy of, is even an insult to, love. What a sacrilege! And yet, after all, we can pray anywhere, not only in church, right? Thank goodness you agree! If, however, *das Wesentliche,* the real thing, happened to you without the romantic decoration, you would be disillusioned, as if you had missed out on who knows what!"

"You're being unfair," I muttered. But even though I myself don't know what I want, and I don't think I have any desire for an "amour," I find myself grateful to him for every sign of interest and attention.

"You'll learn in time. In life in general one can't stick too rigidly to theoretical principles. Life forces one to compromise, even you and even now. Think of what you do in that shop. It's stultifying work, but you can't do anything about it, so you carry on. But still, I'm convinced that you will only compromise up to a certain point and not a jot further, no matter how much pain that causes you. And believe me, you will be hurt!"

"Why? How do you know?"

"I saw you from a distance during the last roundup for snow removal. My pass protects me against forced labor, but for all sorts of reasons I prefer to avoid any confrontation. It so happened I was walking along the street on my way to work during that roundup, and I hid in the nearest doorway. Deep in your heart you consider running away or hiding as undignified, as a kind of cowardice. I saw from that doorway how you walked along quite calmly with your head held high, looking straight in front of you. You were lucky that time, but next time they'll catch you, and when they do I'm sure you will march along carrying a spade and looking straight in front of you in the same way, head held high. And you will work like crazy!" He marched around the room mimicking me.

"Work like crazy for *them!*"

"For yourself, *mein gediegenes Mädchen,* for yourself alone, because you don't know how to do otherwise. Emanuel Kant would love your *Pflichtgefül.* At least you haven't read him yet. *Komm mein Kleines,* come my little one, it's late."

What an evening! I'm scribbling on a scrap of paper by candlelight, because my diary is hidden beneath the piano. I can't get to it over Mietek's and Uncle's beds, and they are both asleep. Our conversation was much longer, but all my comments aren't important. It's easier for me to digest what Alexander was actually thinking when I write it down. Dear God, am I really like that? Am I really preparing a bleak future for myself? Could I change my nature, even if it were possible to do so?

At our next meeting I was afraid to mention any of my beloved poets to Alexander in case he should tease me again about "my" literature, but he brought the conversation back to Rilke and later to the old German ballads. He recited one of them, his deep voice flowing smoothly to the rhythm of the heroic epic. I knew one of the ballads he recited, and I listened quietly.

"I like to listen to you so much. How do you know so many poems by heart?"

"I've no idea! Evidently, I'm brilliant, but then, so are you." He laughed and stroked my cheek. "Why aren't you moving away from me now? There must be some instinct which tells you the difference between a wild man's mad lust and a safe caress."

From now on, he intends to offer only fatherly affection, then? I panicked that it was all over, and frightened myself even more by asking, "Don't you feel close to me anymore? You still like me, don't you?"

Alexander smiled, flashing his white teeth which are strong and healthy despite all the sweets he eats. He kissed my cheek. "And what would happen if I were in love with you? What then?"

"When that happens, we'll figure it out," I joked.

"And what if it has already happened?"

I can never tell whether he's serious or not, not even when his expression is a mixture of affection and irony. He knows my answer. "I would be so happy," I replied, looking straight into his dark smiling eyes as he kissed me.

To be honest, I'd prefer to just talk.

"And you said that you were just a little episode, *Mädchen.*"

"That's right! A nice little diversion once in a while."

"Stop the irony. Besides, it's also your fault. I can't purchase electrical appliances all the time just to pursue you."

"And a lady can't pursue anyone. It's a miracle that we didn't miss each other altogether."

"One never knows," he said, taking me in his arms.

Good lord, why do I never know how to react? Why do I always freeze up?

Luckily, he was touched rather than irritated by how disconcerted I was. He helped me on with my coat, and when we were on the street said, "You have so little time to yourself. You're at Lux all day; the evenings are short because of the curfew. It's a shame we can't walk out of the ghetto and go into town. Would you do it?"

"Leave the ghetto altogether? All by myself?"

"With me. But never mind. Please come over to see me on Saturday afternoon, *meine grosse Unschuldige,* my tall innocent one. I don't want to expose you to evil and groundless gossip. I would be ashamed of myself if people actually knew how innocently we spend our time!" We both laughed. "See, a few small streets, a few steps, and you're home. There's nowhere to enjoy a walk on a beautiful evening."

The pale moon cast a glow on the white frozen streets. I walked at Alexander's side with the snow crackling beneath our feet, agitated and very happy.

23 January 1942

To go or not to go, I deliberated, knowing all the time that of course I would go. I had to go. On Saturday at five I knocked at his door. He opened it with a funny look of consternation on his face and with soot on his hands.

"Nothing is going right for me today! They kept me in the office late, the stove isn't lit, I haven't shaved, nothing is ready."

I took my coat off quickly and helped him to make the fire, and when he went to wash his hands I tidied the room. In a short while we were sitting in armchairs by the fire. Alexander took my hands in his and smiled, sensing that I had something to say.

"You begin. It's your turn today, after my last moralizings."

"Demoralizings," I corrected him, and we both laughed. "What else can you call your attempts to shake my principles?"

"*Ohne Übertreibung.* Don't exaggerate. No one has ever lost their moral principles by becoming less rigid. What's on your mind?"

"Compromise. Who is compromising whom? You mentioned that you didn't want to compromise me. Why?"

"*Kindchen,* I am old enough to be your father. The ghetto is too small and provincial for our acquaintance not to seem strange, or at the very least incomprehensible. There's nowhere to take a walk; in the café it's impossible to talk freely."

"So I am to compromise myself by coming to your apartment! Why don't you ever come to my house to see me?"

"Oh, if that's what's on your mind, I'll come over next Saturday. And now tell me about yourself. I'm tired, I'd rather listen to you than talk myself." He stretched out on the sofa and covered himself with a blanket. "Come here."

I stayed where I was.

"Don't be so stubborn and naive. I'm not going to hurt you."

I sat down stiffly next to him. He covered me with the blanket and stroked my hair which was freshly washed and soft and fluffy.

"You've got nice hair, *wie Seide,* like silk; you're very pretty you know." As always I didn't know what to do. He kissed me lightly on the cheek and closed his eyes. "You still don't know how to kiss. I'm so tired."

"Why don't you take a nap? I can read or write a letter." I got up, and he crawled out from under his covers, too.

"*Süsses Mädel.*" He handed me a block of cream writing paper from his desk, and suddenly he lifted me high in the air as a joke and carried me over to the sofa. I frowned. He stopped laughing and hugged me and kissed my cheek, and because I kept turning my head away he said, "Why are you so young, so pretty, and so silly? Women like you need to be raped! Don't worry, I won't, not you."

"Because you don't care about me!"

"Because I *do* care about you. If I didn't, I would have had you the first day we met. But I valued a friendship with such a *merkwürdiges kleines Fräulein,* such a remarkable young lady, more than a casual affair. Who would guess that you were such an unscaled fortress! If it were not for the war, I could gradually teach you all about love. But things aren't up to me, I don't have the right, I'm not free."

"Aha!"

"There's no 'Aha' about it! Women are the least of it. It's just the war. Sometime you'll learn the truth and you'll understand. Now, get under the blanket or get off the sofa!"

I slipped out of his arms, sat down comfortably in an armchair, put my feet on the other one, lit the small desk lamp, and started to write a letter to Staszka. Alexander read the *Krakauer Zeitung* newspaper, and after a while he fell asleep. He breathed evenly and peacefully, and then he started to snore a little, which bothered me, because I had never heard a man snore before. I dropped the hand with the pen onto my lap, suddenly feeling so sad that I wanted to put on my coat and leave. I recognized the ridiculousness of the situation as well as its charm, but at the same time I wanted to cry. To cap it all off, someone knocked at the door, but remembering Alexander's comments, I stayed motionless in the chair. Oh, if only I could go and meet Staszka on the corner and laugh about this little misadventure over pink Napoleons in a café near Wawel. How could I be a femme fatale under these circumstances? I can't. I can't and I don't know how. I shook with cold by the blazing stove.

Alexander woke up, reached for my hand, brought it up to his lips, and, placing it on his cheek said, *"Gute Nacht, Halinka,"* and went back to sleep. After a while he got up, rested, and sat down opposite me.

"You've been bored here for long enough. In order not to expose your virtuous principles to any more danger, and in order to introduce you to the great world, let's go to the café."

So that's how he had understood what I had said. Maybe he really did want to be with other people, or had decided that I was asking for "public recognition" of our relationship, instead of just wanting to meet him secretly at his place. I don't know. I don't know what I want myself, or why I suddenly felt so bad.

"I don't have the time. I have to go home."

"Always home. You wouldn't leave that home if your life depended on it, would you?"

"By myself? Live in freedom, knowing that my parents were here in this slavery? It's not easy to leave your family. You're lucky that you are alone."

"Perhaps I don't want such luck anymore? Will you go with me into that great world, Halinka?"

"Are you being serious?"

"I couldn't be more so," adding with an ironic smile, *"keine Angst.* Don't worry. I mean the café for now. And stop addressing me so formally. I'm Alex! Turn around for a minute, I need to dress."

He recited a long biblical poem as he changed his clothes. Straightening his tie and swearing at his large collar, he joked, "Don't assume for a minute that

I am a believer. And now look at the infidel with his new tie who is ready to eat you alive."

Cupping my face in his hands, he said in a low voice, "You're a strange girl. It's hard to believe that such naive innocence still exists! Have you really never been in love, nor longed for anyone? Have your lips never kissed anyone, nor spoken words of love? You never held your arms out in desire on long dark nights?" He really did speak like that, as in a film.

I didn't say anything. Had he been speaking in Polish I might have felt more comfortable, but even so, what could I have said? I don't know why I am like this myself. In despair, I exclaimed, "Don't you see? I'm a *femina frigida*!"

He laughed so hard that he cried.

"How else can I explain that I think longingly about you all the time, and then when I'm with you . . . Well, you see how I am."

"I can see that your mind is more mature than your body. Your senses are asleep, and your undeveloped womanliness rebels against temptations it's not ready for. It's as though you were frozen in an impenetrable cage."

"I've already told you that I'm frigid."

"You've constructed a glass wall around yourself which both protects you and keeps you from other people. It will melt under the influence of patient love. But what decent man would take on such a responsibility under the present conditions? A brute may come and shatter your glass house and send you forever into conflict with yourself. And then you would build even more impenetrable glass walls."

My God, what a fate! I couldn't believe my ears, but at the same time I believed his every word.

"What a shame that your formative years have to be spent during a war. If you were ten or twelve, or at least twenty years old, your male-female problems would be less complicated in the future."

"Will there be a future? I think that for all of us here . . ."

"Of course there will. Some are going to survive, and you will for sure, and you'll live for many, many years."

"Happily and with a fairy-tale prince?"

"Oh, you'll always create problems for yourself with unsuitable people. There aren't too many Alex's, and fairy-tale princes can treat you badly, too. Malicious people will immediately see that you're an easy target, incapable of fighting back. They'll elevate themselves at your expense and put you down. But no matter what mud they sling at you, you'll pick yourself up with *reines Gewissen*, a clean conscience. Your little ray of optimism and honesty will steer you in the right direction."

These weren't jokes any more. Alexander talked and talked until I interrupted him.

"Why would anyone other than the Germans try to persecute me? Aren't there decent people around?"

"Of course there are, and they will always value and love you."

"Some prophecy! And what about love now?"

"Knowing the steely resistance of your sacred innocence as I do, I would have to kill you first and then take advantage of you!"

"Perhaps we should change the order? Wouldn't you be afraid of the scandal when they found my violated corpse?"

"No. At worst they'd lock me up." His eyes twinkled happily. "Although aren't we locked up and sentenced to death as it is? Let's speed it up to our own advantage." He looked at me with half-joking, half-serious eyes. Completely confused, I buried my face in his shoulder.

"*Kleines Mädchen*, in your thoughts you are already mine, although you haven't the slightest idea what that means, either in the good sense or in the bad. In body and in spirit you are an unspoiled *virgo intacta*."

"We're back to *The Picture of Dorian Gray* again!"

"You'd better believe it. And you will stay this way even if you have ten children. You have something of *Noli me tangere* in you."

"When he spoke these words, Christ was no longer in the land of the living," I muttered glumly.

"Don't worry. You will be. I have no idea how, but you're going to survive." He stood up and with a theatrical gesture stretched out his arms and recited in a deep voice, "I see a radiance around you and the hand of the Lord above your head."

Walking by his side down the street, I still pondered over our conversation.

"Let me see you smile, *Mädchen*, young people should live and not philosophize about life and death."

"Maryśka and Staszka and I did just that when we used to debate whether suicide was cowardice or heroism."

"Whatever else it is, it's stupid," was Alexander's short opinion, and we laughed. "Even a hard life is interesting, and the world so beautiful. A corpse is a corpse, that's all. However long man lives, he has hope and faith in the unknown future. Curiosity about what tomorrow will bring is the motor driving our lives."

"Maryśka used to say the same thing!"

"At least you had one sensible friend. Come and have a cake."

"I've got to go home."

"If you insist. I'll go visit some friends, but we'll drop by the café regardless."

Although I'm crazy about sweet things these days, I felt sad and couldn't swallow a thing. I felt particularly sad at heart when I shook hands with him.

"Galiczka, Halinka. Things will be better tomorrow." He touched my cheek.

We parted at the corner of my street, and he promised to drop by the shop tomorrow. I went home choking back tears.

The whole clan of aunts and acquaintances was at our house. The large old mirror in its golden frame reflected the people dearest to me sitting around the table. My cheeks were glowing from the cold and from kisses, and the trace of a smile was frozen on my face. It's usual for me to cover unhappiness by being lively and making jokes.

"Halina is in a terrific mood," said Pani Bella. "Oh, you happy golden girl! There's nothing like youth."

Thank God she didn't look at me more closely or she would have noticed traces of tears.

I think he has a wife. Somewhere far away, probably in Russia.

And now it's Friday again, and he's only been in the shop once, and we didn't make any arrangement to meet. I noted down Alexander's observations, partly in my diary and more fully on pieces of paper in the shop (because I then hide them sheet by sheet in the piano music). I mentioned some of our conversation to my parents, who looked at each other knowingly: "Freud."

"Who?"

"Freud. Your Viennese physicist knows psychology. It's a pity that our books aren't with us in the ghetto, because you could have read Freud for yourself. Is all this talking what you do when you go out with him?"

"What on earth do you think we do?" I snapped back.

"I think that you're safer with that *Damenfreund* than you are with any thoughtless young boy," Mama said.

7 February 1942

One day is much like another. One day passes by in a flash, though actually it drags on for hours. As a matter of fact, I have no time for anything lately. At eight o'clock I get up and get myself together quickly to go to the shop. We can't all get up at the same time because there isn't the space. So we gradually fold up first one bed, and then another. Uncle and Mietek get up first and leave at six; then my parents, and then I get out of my corner and go into another to wash behind the screen. The windows are open, the sheets are being aired. My father breaks up the bigger pieces of coal and carries out the buckets of dirty water, while I bring smaller basins of clean water from the tap in the hallway. One of us runs downstairs to line up for bread or maybe even margarine. Sometimes we can get watery milk from neighbors who deal with Aryan smugglers and get provisions through a hole in the ghetto wall in exchange for money, jewelry, or clothing. After that I rush over to the shop, always down the same street, not looking around and not seeing anything. I walk quickly and without thinking. From nine o'clock on, the morning seems to drag in the office. Freezing to death and walking back and forth, I wait for noon when the boss arrives. He's a true lunatic. He swears and rages at the whole world, including his employees. Finally, at one o'clock we close up.

I take the same road home. Shove lunch down quickly—potatoes, turnips, carrots sometimes, and so on ad infinitum. Occasionally I help make a brush, although this "cottage industry" of ours produces more wire-cut fingers than money. And again I rush to the shop.

The afternoon passes by faster somehow. When the stove is lit I sit close to it, and thoughts flow lazily through my mind. Sometimes I sing. I hum well-known folksongs, tangos and foxtrots, or Grandma's old-fashioned Viennese repertoire. Songs are sentimental ("I miss you," "I remember"), heart rending ("Don't ever forget me"), or forceful ("I love you"). I sing myself songs about "only your lips" and "dearest eyes"; about the sun; the blue of the sky; May; lilacs and roses; distant lands; steamy nights; about rainbows of happiness. I sing about all those things that exist for me only in the realm of wishes and desires. I sing about happiness, which is as far away from me as spring is to the present. Except that spring will definitely arrive one of these days, but happiness . . . ?

I sing about all this because I am so gray, ugly, heavy hearted, so ignored and alone; because life flows past me, as if I were forever separated from it by the glass door of Lux, out of which I can see people but never mix with them.

It's strange. Alexander once said there was a glass wall around me, but he meant it in a different way. He meant that I was like one of those hollow Russian dolls filled with ever-smaller ones because there were so many little cages in me and I was hiding in the smallest one. Frightened, but honest, while on the outside I seem so courageous. Not anymore! I feel so helpless.

I can't stand this existence. This gray, monotonous existence weighs me down so much that I am afraid of doing something crazy and stupid out of an uncontrollable urge for change. What's happening to me? Will I be worth anything after the war, or will I have completely gone to pot? Can any change whatsoever be enough to shake me out of this torpor? I've become dulled, like a machine that has worn down from daily use, no longer capable of thinking clearly. I feel like a bored and disappointed, but inexperienced, thirty-eight-year-old woman who is unconsciously still waiting for something, for something that will arouse her and shake her out of her lethargy.

After the shop closes in the evening, I rush back home. Someone always comes over to visit my parents, or else Mietek Garde, Bronek, and some girls I know come to see me. Whether guests are there or not, I make brooms until ten o'clock at night, then wash, and after that there is peace. I can't read in bed very much after eleven, because someone is always trying to fall asleep and the light bothers them. With the darkness comes good, quiet night.

Lately my evenings have been ruined by Felek, who brings bad temper and arguments into the house. He's changed completely since he's been seeing that brat, Genia. Stupid as she is, she certainly knows how to hook Felek and push him into marriage. Her parents came here once to "talk things over." Our parents aren't too keen. They cautioned them that Felek wasn't mature enough yet to commit himself for life; that it won't be until after the war that he'll start studying medicine and music; that the differences between them in background, upbringing, and interests will only increase with time. Even in the ghetto, young people study and read, but it doesn't even occur to Genia to do so. Felek started to teach her to play the piano, but nothing came of it. Her parents are decent, ordinary people. They had a mattress shop in Kazimierz, the Jewish section of Kraków. You could order a mattress from them, talk about horsehair or oakum, and that was the extent of their conversation. A girl I know once laughed at Felek for going out with a girl who had to repeat a year in school and then was taken out to help her mother at home. Because of Felek, I tried to come to Genia's defense by saying that even though I was a very good student in gimnazium, I wasn't sure I'd be able to learn accounting. Truth to tell, though, I don't know what Felek sees in her. She's quite pretty, has a small face, an ocelot fur coat, and thin, spindly legs. She's no match for beautiful, lively Fela, my brother's first love! The two of them used to radiate happiness. There's something weird about his relationship with Genia. People who are in love smile at the whole world, but she is always in a sulk and full of complaints and anger, like an old crow. I only once heard her giggling with that Cesia K., the shaggy-haired blond daughter of a barber in the ghetto. And Felek, who is so friendly and cheery by nature, comes home in a filthy mood. He's learned to swear lately, and he tries it out on me. After a sharp argument which irritated me enough to make my blood boil, I cut in with, "Is that the way you speak to your dumb brat?"

He berated me with a tirade of vulgar curses and foul names and tried to slap me in the face. In total fury, I leapt at him, punching him in the teeth with my fists. I really don't know what came over me just then, my own teeth were chattering so much that I cut myself on the lip. I couldn't breathe, my ears were ringing, and Felek couldn't extricate himself from my iron grip.

"Stop it this minute!" screamed Papa, pulling us apart. Breathing heavily, we looked at each other in stupefaction and horror. What a disgrace! "My children are raising their hands against each other over some stupid girl? My own children behaving like drunks in some gutter? I never thought I'd live to see anything like this!" And Father threw himself down on the bed in tears.

I had never seen my parents in such a state, except after Grandma died when we were on vacation. On that occasion I had been taken out of the room immediately. My father's despair broke my heart. Mama ran up with a glass of water. "Stop being dramatic, calm down." She was the only one who was under control. She always defends Felek.

Papa didn't listen to her. He sat on the bed and said in a weak, trembling voice, "Shake hands with each other, this second, and apologize. This is never to happen again. You are of the same flesh and blood. Felek, this is your younger, your only sister, closer to you than the whole of your future family. One can have many women, even many wives, but you have only one sister. Remember that you are a man, and you are always to look after her and to protect her after I am gone. As for you, don't go for your brother like a tiger! Apologize to each other at once!"

We shook hands. But our mutual, teasing affection for each other has vanished, at least for now. The fond understanding I thought we had preserved even during the times when he wasn't at home turns out to have been an illusion. Felek has always been easily influenced for good and for bad. Let the ocelot coat have him! I know that I am alone in the family, I have only my mother and my father—it's not worth writing about.

Oh dear, I know, too, that it's Saturday; that I'm waiting for Alexander; that I'm alone in the house; that I've prepared tea and cakes; and that it's already five and he's not here!

10 February 1942

I waited for him until six. In the end I ate all the cakes and went out, even though I should have stayed in the whole evening because we had arranged to meet at my house. I grew more irritated with every passing minute; the waiting ruined my pleasure at the prospect of seeing him. My parents went to Aunt Dora's for one of her Saturday teas, and here I sit, bored. Penelope might have waited and waited, but Odysseus wouldn't have inspired the same patience in me!

I went over to the Goldstein's, where on Saturdays their apartment changes into an asylum for a whole mass of acquaintances ranging in age from five to eighty. I smoked a cigarette Ben Goldstein gave me, but I didn't inhale because it makes me dizzy. I watched the little ones, and then I went for a walk with Dziunia and Artur. It was nice out on the street. We stepped through freshly fallen snow and laughed in a carefree way—I no longer cared about the engineer. With me it's always one extreme or the other: either striplings who are too young for me, or a gentleman who is too mature in every respect.

I came home feeling great, but not knowing how to answer my mother's questioning look or how to tell her that I had eaten all the food prepared for the guest. Then I noticed a slip of paper under the door: "I came too late. I wanted to tell you and came to look for you, but the shop was closed."

I fell silent. That man has the curious ability to confuse me. I was dumbfounded, saddened. What was I to do? But I was a little bit glad that my unpunctual gentleman had found the door closed and not a living soul in the house.

On the following morning I sent him a card inviting him for the afternoon. He came to the shop right away, but because of the boss I couldn't talk to him freely. I whispered to him that the boss would be going out any minute and that he should make a telephone call. "I'll come by later," he waved to me and went out. My boss was at me instantly. "What did he want? To telephone?" I was scared of him and said yes. "And you didn't allow him to? You didn't let that Weissberg make a call? Where's your common sense?" With that he rushed out to the street, shouting, "Engineer! Engineer Weissberg!"

Alex came back having no idea what was going on, but took the receiver with a proud expression on his face and dialed a number. The old man left, and Lusia, Alex, and I burst out laughing.

"Can I go now, too? I'll come at seven," he said as he left.

In the afternoon, of course, I developed a terrible toothache and was home by six. Because in my rage yesterday I had eaten all the cakes, Mama made me canapés and black coffee. I put on my blue dress with the lace collar and brushed my hair. Perhaps that large old mirror flatters, but I thought when I looked at myself in it that I looked nice; or maybe that's always the case when a young girl is waiting for a, let us say, loving man.

"*Guten Abend!* Are you alone? You're so heavenly blue, innocent and pretty," he said, kissing me on the cheek. "Where did you disappear to yesterday?"

"Something always has to happen to spoil our meetings. It's not appropriate for a lady to have to wait and wait forever. A gentleman is always punctual."

"A king. Only a king. But no king ever lived in Kraków in 1942. My being late does not mean disrespect." He caressed my hand tenderly and embraced me, but when I slipped out of his arms he drew a deep, dramatic breath, sat down on the sofa, lit the small lamp, and putting his finger through my hair, said, "Why do you always move away from me? There can be only a few reasons. Is it moral scruples about being sinful?"

"Not at all. I haven't had a religious upbringing either."

"Ah, so it's scruples about propriety. 'A young lady from a good family is not supposed to behave like that'; or perhaps you're simply too young."

I rested my face on my hands and agreed.

"It could also be a form of false pride, or else a fear of men?"

"Maybe," I murmured without conviction. Moral scruples? Physical ones? To tell the truth, I felt no need of a man's embrace. Why can he not understand that his presence gives me pleasure in and of itself, without physical contact!

I got up from the sofa and pulled my dress down, a bit embarrassed that he was looking me over from head to toe.

"You're very graceful," he said in surprise, "but you're only a baby, a little baby, and I'm forty years old." He looked around. "Your little room is very pleasant, you've even got a beautiful asparagus fern in the window. What books do you have?" He reached up to the small shelf where there are only a few of our books, the rest of them are with my nanny. "Polish poems? No, a translation of François Villon," and he began to recite "Le Grand Testament" in French.

"This literature, somehow, doesn't affect you. What else have you got?" and he burst out laughing, "Laclos! But our liaison isn't dangerous, is it?" he winked knowingly. He looked through Stefan Zweig's *Amok* and grew serious. Despite our best intentions, our conversation did not flow well and the atmosphere was tense. It improved only when we sat down to the table. Suddenly my father showed up covered with blood and mud. He had fallen down on the way to my aunt's and looked so bad that he should have gone to bed immediately. Now the conversation fell apart completely, becoming sad and uneasy. We went out for a walk. I was afraid to go to the café because the boss might be there, and so we went into the pastry shop. Alexander mentioned that he might be traveling somewhere soon. I gathered all my courage and allowed that when I don't see him for a long time, I miss him.

"*Na, bitte*, so why don't you fall in love with me? These days nothing is left except love."

"Why not? Because it would be senseless. It would be pointless, like everything else I do."

"Those long legs of yours would lead you to any goal, if you only knew how to use them," he chimed in with a wink, while I shook my head. He laughed, amused by the disgusted expression I had put on for show.

"Who's thinking improper thoughts now? I was simply referring to using your legs to walk toward your goal."

Right! Who'd believe that? But I stuck to my argument. "Is it so weird that I don't want to open myself up to unnecessary worries, fears, and betrayals? Such a love couldn't bring anything else."

"Why? Man hopes, dreams, and knows he's alive. While you . . ."

"While I," I resorted to joking, "if I told you I loved you, I would hear right away that I was just a little 'baby'!"

"How do you know?" he said, growing serious. "You can never know. However, you really are too young to appreciate that the anticipation and the pursuit are sometimes more important than the attainment of the goal."

"And those terrible pangs of yearning when one has to wait too long?" I asked. He grinned broadly:

"There's no real need, *Kindchen*, for lengthy yearnings. So long. When you have a yearning for me again, let me know. Good-bye."

He had barely left when I started to miss him. What is this? I don't love him—I really don't love him. I don't know him; I don't know what kind of a person he is. I feel good when I am with him and bad when I'm not. But I'm not going to get in touch with him. Let him miss me and get in touch with me. He's right, in a way, about my "false pride."

On the way home I discovered that my poor father had not fallen at all. A drunken soldier had been roaming through the ghetto and had beaten him mercilessly.

14 February 1942

I came across some letters from Janek Miller. When he had been in Skała and I had been in Kraków we had had closer contact with each other than we do now that we are both rotting in the ghetto. I bumped into him once as I was leaving the shop. He was waiting outside, short, slight, ugly, and unkempt. He looked like a dwarf beside me. He raised his beautiful dark eyes up at me and said with a sad smile, "I feel as though I'm walking with the tower of Our Lady Church." Poor little Janek.

There has been no heat in the shop for over a week. Given that our hideous shop is always freezing anyway, the cold is positively arctic now. Our good boss brought us a tiny electric stove which isn't big enough even to warm our hands, and he curses us heartless scoundrels because we keep it on all day. The dreadful cold, the hopelessness of my job, and the lack of any prospect of change have a depressing effect on me. When by early morning my legs are freezing, when I turn blue and swell from the cold, I think with hatred about my boss, that mad offensive vulgarian. For all my sharp tongue, I don't know how to respond to his idiotic, insolent yapping! On Friday, after having had a row with the old man, I went to the public baths without asking for permission.

I arranged to meet Ena at the café on Saturday. She's the twenty-something-year-old pleasant and clever aunt of my little Rita. As we waited for our turn to bathe we sang tangos and some of the popular ghetto songs, and we decided to go to the café to hear their composer sing them.

We also decided to invite the engineer along to act as our male escort. I scribbled a few words quickly on a piece of paper which I planned to leave on his door if he wasn't home. I wavered a bit on the dark stairs when I heard sounds coming from the room, but at that moment his door opened and Alex came out. I blushed, crumpled up the note, and told him why I had come. He stroked my cheek, "Of course, I'll come! Naturally!" He kissed my hand and I left.

The next day I picked up from the seamstress my blouse and suit—the one that had a sealskin collar until furs were requisitioned—and I got ready to go out. A hitch! Ena got caught for forced labor. I don't have anyone to go with. I'd feel foolish going by myself. My parents would have to give up their concert at the orphanage, and Papa didn't want to. I wrote a note saying that I couldn't go and that he was not to be mad at me, and I went and left it on his door. Then I came back home. Meanwhile, Papa had changed his mind: "We'll go to the café." Too late, I'd already canceled the meeting.

Mama couldn't understand what had come over me and said I was behaving stupidly. But I had had enough of everything and everybody, most of all of myself. I changed out of my clothes in a fury and put on my Cinderella rags again and sat down at the piano, which had been returned to us yesterday. To drive everyone out of the house, I started to playing a loud foxtrot and then remembered that our old next-door neighbor who had a bad heart was dying. I no longer remember what, but I went on playing and playing. Tears came into my eyes. I wasn't even sad anymore, I wasn't at all choked up, not a muscle moved in my face, and yet tears flowed down my cheeks. Mama and Papa left me alone with my best friend. I played until late, luxuriating in the peace and quiet of the empty room.

It turned out that the engineer had gone to the concert instead with a good friend, the beautiful young clerk from the council whose husband is not in the ghetto, and who is supposedly on very close terms with Alexander. He spent money left and right and apparently had a wonderful time. I wasn't surprised, even though it hurt—now, that's a bad sign! Why should he sit at home alone? *Liebe war es nicht, es war ein Scherz,* It wasn't love it was only a joke. After all, I'm not yet eighteen and I'm nothing, just his *verträumtes kleines Mädchen,* someone with whom it's pleasant to spend an evening now and then because there is a certain charm to "the freshness of youth" and I am an occasional plaything. As for me, I suffer.

Cambridge, Mass.

Alexander never appears in my diary again. I strictly forbade myself to think about him anymore, and I never referred to him again.

Until now—and now I am ready to fall in love with him as I was unable to do then in the Kraków Ghetto, when he represented for me the pinnacle of my dreams.

I was impressed that "an engineer like that" would devote his time to me, but I was not able to overcome my shyness in the face of such a grown-up situation. I was convinced that "nice" young girls did not pay calls on gentlemen or accept meals from them in cafés and restaurants, and so I regarded such overtures on his part as disrespectful and placed obstacles in his way. A proud Cinderella in her mother's high heels—a completely impossible creature!

Aside from my parents, Alexander was my authority figure, the most important person in my life at that time. I quoted him verbatim, even down to his German expressions. I adored him, but I kept myself in check, fearing that I would not be able to control my emotions and that he would ridicule them—and that would have been completely unbearable. Feeling, as I did, absolutely inferior to him, I could not imagine that Alexander could have entertained any deep feelings for me.

And yet that mature man must have felt genuine interest, otherwise our amusing meetings would have been deadly dull for him and he wouldn't have been able to summon the angelic patience and delicacy he did in his dealings with a naive and inexperienced, albeit thoughtful, girl.

How prophetic his words were! It is as though he foresaw the difficult, if not tragic, turns my life would take and the mean people waiting to take advantage of my trust and to do me harm.

If after that time I ever met Alexander again in the ghetto, it was only in passing on the street and with a wordless nod of the head. Nothing else. No "good morning" or "good-bye." The engineer disappeared soon afterwards, and it was only after the war that it emerged that he had been closely connected with the Polish Underground movement. A distinguished Polish lady rescued him from danger and hid him. Later he lived with her in Paris.

Had I only known then what I found out in 1990!

My book, Images of the Lost World, *was about to be published by Oxford and I went to England to check on the illustrations with the editor. Through a friend with whom I stayed in London, I met another Polish woman, Stefania M., who had read my diary in Polish and phoned me to say, "If you'd like to see a photo of Alex Weissberg, come and see me."*

I went and was soon looking at a photograph of Alexander taken in Velden in 1952. He had not changed in the ten years since I had last seen him, except that his hairline was receding slightly from his high forehead. There he was, sitting on a bench, holding a lion cub on a leash by his side. The same familiar twinkle in his eyes; the same broad smile revealing his healthy teeth!

"Alex was my friend's husband," Stefania said. "She met him in the Underground movement and fell madly in love with him. She helped save his life by hiding him. Have you any idea who he really was? Look at

these books." She pointed to five books published in 1951 by Alexander Weissberg-Cybulski. Each was in a different language: Conspiracy of Silence (London); The Accused (New York); L'Accuse (Paris); Hexensabat (Frankfurt-am-Main); and Wielka Czystka (Paris).

I had heard of these books but had not associated them with Alexander. I had read none of them, because I remained in Poland until 1960 and such literature, of course, did not reach a country under Soviet domination.

Later on, during the radical sixties and seventies in the USA ("better red than dead"), the truth about the Soviet Union and the stories of the Great Purges fell on deaf ears. At that time, after all, the United States represented ugly imperialism, and the USSR was regarded as the benevolent protector of the oppressed. Arthur Koestler's Darkness at Noon, although based on fact, was a novel, and as such could be dismissed. Alexander's book, written while Stalin was still alive, was the very first eye-witness report to disclose publicly the "Big Lie" and to denounce Stalinism. So-called revisionist literature like his was read only by experts, and otherwise it collected dust in libraries for another twenty-five years until the time of dissent.

I read all 518 pages of The Accused night and day, learning more from it about the enormous crimes, cruelty, and political perversity of Stalinism than I had from the writings of that celebrated icon of American colleges, Solzhenitsyn.

Now that this monstrous empire has fallen apart, devastated and demoralized by seventy years of terror and corruption, one wonders how it was possible that a world that had known these things since 1951 could have maintained any illusions about the "paradise" that was communism?

In his preface to The Accused, Arthur Koestler introduced Alexander. His family had moved to Vienna from Kraków before the First World War. He had studied mathematical physics and engineering there before becoming an assistant lecturer at the Berlin Polytechnic, where he was considered one of the most talented young scientists. At seventeen, he became active in the socialist youth movement and then joined the Communist Party. In 1931 Alexander was approached by the Ukrainian Physical Technical Institute in Kharkov and moved to the USSR. This institute had the largest and best-equipped experimental laboratories in Europe. Most of the scientists working there were foreigners. With some of his colleagues, Alexander founded and edited the Soviet Journal of Physics, and in 1933 he was put in charge of the construction of a large experimental plant of which he was to become the director.

He and his wife separated in 1934, but he rushed to her aid when she was arrested two years later. He was imprisoned himself in 1937, charged with "having recruited a gang of Nazi terrorists to assassinate Stalin and Voro-

shilov during a hunting trip in the Caucasus and, in the event of war, to blow up the main industrial plants of the Ukrainian capital." All of his colleagues soon followed him to prison.

In May 1938 Albert Einstein, who had invited Alexander to Pasadena, wrote to Stalin on his behalf. Three Nobel Prize winners, Irène Joliot-Curie, Jean Perrin, and Frédéric Joliot-Curie, also wrote to State Prosecutor Vishinsky on his behalf and on that of his fellow scientists. Their imprisonment, they said, "has shocked scientific circles in Europe and America. . . . Professor Einstein in Pasadena, Professor Nils Bohr in Copenhagen . . . [and others] are interested in their fate and will not abandon this interest. . . . They are sincerely convinced that the accusations made against Weissberg are absurd and must be based on a serious mistake which must be corrected at once for both political and personal reasons."

In the wake of the notorious pact with Ribbentrop, made on 23 August 1939, almost on the eve of the Second World War, the Soviets handed over all the German nationals they were holding in prison, including Communists and Jews.

"On January 5, 1940, on the other side of the bridge over the river Bug, the representatives of another totalitarian system awaited us—the Gestapo," wrote Alexander in The Accused. *"For three months I was held by the Gestapo in various prisons in Biala Podlaska, Warsaw, and Lublin, and then I was released in the Cracow ghetto. When the extermination of the Jews began in the spring of 1942, I went underground. In March 1943, the Gestapo caught me and put me into the concentration camp in Kawencin. With the help of friends in the Polish Underground movement, I succeeded in escaping, and I remained in hiding in Warsaw, where I took part in two insurrections against the Germans. . . . On January 17, 1945, Russian troops occupied the suburb of Warsaw where I was hiding and I could again walk the streets. Eighteen months later I left Poland and arrived in the Swedish port of Malmö, setting foot on free soil for the first time in a decade."*

From the first page of his book, which I read in German, I recognized Alexander's style, his lucid and trenchant way of reasoning. There he was, very much in control despite the illogical horror which was sometimes, in its absurdity, amusing. There he was, witty, still good natured, and compassionate. Our conversations in the ghetto acquired much deeper significance for me after I had read his book.

Of course, I searched for traces of things I knew about, and found them right in Koestler's preface:

"Alex made the impression of a prosperous and jovial businessman . . . with a great gusto for telling funny stories and a curious liking for sweets— there were little trays with chocolates around, which he kept gobbling

absent-mindedly by handfuls. . . . I don't know a single person who, after three years in the hands of the KGB and five years hunted by the Gestapo, has emerged physically and mentally so unscathed and pleased with this best of all possible worlds as Alexander Weissberg. . . . He still looks like a prosperous businessman, with a fondness for Viennese coffeehouse stories, munching pralines or his favorite Turkish Delight."

Most moving of all to me was Alexander's recollection of the endless time he spent in solitary confinement in his tiny cell: "For two hours I tramped around in my cell counting the steps. . . . Soon I began to sing, noting how many rounds it took to complete the song. . . . The singing helped to soothe my nerves. For the two hours after that I recited poetry. I have a good memory, and I knew many poems by heart. I recited almost the whole of Rilke, the Buch der Bilder, *the* Stundenbuch *and the* New Poems. . . . *I have a selective memory, and anything that seemed to lack rhythm and beauty I have forgotten, which meant that I often had to supplement poetry with inventions of my own. Stefan Georg, Christian Morgenstern, and others also served their turn. I took delight in the pictures their verses conjured up and in the beauty of the words themselves. The two poetry hours were the best of the day.*

"Another two hours were occupied with mental mathematical and physical calculations. I began to think about numerical problems for which previously I had had neither time nor inclination. . . . And the rest of the day I devoted to the architectural plans, housing problems, which had become a hobby of mine."

And, finally, the young Komsomolka, Sima: "She had brown-blond hair, . . . sparkling blue eyes, magnificent white teeth, and a wonderful complexion. Even more captivating, however, was the grace with which she moved: a little shyly, almost childlike, and completely captivating. She was in the first splendid flush of her youth. The expression on her face was childlike. . . . She was not in the least forward or flirtatious and she was even a little reserved toward men. . . . We grew more and more friendly. . . . I was happy in her presence, but no physical intimacy bound us. I was many years her senior, by no means an impossible gap, but I hesitated to establish a relationship that would, in all probability, be brief, and would, I was certain, be deep and unsettling for her. . . . Her loveliness and her youthful vitality were a constant joy to me, but we never became really close. . . . We went for a walk. It began to snow. . . . Her hair was soon covered with snowflakes. She looked radiant. . . . We looked out from the top of the hill over the whole town which was spread before us. . . . I hugged her and kissed her pink cheeks. . . . The next day, she didn't come as she had promised, and I never saw her again."

This is the only romantic episode in his book. It is almost a carbon copy of our first meeting. I was not his first "childlike" girlfriend. Perhaps he was thinking of Sima when, also at Christmastime, we went for a walk on Krzemionki hill and looked out at the city of Kraków. Or perhaps he was recalling our evening when, after the war, he wrote about that walk with Sima in Kharkov. No one can ever know. Alexander is dead and so is his wife and even her friend who gave me his photograph.

18 February 1942

I went to snow work on Monday. Because no one woke me up, I got up at the last minute and hurried into my clothes, swallowed a little tea, and rushed over to the *Arbeitsamt* with a piece of dry bread in my pocket. I met Dola W. there and we both turned in our *Kennkarte* and then clambered into the large covered truck. We drove toward the airport as though into the unknown. Three-quarters of an hour later we were there. What a sight! What a long forgotten sight! Spreading fields, lots of open space, and spruces sprinkled with snow. As I marched across the field toward the pilots' barracks, I drank in the clear, dry air with pleasure. It looked like a whole town of barracks, larger than the ghetto, and clean. Pilots were milling around everywhere looking at us with curiosity and friendliness. We die of fright at the sight of uniforms, but here the young pilots seem to look at us in a friendly way without noticing our armbands. Some of them asked what they were, but I didn't answer because I thought they were kidding. It's impossible that they didn't know. The officers wondered what to do with us. Some of us went to clean one barracks, others to another. A tall airman came with us. He was nice because he lit the stoves himself while we were supposed to sweep up, which we did, singing. There weren't enough brooms for all of us, including me, so he left us by the stove to have a rest. One of the girls swept a hundred złoty out from under the wardrobe and gave them to him, but he didn't even know what kind of money it was. After work, we all sat by the stove. The soldiers had just returned from France, and they showed us photos and told us about their families. I felt a bit like our maid, Janka, who used to go to the army barracks to meet boys.

At noon—lunch! We marched across the field again to a canteen on the first floor of an enormous hangar. We were given a soup consisting of kasha, macaroni, and a tiny bit of meat. I went downstairs with Dola intending to buy tea, but the airman in charge, an older *Unteroffizier* named Klemens, invited us into his office for coffee and to listen to the radio. Poles work in the office, the two in blue overalls, Polonczuk and Bial, who is an ordinary vulgarian with a Hitler mustache. They are our *Vorarbeiter*, foremen.

Klemens is older and very polite. When he discovered that we didn't have a permanent placement and that the *Arbeitsamt* sends us out to different places each day, he wrote down our names and indicated that we were "necessary" to him because he needs a group of regular workers who know German. After an hour, we were summoned by telephone back to the barracks for conversation by the stove. Is this why we need German, to listen to stories about "*meine Heimat,*" my homeland? But it was all so different, so much more interesting than the dreary ghetto, that I stopped being outraged by the interaction between our girls and the soldiers. Horse-drawn sleighs finally arrived at the barracks, and we had to load them with straw mattresses. Dola and I climbed up to the top and drove to the other end of the "town" of barracks. Standing on top of the mattresses, I stretched out my arms, took a deep breath of the clean air, and unexpectedly burst into loud, happy laughter. It was almost embarrassing!

"*Schau, das ist die Jugend!* That's youth for you," the younger airmen standing around whispered to each other, while I thought how little it takes to make young people happy! We are so kicked around and beaten down that a little fresh air and sunshine, a friendly smile, a kind word, and a friendly look give us pleasure. For that moment I felt almost as carefree as I felt before the war.

"Unload the straw mattresses!" "Our" airman from the morning helped us, together with some of his friends. He smacked me on the arm as a joke, and I threw snow up his nose. "Bravo," shouted the airmen, and a snowball fight started. One of them, Hans, a very young, dark-haired man with big blue eyes and an intelligent face, made a strategic retreat and drew us with him into the barracks. "Disgraceful flight," shouted the man we knew, while I yelled back, "*Nec Hercules contra plures!* Even Hercules cannot help against so many!" since there were only three of us. The dark-haired airman slammed the door, and, winking at me, shouted, "*Hannibal ante portas,* Hannibal at the gates!" Sonia didn't understand. "What are you talking about," she asked? "Speak Latin," he replied.

We had to move furniture into two rooms. The beds were so heavy that he called some more soldiers to help. "This isn't work for girls," he said, and we were left to sweep the floors while they erected bunks. A beautiful black dog came up, straight to me, of course, but how could I play with a dog when I was supposed to be sweeping? I suddenly felt very tired. Whistling Brahms, dark-haired Hans approached me.

"What a long face! Are you tired? Don't you know how to sweep? You do it like this," he said, taking my broom. "I'll feel better in a minute," I said, but he didn't give the broom back to me and cleaned the area himself. "You've had enough for today. Have a rest!" I stood by a side window. The snow was violet in the dusk. In a second he was by my side again and pushed me away with rough concern. "You'll catch cold, the window is open." By now the girls had finished arranging the mattresses and had gathered by the stove. Hans gave us cigarettes and flicked through an illustrated newspaper. On the front page there was a picture of a smiling German girl and a title, "She's thinking about you, friend!" Hans read it out in a cold voice, shrugged, tore the paper up, and threw it into the stove. He turned to the window, whistling, and shook hands with me when we said good-bye.

I went slowly to the office to collect my hard-earned three and a half złoty, and at eight o'clock I walked slowly across the snow-covered field through raging wind and frost to our truck. We loaded ourselves onto the open platform and started for home. The girls sang the whole time, and I did, too, but sadness came over me suddenly. It's clear why. But why Hans? Does he also not understand this storm of events, this madness? Does he feel lost and small in this terrible turmoil? Does he also think that his youth is going awry, that he is tangled up in life and being stripped of all illusions and ideals? He belongs to a nation that is winning, that controls so many nations; he's an airman, he's young and attractive; he ought to be as arrogant and proud as the rest of them. But he is gloomy, and his bright eyes are sad. Why?

24 February 1942

Chance is always kind to me, especially in regard to work. (Knock on wood!) In order to make money, young girls borrow other people's *Kennkarte* and substitute for them at work. But my parents think that doesn't make sense. I certainly wouldn't be able to pretend that it was my *Kennkarte*, and even if I got away with it, who knows where I would land working myself to death? So my parents don't want me to become someone's slave simply because some people live like millionaires at other people's expense. I really did catch cold at the airport, and I haven't been to Lux all week. As a result I'm fired as of the first of March—in a few days, in other worlds. Actually, I'm happy about it. I'm not going to be out of work for more than three or four weeks, and those daily tasks which we are obliged to perform are, in spite of everything, a kind of change for me. That's how I felt yesterday.

I called for Dola, that splendid worker, before eight, and we went to the *Arbeitsamt*. There was terrible disarray there, and I don't know how it happened, but even though we gave our *Kennkarte* in together, we got separated. I climbed into a truck and began a conversation with one Stefa, a quite nice nineteen-year-old girl. After driving for half an hour, the truck came to a stop and volunteers were called for, five men and five women. Three old women and a few men crawled out, explaining that they "weren't very strong." After thinking it over for a few minutes, Stefa and I jumped out. I didn't want them to say that Jews always try to avoid work. As I was jumping out of the truck, I slipped onto my rear in the muddy road. It didn't matter. We marched to the fort on Kamienna, to the *Sammelstelle* field hospital. Our *Judenmeister*, a dried-out old ruffian with big ears, led us to a shed and told us to carry coal. Someone else brought out brushes and cleaning rags. I had just decided to go off scrubbing with Stefa when one of the male nurses announced that he needed one of us to help him. I can manage one of them, I thought, and went off with him. Then another one showed up, also middle aged. They looked decent because they were soldiers and not *Totenkopf* or Gestapo or SS. We spoke to each other as we went upstairs to a ward to fix the planks on camp beds for the wounded. A new transport was supposed to be arriving tomorrow. The nurse carried the planks while I carried a hammer and nails and we worked, that is to say, he hammered things. The Polish women who work at the fort washed floors and replied politely and with a smile when I said "Good morning." The man I had seen earlier joined us, and we hung around there all morning while my fellow Jews carried coal and washed toilets. "I'm not going to leave you, because if I do you'll have to carry coal and that's not women's work," he reassured me. What a gentleman! He told me about his home, wife and child, and showed me photos of them. Then he went to fetch a pencil to see if I really could write in Gothic script and told me to appear to be working if anyone came. He came back bringing me a mandarin orange.

"It's time for you to go to lunch, now, because we've finished here, but the blankets will arrive in the afternoon and we'll work together again."

I went downstairs, where our respected *Judenmeister* ordered me to carry heavy buckets of water from the kitchen across the enormous courtyard. My arms ached, but when I was refilling the buckets in the kitchen I joked with the Polish women so as not to show that I was half-dead with tiredness. They even helped me because, as they put it, "You are so nice. You don't look like a Jew at all, and what pretty teeth you have!" I made some kind of witty reply, but it hurt me to think that if someone did look like a Jew it was all right to debase and beat them. I took the buckets and then returned to the kitchen because the *Judenmeister* had brought lunch (a delicious, though slightly oversalted and very greasy, pea soup with bacon). He deigned to talk to me, claiming I had a *Kopf, Jugend und Humor*, a head, youth, and humor. Stefa decided to stick with me, and we washed the dishes after lunch, chatting with the Poles as we did so and with the "Mandarin," who seemed to have fallen in love with me, as Stefa said. On the other hand, I had noticed a difference in the way they treated us and the Aryan girls in the kitchen. They were servants, while we were "young ladies."

After lunch Stefa and I sat over a box of briquettes which had to be unloaded. The *Judenmeister* and the "Mandarin" were with us, of course. The rest of the "Juden" were chipping snow and ice off the driveway. At one point a big red bus pulled in, driven by a Polish tram driver. A very young soldier jumped out and reported that the blankets had arrived. Stefa and I carried coal then, and one of the office clerks counseled us strongly not to touch the blankets because they were filthy and full of lice. "Don't worry," I whispered to Stefa, "as long as the 'Mandarin' is with us we won't be overworked."

After a while the *Judenmeister* called two men and us over. "We're driving to Grzegórzecka Street to fetch blankets!" We squealed with joy, because the ride itself was worth it. The "Mandarin" sat down next to me and slipped oranges to me and Stefa. The other young soldier sat opposite. He was a handsome young man with lively, masculine features and a tanned face which revealed sparkling white teeth when he smiled. His hair was blond and he had thick black brows and lashes. Hans from the airport had steely gray eyes, while this one had sapphire blue ones. Even our boys in the ghetto are very handsome, and Poles are generally good-looking, but now everyone looks poor and oppressed. The "Mandarin" smiled benevolently, in a fatherly, knowing way, as we bantered with one another and bundled up heavy, steamy, disinfected blankets for the other Jews to load onto the bus. The work made me hot. I turned lobster-red and took off my hat and jacket. When the bus was full, the five of us sat next to the driver, the other Jews climbed into the back, and we took off with the horn blowing. The driver delegated me to give the turn signals, and the constant blowing of the horn delighted me. Speed, movement, that's my idea of life! The handsome soldier smiled happily, and the "Mandarin" tolerated my *kindische Freude*, my childish pleasure, very nicely.

At the field hospital, we unloaded the blankets, the others carried them to the wards, and we went back for more. The "Mandarin" didn't go with us that time, another youth did, a soldier whose turn it was on duty. This one sat down next to me, and in the purest Polish tried to set up a date at the Hawełka! He asked for my address in the ghetto and wrote it down on a matchbox. I was amused to no end by this twenty-one-year-old child. When he got off at the tram stop, the handsome one sat down in his place. He's called Franz Lüssen, is twenty-two, and was on the Russian front for seven months.

"I've got a short memory, too, so I'll write down your address. *Ich mag dich gerne, du bist nett.* I like you a lot, you're nice! See, when we're riding on this bus we think of ourselves just as young people, and not of the fact that I'm a soldier and you're . . . I wonder whether we'll meet again? I'd like to."

"Why should we?" I smiled. "It's sufficient that we feel good for a moment, and I will remember this episode. Of course, we won't see each other again."

Smoking cigarettes and chatting like this, we arrived back at Grzegórzecka

Street. Hospital trains stood there, and the loading of blankets began, but no one counted them. An *Unteroffizier* jumped out of the disinfection wagon and started to scream at our Franz. He made some kind of reply; their conversation grew faster and more heated, and the *Unteroffizier* made as though to strike Franz. The poor kid went white and muttered "Jawohl!" He walked this way and that grinding his teeth, but when he got back into the loaded bus he had regained control of himself and even smiled. Sitting beside me, he played with my hand, took the ring with the HN monogram off my finger, and tried to put it on his own, "as a souvenir."

"And what am I going to have as a souvenir?"

"What do I have to give," he joked with a mock-serious expression, "I'm only a poor man."

"Yes, but if I'm giving you something, actually you're taking it, then you have to give me something in return."

"So what are you going to do about it? Cry? Scream?"

"No, I'm just going to think . . ."

"About me? What?"

"That's my business." My expression changed. He seemed human enough, and yet here he was, taking the gold signet ring Papa had given me, and I could do nothing about it. Perhaps he was just teasing me the way Felek does.

"Just so we don't lose each other forever, here's my address."

"I'll bet! It's probably not real."

He was surprised by this and showed me his military I.D. card with a photograph. He lives on Juliusz Lea 54. Somewhere in those avenues is the Gestapo. He wrote the address down on a piece of paper and put it in my hand. Then he wrote my address in his notebook.

"I'd like to visit you there. Perhaps it'll work out."

As we unloaded the blankets, I joked to Stefa that it was a shame that I didn't have any diamonds, because then, perhaps, he would love me better. The driver agreed that this was an engagement and got ready to leave.

"Joking apart, what about my ring?" After some lengthy good-natured bartering, he took it off his finger and gave it back to me saying, "a fine engagement this is!"

"It would only be for real if I gave you the ring myself."

"When?"

"If I fall in love with you, but that's impossible!"

"Why?"

"Because it's not allowed! *Verboten!*" I stressed the word. I was being serious now.

He smiled sadly. "There are many things we do which are not allowed. When it comes to love, to . . . Oh, *Mädchen . . . Auf Wiedersehen, Alles*

Beste." He squeezed my hand several times and gave me a lingering look. I jumped off the steps of the bus and it took off. The "Mandarin" stood at the fort gates watching us with understanding and kindness; the *Judenmeister* called for the two from the bus, while the rest of the Jews lugged the blankets up to the ward. Panting and grunting, Stefa and I staggered up to the ward carrying a bundle between us. Several orderlies, the "Mandarin," and the *Judenmeister* were already up there.

"You two are going to fold the blankets and not carry them," ordered the *Judenmeister* (What a favor!). He folded them himself, muttering to me that I should consider myself very lucky because he's normally quite a *Judenfresser*, a Jew eater. The girls were singing, "I don't need millions, only love and music," and I argued that all three things were good. I didn't actually need millions, but I did need enough money. The *Judenmeister* chuckled, "You're never going to have millions, you're only allowed to own two thousand złoty."

Finally, after six in the evening, having received 2.95 złoty, we walked from this end of town to home. It was dark and warm. The day had been beautiful, almost like spring. Franz said that he would come to the ghetto tomorrow at seven, but they don't let anybody in, and if by some miracle they did, what an embarrassment it would be! The very fact that we can leave the ghetto and see Kraków and people is a break for us, but we still had to perform very hard physical labor, and I barely staggered home. I didn't have the strength to talk, and my whole body ached so much I couldn't move. I fell into my bed and slept like a log.

2 March 1942

I don't work at Lux anymore. At last! I wonder how many more times I'll change jobs during the war? How many more disappointments am I going to have in life? I shake my head sadly. A few days ago I floated on "the wings of youth," and no one could keep me down. Today I feel weak, tired, wrung out like a damp mop. Why? It's been a year that Staszka has been gone. I'm all alone. That Franz really did send me a card telling me that he had tickets for the theater and that I should call to find out where we should meet. Is this a trap? Does he really not know what is going on? I wouldn't have gone out with a German soldier anyway, not even a decent one. Here in the ghetto, meanness and selfishness offend me even more, and each time I meet up with them I'm hurt afresh. I should be used to the fact that people are wrapped up only in themselves, but somehow I'm not. For example, our neighbors who are ordinary people, but very wealthy ones, send both of their daughters out as substitutes on snow work. "Let the girls earn a little," they say. My parents have also changed their position on this by now; it has become so normal that they would not be opposed to it. But how do you find substitute work, how do you compete with my neighbors, for example, who stand in front of the *Arbeitsamt* all day in a group snatching other people's *Kennkarte* away from them? They wouldn't let me have their jobs because they have to work to pay for important things like manicures and hairdos, while I only have to work for bread and marmalade.

Even my own work is wearing me out. I have a cold yet again, my throat hurts and my back hurts, and what's worse, I've started crying. It's the beginning of spring and of my *Weltschmerz!* I'm demolished, miserable, and choking with tears. I don't have the strength or the desire to do anything. What's going to happen?

10 March 1942

I am now unemployed. Four times a week I have to report for forced labor assignments and once a week for block work. Since I have finally recovered from the flu, this does not worry me much. In fact, work is a kind of distraction for me. Sad, but true. The trouble is that there is no pay. There is no money at home either—we are simply destitute, with nothing but misery. I cannot bear it anymore! If only I could break away from here! If only we could leave and go anywhere, even to forced labor in the countryside, on a farm! I cannot stand it anymore, I really cannot. Worst of all is that in our distress we harass and torment one another. The four of us, so close at one time, have stopped understanding each other, as though we were each locked in our own separate worlds. Felek hardly ever drops in, and when he does he is tense and gloomy and complains. He is full of ridiculous demands. He just comes to eat and to sleep and often starts quarrels that upset all of us. What makes him so angry? Maybe he is not ready to get married, though Genia applies pressure with her fried cutlets. I would never have believed that Felek could fall for a girl as dull and common as she, pretty though she is. Felek earns a lot more than any of us, but he never has any money and his shoes are completely worn out. He seems to hate the whole world because he's hungry, but who isn't nowadays? It's been so long since we had butter to put on our bread, eggs, or coffee with milk and sugar on the table. And poor Mama! How worn out she is, how frightfully thin and overworked! My father . . . No, my helplessness drives me crazy. There is no way out, simply NO WAY OUT!

How I wish I could run away from here! True, we are not the only unhappy ones in the ghetto, but we seem to be more desperate than anyone else. And I am ashamed to admit it, but I pity our enemies instead of hating them, as I should. In fact, in spite of everything, I feel sorry for all these Hanses, Pauls, or

Heinrichs. Each of them has had his own private life and dreams brutally disrupted by the war. I pity Sepeln, our truck driver from the *Fliegerhorst*, the Air-Force base, a kind, older soldier whose adolescent son is fighting in Russia. I pity the young French civilian forced laborers here at the *Fliegerhorst*, far away from their own country. I pity twenty-two-year old Franz, my admirer from the field hospital on Kamienna Street, who was sent to the front a week ago and who has again written me a postcard. And so, here I am, weeping now not only for my mother and father, for Felek and for my own wretched youth, but also for Franz and old Sepeln's son, and I beseech all the gods for a quick end to this legalized murder and lawless violence, this war.

23 May 1942

What a lofty plea! What possible good can it do!

Cambridge, Mass.

The sarcastic sentence above ends the first notebook of my diary. Aside from my personal entries, I had copied into it aphorisms and thoughts from Polish, German, and French poems, as well as my own poetry, the titles of books I had read, and even excerpts from a history of French literature.

The notebooks that followed were no longer in the form of a diary. It was as though I had suddenly grasped that the incomprehensible which was happening to us must be recorded, regardless of the danger such a document represented. I kept writing in a different form, in the third person, substituting "she" for "I," so that if the document were found during a search, it could be easily dismissed as just a trifle, a fictional or fantastical story, as nothing real. This boundless naiveté of mine bears testimony to how, in 1942, I still believed in law and order. As if the Germans needed an excuse to murder us! In fact, by 1942 the knot had already tightened. Every morning after waking up I felt it almost literally at my throat. We were held at bay by an irrational predicament which transcended accepted ethical principles and logical norms. The ghetto, divided into blocks each of which was ordered to work on a particular day of the week, had already become a labor camp, although there were as yet no barracks and there still existed something like home. Only this home, which at any moment a villainous German criminal, a Latvian, a Wlasovian, or a Jewish policeman could, with impunity, break into, could not provide a sense of security anymore. The family nest, thrown onto a dead branch and exposed to all four winds! And the chilling awareness that my parents, too, were helpless, that anyone could humiliate them, yell at them, mistreat them and beat them up and the world would not fall apart and my heart would not break. It was the worst time for me. I hated the ghetto with all my strength, but we were still together, although only from evening until morning.

At daybreak I rushed to the truck that drove us to the Fliegerhorst, clutching a small slice of bread wrapped in a piece of clean paper by my mother ("Just don't throw the paper away, don't forget to bring it back for tomorrow!"). On payday I used all my meager earnings to buy a loaf of bread and some butter, bought it illegally in a little store outside the Fliegerhorst. Out of necessity, my parents had overcome their objections to the nature of my work. I was the maid for the most menial jobs, scrubbing the barracks and latrines, exposed to the advances of the boorish recruits. On the one hand, the armband with the Star of David protected us from them because the soldiers were afraid of being accused of Rassenschade, racial shame, but on the other hand, it also exposed us to humiliation and exploitation by anyone at all. I already knew then that there was no point in fretting about what had been imposed by temporary circumstances, temporary, because the war wouldn't last forever. Still, for now we often had to work together with Polish laborers from the outskirts of Kraków or from neighboring villages— better class Poles did not work for the Germans, at least not as scullery maids. Our presence at the Fliegerhorst gave some of them—like Wisia-Kurwisia (Vicky-Hooker-icky), for example, a miserable two-bit whore with rheumy eyes—a sense of superiority. After the painters finished their job in her barracks, we had to scrub the floors, while she sneered at us with the Polish foreman. It was my "baptism of fire." Even in the ghetto, in our little one-room flat, the parquet floor was waxed. "Scrub the shit-house!" Wisia ordered me to the toilet, and she flung down a pail of water. I touched with abhorrence the stinking rug which dripped dirty water. I tried clumsily to stanch the loathsome torrent of rinsings, while Wisia, leaning on the door frame, scoffed, "Look at yourself, Little Princess! Your Jewish reign when I stood under the lamppost on the street and you were at school is over. I am the lady now, and you are up to your elbows in work!"

"Fuck off, Wisia," Bordzia moved her out of the way. Bordzia was at home here, she had worked at the Fliegerhorst for a long time. As robust and as pretty as a peasant girl, Bordzia was impudent and saucy and not afraid of our Vorarbeiter, our foremen. Smoking cigarettes and spitting through her healthy teeth, she talked back at them in their own insolent language. They liked her because she was "one of the boys." Bordzia's vulgar behavior and her bald-faced aggressiveness offended me, but now it was she who grabbed my dirty rag, wiped deftly here and there, and immediately the toilet was clean.

"Thank you," I whispered, surprised and embarrassed.

"Have you gone nuts! You would have screwed around here all day; you'd do better to write us a song!"

In fact, the whole ghetto was singing my songs, and later they were sung in all the camps where there were people from Kraków.

After the Jews had been relocated in the ghetto and later deported to the camps, the ancient quarter of Kazimierz in Kraków was "Aryanized." Miodowa, the main street there, becoming an avenue of cheap prostitutes. After the war, a dormitory for Jewish students stood near Miodowa Street. I was living with my mother, but I used to go there for lunch and supper. Returning home one evening, I ran straight into Wisia! She hugged me with joy and explained to her associate, not without some pride, that I had worked for her at the Fliegerhorst.

"Where is Bordzia?" she asked. "It's a shame that she perished, but at least you have survived. I walk here every evening, and I've spotted you a few times and thought that it must be Halinka. And you," she pointed to my academic beret, "back in school again?"

I refrained from saying: "And you? Back on the streets again!" and even gave her a polite "good night." Her short period of prosperity and of my endless Gehenna were both over.

May 1942

Suddenly, life has become uncomplicated. Easier, though mindless. Every morning, we race to the large open trucks that are waiting in front of the *Arbeitsamt* to take us, skidding from side to side at every curve, to work in the city. We fall on top of one another, squealing and laughing. The indignant, but still dignified, among us who still address themselves as "Doctor," "Professor," or "Attorney" look down with disapproval at us young girls singing, to the tune of *Rosamunde*, "for a bowl of soup and a slice of bread, the girls from the *Fliegerhorst* give you what you want." They acknowledge, rather more graciously, my own song to the same tune about our dislike and avoidance of work at such German institutions as the *Bauhof* on *Bosacka* Street where Jews are forced to take on the hardest, most menial tasks. They are also beaten, tormented, and ridiculed—as though it were not enough to have to slave for a drop of soup and a piece of bread.

> One truck came from Bronowice
> two from air-base Rakowice
> covered coffins from the Lazarets
> came to take the women.
> Get to work! Get to work girls and boys!

So Jews and Jewesses rush to their *Kommando*
because suddenly, like an evil ghost
arrives *Bauhof* and *Bosacka,* and
everyone runs far away from here! far away!
Let's now embark quickly and let's drive away
with good humor despite the dusty wind
let's leave with relief the ghetto gates
Good-bye! Farewell!
And now "free"—let us sing aloud
whistling at our bad, wretched fate.
Smile at the sun, for once it will shine for us again!
although tonight we still have to return
to the closed ghetto gates.

Two trucks rattle along Rakowicka Street and across the fields to the small red guardhouse of the *Fliegerhorst Kraków-Rakowice.* The soldier-driver reports how many Jews he has brought up here today; the bar across the street is hoisted, and he delivers us to the *Unterkunft,* where twelve girls jump down, and the jovial *Unteroffizier* Klemens assigns work for us. We scrub and clean the guardhouses, the soldiers' and officers' barracks, the hangars, and the offices and canteens. Whoever has a permanent job—if anything can be considered permanent these days—organizes her work so as to have some free time. Erna fixes runs on silk stockings for money. Bordzia, spitting out curses, grabs a pail as though to collect wastepaper on the streets with a stick; in fact, she is going to visit Sonia G., Hanka F., and Rosi Schwarz who wash and press the officers' laundry in the small house beyond the *Richthofenkaserne.* Rosi's family was deported to Poland from Berlin about a year before the war. She quickly learned to speak Polish. She is a strikingly beautiful girl, tall with golden-blond hair and long, slender legs. She has delicate features, a radiant complexion, and an enchanting smile which shows her straight and truly pearl-like teeth. No wonder everyone is in love with her, even more so because she has a low, melodious voice and sings Zarah Leander songs splendidly. Our other "peaches and cream" beauty is Hela Fuchs. We of the *Unterkunft* look neat and clean, not like those of the *Landwirtschaft* who work in the fields, or at construction sites, or with coal in the *Kohlenlager.* The men in their worn-out suits or overalls look pitiful, apart from those who work in the sewing room, and only one of them is a tailor by profession.

I am part of the so-called Flying Brigade, meaning that we plug up all the holes, working at various jobs. Sometimes the work is easy; sometimes very hard, dirty, and tedious. Sometimes our boss for the day is mean, but sometimes he is nice.

Now that it is late spring, the nicest part of the day is the ride in the open truck through the city to and from Rakowice. We come back refreshed by the fragrant breezes from the fields. Sometimes Mama meets me at the ghetto gate, and once I brought her a few of the wildflowers that grow along the runways. She was so thrilled with these that today I picked some of the cornflowers which have just come into bloom. It was already late and the girls did not want to wait for me.

"Come quickly! The truck won't wait for us! It's six o'clock and she's picking cornflowers!" yelled Erna, irritated.

We ran to the overcrowded truck, which drove off immediately. I looked back at the fresh grass of the airfields strewn with wildflowers and at the small windows of the aircraft shining reddish in the setting sun. The truck rumbled swiftly through the city and soon drove into the small dusty streets of the ghetto. Our noisy crowd disappeared through the doors of the tenements.

My bouquet contrasted sharply with the pitiful, dilapidated houses. The children playing in the alleys and stinking courtyards ran after me, calling out with curiosity, "How pretty! What is it?" I had to stop and smile. "Don't you know? Bachelor buttons—cornflowers!"

"Cornflowers," repeated a little girl, looking at them in silent wonder. I took a few flowers and put them into her tiny palm. Immediately, several small, dirty, hands reached up to the flowers. "Me too! Me too! I want a cornflower, too!" The children admired the blue flowers, and one asked resolutely:

"There are bomber-planes in the *Fliegerhorst*, is that where these flowers grow too?"

"Oh, no! They grow everywhere, by the roads, in the meadows, in the wheatfields."

"In wheatfields?" wondered the youngest, Irenka, not yet three years old. Michas, a very bright eight-year-old boy gave her a look of contempt:

"Sure! They grow in the wheatfields! I was in the country once and saw plenty of them. And a forest, too!"

"There are wolves and witches in the forest. My nanny read that out of a book to me at home in Kraków," Ritka whispered timidly.

"Stupid! Wolves and witches are only in books to frighten children so they will behave."

"Michas is right. There is nothing to be afraid of in a forest. Has any one of you been in the woods?"

"A forest is green, rustling, and fragrant," Ritka chanted with the solemnity of a good pupil in a classroom, while the children listened in rapt attention.

Michas had to throw in his remark, "and cows graze in the meadow in a clearing!"

"Cows? What are cows?" asked Irenka. Some of the older children burst out laughing. I tried to direct her to the right answer.

"Do you drink milk?"

"Of course I do! My mother sells milk to the people in this house," she said proudly.

"Well, then, where does milk come from? Who knows?"

"I do!" squealed Irenka. "Milk comes through the wicket in the ghetto wall. A peasant woman brings milk every morning at five!"

At that I burst out laughing, while the perplexed children looked at me in surprise. How could I laugh at such an obvious fact?

"The peasant woman does not make the milk." I turned to an older boy, Big Jurek, for help. "You went to school, tell them where milk comes from."

"Milk? You milk cows, that's all!" and he went back to playing hopscotch.

"Indeed," I agreed, and was about to go on, but how could I explain a farm to children for whom "forest," "meadow," and "cornflower" are empty, meaningless words?

"Please tell me," whispered a little voice, "*there*, where those cows and fields are, is *there* like here?" Irenka pointed to the confined and littered courtyard.

"Oh, no! Of course not!"

"So, what is *there?*"

I hesitated. For these children, that other beautiful world is a magical kingdom, a fairyland known to some of them only from pictures and books. How to describe for these children the fragrance of resin in the woods? The sound of singing birds? The taste of wild strawberries? Perhaps it is better not to open these light or dark curious eyes to the beauty of the world, only to have them hurt even more by the ugliness of this gloomy and dirty courtyard where even the anemic wild lilac bush in the corner is wilting for lack of sun.

"I have to go," I said quietly. "I will tell you on Sunday."

"Will you bring us flowers tomorrow?"

There is very little time between our return from work and the curfew, so I rarely keep my diary now, but these unfortunate children . . . I had to write down their words instead of helping Mama with the supper. My poor mother also has no time for herself. Quietly and with great efficiency, her small hands remove obstacles and smooth our life as much as possible. Mama knows and remembers and cares about everything, from the most serious things to trivia such as my lost bobby pins or my scattered letters and notes. Shame on me! I would do better to help her now.

Cornflowers! How early they bloomed this year—the end of May.

Where did all the people in the ghetto come from all of a sudden? We are stepping on each other's toes. To my great joy, even Maryśka Kranz showed up. It's too bad that it was only for a short while, just to get a break from pretending to be an Aryan. Her hair is now bleached a platinum blond and she has false Aryan papers. There is a new registration for "blue cards" for people who are in the ghetto illegally but can now get I.D.s and permission to stay. Our I.D.s had to be stamped as well, and enormous crowds waited for these stamps from early in the morning until night. We could hardly move for the crowds, and the O.D. organized a one-way system for the pedestrian traffic in the streets.

Perhaps a change for the better is in the air? Perhaps the ghetto will be enlarged by a few streets in order to accommodate all of us?

At the same time, a rumor has started about a relocation. So far we have only had "Actions" and roundups.

On Sunday, Mama and I cleaned our apartment, and after lunch we went with Aunt Dora's sisters to Krzemionki, our one grassy hill. Dziunia and Bronek quickly joined me there to enjoy the nice weather of these "last days of Pompeii."

"Leave me alone with your horrible prophecies! Stop that constant doom and gloom!" I stretched out on the grass and looked up at the clear blue sky. Suddenly, there was commotion and screaming. "The ghetto is being surrounded!"

I jumped up. And indeed! Clearly visible from our hill, a detachment of SS marched toward the ghetto; the spearhead had already reached the gates. The soldiers marched in line, in full military display with rifles at the ready, as though into battle. The ghetto seethed. We could hardly push through the overcrowded streets.

Up in Dziunia's apartment we looked out the window that faces the Aryan side of the street. We noticed how densely the walls were surrounded by police, who stood there shooting up at the windows facing the outside world. Broken glass was everywhere.

No one slept. Whoever had not received a stamp on his I.D. was to be evacuated.

At six o'clock in the morning, the announcement came: people who are to be deported can take along twenty-five kilograms of possessions and twenty-five złotys. They must leave their apartments open with the keys in the lock. At seven o'clock we heard screams and weeping on the streets, and from the corner window we saw these unfortunate people with bundles on their back and children in their arms being pushed and beaten with rifle butts. They were led to the railroad station in Prokocim and into freight trains heading east.

The other girls from the *Fliegerhorst* who live in our house were all set to go to work. I did not know whether I should stay home or join them. Mama ordered me to go. The *Fliegerhorst* trucks had been forbidden to enter the ghetto today and were parked outside the gate.

The day at work was torture. When we returned in the evening, the second transport had already left the ghetto, followed by horse-driven wagons carrying water for people waiting at the train station. They were hardly gone before the workers from the *Baudienst* emptied their homes, threw pots, pans, and odds and ends onto the street, and loaded tables, beds, and wardrobes onto trucks. They ransacked the homes. Overturned and piled up furniture. What a terrible vision of abandonment.

Rifle fire was heard throughout the night. The *Sonderdienst* kept shooting at unbroken windows. This is the third day of tensed nerves. Mama saw me off to the truck. On the way, we noticed an SS detachment marching into the *Plac Zgody*, Concord Square. A sense of foreboding gripped my heart. Mama said, "What pure irony; *they* and the name of this square! Some beautiful concord!"

Orderlies were transporting old and sick people to the hospital; some people believed that they would be secure there. Meanwhile, Papa has called his garbage *Kommando* to report to work and even admitted some strangers, knowing that not working means deportation. Mama kissed me at the gate and went home.

When we returned in the evening, we were shocked by the unusual silence in the ghetto. The streets stood empty. The weather had been beautiful and sunny today, yet the pavement was wet, as though it had rained. Streams of dirty red water flowed through the gutters. On *Plac Zgody* a garbage truck rattled along the cobblestones, followed by hospital orderlies looking like butchers in white smocks splattered with blood. I spotted Felek among them. With one blood-covered hand he was holding a sheet down over the wagon, and with the other clean hand he held a piece of bread wrapped in paper, which he chewed hungrily. "Dear Lord! What has been happening here? Where are our parents? What are you doing?" I cried. "Mama is at home," he said. "She just gave me supper. What am I doing? Someone has to remove the corpses!"

Horrorstruck, I noticed legs and arms sticking out from under the sheet. I sped home, jumping over pools of blood at the corner of Dąbrówka Street and our dead-end street, Janowa Wola. DEAD END, indeed! The wall of the corner house had been chipped up to the second floor by bullets. The end of the world! I barged breathlessly into our room and straight into the arms of my parents. Mama told me that the pedestrians had been dispersed, all inhabitants forbidden to leave their homes, and a systematic evacuation had proceeded from street to street, to the deafening roar of shooting soldiers and the screams and wails of the victims. Mama had not been able to sit still, so she went on tidying the room as usual. She displayed her documents on the table and waited. In a corner behind the wardrobe, she had lit candles beneath the portraits of her parents. From behind the window curtain, she surreptitiously observed what was happening in our dead-end alley. "From every house people ran, beaten with whips and rifle butts. They clutched their pitiful bundles in terror as a fat officer ordered them to kneel by the corner house and killed them with a single shot. Bodies fell, one on top of the other, until there was a mountain of corpses!"

Now I looked through the window and noticed some scattered bundles and an artificial leg.

"Neuman, Abraham Neuman. You know, the famous tall artist who limped, and Gebirtig, who taught you to sing his song 'Rajzele'? They were friends, both of them old and sick. They were walking at the rear. Neuman did not kneel, but was about to strike the commandant with his walking stick. They shot Gebirtig, too. What criminal madness!" Mama's blue eyes glowed with nervous excitement as she spoke. "And then a miracle happened."

A miracle, indeed. Because when the infuriated soldiers thundered into the house and kicked open our door, they suddenly grew silent. In the neat room, my mother stood quietly by the table, pointing to her documents. The Germans barely looked at them and left, closing the door behind them. Later, from the neighbors' window, Mama watched the SS soldiers marching out in precision, their studded boots beating loudly against the paving stones. Behind them, others drove a defenseless mass of evacuees with screams, beatings, and shootings. The rear of this *via dolorosa* was brought up by yet another SS detachment singing loudly like conquering heroes.

Heroes!

The ghetto was surrounded by the SS for the rest of the week. The dead were buried in a mass grave in the Jewish cemetery in Płaszów. No news of the transport, except that before the train left the station for the East, the people in the overcrowded, locked boxcars were fainting for lack of water and air.

Meanwhile, the *Judenvernichtungskampagnie*, the campaign to annihilate the Jews, is raging all over the General Government. During the deportations from the small towns and villages, people were kept outside in the heat and rain for several days before empty wagons arrived. In Mszana Dolna, people were robbed of all their meager belongings and forced to dig a mass grave before being shot on the spot. And this was supposedly just a resettlement to Russia or to the Ukraine for work!

On Sunday, a new registration, to check who is left after that memorable Thursday. There had been so much talk about the little "blue pages," and now, indeed, they have been pasted into our *Kennkarte* as proof of permission to stay in the ghetto. Not all of us were given this privilege, and the people who weren't were taken immediately to a transport, but at least without any shooting. One-third of the ghetto inhabitants have disappeared: 6,000 were deported, 12,000 left to work, and 130 were killed.

The ghetto has been turned into an *Arbeiterviertel*, or workers' quarter. It seems deserted, except during the morning and evening rush to and from work. There is no one who does not work. All of us, men and women, toil as craftsmen in workshops, as cobblers, tailors, carpenters, electricians; we produce military uniforms at the Madritsch factory and pots and pans for the German army at Schindler's enamel works; we clean the field hospitals, the military and police barracks, we sweep the streets—all this is supposed to teach us, lazy bums, to become useful human beings. What a noble pedagogical method!

A week later—a new shock. The ghetto, which is composed of a few streets, has to become even smaller! Just three streets, separated by barbed wire from the rest of the city! Battles at the helpless housing office, which ordered eight persons to a room! Because of the curfew, homeless people sleep in hallways or on the piles of their belongings and furniture, which have been thrown out into every courtyard.

We had moved temporarily to Aunt Dora's when suddenly the Germans added two more streets; luckily, one of them was ours. The tenants had until 8:00 P.M. to return to their previous homes. Rivers of people tried desperately to do so before curfew. After two sleepless night, Papa and I could hardly drag the wheelbarrow with our bundles. Next day, overtired, I fell asleep on the truck taking us to the *Fliegerhorst*.

I worked at the guardhouse with Irka; I was sweeping the hall when a pilot stepped out of the office and inquired eagerly about what was going on in the ghetto. What words could describe how we are being driven to slaughter? Worse than cattle. Why? What fault is it of ours? "Girl, you know why, don't you?" he whispered.

Of course, I know—we are Jewish. Suddenly, with the broom in my hand, I straightened up, as though the suffering of my nation had given me strength and pride. At this moment I realized what a powerful bond common suffering is. *My* nation! My *Jewish* nation, no longer just my *Polish* nation, as I had felt until now. No one refers to me now as "that girl" or "that young Polish girl," but as "that Jewish girl" or "*die grosse blonde Jüdin*," the tall blond Jewess. The young pilot took a pack of cigarettes out of his pocket and awkwardly put it on the window sill. I did not move, hardly restraining a contemptuous smile. He muttered, "*Ich kann doch nichts dafür,* I can't do anything about it," and went back into the office.

We collected our pails and brooms and left for lunch, leaving the cigarettes untouched on the window. Irka could not forgive me. "You didn't take them and you didn't let me do it. You wouldn't have asserted yourself like that in front of an SS man. He didn't mean any harm! Look at you, an honorable scullery maid!"

Yes, an honorable scullery maid!

Erna Neiger is mothering me at the *Fliegerhorst,* and my parents worry less because there is someone to keep an eye on me. I like Erna a lot because she is nice to be with, resourceful and, as they say, "good for dancing and for praying. Scrubbing a floor?—only barefoot. House cleaning?—thoroughly, but fast. Cooking?—only gourmet. Drinking?—only vodka. Falling off a horse?—only the best Arabian." At twenty-six, Erna is the oldest of our dozen girls from the *Unterkunft.* She takes good care of her father and younger sister who work in the ghetto. In our free moments, she knits while I read. She always looks elegant and likes to have fun. She invited me to a party yesterday evening. A tiny room, a gramophone hoarsely playing old records, people dancing huddled together. I have learned how to smoke cigarettes, but I cannot stand the taste of alcohol—besides, it does not make me happy, quite the opposite. The lights went off and people kissed in every corner—I sneaked out and went home. Today, Erna said with a resigned sigh, "You are condemned to eternal virginity! What do you need it for?"

Again, an ominous rumor about a deportation is going around the ghetto. People are sending their children away to the Aryans, while small babies and toddlers found in fields or barns in the nearby villages are arriving in the ghetto. The Germans deported or killed their parents. These nameless children sit on triple bunks in the orphanage, sadly chewing stale bread. Some of them come from mixed marriages, like Lilly from Berlin. Her Jewish mother died and her father, a German soldier, left the child in a boarding school in Zakopane. Monthly payment for the child stopped when he fell in battle. The school board discovered the Jewish parentage of the child from her papers and sent her to the ghetto in Kraków. The little girl stood for hours by the barbed wire, her serious dark eyes searching the Aryan street silently, except once when, seeing some Wehrmacht officers in an open carriage, she screamed, "*Vati! Papa! Nimm mich doch mit!* Daddy! Papa! Take me with you!" When I stopped by the orphanage to pick my mother up in the evening, I found her trying unsuccessfully to calm this crying child. We both tried to play with her, but in vain. We went home in silence, overwhelmed with sadness.

I now have an official sister-in-law—Genia. Her family insisted on an Orthodox wedding, so Felek stood under the canopy in a hat and with a white caftan over his suit, while her mother and Mama walked around him seven times with Genia. Felek has a tiny room at the hospital, but for now he sleeps at Genia's.

Today, Felek went with me to the *Fliegerhorst* to tune the grand piano in the canteen. I swept the floor while Felek fixed the strings and played, more for himself than to check the instrument. The piano came to life, and the pilots surrounded Felek in amazement. When they left, the manager brought us soup, coffee, and bread. Sitting at the side table in the empty hall, we had a heart-to-heart talk, which we have not had for a long time. The radio played "Orpheus in the Underworld."

"He was in hell, all right. But what hell? He should change it for ours!" Felek joked and went to the radio. "This is lousy. Let's find real music."

"Don't touch it—they might think that you are listening to the BBC."

"A great idea," Felek winked, turning the knob. I froze when we heard some Polish words mixed with a squeaking sound, soon jammed by a German military march. Felek shrugged his shoulders, found some Bach, and came back to our soup. The rich sound of an organ filled the large hall. The manager came back, put some chocolates (!) on our table, and grumbled, "*Was für eine Musik ist das! Wir sind nicht in der Kirche!* What kind of music is that, we are not in church!"—and changed the station to dance music.

Autumn 1942

At the end of October, we returned from work to find great turmoil in the ghetto. The exact area where we live had to be evacuated this evening. People were pushing through the crowd with their belongings in their hands. I spotted my parents: Papa carried a knapsack and dragged a suitcase, Mama carried some boxes. I took her bundles. We left our luggage with Aunt Dora's sisters and went back for more. Fighting our way against biting wind, cold rain, fog, mud, and the mass of people, we reached our place—that small half of a room! What a heartbreaking view—a stripped, pillowless bed, the empty wardrobe standing open, kitchen utensils thrown out of a drawer in a hurry. I gathered together my "treasures"—diaries, poems, photographs, letters, a few books—ready to go back again to the other side of the ghetto, when we heard that a week's extension had been granted. What a relief! Only for a week, though.

Too tired to bring our things back, we decided to cover ourselves with coats instead of blankets and to sleep for as long as we could. Before midnight an O.D. arrived to register who works where—and soon the list for the resettlement was ready. Hearing the sound of heavy boots thumping up the stairs, I stood at the open door. Mietek G. was there with a group of O.D. men who had arrived to deport people on the list. Mietek knew what I thought of the O.D.s. He and I had not been in contact since he had put on their uniform and high boots and joined them, but now as he passed me, he whispered, "Tell Lola R. to hide somewhere, and you hide, too."

I dashed upstairs to warn my colleagues from the *Fliegerhorst*, but I did not even attempt to hide. Where? I could not force myself to crawl under the bed, and instead I stood at the open door, watching the O.D. men pushing distressed and crying people down the stairs. Frightened, Mama and I hugged each other, knowing that if . . . then together. Mama cried, begging me to save my young life, and I cried too, but I knew that I would never let her go to her death by herself and that she would never leave me either. The O.D. men came back again for an additional quota. The night was endless. Finally, a pale and foggy morning brought with it an order: "Everyone to the *Arbeitsamt!*" We ran out of the house. Two hours later, everyone in our section of the ghetto was automatically, and without any segregation, sent to the transport.

From across the street, Papa, who had been at work all night, ran up to us, out of breath. His face was wrinkled and gray when he embraced us. He took Mama with him to his garbagemen and told me to stand with my *Fliegerhorst* group. On Józefinska Street there was an enormous crowd, sixteen abreast, with signs: *HKP, Bauleitung, Montellupich, Madritsch, Fliegerhorst.* The garbagemen from the *Strassenreinigung* held up a large broom instead of a sign. People greeted each other, weeping, "I lost my mother, my sister, and my brother"; "They took my father away"; "My wife and daughter had to go, while they beat me up and threw me off the transport. I am alone, all alone."

We stood for a few hours, freezing, unsure whether we were waiting to go to work or to be deported. In any event, I decided to eat a piece of bread which my mother had slipped into my pocket. Hela looked at me with amazement and disgust. "How can you eat? She's chosen this time to gorge herself!"

"Especially at this time," I answered, and swallowed the last morsel, putting the empty paper bag into my pocket. "Who knows what is going to happen to us? Such delicious dry bread with slices of frozen turnip should not go to waste!"

We stood crowded on the street, while SS officers strolled along the sidewalk, glancing at us with cold contempt, whipping one person or another and shooting into the air. They began to decide our fate by segregating us at the gate of the ghetto on the corner of Limanowski and Węgierska Streets. People held their breath in the deadly silence, interrupted only by rough German shouts. My heart leaped into my throat, beating wildly. We had already approached Węgierska Street and could see that not all the people were going through the gate, that some were being pushed into the entrance of Number 14. At first, we supposed that they were the lucky ones who were going to stay in the ghetto, but soon we noticed that the regular trucks, the ones that transported us to work every day, were waiting outside the gate. We prayed to get there as soon as possible.

The last people to go outside to work were two rows ahead of us. Shouting, beating, and shooting, the SS men forced us into the large courtyard. The mass of people squeezed into the overcrowded space was so large that the glass in the windows of the ground floor apartments shattered. "This is the end," flew through my mind. "We are going to be trampled to death." I could not breathe. Where was our group from the *Fliegerhorst?* Then I noticed Bordzia, her face gray and tense with terror. Next to her were a few of our girls. What a relief! Perhaps the *Fliegerhorst* would intervene on our behalf. After all, the transport was not leaving immediately. Maybe we would be taken to some work camp. After all, we were all young.

"They are going to kill us all! Oh, God!" Bordzia burst into wild sobs.

"Stop it at once!" I snapped. I was stone-cold, but I knew that I would break down if I allowed myself the luxury of a single tear.

"Look, over there, people are speaking to the officers, showing their papers and being released," Hala Faden called out. "Let's go there!"

We tried to push through, and then the SS men shot straight into the dense crowd. People moved rapidly back and forth and ducked helplessly. The shots echoed from the walls of the building. Horror appeared on the faces of my friends.

"Hunted animals at bay," came to mind. "Is it really possible that I won't see my parents and Felek again?"

Bordzia must have had similar thoughts, for she whispered, "I knew yesterday that it was my last day at the *Fliegerhorst*."

"Don't worry! Look, the sky is clearing! It is going to be all right!" I consoled her and myself idiotically. But, in fact, the rays of sun looking shyly into this dismal courtyard had evoked a fleeting thought: If I can only get out of here, I will survive the war!

A few officers held council at the hallway gate. One climbed on a garbage shed and from this podium screamed, "*Ruhe!* Quiet!"

We held our breath. The pages of a book left behind on an open window rustled in the wind, breaking the frightening silence.

"OK, all of you—go home!"

No one could comprehend at first. Then cries of relief and gratitude. It is over! They have let us go! Only then did tears fill my eyes.

"*Ruhe!*" bellowed another officer, shooting into the air. "Go home, pack your bags, and report here in an hour with your families! The German city of Kraków has to be *Judenrein,* cleaned of Jews! Whoever tries to hide will be shot on the spot! And now: *Raus! Los! Los!* Out!"

Bullets were fired at us from all sides. The pushing mob almost broke the wide entrance gate. I don't know how we got out into the street. We promised to stick together. Bordzia called out, "Don't get lost! We all will meet on this corner in an hour!"

My head felt empty, my knees like jelly. I leaned on the wall looking at the other, now Aryan, side of Limanowski Street beyond the barbed wire. People were going about their business, standing in front of the stores. Lux, where I had worked, was still closed. Someone was shaking a rug out of the third-floor window next to which pillows and blankets were being aired. Everyday activity there, while just across the street, here in the ghetto, Judgment Day!

I noticed the shiny car from the *Fliegerhorst* parked at the gate to the ghetto. Our major must be intervening for his three hundred Jews! Perhaps . . . Perhaps. He talked to the guard at the gate but was not allowed to enter. Of course, this is the dominion of the Gestapo and SS, and the *Luftwaffe* had to drive back to the city.

I did not have the energy to go home and pack, as I was supposed to do. Wild screams, shooting, loud cries and moans. An SS officer was galloping down the middle of the street and shooting in all directions. He stopped close by the gate, just in front of me. Standing quietly alone at the wall of a building, as though I were waiting for a streetcar, I was a perfect target. I glanced indifferently at his enraged face and turned my head away. Bang-bang-bang! Shots rattled—but not at me! The SS man clumped off in a different direction, while an O.D. man ran up to me shouting, "Run straight to the *Judenrat,* your parents are worried sick about you!" "We were ordered to report here with our things," I said. "Hell, von Mallotke almost killed you! Run to the *Judenrat,* damn you," he yelled, grabbing my arm and pulling me away.

The covered trucks of the SS arrived and rumbled toward the Plac Zgody. Some stopped in front of the hospital so that patients on the stretchers could be thrown inside, one on top of another. Two nurses were carefully leading out a sick man while an SS soldier, shouting *Los! Los!* and beating him with the butt of his rifle, pushed the patient and the nurses into the truck and locked the flap. A woman was loaded onto the other truck, screaming in pain. "Damn it! She's in labor! The poor wretch could not have chosen a better time for such an event!" cursed my O.D. man, banging at the closed gate of the *Judenrat* and shoving me inside. Like an automaton I moved to the sanitation office on the second floor.

"Halinko, my child!" Papa enfolded me in his arms. I sat next to Mama in a corner, away from the window, but close enough to look down at the street.

The trucks were now in front of the orphanage. The older children climbed in by themselves, the small ones were thrown inside like baggage. From the hall downstairs, someone called out that all the patients in the hospital for infectious diseases and the residents in the old peoples' home had been shot. We all sat dazed and tense, waiting for our turn to come, when we heard the scream, *"Alles Raus!"*—the German invitation to the transport.

It must have been a nightmare, this day. It couldn't be true.

I haven't seen our girls, in fact, no one returned to this accursed courtyard. Everywhere German SS soldiers, Ukrainians, and Latvians. At about four o'clock a long convoy of covered trucks left the ghetto, followed by the SS marching in rank and file. They looked like clerks going home after a day's work at the office. The "Action" was over. Furtively, people came out of their hiding places and appeared on the deserted streets. We did, too. Acquaintances fell weeping into each other's arms. Others who were just now returning from their work outside discovered the tragedy: instead of coming back to their families, they found empty rooms. Everywhere there were sounds of crying mingled with sounds of joy when people found their relatives and friends. Happily, we found Felek near the hospital; he was splattered with blood. We stayed at the hospital with him, because our part of the ghetto was still cut off. Some of our possessions, including my diaries and treasures, were at Aunt Dora's sisters, but they had been taken away. So have the aunts from Crown-Soap, and Uncle Ignacy and little Jurek. Gone, too, is Bordzia.

Each footstep echoed through the empty hospital. People ran around in search of their families and were close to madness when they heard how cruelly their sick children, parents, or siblings had been deported to who knows where.

I could not sleep, and I left the stuffy room. I wanted to open the window but had to back off. In the pale light of the moon, deep down in the narrow well of the courtyard, thrown one on top of another, heaps of corpses mingled in their last embrace. Blood dripped from this macabre mountain of murdered people, staining the courtyard with dark puddles.

That night I wrote a poem about the October deportation.

I crouched at their sight
like a beaten hunted dog
I squeezed into a crowd
stupefied and terrorized.

by their screaming by their glances
insolent and scornful
by their icy hateful
steely eyes

thousands of beings depend
on one wave of a finger
thousands of eyes young and old
hang on the wave of a finger
right—left
life—death
right—left.

a fist with a whip
reigns
over the masses
of women
children
men
old and young
sick and strong.

Will it smash to death
humans—outlawed
who so helpless
and defenseless
just wait.

Heavy German fist fell
on the stooped
shaking backs.

Scream and moan and women's cries
Blood and tears mix
on the pavement
The old and sick—a bullet in back
straight to the heart

The crowd—into the trucks
Out! to the transport
Where to?
Where?—to death.

Brain in the gutters. On the streets
heaps of corpses, legs, and arms
and smashed heads of little infants.

Where are you, dear Lord?
Where are You?

Cambridge, Mass., 3 July 1986,
the one hundredth anniversary of the
unveiling of the Statue of Liberty

Whenever I looked through my diary after the war, I refused to read about the deportations. Now, after forty-three years, I transcribe the yellowish pages on my balcony filled with flowers. The first morning glory opened today, and the pouring rain of a sudden thunderstorm destroyed the delicate blue petals. Unlucky flower, like a human being born at an unfortunate time. Soon the sun shone again and painted a radiant rainbow all across the sky.

An analogy? In those other times this would have been a "sign." My own notes are inadequate compared to that which has been etched forever in my memory, in the sharpest of detail. Sight and hearing absorb things faster, and more precisely, than thought. Bordzia's swarthy face, her snow-white healthy teeth, the twinkle in her dark, smiling eyes; the taste of bread filled with frozen turnip; the bang and the splash of the small infant's head—an SS man had torn the little bundle from its mother's arms and had smashed the baby against the wall at the very moment when von Mallotke rushed toward me. There is a limit to feelings. I was beyond fear, then. Did that brute, drunk with blood, realize that there was no fright in me? He backed off, as a raging dog does when his victim suddenly confronts him. No human reflex had caused him to spare me; he just turned around and went on killing others. What had saved my mother during the June deportation? Surprise? The unexpected sight of a neat room, like an echo of a normal life, in this raving madness of chaos and murder?

We tried in vain to find sense in this utter senselessness. The norms regulating the life of a society, the ethical, legal norms of logical reasoning, simply did not apply. Like being forced to move from one part of the ghetto into another and then, after an hour, back again to where we had come from. Was it because a train had not arrived on time from Treblinka or Bełżec?

A constant seesaw: relief—tension; a glimmer of hope—the depths of despair. Terrorized beyond comprehension, deceived by every German order, by every word at every moment, we became a trifle for our murderers.

November 1942

We have moved again, for the third time during the war. Our apartments have shrunk gradually, but the latest one is the worst, a gloomy hovel on the ground floor at the back of a house where the sun never shines. The one room and kitchen stink of damp mustiness, the smell peculiar to poverty. Everything was scattered around when we entered; a few chipped mugs on the stove surrounded a pot of ersatz coffee. Obviously the former tenants had not managed to drink something warm before being deported. We moved the furniture and other things out into the courtyard. Some people took them immediately. Let them have it. If they don't take it, the *Baudienst* will take it for the Germans anyway.

Mama tried to cover the ugliness of this dark room with the last of our nice things, but I don't like this place and prefer to be at the *Fliegerhorst*. At least it is peaceful there, while in the ghetto—or in what is left of it—it is always tense.

I miss our piano, lost in the other part of the ghetto. How strange that after such tragedies, and in the midst of not knowing what is going to happen tomorrow, I can even think about playing the piano. But music lets me forget our misery. True, it should never be forgotten, but to live in constant terror is beyond human endurance. One has to relax. Music like velvet, like a cat's warm paws, can sooth my tormented soul. The piano in the canteen pulls me like a magnet, but I am forbidden to play.

December 1942

The period in the ghetto between the October deportation and the billeting into the barracks has been the worst for me. Not one day has passed without roundups and shootings. Prisoners from the neighboring camps, dirty paupers in rags, their only possession a small bundle, fill the kitchen for the utterly destitute, steal whatever they can and run away, beaten and kicked by the O.D. men. Deprived of soap, a bath, and a change of clothing, overworked, hungry, and tired, they are so wretched that one can hardly blame them. The O.D. men take people off the streets to construct barracks at the Jerozolimska cemetery in Płaszów. It is a dangerous place to work. The SS foreman tortures his laborers and shoots them indiscriminately, like von Mallotke in the ghetto. He simply takes the passers-by into his car and shoots them in Płaszów. No one is sure what is going to happen from one minute to the next.

A nightmare without end.

A madness over false Aryan papers. Whoever has money can buy them, others take a risk and bluff. Many who get caught with false papers—thanks to Polish informers and sometimes to Jewish denouncers—lose their lives. It does not serve as a warning for the others, who still try their luck. We all have much bleaker prospects and nothing to lose. I always disliked the ghetto, but now I hate it, I HATE IT! The sunny days of fall are over, and the sky is hanging low over the city, full of dark clouds. Dampness seeps into the streets, houses, clothing, even into the soul. Returning home after work in this slimy fog, I stumble through puddles in the dark courtyard and reach the gloomy room, scarcely lit by a carbide lamp—we are forbidden to use electricity between six and eight in the evening.

We share this room with engineer Izek, husband of Aunt Rega from the Crown-Soap factory. She was looking after her younger sister Mila and went with her on the transport. The children were in hiding and are now with us: Mila's eight-year-old Henio and Izek's children, Rysio and Felunia, who are even younger. Their nanny sleeps in the kitchen; she is a mature woman from a small town in the Tatra mountains. She looks and talks like a peasant and certainly could survive somewhere in a village. Izek pays her well and promised to take her in time to the *Julag* camp in Prokocim. Every evening after Izek returns from work, the children stand in front of him while the nanny reports who was misbehaving. Today it was Rysio. From my bed in the corner, I see how obediently the little boy approaches his father to be slapped on his outstretched small hand, reciting, "Thank you Daddy for punishing me when I deserved it and teaching me how to be a decent man." Izek kisses each child, and all of them sit down to eat soup. My parents had different educational methods. They never slapped us.

Cambridge, Mass.

Izek did, indeed, take his children and their nanny to Julag, *but unfortunately not for long. The SS men from Płaszów soon arrived to liquidate the* Julag *camp and shot all three children, one after another, in the presence of their father. He was allowed by cruel fate to survive the war, the only member of his entire family who did.*

December 1942 cont'd.

The billeting of people who work in the city was announced on 4 December. It had been expected for some time, and we are even glad to leave the ghetto. On the eve of my departure for the *Fliegerhorst*, I suddenly realized that it meant the end of our family life together. I will be all alone from now on, without the support of my home and without my parents' advice; I shall have to decide about many things, to take care of food, laundry, money. Mama's good, wise eyes won't watch over me, her caring hands won't smooth my daily life. I won't be able to kiss her and Papa good night. I am going to be all alone among strangers. There is one consolation, though; I hope to visit them on weekends.

Gathering my courage, I mentioned my worries about parting from my parents to our boss at the *Fliegerhorst, Unterkunft, Unteroffizier* Klemens.

He is understanding and good to us all, our "Uncle" Klemens—perhaps it would be possible to bring my family to the *Fliegerhorst*, but it is not up to him. The *Arbeitsamt* in the ghetto decides on workers, and without money and connections in the O.D. it is impossible to get on the list. Alas, alas.

Mama packed my suitcase and reminded me, "Here is a box with needles and thread, here are your toiletries, soap, toothbrush, and toothpaste. Do you want my high-heeled pumps, in case you go to dancing?" I burst out laughing. "Dancing? This is a forced labor camp! An *Arbeitslager!*" "So what? You are all young and should have fun, no matter what the circumstances. Take the pumps, just in case," Mama decided. "Did you fasten the buttons on your pajamas? Tell me what else you might need, don't wait for me to figure it out for you."

In my helpless despair, I stopped what I was doing, and, overcome by sadness, hugged and kissed her.

No one was allowed to go to work next morning; the ghetto was closed. The trucks from the *Fliegerhorst* waited at the *Arbeitsamt*. We loaded our luggage amid loud confusion. A quick good-bye and a jump on the truck. From there, holding back tears, I looked down at my mother. "Mommy! Mamusiu!" She stood there, poor darling, a kerchief on her head, waving to me and smiling bravely, her tired blue eyes full of love. "Cover your face against the cold wind during the ride!"

"Mamusiu!" A desperate, soundless cry choked me. I could not pull my eyes away from her worried pale face, until I could no longer see her through my tears as we left the ghetto. At this point, I noticed many strangers around me, young people and older ones. Where had they come from? My poor parents alone were not on the list.

Covered with snow, the *Fliegerhorst* seemed empty. The trucks stopped in front of two large barracks. I walked quickly into a room with two windows and six two-tiered bunks and put my suitcase on the top one. Erna is on the bottom. Our boys helped to unload the straw mattresses, military wardrobes, chairs, and tables. The room was icy-cold. Erna lit the fire on the stove and we all felt a bit more cozy. In a small room across from ours, girls scrubbed the floor, hung a white window curtain, and put out a colorful tablecloth. We did, too. A few pictures on the wall turned our crowded room into a kind of home.

During the day, "Uncle" Klemens and our inspector checked to see whether there was enough furniture, water pails, brooms, and kitchen utensils. Our rooms were orderly and clean when they arrived in the evening for official inspection. Both were good natured and jokingly tried to ease our transition into the camp. In all this excitement, I almost forgot about the ghetto. If only my parents were here with me I would be happy!

Once in bed, we began to organize ourselves in this new situation. Understandably, Rena and Dora had the authority. They were the oldest, married before the war, both of them good looking, Rena with a short haircut, Dora with long locks and gray eyes like a cat. Both are witty and energetic. Rena, an attorney with a degree from the University of Kraków, is a born leader. "This is our home now and we have to take care of it," she said. "A different person each day will be on duty. She will fetch hot and cold water, coffee, soup, and our rations. She will light the stove and mop the floor. We'll start at the first bed from the door, so tomorrow Julia is in charge!"

"Me?" Julia stuck out her long thin nose from under a heavy feather comforter. "Thanks a lot! Why me?" "Vivat, Julia the First!" we all laughed, so loudly that our neighbors knocked on the wall and shouted, "Shut up! Let us sleep!" We shouted back, "Sorry! Sweet dreams!"

I could not fall asleep on my hard straw mattress. We were here like shipwrecked people, all 180 of us in these barracks, deprived of our private family lives. Still, this very first day away from home seemed much better than I had imagined; I almost felt guilty for laughing and enjoying the new situation while my parents were certainly worrying about me. My dearest of all, don't worry, and have a good, peaceful night!

The following morning, I jumped out of my bunk at half past six and lined up for the washbasin. Next to me was Hela, nervous because "This is taking forever, and I need time for makeup, for my brows!"

"Runka, move over or go back to bed! You are so fat that you take up half of the room!" Runka ironed a lace collar on the table and smiled with all her dimples.

"Heavens, look at this table! The tablecloth is rolled up, the toiletries are mixed with the food and combs! Girls, are you mad?" yelled Rena and bent over the slop pail, brushing her teeth.

The *Lagerführer* of the female barracks, Dora's friend, entered the room with a pot of hot coffee. Half-dressed girls screamed from every corner. He covered his eyes: "I can't see anything. Send someone for the food, please."

"What are we getting?"

"A half pound of bread and a quarter of a pound of marmalade."

"Great!" And we bustled about breakfast. Soon he called, "Come out, please, we are marching to work!"

Only those girls on duty and a few older women remained in the barracks. They cleaned the kitchen and the small bathroom building. Unfortunately one of them, the mother of a young child, had to return to the ghetto after a few days. Sunday afternoon was free. We changed into nice dresses and went to visit the men's "hotel." It was a bare military barracks, with nothing of the "female touch" that ours has.

I made a small shelf over the bunk for my odds and ends and for a green plant. Our room looked nice as long as there were only two or three of us in there. When everyone came home, it was too crowded around the table and the stove, and too noisy. Later we had visitors: our boys. I played harmonica for them, and we sang and danced. Mama was right about packing her pumps.

The very thought of my parents made me feel guilty again—how could I feel peaceful and safe here, away from them?

The men left at 8:00 P.M. There was plenty of time to read, to wash and sew, to sing and to recite poetry. Not without reason was our room called "Olympus"!

The two barracks together with the bathroom, laundry, and nearby kitchen were soon enclosed by a barbed-wire fence. Our living space inside the fence is rather limited. At the gate stood, first, a pilot, and then, a German *Obhut*. So much for our free walks after work. That is over.

Christmas is coming. The soldiers are going home for the holidays, and those who stay here are treating their serving maids to the goodies their families have sent them. I feel uneasy accepting anything material, as though I were a real servant. Well, Lola R. (who was saved by Mietek during the October deportation) and I have nothing to worry about, because we work for lower-ranking soldiers beyond the runways at the *Fliegerkaserne*. They have left for the holidays, or for the front, and the barracks is empty.

An old sergeant in the office ordered us to clean the large bathhouse. Our feet were frozen stiff on the concrete floor. With a feeling of revulsion, we scrubbed the wooden crates, which were all gray and grimey. We went to the office to ask for soda and hot water, but the sergeant shouted, "What a nerve! Those Jewish folk! Our soldiers are freezing in Russia and these damned broads want hot water! Out!"

We scrubbed as best we could. In the afternoon, the sergeant came to see our work, and of course, nothing we did was right. We had to lift the heavy crates and scrub them and the concrete floor again, while he stood there shouting, "I will teach you, you lazy Jewish whores! I promise you will work here until doomsday!"

Finally, he ordered me to clean the stone steps outside the entrance. I swept them with the broom, but he began to rave: what kind of Jewish work is this? He grabbed my broom and hit my arm with the handle. No one had ever hit me like this before. The humiliation was worse than the pain and made me furious. I could have killed him. From the hallway, Lola watched in fright as I stood there full of hatred. The sergeant fetched two pails of water and with a swing splashed the water on the stairs and at my feet. I sponged up the streams of icy water, my bare hands almost freezing to the wet rag, while he stood at the top of the stairs enjoying his almighty power. Until dusk, he kept finding other things to be done in this bathhouse.

At last, we put the brooms into a locker, and he pushed us out through the back door, where there was no path. Falling into the snowdrifts, we reached the road, which was hardly visible in the darkness. I looked back with hatred at the bathhouse; my tormentor stood in the brightly lit doorway, then stepped down, shaking his fist at us, and, at that very moment, slipped and fell down the icy steps! We burst into loud laughter and ran to our barracks, frozen but happy.

The next day I showed "Uncle" Klemens the oblong blue bruise on my right forearm and asked him for a transfer to another job.

"I won't send anyone to work for him!" said Klemens and at once telephoned the *Fliegerkaserne*. To my surprise, his short conversation, angry at first, changed into laughter. He turned to me, amused. "Your sergeant fell yesterday and broke his right forearm. *Sehr gut.*"

On New Year's Eve, people decided to celebrate with an ocean of alcohol. I don't like vodka, and instead of being happy, I was sad. What could I expect from life? Nothing good. And my family? Would we all be alive next year? With such melancholy thoughts, I went to sleep on my upper bunk. A tug on my blanket woke me up in the middle of night. Surprised, I recognized "Uncle" Klemens. "I wish that you all survive the war; I wish we could save you! *Alles Gute!*" he said, and shook hands with each of us. Klemens visited every room in both barracks. He, too, must feel lonely away from home, and he had come to us as to his family. We were all touched and grateful.

15 January 1943

I have a cold and am staying in my bunk and looking at our "Olympus." Young and intelligent, we all seemed to be compatible roommates, and at first we were delighted with ourselves. Later, the differences in education, milieu, upbringing, and character showed up. One gets to know people best by seeing them when they are upset and quarreling; a boor will swear and shout dirty names; a bitch will spit venom, but a well-bred person will still act courteously. Despite everything, I have got used to our "Olympus" and would not like to change it.

More gloomy news from the ghetto. Two young girls were hanged because they were afraid of staying at the barracks on Jerozolimska Street and had hidden in the ghetto. A large camp is going to be established in the newly built barracks at Płaszów.

Sunday, after cleaning the streets of the *Fliegerhorst* for two hours, we visited the ghetto. We walked seven miles, there and back. I cannot stand it that my parents are left in the ghetto. Even Izek B. and the children are in a camp in Julag, and Mietek is, too. I did not manage to see Felek. I am dead tired, too exhausted to think, let alone to write.

In one of the hangars, the major has organized a first-class waiting room for the pilots. "Uncle" Klemens sent Inga and me there because we both speak fluent German. With our pails and brooms, we traveled to work in style—in the major's elegant car, together with our inspector, who squeezed himself between the window and us. Our job is to serve coffee and to clean two large halls full of tables and comfortable chairs. We do our best! On every table there are fresh flowers and a large pot of coffee surrounded by blue cups and saucers, with newspapers and illustrated magazines at the sides. The radio playing soft music inside the nicely decorated, well-heated rooms creates a relaxed atmosphere on a frosty winter day.

Between six and eleven in the morning, and from two to five in the afternoon, we scrub the tables and the floors, wash the dishes behind the screen in a corner, and take turns serving coffee. If one of our "clients" is arrogant, we give him the "one with whipped cream," that is, we spit into the cup before pouring the coffee and serve him first, so that no one else gets this drink by mistake. So far, the major's inspections have brought praise for the cozy *Aufenhaltsraum* and for us, the waitresses in white aprons. Once a few soldier-waiters from the casino catered fancy food, and the major told us to remove our Star of David armbands because a squadron of top military officers was arriving. A huge fat man in a fancy uniform—Göring?—came in with a group of stuffy generals to bless the pilots leaving for the East. They left plenty of good food, sweet oranges, and apples. On principle, we never accept hand-outs, but sometimes someone leaves cigarettes, candies, bread, ham, and, one time, sardines and real coffee in our maids' corner.

Today was a gloomy winter day. We moped around all afternoon, which dragged on endlessly, until the door opened and a bunch of young pilots burst in with a happy noise. Joking and laughing, they threw their parachutes into the corner, unpacked their knapsacks, ate their sandwiches, and drank our coffee. One played accordion and everyone joined in singing. Not knowing who we were, the pilots invited us to dance. We declined, pointing to our Star of David armbands. They did not understand, but stopped insisting on "just one tango." We went to our corner behind the screen, fully aware of our exclusion, of being deprived of the natural expression of youth. The pilots played and sang well-known tunes about a house under the stars on a mountaintop; about the star of Rio; about the stars in their homeland—as if those same stars did not shine all over the world!

The afternoon passed quickly. At five o'clock, we put on our coats furtively and left, trampling angrily through the fresh snow. Inga stopped abruptly. "Say," she asked, "and where is our homeland?" "Where?" I repeated, and pointed to our barracks with the guard at the gate.

Two women were sweeping the path to the bathroom and Pani Z., bundled in a warm shawl, was walking her small white crop-tailed dog. Snowflakes had changed the barbed wire into a lacy fence. Blue reflectors from the runways and the reddish shine from our windows illuminated the snow. We smiled at each other sadly, entered the gate, and soon lost ourselves in the busy evening life of our barracks.

The end of the ghetto is only a question of time, perhaps a few weeks. People are aware of it, and yet they do not seek rescue, because how can they, to where could they escape? Young people take the risk, though it is almost impossible to survive without documents, money, and contacts. We are all exhausted, constrained by family obligations and collective responsibility; it seems that we are waiting passively; helpless, resigned, deserving the contempt of the Aryans. "Frightened and shaking like a Jew," is the saying. Little do they know that we care and worry not only about ourselves, but also about our family, our friends, and our community.

I have been to the ghetto twice for short visits, and it saddened me desperately to see how haggard my parents looked. I miss them so much! A young doctor at the *Fliegerhorst* who knew Felek referred me to the hospital in the ghetto because I have a sore throat all the time. Klemens let me go with a group of laborers from the *Kohlenlager* who had to transport some supplies from the city and were going through the ghetto. The day before I had bought two eggs from the Polish girls who work at the casino and asked Erna to fry an omelet with margarine. Decorated with my ration of marmalade and sprinkled with sugar, it smelled delicious and looked like a cake. Wrapped up on its plate, it should have stayed fresh in the cool window. I could not sleep because of the excitement of meeting my parents in a few hours! But the excursion was delayed for three days. I checked my omelet every day. It had fallen and no longer looked so inviting, poor thing. I tasted it to make sure it hadn't spoiled, but it was still so delicious, I could hardly stop myself from nibbling at it. Finally, we got to the ghetto and I went straight to the orphanage. There were about six hundred children whose parents worked all day or had been deported. What miracle had saved these children? I inquired about the ones I knew—Ritka, the children from Traugutta 13, "black Michaś," little Irenka, Stefunia. None of them was there. Their young mothers did not abandon them, they had gone with them to the transport—where were they now?

My mother was not at the office, so I ran home.

No one paid attention to the tiny buds on the trees and the spring fragrance in the air. The streets were full of nervous people carrying bundles to the trucks from the Kabel factory, which was transferring its workers to the barracks in the factory today. Who cares about spring if one is losing home and family? I searched for my cousin Fredek Nelken, manager at Kabel since before the war, but could see neither him, nor his mother, nor his siblings, Zygmunt and little Jadzia. In our hovel, Mama was bent over the washtub laundering linen in preparation for the move to the barracks on Jerozolimska in Płaszów. The suitcases stood in front of the open, half-empty wardrobe. Desperately sad, I helped Mama with packing. When Papa arrived, we ate soup and my sunken omelet and stared at each other in silence. Then Papa rested on the bed while we squatted around the small iron wood stove, our eyes fixed on the flames. Darkness lurked behind the window. Then the weather changed, the wind blowing wet snow. I had to go, and not knowing when I would see my parents again, I threw myself into their arms embracing them with all my might.

Papa walked me to the corner and returned to his work. Waiting for my ride, I held back tears, but once on the truck, I wept all the way to the *Fliegerhorst.*

Spring 1943

No hope that anything can change for the better. The Germans liquidated the ghetto on 13 March. They killed the sick patients in the hospital and the children in the *Kinderheim.* Cruel Latvian guards arrived from the Stalowa Wola camp, and, together with the raving SS men, surrounded the columns marching to Jerozolimska Street. People holding the remains of their belongings were beaten, whipped, kicked, and shot. Those who were still in Ghetto B were herded to Plac Zgody to be killed there, or deported to Bełżec or Sobibor. Genia hid herself at Felek's, and he later smuggled her on to Jerozolimska Street with the hospital personnel. Her parents, younger brother, and little sister all perished in the massacre.

The camp in Płaszów is situated in the Jewish cemetery. We hear all the time about constant roll calls, beatings, and public executions by hanging or shooting for any or no reason. As long as people go out into the city to work, there is still some communication between the camps, though carrying letters or food is punished with death. Death is the one and only punishment for everything: for smoking cigarettes, for wearing a bra (!), for hiding money. The camp was closed for two days during a search for money, gold, silver, jewelry, watches, and fountain pens. All these were taken away. Whatever people had struggled to save they now lost, and a few people were shot. It is forbidden to own more than a change of underwear and one suit or dress, which is now painted from top to bottom with yellow checks for those who work outside or in red for those staying inside the camp. People sleep on three-tiered bunks, two hundred to one barrack, get soup from a single kettle, share the latrines and the communal bath, stand at dawn and late in the evening for endless roll calls, and work twelve hours a day.

I cannot even imagine my parents living there. They work outside the camp liquidating furniture and everything else left in the ghetto. Our Jewish "estates" are being thoroughly recorded and exported to Germany. I beg everyone to take me to the ghetto with a special permit. Once Klemens told me that a truck was going by there with workers from the *Landwirtschaft*. I had no time to take anything and ran empty handed just to see my parents. We went through the main gate, which had not yet been demolished, as the other ghetto walls have been. Mama was working in the office of the warehouse— but the soldier did not let me in. An O.D. man went with me to the hallway of a big house on Limanowski Street and promised to let my father know of my visit. Soon he arrived, poor Papa, haggard and miserable in workers' overalls, which seems to be the national costume for Jews nowadays. I fell into his arms, sobbing. "Halinko, Halineczko." Papa stroked my hair and caressed my cheek. An enormous German appeared at the entrance door. Papa pushed me into a dark corner, and, standing at attention, reported on the number of tables and chairs delivered to the warehouse. The SS man cracked a whip, shook it at my father, and left. I knew that this SS man was torturing and humiliating Papa. I could not let go of my father and cried sorrowfully over him, and with hatred toward this German, and with guilt that I had a much easier existence at the *Fliegerhorst* than my father had here. Lord, dear Lord, watch over them, have pity on my parents.

The fresh, young green of spring has arrived at the *Fliegerhorst*. A few weeks ago, I thought I would never smile again, ever; today I am joking, laughing, singing, and would even be dancing if there were anyone to dance with. Most of the time there is no one. Some of the boys are interesting enough to talk with, but Inga and I have agreed that if our entire life were limited to the *Fliegerhorst*, we would die virgins. Every day the same routine. Up at five, run to the kitchen for hot water to wash, a quick breakfast, and then off to work at six, before everybody else gets up for roll call at seven. Work until noon, one hour for lunch, work until five, then one hour of street sweeping and return to our little camp. The barracks are noisy and busy: quarrels over the washbasin for laundering things; quarrels over space to cook on the electric plate; eating supper; visiting friends; filing out for the roll call; an evening walk the length of the barbed wire; gazing at the clear sky, or the runways, or the airplanes in front of the hangars; and then good night. On Saturday afternoons we all take showers at the bathhouse where the vile old sergeant broke his arm. Sunday afternoons are free, but not this week—our Saturday bath has been rescheduled for tomorrow.

Feeling great after the bath, we sang happily as we marched back across the runways covered with fresh grass. Nearing the barracks, we suddenly fell silent at the sight of an enormous SS officer and an O.D. man at the gate. It was the commandant of Płaszów, Amon Göth, the man who had committed the massacre at the ghetto, standing with Chilowicz, the head of the Jewish camp police. Klemens and our inspector gave us a quick nervous glance. In their grayish blue *Luftwaffe* uniforms, they seemed to us an island of hope against the swarm of green SS men who surrounded our barracks.

We were informed that as a subcamp of Płaszów, we were compelled to obey the same regulations. Therefore, we had to give up our jewelry, watches, gold, and silver. I stood near the open door, and with a heavy heart, threw my gold ring with my initials on it into the large laundry basket. The ring had been a present from my father on my thirteenth birthday. A giant German whose face was so large that it looked as though it was under a magnifying glass jabbed me with his whip and pointed to my ears. Obviously, he wanted my forget-me-not turquoise earrings which I, like every girl, had worn since birth. I had never removed them and could hardly take them off. Erna helped me, whispering, "Hurry up, or he will pull your ear off along with them!" We were ordered to line up outside to have large squares with the Star of David and a five-digit number painted in thick yellow varnish on the front of our clothing. My number ended in eighteen, and old Mr. Seligman said that was good luck, because in Hebrew eighteen means "life." Our underwear was stamped with the Star of David and a black notation, *Arbeitslager Płaszów*, Labor Camp Płaszów. We all looked as if we had escaped from a circus, except for Julia who had a yellow dress to begin with—too bad my dress was blue. I wondered, who will wear my earrings? And my ring? A Helga or a Nelly, so that the initials "H.N." will fit?

Someone has escaped from the *Bauleitung camp*. He did not show up at the carpentry shop nor at roll call. Friends opened his locker and found it empty except for the tefillin, a prayer shawl, and a prayer book, symbols of Jewishness which he had left behind. Two days later the SS authorities from Płaszów arrived and shot Dr. Künstler, the *Bauleitung*'s young physician on duty. The new one, Dr. Tilles, was assigned to us at the *Unterkunft*. I was his first patient because I had a terrible cold. He told me to stay in bed and I slept nonstop, until a sudden commotion in the hallway woke me up. Klemens burst into the room. "Inspection from Płaszów! *Raus aus dem Bett!* Everybody up and out! Quick!" and he rushed to warn the other camps at the *Fliegerhorst*. I jumped down from the bunk, snatched my painted dress, and moved the table in order to scrub the floor, as if I were on duty. There was no time to fetch water from the bathhouse, because heavy boots were already thumping inside the barracks and I heard loud commands: *Achtung!* Attention! I grabbed a pail full of the morning's coffee and emptied it on the floor.

My back to the door, I sponged with such zeal that it took awhile before I straightened up and stood to attention. An SS man waved his hand, and they all went into other rooms. Later, Klemens explained that the *Bauleitung* had warned him about these so-called inspections when SS men arrived unannounced and shot everyone inside the barracks. In a serious tone, he said quietly, "Run away, child, save yourself, escape while you can! *Schade um dein junges Leben.* Run away. Go!"

"How can I do that? There is such a thing as collective responsibility! When a few people escaped from the Liban quarry, not only their families but the entire *Kommando* was executed. Is it fair to be free at such cost? Can freedom gained at the expense of innocent victims bring happiness?"

Klemens shrugged his shoulders and sighed. "And yet, people do run away. The *Luftwaffe* is not the Liban quarry. You are young, save yourself! In the meantime, you are going to have a new job helping the old civilian, Paul Müller, keep the files in order. Report to him tomorrow at the first hangar."

Cambridge, Mass.

Paul Müller saved my diaries, poems, and photographs. He did everything to save not only me, but also my friend Inga and her mother. It did not work because the SS authorities from Płaszów acted more quickly. The Flieger-horst employed several German civilians, mostly older men unfit for military service, as low-ranking clerks, foremen, mechanics, or drivers. Paul came from a small farm in Upper Silesia and was in charge of the warehouse for spare aircraft parts. He was of medium height with a plain peasant face and graying hair. His sharp pale blue eyes were sometimes gleeful and sometimes shrewd and sly. He was rather taciturn, spoke in a quiet voice, hardly ever smiled, and then, only with his eyes. He gave me his desk, seating himself at the table next to it. After explaining how to record and file orders, he reminded me that when there was an inspection I should grab a rag and dust the shelves. Whenever someone arrived with a yellow slip ordering screws, cogwheels, clamps, or shafts, Paul would put on his wire-rimmed glasses and know at once what was wrong with the JU-88 or HE-III. Unhurried, hands in the pockets of his overalls, he would go to the locked hall, while the "client" waited in our office. Paul brought what was asked for, though he grumbled the whole time and got rid of the suppliant as quickly as possible. At noon, he would bring two canteens full of good food from the mess and put one in front of me, close the door and hang a sign outside that said, "Lunch break." During these breaks I wrote my "novel," my diary. Müller did not inquire too much about what I wrote, and he even gave me a few office copybooks for my Liebesgeschichte. *The "novel" was extremely important, not only to me. Every day, I felt obliged to write another chapter, and every evening on our "Olympus" the most responsive audience in the world gathered to listen to my reading—about us. The romantic love story was not exactly true, but everything else dealt with our reality. It was the chronicle of our life.*

I kept my treasures—diaries, poems, and photographs—in my desk drawer in the office, where they were safe from inspections and searches. With time, I learned to trust Paul, though I either joked or kept silent when he alluded to escaping. One day he found a handbag which had been left behind in the canteen by a young German telephone operator, and with a sly smile, he showed me her Kennkarte: *"Here is my plan. That girl, that 'officer's mattress,' will get a duplicate. This is your* Kennkarte. *Give me your photograph. I will copy it, paste it on, and you will be free."*

"What about the official stamp?" It covered half of the photograph. With a shrewd expression, Paul came up with a solution. "A hard-boiled egg! Just roll a hard-boiled egg over it and the ink will stick to it! Just roll the egg over your photograph and it will be OK!"

"And then?" I asked, quite amused, for who could take this seriously?

"Then we both leave the Fliegerhorst. *My flat is nearby, my landlady knows that I am expecting a visit from my niece. Then I take you to my farm in Silesia."*

"And then Frau Müller kills me and beats you up! You had better return this Kennkarte," *I said.*

With great regret, Paul returned the handbag to the canteen. A few days later he left for a week's vacation and came back with a letter to me from his wife. "We do not have children and, with Paul away, the house is empty. Our countryside is nice, you would like it here. I know that you are a decent girl and I would be glad to take you in. In the meantime, enjoy my Apfelkuchen." With a triumphant glance, Paul opened the package with the apple pie and watched my reaction. I believed that he really did want to help me, and I wrote a letter to Hanka Łętowska. In order to make her trust Paul, I gave him my "treasures" to deliver to her. Next day, Paul told me how frightened Hanka had been when she saw an older German civilian at the door of her apartment and how quickly he had convinced her of his best intentions.

"Hanka has good contacts," he said, without mentioning any Polish patriotic organization, "and she works at the City Hall, so a real Kennkarte *is not a problem. I will take a few of your things to her, as well as any of your clothes that were not painted over."*

He planned to get me straight from the Fliegerhorst *to the train to Silesia, and he wanted to do it soon, at the beginning of December, since police checks were most stringent around the holidays. I composed a letter to my parents, which did not make sense at all, but in which the first letters on the left-hand side, when read from top to bottom, gave Paul Müller's address. Hanka smuggled the letter to my mother and brought her answer back to me. My mother worried whether the pressure of pretending to be someone else would not be too much of a strain. If only my parents were not in Płaszów, where they could not be helped, too.*

Paul knew how close Inga and I were. At my shy request, he promised to get false papers for her and her mother. "I am doing this for you. People pay a fortune for papers, and I will get them free, but that is all. As soon as they have left the Fliegerhorst, *they are on their own."*

We waited for their documents. Mine were ready. Müller took another vacation to prepare my journey. He gave the office keys to the officer at the hangars and sent me back to the Unterkunft. *It was safer for me and for him not to work together. With a group of our girls, I cleaned the barracks of the middle-ranked pilots, knowing that soon it would all be over. Strangely, instead of joy, I felt profound sadness: Here I am, a rat, fleeing the sinking ship.*

I scribbled what follows on a few pages, which Mama sent to Hanka from Płaszów. Here they are:

I tried to imagine the small details of my new life in freedom, though deep down I doubted I would ever dare to escape. Was I already used to slavery? Perhaps I cannot live free anymore? Each uncertain glance, each awkward action, the signs of nervousness typical of those who live in constant danger would betray my identity. Mama warned me about this, knowing my inability to lie. So far, the *Luftwaffe* had indeed covered up the disappearances of a few of us—at least I did not have to worry about endangering my colleagues.

Winter 1943 arrived, with December snowstorms and winds blowing wildly over the runways when we returned to our barracks in the evening. Inga grabbed me at the gate in great excitement and whispered, "The papers are here! Paul stopped at the *Aufenthaltsraum*. Tomorrow evening we will be free! Are you happy?"

"I don't believe it!" I did not know what else to say.

"You silly thing! Remember, tomorrow evening!" We went to our rooms. The usual noisy activity prevented me from falling asleep. I jumped down and went to Inga's room. It was larger than mine and filled with many more women. We climbed onto her corner bunk. "Inga, what is going to happen to all of them?"

"Nothing!" Inga banished all doubts categorically. "Two weeks ago eight people escaped from the *Landwirtschaft* and it was covered up as an accident. Stop being hysterical!"

"You're right, I am talking nonsense. Good night!" We smiled at one another.

TODAY!—that was my first thought right after awakening. Today, Wednesday, opens a new chapter in my life! I looked out of the window. For the first time in many days, the sky was clear and a bright sun gave the frost-covered glass a golden shine.

"What a holiday! Halina is the first to be dressed and the first to make her bed!" Erna laughed.

"A great holiday, indeed, because our nonstop talker is so quiet today," added Dora S.

A sudden commotion in the hallway interrupted our joking. A neighbor barged into the room. "Heavens! We can't go to work! The watchman has locked the gate! The SS-men are coming!" My heart froze, and I surprised myself by bursting into mean, bitter laughter. Lola, her eyes full of tears, cried out, "Have you gone mad? What are you laughing about?" "I am laughing at myself," I answered frankly.

We soon knew: the camp at the *Fliegerhorst* was being liquidated. "Pack your things," we were told, "and wait for the SS-men from Płaszów."

I had nothing to pack. My things were at Hanka's. The suitcase I had here was almost empty. I ran outside to a corner half-covered by evergreen bushes behind the laundry and the lavatories and looked at the snowy runways shining in the sun. I folded my hands and whispered a prayer more ardently than ever before, a prayer without words, just invoking the Lord over and over again. Suddenly, behind the barbed wire, in the bushes, I noticed Paul Müller!

He stood there with his toolbox. "I am going to cut the wire! Run away. Now! Quick!"

At that moment, trucks pulled in and SS-men immediately surrounded our camp. Paul moved away from the bushes but stood at the side, watching. "It is the end," I thought, and returned to our barracks. Klemens pushed me into our room. I did not know that Julia had hidden herself under the bunk. The women were ordered to wait at the side. People ran crying from one group to the other. I stood there amid the shouts and the beatings. One truck carrying our men drove away, while the women climbed into the other. From inside the covered truck Inga and her mother screamed: "Halina! Don't escape without us! Don't leave us! Come along!"

"I am coming, I am coming," I whispered to myself rather than to them. Klemens shouted, "Nelken, where are you going?"

Deafening screams from the SS-men. I moved toward the truck mechanically and climbed in. The major and our inspectors stood in silence next to a handful of our people who were being left behind for a week or so to dismantle the camp. Klemens came up to the truck, sadness mixed with anger in his eyes. Then the trucks drove away, hardly stopping at the guardhouse. The silhouette of Müller with his toolbox flashed by my eyes as he waited at the gate with a fierce expression on his face. The gate went up, letting the trucks through, then went down. I wished the world would end. A tire burst with a loud explosion. The driver swore and got out to fix it. I stood next to the tailgate among the SS men who were escorting us and could not help looking straight at those plain, cruel faces. Our life depended on such men.

The watchtowers of Płaszów, their barbed wire stabbing the sky, drew nearer with every second. The gate shot up like the hand of a clock measuring my new life which should begin today—Wednesday.

Płaszów. Barbed wire, wire, wire jarring the eye and pulling heart and soul apart. Wherever one looks, there they are, the straight rows of wooden barracks divided into large rectangles by narrow paths. Tall watchtowers equipped with blinding searchlights keep the camp in constant check. Against the sky, the black lines of barbed wire resemble the musical score for a mournful chorale of captivity.

The short winter day comes to a close. The hopelessly long day of hard slave labor comes finally to a close. The pale sun paints the last yellowish shine upon the barracks, barbed wire, and gates—it is all unreal.

Dusk. Sadness drifts from the dark corners of the barracks. Rattling machines and talk quiet down. Hands stop work. People glance through the windows and quickly turn their eyes away from the barbed wire and the barracks, away from the hateful view of the camp.

I sit at the table next to a wood stove on which someone is secretly boiling potatoes. We are tufting mattresses piled on the table. Across the table sits a pretty girl, Hanka Szklarczyk. At the end of the table sits Genia, Felek's wife, a prominent person here because her parents owned the mattress shop which is a part of this Płaszów upholstery cooperative. At the next table, someone gives a detailed account of yesterday's execution. I ask shyly, "How come? Why were they shot? For what reason?"

A loud burst of laughter. "Why? What a question! Just because! Because the Germans feel like shooting us! You must be a *Zugang*, new, from the *Fliegerhorst*, where you were in heaven!"

I hang my head. With the Kapo's every roar I cringe, afraid to move. I am sinking into a dark abyss of cruelty and death. Nothing but despair.

"Five to the latrine!" screams the Kapo.

Hanka drags me along. Time will pass faster if we go. We step out on the muddy path. Many other "fives" are there; it is forbidden to walk alone, only in fives and not too often.

The stench, and the sight of a plank going the length of the barracks, and the long lines in front of the few holes make me sick. Someone hurries the women. "Shit faster, it'll be time for the roll call in a minute!" I am unable to get near the plank and move away. Hanka, always composed, pulls her pants down and says, "Don't worry, you will get used to it."

"Never! I will never get used to it! I don't want to get used to it!"

Helpless fury boils inside me. Hanka shrugs her shoulders, and we both go out and wait for the other three in our "five." From the O.D.'s guardhouse a trumpet announces the end of work and the return from the camp's work area to the *Appelplatz*. In our workshop, people seem to have come more alive. They collect their knapsacks, form themselves into rows of five, and begin the evening march to the gate of the "living quarters" of Lager Płaszów.

Cambridge, Mass.

This was the last original prose from Płaszów. What followed were poems written on scraps of paper, or in my tiny notebook, or, toward the end of the war, on the wooden plank of my bunk; poems that I have forever held in memory.

1. The author's grandmother, Rozalia Barber, 1909.

2. Regina and Emanuel Nelken, the author's parents, with her brother, Felek, ca. 1923.

3. The aunts, 1915. *Left to right*: Hella, Regina (the author's mother), Bronka, and Lola.

4. The author's family home at 7 Długosza Street in 1984, utterly ruined by neglect under communism. The city of Kraków still delays the return of the house to the author.

5. The courtyard balcony, 1984.

6. The author and Maryska K. (Wawel, March 1939).

7. School performance, May 1939. The author is standing in the center.

8. Hela B., the author, and Rila, in Wawel, two days before the outbreak of the Second World War, 29 August 1939.

9. The author with her father and her friend Staszka, all wearing armbands with the Star of David (Kraków 1940).

10. "Why?" the author's drawing on the first page of her diary, 20 September 1940 – March 1942.

11. Main gate of the ghetto in Kraków, as seen from the "Aryan" side, 1941.

12. "Wild party boys," 1941. *Clockwise from the top*: Lonek, Ksylek, Stefan, Jurek, Józek Hollander ("Netherländer"), and Mietek.

13. Alexander Weissberg in France, 1952.

14. A poem, "Olympus," illustrated by the author (Fliegerhorst-Kraków, 1942).

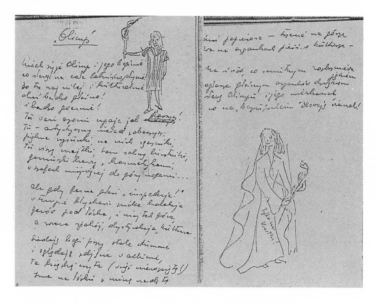

15. Prisoners at work, Concentration Camp Kraków-Płaszów, 1944. (Photograph courtesy of the Komisja Badania Zbrodni Hitlerowskich w Krakowie, *Instytut Pamięce Narodowej* [Commission for the Investigation of Nazi Crimes, the Institute of National Memory]).

16. Female prisoners at work, Concentration Camp Kraków-Płaszów, 1944. (Photograph courtesy of the *Instytut Pamięce Narodowej* [the Institute of National Memory]).

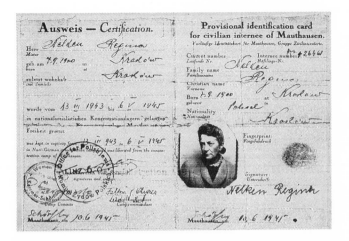

17. Regina Nelken's identification card from KL Mauthausen, showing her Auschwitz tatoo number, A-26461.

18. Feliks Nelken-Gwóźdz, M.D. (Munich, 1950).

19. The author's cousins
Mietek Barber and Gyury
Hegedus in the uniform of
the Israeli Brigade of the
British Army (Brussels,
1945).

20. Jewish monument
erected in 1946 in KL-
Kraków Płaszów.

21. Baron Ferdinand von Lüdinghausen and the author just before her lecture at the Alexander von Humboldt Foundation (Bonn, 1976).

2 BEHIND BARBED WIRE Płaszów, Auschwitz, Ravensbrück

Zwangsarbeitslager Kraków-Płaszów 1943–1944
Konzentrationslager Kraków-Płaszów 1944–1945

Concentration Camp Kraków-Płaszów was a tremendous shock. We went straight to the sauna, the showers, and we waited in the nude, first for our clothes to come from delousing, then to be registered. At news that the *Fliegerhorst* had been liquidated, people had gathered around the sauna building, among them my father, who worked now as a laborer inside the camp. I hardly recognized him as the haggard man in overalls holding a shovel. But the O.D. at the registry still respected my father and at his request assigned me to my mother's barracks, which housed the office workers, and to the upholstery shop, where mattresses were being made and where Genia worked.

After the evening roll call, there was a little time to visit my family. Mama brought a laundered shirt for Papa to his barracks and a piece of cheese for Felek and Genia, who were staying together at the hospital in a cubicle just big enough for one bed.

The women's barracks were on the hill, to the left of the main *Lagerstrasse*. My mother slept on the lower bunk between her friends, Bronia F. and Regina W. I stuffed myself in between them as into a drawer and hung my clothes on a string which my mother had ingeniously attached with two nails to the bottom of the upper bunk. Snow drifted over our heads through the slits in the boards of the barracks.

Bewildered and ice-cold, I wrapped myself in our down quilt from home. At least I was next to my mother. A trumpet sounded taps. Lights out. The dim bulb in the middle of the barracks went out. Night, silence.

In the dark of five in the morning, the trumpet sounded again. Outside, someone sang the vulgar version of the reveille. At once, there was a wild commotion in all the bunks. My mother poured some water from a small bottle onto a hankie to freshen us up.

My mother worked outside the camp and she washed herself and our clothing there during lunch. Now, she dressed herself in a jiffy and helped me to get ready. Bent in two like a pocketknife, I could not find anything in the dark. When I finally emerged from the bunk, Mama quickly made our bed.

"Mister Coffee" showed up, and, while selling us cups of a hot beverage that tasted like hot dishwater, told us what the weather was like outside.

An O.D. man outside yelled hoarsely: "Block elder! Take your whores to roll call! Quick, you miserable sluts! Stand here five abreast! Don't drag yourself like dead fish! Move! Move! Damn you, move!"

Not for a single moment was I free of a sense of total defeat. Deeply unhappy, I could not even look at the white roll with kielbasa which Mama served me that evening on a napkin neatly spread on the bunk. "Oh, to hell with your elegant supper!" I snapped.

"What kind of talk is that?" my mother exclaimed. "How dare you use such vulgar language!"

"What do you want from her?" remarked Bronia. "Everybody talks like that. Is she supposed to behave well in here?"

"Especially in here!" my mother replied, emphatically. "Anyone who swears, steals, cheats, or beats others hands Hitler victory on a silver platter. The Germans want to turn us into the lowest of the low! Don't you dare stoop to swearing!"

"I cannot stand it here!" I wept aloud. "It's killing me! I can't stand these barracks, the crowds of people, this constant noise, the latrine! The endless roll calls! Frostbitten feet! Stinking soup! I can't stand this! I am going to kill myself!"

Regina W. leaned out of her bunk and yelled at me, "Shut up! You won't have to kill yourself, they'll do it for you, just you wait and see! There will be one idiot less here! Look at her! Here just a few days, and the princess falls apart! And what about us? Do you think we love this camp? But we have to carry on, because whoever gives up won't survive! Your mother risks her life smuggling food into the camp for you, and you dare to make a fuss! You ought to be ashamed of yourself!"

I *was* ashamed. I lay heartbroken, sobbing and unable to fall asleep. Mama whispered to me, "It's true, we stand at roll calls for hours, but they have to stand as long as we do. So who is whose slave?"

"They have good boots and warm clothes," I replied bitterly.

"Think about something nice: vacations before the war, the teacher you liked the best, the interesting books you have read. Think about anything but this camp. No one has power over your thoughts, no one! This is our freedom. Good night."

My brave mother kept our whole family together with her fortitude, her common sense, and her profound wisdom about life. She would not accept that the present was not worth caring about because everything was only temporary, provisional.

"Nothing lasts as long as 'in the meantime,' but in the meantime one has to live like a human being" was her saying, and, first in the inhuman conditions of the ghetto and now in the camp, she strove for her family's human existence. Nothing was too difficult for her, not washing, not mending, not consoling without cheap sentiment. She, too, froze during the roll calls, but she did so without complaining; she tried to shield me from the icy wind and to turn my attention away from our misery.

"Look at that sunrise! They don't see it, because they have to count us and look for a new victim to beat! But we are able to admire this natural wonder."

The *Aufseherin*, the female wardens, in windblown capes ran between the rows of inmates like black crows. No one wanted to be in the first row. Sometimes I could not avoid it. My mother, standing behind me, whispered:

"Stand up straight, keep your chin up! Don't show them that you are afraid. They want nothing more than to terrorize us into madness and to make us lose all human dignity. Look at Kraków, not at these witches. Soon we shall march out and you will warm up."

I continued to feel worse and worse, though people around me were rather friendly. The Kapo of the upholstery shop, Roman L., gave me paper on which to write my poems. He was lenient about the work of our group, which was made up of the youngest girls. Once he gave us a bowl full of hot water for washing up. One by one, under a table covered with a mattress, we all washed ourselves in the same water with a scrap of a soap and then dried ourselves on the same towel.

The night shift was torture. I met my family only in passing, and at a distance, either during the roll calls, after which they went back to the barracks and I went off to work, or in the morning, when I collapsed half-conscious on the bunk. Mama left bread for me for breakfast there.

Once I found under the pillow a letter from Hanka L. smuggled in by my mother. Hanka wrote that if I could only work outside the Płaszów camp my escape might still be possible. If not, she would send my winter coat and sweater to my mother. Before I could think about it, I fell asleep. A sudden commotion in the barracks woke me up. An O.D. had come to pick up people to work in a small camp, *Luftwaffe Nachrichtengerätelager*, near the enamel factory owned by Schindler. I jumped out of the bunk and was barely able to scribble a few words to Mama. Still sleepy, and without thinking, I found myself with a small group of people on a truck moving quickly through the city toward the railroad bridge over the Vistula River. Once there, we walked into the camp through a small gate, passing by a guard who whispered to me in Polish, "Miss, what are you doing here? It is me, Nenko, your neighbor from Długosza Street!"

An officer counted us and sent us to work. There were about sixty people in the camp, perhaps twenty women among them. They loaded the train with telecommunications materials—telephone poles, iron transformers—which they had to carry on their shoulders. The iron tore their clothing, which was in tatters. People inquired about family and friends in Płaszów. The newcomers answered gladly, but not me.

Not saying a word, I worked automatically, without looking at anyone. A lucky chance had brought me here. Just beyond the gate was a normal street with pedestrians. It was much easier here than at the *Fliegerhorst*—and Nenko could let Hanka know where I was. I can escape from here! With my "Aryan" papers, my "good (non-Jewish) looks," and a secure place to stay, anybody would do it. I did not know anyone here and I didn't want to know them. I did not have any ties or obligations, any family or friends who might pay dearly for my escape.

My family! With an aching heart, I thought about my mother. I had not had time to make the bed or to say good-bye to my parents. Who knew when I would see them again? I bit my lip in order not to cry out loud.

At that moment, a woman loading transformers nearby came up to me, and taking my hand, said, "Don't worry so much, child. I cannot look at you torturing yourself so much. Somehow things will turn out well, they will!"

Furiously, I pushed her away and burst in tears. Zosia put her arms around me and whispered soothingly, "There, there, everything is going to be fine!" I was shaking all over, sobs tearing at my heart. I could not escape now. I could not endanger this woman. Her goodness of heart stood between me and my freedom.

The *Hauptmann* who was camp *Kommendant* lived in Kraków and rarely came for inspections. *Oberfeldwebel* Krak, some *Unteroffizier* called Mai, and a few ordinary soldiers ruled the camp. All of them wore the gray uniform of the *Luftwaffe,* but the uniform was all that connected them to any air force. They were lowly clerks, shirkers from some outback, puffed up with their power over a group of around eighty slaves.

A few privileged people in that small camp worked in the office, kitchen, and laundry, while we moved the *Stappel,* the piles of transformers by the railway. Long lines of freight wagons arrived here, loaded with heavy scrap iron—telecommunications equipment which had to be unloaded and then reloaded for transportation to the eastern front. Once they even made us women haul telegraph poles as a punishment for the escape of three of our colleagues.

For a few minutes, our daily walk to work led us through freedom—a short stretch of road behind the railway viaduct leading into a second field enclosed with barbed wire, where the piles of transformers lay. After a week, like everyone else, I had holes worn into my coat by the transformers. At work we walked in pairs with the transformers on our shoulders and told each other stories from books or from films. The youngest group of girls had not yet had any experiences to recount. Zosia worried about her little girl who was being hidden by somebody. Lawyer Schlang and his wife thought about their young son who was also somewhere outside Kraków. They knew my parents, and Pani Schlang took me under her wing. We shared a bunk in the bigger barracks. The bunks stood by the wall opposite the door. On the left were benches and a table; on the right there was a bit of free space for bowls, pails, and clothes. The camp "aristocracy" slept in the middle bunks; on the "third floor" slept nice Anka Pechner, a doctor's daughter, and Bronka Kaplan, a dentist's daughter. In the other, smaller barracks, Zosia shared a bunk with Jaśka and Irka, who had come with me from Płaszów.

In addition to the normal square painted on all our coats, Jaśka and Irka had a large red circle on their backs, a sign that they had been captured in town and had to be watched as "escapees." Jaśka had escaped from the massacre in Lwów and had worked in a restaurant in Kraków. She told me that one of the Polish girls in the kitchen there sang, "So Jews and Jewesses hurry to your labors in the morning"—my song! We used to sing it as we drove through town in the trucks, and the words soon became well known. But Jaśka had been terrified that the words referred to her and that she had been discovered. In terror, she dropped the plates she had been carrying—and it was then, apparently, that someone had turned her in.

Jaśka had a beautiful trained voice. She had gone to a conservatory. She would sing us "Wo die Lerche singt" and operatic arias to the accompaniment of my whistling. She, Irka, and I stuck together, and Zosia mothered us.

The men's barracks was separated from ours by barbed wire, but until nine o'clock at night whoever wanted to talk through the wire—not me—could do so.

I was overcome by a terrible psychological weariness. Anything was better than thinking. Hanka sent me some warm things. Mama sent me a small pillow, a letter, and a small piece of kielbasa, perhaps five ounces. I ate that delicacy with my bread for several days and read the letter every evening.

One time I was just reaching under the straw mattress for it, when Krak unexpectedly walked in for inspection. The women were at the table eating soup. The Block elder yelled, Achtung! Before I had managed to slip out of the bunk, the others were standing at attention. I was only a second too late, but old Krak mumbled that I didn't seem to be in any hurry. Before I could reply, he picked up the metal bowl of soup, threw it at me, and missed. I couldn't control my nervous grin. He screamed and aimed every single bowl on the table at me, but to no avail! He would have been a wonderful marksman at the front! Finally, he screamed that I was to report to him in the office the following day and walked out, slamming the door.

I couldn't sleep and the next morning stumbled out for the *Appel* with a heavy heart. When everyone marched out to work I tried to go, too, but I was called back to Krak's office. He closed the office door behind me and opened his maw. He screamed at me in a strange dialect I didn't understand, but in any event, what did it matter? Finally, he lashed out and tried to hit me across the face, but he couldn't reach and beat me across the arm. He kicked me into a corner of the office: *"Da stehen bleiben!* Stay there!" and walked out. I was to do time out in a corner?

But Krak returned right away with a small stool. He put the stool down in front of me and stood on it—and only then did he begin to beat me around the face, so hard that my head rolled around like a ball. He deafened me. My teeth cut through my cheek. Nobody had ever before hit me in the face. The physical pain was horrendous, although at the same time I almost felt a desire to laugh! That stupid Krak was much shorter than I was. He even stumbled as he was hitting and had to grab onto the lapels of my coat to prevent himself from falling over. At last, he came down from his high perch and pushed me out the door.

Swollen and half-conscious, I returned to work. Everyone felt sorry for me, but I heard their voices as through a fog. Zosia soaked a handkerchief in water and put the cold compress on my face, reassuring me, "Never mind, child, it will heal before your wedding."

Spring arrived. On the road beyond the barbed wire, young couples walked toward the Vistula River. We sat on the barracks' stairs and talked. Krystyna from Rzeszów, had somehow acquired beans and potatoes, which she boiled and mashed and put on bread. She treated us all to some, and they were delicious! Krystyna looked like "Huculka," a Carpathian peasant, and she hummed the melancholy "dumka" folksongs from that region. Jaśka and Irka sang tangos. Zosia softly hummed a lullaby. It was the clear, warm evening of 2 May 1944. A light breeze from the Vistula carried the fragrance of willows. I read my poem about spring and freedom.

By then we knew everything about each other. One of the three "escapees" asked, "If you had the same chance now, would you escape?" "I don't know," I replied honestly. "Perhaps." "Heavens!" all three of them shouted at me in self-righteous indignation. "What about collective responsibility? We are to be shot for the sake of your freedom? Is your life more important than ours?"

The next day, they disappeared, all three of them. All of them survived the war. And we?

Their escape was detected during our lunch hour. Alarm. Roll call. Tense nerves. And not only among us inmates. The soldiers were afraid of Krak, too. Standing at attention in front of the captain, Krak mumbled our numbers. The captain swished his crop, squinting nervously at the SS-men from Płaszów. Just to be on the safe side, he ordered us to count off, and every tenth man had to step out. Then the whipping began. Young Henek bit his lip and took the merciless beating, standing proudly erect. But old Seligman screamed shrilly at the first lash, squirming around and lamenting very loudly in all the languages he knew: *"Warum! Herr Hauptmann, warum schlagen Sie mich! Fa wues mich! Dlaczego!"*

The clatter of an incoming train drowned his shrieking and the SS-men's screaming. An endless line of wagons arrived at the siding with orders for immediate reloading and express shipment to the eastern front. This transport saved us from a mass execution. We worked nonstop for forty-eight hours without food. No one complained. Anything is better than a bullet. And besides, the front was obviously coming near! At last! At last!

It is unbelievable the degree to which the camps were isolated from the world outside the barbed wire. No one at the *Fliegerhorst* knew about the Warsaw Ghetto uprising. Those who worked for the military were better informed about what was happening on the war fronts than what was happening in any of the camps near Kraków. Contact with the outside world was very limited and dangerous, and so was communication inside the camps. One knew only one's nearest neighbors from the barracks and the few people with whom one worked. I lost touch with the girls from the *Fliegerhorst* when we got dispersed among different barracks and work assignments in Płaszów.

Mr. Nenko became my guardian angel. He smuggled small parcels and letters from my mother and Hanka L. via our maid from Długosza 7, Janka, and he also smuggled out my letters to them. Hanka let me know that Paul Müller had shown up at her place completely drunk and swearing that it had all been the fault of those two rotten women, Inga and her mother, because I could have successfully escaped a week earlier had it not been for them. When it became clear that I could not escape, even from this little camp, he asked for a transfer and left Kraków. None of us ever saw him again. After the war I tried in vain to find him and his *Kühschmalz*.

At the end of May, Nenko brought me a letter which I immediately devoured with my eyes and which left me wailing with pain. On 13 May, my father, returning from work for roll call, had been taken along with his entire unit on a transport. Felek had tried to smuggle Papa through a side door into the hospital when an SS-man threw himself at him and knocked my brother down. Papa had been sent to Birkenau, supposedly to the "match factory."

We had heard rumors about Treblinka, Sobibor, and Auschwitz; we had heard that people were burnt there, but no one seriously believed it. We had not heard of Birkenau. It sounded innocent, and it was comforting to think that Papa had been sent to work in a factory. But why a match factory? Were matches such an important military industry?

How could I have known that the gas chambers of Auschwitz were located precisely in Birkenau? Though I was heartbroken that he had been deported to a place I did not know, I hoped it was a safe one. In fact, when my father's transport from Płaszów got attached to the death transport from Hungary, my poor father went straight to the gas chamber. That was the first transport to become immortalized in photographs by SS officials and scrupulously documented in an album. The album was found after the war and published by the Beate Klarsfeld Foundation in Paris.

A few days after those three girls escaped, we received uniforms from Płaszów: white and black for men; gray with dark blue stripes for women. The men's uniforms looked like pajamas with a funny beret. The women's garments were a straight sack with a collar and three buttons, an equally formless jacket, and a piece of white cloth for a kerchief. When we stood in even rows at roll call, we immediately turned into a gray wall. This, to German eyes, was *ordentlich,* orderly—unlike our civilian clothes, which a year earlier had been painted in a yellow checkered pattern and which made us look like circus clowns.

That same evening, we tried to alter the striped sacks into nicer looking dresses. For a few days we came down with sewing mania. We stayed up until midnight, creating "model dresses," borrowing the only available pair of scissors from one another. I cut my sack in two and made a pleated skirt and a shirt shirred at the waist. I sketched my "model" in a letter to Mama, but instead of being proud of my suddenly discovered practical talent, my mother was seized with fear, for she knew what was in store for me.

The female warden from Płaszów arrived while we were at work. We were ordered back from the field, and, standing at attention in front of our barracks, we heard the murmur inside. Suddenly I heard my name, which was written, as was everybody's, on my bunk. As soon as I entered the barracks, the *Aufseherin* beat me all over my body, yelling and brandishing the remains of my past splendor, a pink silk nightgown, and the remains of my present misery, the leftover pieces of my cut up uniform.

"*Unerhört!* Outrageous! They sleep in silk lingerie between sheets under quilts and dare to cut *Wehrmachtsgut!* army property!" She threw our civilian clothing out of the bunks, checked who had altered their prison garb, and, because each of us had sewn folds or pleats, beat us all. Finally she ordered me to sew my uniform back together as it had been before. Otherwise, at the next inspection she would take me to Płaszów and lock me into the bunker. For now, she just took my silk nightgown.

Someone from the office took pity on me and gave me another striped sack from the store. I wore this prisoner garb in its pure ugliness with a blouse underneath it, because it was very itchy.

The camp uniforms were as stiff and as coarse as if they had been woven out of stinging nettles. They were sweltering in the sun, did nothing to protect us from the cold, and soaked up water when it rained, turning slimy and holding moisture for weeks.

"Since they gave us uniforms, they are going to leave us in peace," proclaimed Pani Niunia, one of the inmates. Logically speaking, she was right, but they used no logic in their dealings with us. Still, people wanted to believe her, for they were afraid of Płaszów. And so, when trucks of SS-men arrived in this little camp, there was a feverish running from one barracks to the other and loud lamenting in every corner. Amid the great confusion, I picked up a few of my belongings and stood quietly at the side of the *Appelplatz*. An older SS officer called me over by swishing his crop: *"Du, Grosse, weinst du nicht?* You, tall girl, why aren't you crying?"

"One has to work everywhere," I answered calmly, because I did not care about this camp, and I was looking forward to seeing Mama again.

"Do you have any money?" he asked me. What a question! It was forbidden under sentence of death to have money. Still, people did hide some, and I did have some small change. "Yes, I do, twenty groszy, which I use as fasteners for my stockings because my garters have been torn off." And I reached into my bag, ready to show him.

"Take these two złotys, a lump of sugar costs that much in Płaszów," he said, and pressed the money into my hand. I did not know whether I should take the money or not. A kind-hearted SS-man?

Płaszów Again

Déjà vu . . . We arrived at the sauna.

A bath. Delousing. Waiting in line for the assignments to the barracks and work. I was about to approach the table with O.D. men in charge when the same older SS *Hauptscharführer*, Schuppke, pushed me aside: *"Die Grosse bleibt in der Sauna!* The tall one stays in the sauna!" And so, I was given the best place to work, since in the sauna one could bathe and do laundry every day.

At the next table I received an assignment to Mama's barracks because the O.D. in charge was the young technician from Lux, a little nobody then, and now a *celebrity!*

At the roll call, I stood with the small group from the sauna. Afterwards, I ran over to Mama, who was now in a different, much nicer barracks. All the women here knew each other and welcomed me joyfully, while Bronia and Regina embraced me like their own daughter. I told them how good this Schuppke had been to me. Mama shook her head. "Very good, indeed— now. When he was *Kommandant* of the Rzeszów Ghetto, he killed nearly everyone there except for a small group of people whom he brought into Płaszów."

Only a few people were left at the *Gerätelager* on the Vistula River. The Hungarian Jews were taken there every day from Płaszów, where they had been transported from Auschwitz, women and men with shaved heads, wearing striped clothes. They knew neither the city, nor the language, nor the people. It was clear that not one of them could escape easily. After being in Auschwitz, the women were terribly afraid to go downstairs into the showers. When I was on duty, I let them shower in warm water for ten minutes instead of three. I knew that a bath was our only luxury and that some of the nasty sauna attendants deprived people of it.

One day, the Hungarian women were waiting for their clothing to come back from delousing and were jabbering away loudly in their own language. Suddenly, the sauna boss, SS-man Lutz, burst in among the naked women with a hoarse roar, "*Ruhe!* Quiet!" And then he left, banging the door in full appreciation of his power and their fright. The women froze in terror, unhappy and lost. It seemed that everyone here screamed at them, even some of the fine Kraków ladies who enjoyed humiliating them in order to elevate themselves. On this day I asked in German if they would like to sing a Hungarian song. One shy little voice was soon joined by others in a soft melancholy tune from the *puszta*. Many wept quietly. I tried to cheer them up by saying that one day we would all return home, and then Lutz showed up again. This time, he asked, "What did you do to them that they are so quiet? From now on you are in charge of all the women's groups!" He looked around and selected six girls to clean the sauna under my command. I could communicate in German with only one of them. She was a philosophy student from the University of Budapest, and she became my translator.

It was time for lunch. Mama had given me an egg sandwich for breakfast, and my young "Philosopher" had nothing, so I shared it with her and asked Lutz for additional soup for my workers; he agreed and even added bread. Then we all scrubbed his office with rags and brushes, I could not let them work alone and just stand there watching them as Vicky-Hooker-icky had once watched me!

The "philosopher" and I became friends, to the extent that a friendship could develop in the few weeks that we worked together. Little did I know that we would meet again, or where! But soon I was transferred to the SS-*Krankenhaus*, the infirmary for the SS and for the bandits of lesser rank: the Latvian and Ukrainian guards at the Płaszów camp. The Hungarian girls were transported back to Auschwitz in August.

During roll call now, I stood with the group of clerks and maids working for the SS "brass." The *Appelplatz* stretched from the women's barracks down to the main road and around the "Chujowa Górka," the execution hill, and along the barbed wire of the Płaszów camp for Polish inmates. There was a gate that divided the inmates' living quarters from the working part of the camp. We were counted at this gate twice a day. To the left, the road led to infirmary, to the administrative offices, to the barracks for the SS, and to those of the Latvian and Ukrainian guards. To the right were the villas of the *Komman-dant*, Amon Göth; of the *Oberarzt*, head doctor Blanke; his lover, *Oberauf-seherin*, chief woman warden Else Ehrich; and the apartments of the SS officers and the SS women wardens. The other side of the road opened onto a beautiful panoramic view of the city of Kraków. The road turned right to the *Arbeitsgelände* and the craftsmen's barracks. Military uniforms sewn at Madritsch were the only real production at Płaszów. Otherwise, the camp's chief occupation was to dispose of the belongings that had once been owned by people who had been killed. In truth, anything of value had already been plundered by the SS, but the rest, in accordance with the German mania for eternal selection and counting, had to be carefully sorted and sent to the Reich. The SS garrison's main occupations were long, constant roll calls, the punishment of inmates, and executions.

Once we had been counted, I passed through the gate and marched to the infirmary—I, the humble cleaning maid, accompanied by the secretary, Madame Jeanette Suchestow, known as the "Polish Mrs. Wallis Simpson." She was a big, vivacious, and handsome woman, the wife of a rich businessman from Drohobycz and known internationally for her long-standing romance with a leading Polish aristocrat, Prince Radziwiłł, who had fallen madly in love with her. Jeannette showed me a photograph of a hunting party in Białowieża, one of the Radziwill estates. There she was in a hunting costume, surrounded by the cream of international society, standing between the prince and Hitler's marshal, Herman Göring!

All the SS-men were extremely impressed by this photo. Klara Bauer, who had also arrived with the transport from Drohobycz, told me how Göth had found Jeanette on the transport list and had ordered her to step forward: "Here, Frau *Grafin*, Countess, work with dung now!" Without a word and without any hurry, Jeanette loaded the wheelbarrow, shovelful by shovelful, holding her head high and looking straight ahead with regal dignity—even the

SS men stopped laughing. The *Oberarzt* Blanke took her on as his secretary. Unfortunately, her fifteen-year-old son was deported to Mauthausen in Austria and perished in the quarries.

The *Oberarzt* Blanke seldom visited the infirmary. He had come to Płaszów from Majdanek—obviously, his task was not healing. *Oberscharfuhrer* Hermann Büttner, with a few young SS men and a Polish inmate sent there from Auschwitz, was in charge of the infirmary. None of them had any medical degrees or knowledge, except perhaps Staszek, the Pole, who knew common remedies and dressed wounds skillfully. I asked him about Auschwitz and the strange rumors I had heard, but Staszek cut me short. "It's better not to ask. May you never see Auschwitz."

Once Staszek and I walked together along the *Lagerstrasse* to the barracks, where I cleaned Büttner's room. We met the Block elder from the Polish camp, who told us about the recent roundup in Kraków. "They have brought in completely innocent people whom they caught as they were leaving church after a wedding! I now have to house a priest, a bride in a white veil, a groom, and all the guests! They won't forget their wedding night! A honeymoon in Płaszów!"

Kamila, a young girl from the Polish camp, cleaned the quarters of the SS women wardens. We shared the "news from the latrine," a source of camp information and trades and exchanges. Kamila worried about why she still had not been released, even though her prison term was over. "And why have they kept me here? For nothing! I only hope my fiancé does not get bored waiting for me for so long! And you, Halina, do you have a boyfriend?"

No. There was no time after the roll calls to meet friends who were dispersed among the different work *Kommandos* and therefore among different barracks. Casual acquaintance needs time to develop into a deeper relationship. Besides, it was not only I who curbed my feelings; nobody wanted to get seriously emotionally involved, in self-defense against the pain of unavoidable parting. Still, I did once agree to meet a boy who swept the *Lagerstrasse.* We used to banter with each other every day on the way to work. He was witty and friendly, and we planned a date for after the evening roll call at my barracks. Later I wrote a little poem.

He ran breathlessly. With awkward affection
he whispered: "My poor golden sweetheart,"
glancing around to see no one was watching.
Our hearts pounded loud.

The love of two young ones blooms in the spring
with lilacs and jasmine and violets in May,
And ours—by the garbage at the corner of a barracks.

Love is not for us. We guiltless convicts
do not know tender words, caresses.
Our world—cruel in its naked brutality—
has no illusions.
I don't want love—but beg you with my eyes:
Give me courage!

You lower your lids. I know that we both
search in each other for strength and for help.

You turn away—and like an old man
with heavy steps and a clatter of wooden shoes,
Disappear into the darkness of night.

The covered trucks often drove along the road by the *Kommandantur* straight to the "Hujar Hill," so named after the SS-man Hujar, who carried out the executions of Jews and Poles brought here from the Gestapo, from the prison at Montellupich, or from the suburban towns and villages. They were ordered to stand naked at the edge of the ditch around the hill, and as soon as the shooting and the last screams were finished, a backhoe filled the earth over the still-twitching corpses.

Once, during morning roll call, a group of Jews who had been discovered in hiding arrived at Płaszów. They walked to the top of the execution hill, women, children, and men, two of them with prayer shawls over their heads. They all cried aloud, *Schema Israel! Adonai! Adonai!* Even a stone would have shown them mercy. Jeanette and I walked along the *Lagerstrasse* to the gate in silence. Only our Pole, Staszek, was in the infirmary. "Our medics have gone to the execution," he said. "The soldiers got a double ration of vodka for actively taking part, so the *Scharführers* have also developed a craving for shooting."

I was sweeping the sickbay, when a young SS man named Fischer staggered in with a colleague, finishing a sentence: ". . . and he refused to crawl into the ditch! And did you notice that young, pretty one with the old bitch? She calls out to me, 'You have a mother, too. Have pity! Have a heart!' *Ich habe kein Herz! Zang-Bang! war sie aus!* I don't have a heart! Wham-bang and you're gone!"

Büttner came in with a sheaf of papers to be signed. As head of the infirmary, he took part in the executions, and he had to sign off on the death certificate, just as on a legal verdict! He was deathly white and he barked at Fischer, "*Sie sind betrunken! Geh'n Sie schlafen!* You are drunk! Go home and sleep!" As Fischer walked out, Büttner muttered, "*Zwanzig Jahre alt und auch schon ein Mörder geworden!* Twenty years old and already a murderer!"

Do you still believe in miracles,
nobleness, power of goodness?
Do you still believe in God?
Do you really? you idiots!

Did it still seem to you
that everything will be all right?
You lift your hands to the sky
Oh, God!—you beg and cry

While God, who made us equal
from the same clay, young and old,
sent us such cruel punishment
without our fault!

Powerful great and severe,
He sent us all into the depth
of darkness, despair, and torture!
God unforgiving till death . . .

Christ was supposed to redeem
all human through His death.
But we, in tears, pain, and blood
have to save us *ourselves.*

Büttner was about thirty years old and a clerk by profession, employed in
the health service in Salzderhelden near Hamburg. I have no idea how or why
he got into the SS and onto the staff of the concentration camps. *"Dumm aber
anständig,* dumb but decent," is how Jeannette Suchestow characterized him.

He differed, indeed, from his colleagues. Every German in Płaszów, even
the female wardens, and every Kapo, Block elder, and O.D. screamed in
hoarse, drunken voices. Büttner, however, spoke in a normal tone. While the
faces of the SS were twisted into ugly grimaces by their contemptuous, mock-
ing sneers, Büttner's smile was friendly, human, polite. If ever he wound up
on the *Appelplatz* at roll call, he walked between the rows with the normal,
unhurried, gait of a civilian who had somehow been dressed up in a uniform,
muttering quietly, "It's going to be OK."

Reality, unfortunately, proved otherwise.

In truth, in 1944 Płaszów turned from a slave labor camp into a concentration camp in which the rules regulating those cruel institutions curbed what
had been up to then the absolute power of the murderous Amon Göth. He
continued to murder, massacre, and rob his prisoners, but he had to account
for his actions and to justify them to the authorities in Berlin. In truth, too,

the eastern front was rapidly approaching, but, as had been the case in the ghetto before the deportations, there were suddenly very many of us in the camp. Transports of prisoners from the liquidated outcamps of Płaszów arrived one after the other—from the camp of Wieliczka, for example, where four young boys hid themselves in the salt mine before the evacuation. Polish miners informed the Germans and dogs sniffed them out. Herded in from Wieliczka, the boys awaited their verdict in the bunkers of Płaszów. They swung from the gallows. I knew two of them from the *Fliegerhorst*: Zenek Fuchs, Hela's brother, and Roman Spielman, who—a badly shaken Büttner who had been present at the execution told us—threw himself at the executioners, cursed them, and spat in their faces.

Now a sickly smell rose over the whole camp, a smell of burning meat or bones—an odor of decay. In a panic to remove all traces of their presence, the Germans uncovered the mass graves on the terrain of Płaszów and burned the thousands of corpses of the people murdered in the liquidation of the ghetto and the executions on Hujar Hill. On the way to and from the roll call, each one of us hauled wood for the pyres. Seventeen wagons of ashes were taken out of the camp. Perhaps that gave rise to the macabre jokes that we would all be turned into soap; that the letters RIF embossed on small bars of soap stood for *Rein Jüdisches Fett*, Pure Jewish Fat; that although we are being deported to different places, we would meet again nicely wrapped on a shelf in a shop.

All at once, transports started to leave one after another. First the Hungarian women back to Auschwitz, after them large transports, men and women separately, to Ravensbrück, Auschwitz, Flossenbürg, and Mauthausen.

The muttering about a transport proved to be true when we noticed a freight train on the siding and were assembled for the roll call earlier than usual. Standing with my group on a higher elevation of the *Appelplatz*, I saw the Kommandos arriving and positioning themselves in rows in their places, leaving a path for the Command in the center of the *Appelplatz*. The SS-men and the female wardens passed through here, while the German Kapos and the O.D. formed a cordon along the *Lagerstrasse* at the bottom.

My mother worked in the *Juden-Vermögen Abteilung*, a Kommando that came directly under the *Höhere* SS *und Polizeiführer*, the higher SS and police chief. She was in charge of the records of goods delivered to the German dignitaries. The *stinkende Juden*, the stinking Jews, had to be removed from the face of the earth, but our bedrooms and living-room furniture, our pianos, carpets, paintings, and clothing were eagerly stolen in full awareness that this constituted cheating the authorities in Berlin. A complicated bureaucracy served this end, and it was not so easy to replace the clerks. Accordingly, the office personnel was in large part untouched until the liquidation of the camp in 1945. For that reason, I was not worried now about my mother, but I kept a keen eye out for her and her office mates to arrange themselves for the roll call. Finally! Arriving late, they joined the last rows at the foot of the field, not their usual place. Suddenly, the SS men's screams ordered us to sit on the ground, their threat of *umlegen*, killing, preventing us from escaping from one group to another.

Uneasy, I watched tensely as the *Kommandos* at the bottom of the *Appel-platz* got up, and, instead of passing along the middle aisle up to the women's barracks, as was usual after the roll call, turned straight onto the *Lagerstrasse* in the direction of the gate.

There are moments when reason disappears and only instinct is left. Suddenly, without thinking, I jumped up and sprinted along the crosswalk in broad view. Shots burst out, bullets ricocheted, and one hit Pani Preger in the leg. Behind me, others followed in a wild run, but shots stopped them. I had just reached the road. "Orphan," a German Kapo who had acquired this name because he had been in Dachau for murdering his parents, mercilessly struck the women who were massed together in this terrible confusion. Noticing my mother in the distance, I tried to break through the cordon of Kapos. Viennese Tony, who knew my mother from her office and me from the infirmary, shouted, "*Weg! Raus!* Out! Get out!"

"My mother's there! I want to go with her!"

"Clear out of here, as you value your life! I pushed your mother out of the line, but that son of a bitch, 'Orphan,' struck her, and now she is already on the other side of the gate! *Raus! Los! Los!*"

I elbowed my way to the gate. The SS officers, Dr. Blanke, Schuppke, the female wardens, and others stood there, and to the side, by the wire, was Büttner. Amon Göth lorded it over everyone as he walked to the siding. The cordon of SS guards surrounded the mass of people going toward the train. I was seized with fear. Even if I managed to get through the gate, how would I find Mama in this crowd? Blanke noticed me. I was always frightened of him, but now I was past caring. "My mother is in the transport, I want to go with her, *bitte*, please." "You have to clean the infirmary. Get out of here!"

I moved to the side, but I didn't leave the barbed wire, and I stood face to face with Büttner on the other side! "I sent 'Stuka,' as though at Blanke's orders, to look for your mother and to take her back to your barracks," he whispered. "Kapo Tony is also looking for her. Go away!"

I moved a few paces away and sat down on a boulder without letting the gate out of my sight. "Stuka" was a good-natured, fat *Aufseherin*, but how would she recognize my mother, lost and helpless as a child, amid the thousands of women? I suddenly realized that for the first time our roles were reversed, and I had become responsible for her. But only a miracle could save her.

Suddenly I heard someone say, "You're sitting here, Halina, and your mother is going mad in the barracks because she thinks you've gone on the transport!" Hardly able to believe it, I ran to our barracks, and we fell into each other's arms. Apparently, my mother's not very large work detail had stood at the roll call with a *Kommando* that was to be liquidated, and she and the others had been gathered up for the transport with that *Kommando*. "Orphan" had indeed beaten her across the back. They had all been loaded into the wagons and ordered to undress and to leave some of their clothing on the track. Stuffed into the overcrowded boxcars, the half-naked women were fainting from the heat. Just then, Felicia Bannet had heard someone calling, "Regina Nelken," and she pushed my mother to the front. "Stuka" was standing there surrounded by three women, each of whom claimed to be my mother and saying that they had a daughter. But, of course, only my mother herself knew my work detail. Tony, running up from the other side of the boxcar, finally settled the dilemma.

From her bunk, Jeannette pointed out that my mother was wearing only her slip and that men were coming into the barracks looking for their families, our Felek among them. Taking cigarettes, soap, and two tomatoes from Büttner, I went around the barracks to do a trade. I was able to bring back a skirt.

My head felt dizzy. I stood by the wire fence looking at the starry sky of that hot summer night. Thanks be to you, Oh, Lord. I saved my mother. She is with me in Kraków and not on the road to Auschwitz.

I learned later that that unfortunate Płaszów transport was sent to Stutthof by Gdańsk and they all drowned in the sea.

We used to think that these transports were Hitler's revenge. News about the unsuccessful attempt on Hitler's life was too much to take in. That it had even happened! And why for goodness' sake had it not succeeded?

"The son of a bitch is lucky," Mister Coffee commented in the barracks in the morning. "Literally. Those bastards are experts in nit-picking details, but something as important as this they blow! I haven't got any change, honey, I'll give you coffee for free tomorrow."

For Hitler, fate decreed not an easy death with a claim to martyrdom, but the death of a lousy rat in his underground cellar, a slow agony among the ruins of his country and his nation.

The uprising broke out in Warsaw, the Russians stood on the banks of the Vistula, heaps of exhumed corpses blazed in Płaszów, and new ones arrived from the hands of Amon Göth. On 13 August, he rid himself of the group of prisoners who had enjoyed the highest power in the camps. They knew a lot about the huge transports of stolen goods which he had sent off for himself to Czechoslovakia. To be safe, Göth ordered them to be shot together with their families, and to make a terrifying example of them, he ordered them to be laid out in the ditch by the *Lagerstrasse*. The whole camp marched past, like a military parade, while the SS men watched to make sure that no one turned their eyes away, that everyone read the sign, "These bandits were armed and wanted to incite a prisoners' riot." Even in the morning, these powerful dead men aroused fear, and everyone preferred to get out of their way. Now, in the scorching heat of August, swarms of flies rose above the corpses. *Sic transit gloria mundi.*

And not only for them! Exactly a month later, on 13 September, Amon Göth was arrested by the authorities in Berlin for unlawfully amassing a great fortune for himself. Not for murdering and massacring, not for terrorizing thousands of people a day, but for plunder not reported, not forwarded to Berlin!

With Göth, or without him, it was evident that Płaszów was in the process of being liquidated.

After Göth was gone, the prison diet improved a little. We received powdered milk, and eggs and sugar once, and the whole camp rang with the whipping up of "kogel-mogel," a kind of custard. That was a camp delicacy. Mama sometimes brought eggs for us when she worked outside the camp, but before he fell out of favor Göth had arranged the transfer to Płaszów of her "Kommando," whose independence had been a thorn in his side. My mother had just enough time to convey my writings and poems to Hanka Łętowska, and after that our contact with Kraków was broken completely.

It was not only we who feared the transports. The Germans did, too, and how! They sat here *"wie Gott in Frankreich,"* like God in France, as their saying goes, omnipotent, dominant, accountable to no one, particularly the women. The *Aufseherin*, the female wardens, were our plague, starting with their boss, Else Ehrich. The lover of Blanke, she shared with him a noble past in Majdanek: he, the chief of the crematorium, selected people for the gas chamber; she, with a smile, led children wholesale into the ovens. We all knew Alice Orlowska, a thickset, enormous bitch with a gravelly, drunken voice, close-cropped yellow hair, and painted eyes, always with a cigarette between her teeth and a little switch under her arm. She operated on the main street of the camp by the laundry where, as a boss, she shouted, beat, and drank vodka. She had studied, masculine movements, rolling her heavy rump from side to side as she walked between the rows during the roll calls. Any woman who came within her range of vision was lost. She whipped women so mercilessly with her crop that they lost consciousness, and when they fell over she pulled them by the hair repeating, *"Wir werden sehen wer eher müde wird ich oder du,"* We'll see who gets tired first, you or me. Another warden, Luise Danz, tall, slender, and with a gaunt, boyish face was a specialist in punching jaws with her fist and at the same time bringing her knee up into a stomach. The woman she was mistreating fainted immediately. The caricature of a fat cow, Ehlert was in charge of potato peeling and knew how to hit no less than the others did. All of them hit, with the exception of two Dutch women, "Willy" and "Peter," and of kindhearted, fat Stuka. Each one of them had an SS man to carouse with and take to bed; and a return to the Reich did not exactly beckon. The independent rulers of Płaszów turned into gray cogs in the wheel of Auschwitz.

Whatever anyone wished for, the camp was being liquidated. On 15 October, a transport was leaving for Gross-Rosen. The men stood on the *Appelplatz*, the women milled around in the distance, my mother and I and Genia did, too, because we did not know what was to happen with the hospital.

Felek and Rysiek Ores were the youngest of the hospital personnel, orderlies for all work, easy to replace, but even "irreplaceability" was no criterion. Worried about my brother, I cried in the broom closet at work. Our Pole, Staszek, tried to console me. He was anxious, himself, because the Polish camp in Płaszów was under the same rule as we were. And again . . . Büttner. He wandered around the *Appelplatz* and took this one and that one out of the lines. He walked up to the hospital group where, by reason of his position in the SS *Krankenrevier*, he knew people personally. He knew that most of the doctors, if not all of them, were safe from the transport. He dragged Felek and Rysiek out, drove them onto the road, and with his eyes showed Felek the direction in which he should flee, then yelled, *"Los! Los!"* to cover himself. Felek ran at top speed toward the hospital, all the more so because he could hear boots thundering behind him. He didn't know it was Rysiek and not a Kapo. Behind them tramped Büttner as though he were chasing them. Both Felek and Rysiek remained in Płaszów until the camp was completely liquidated three days before the liberation of Kraków on 18 January 1945, considerably longer than we did.

There was one transport everybody wished to go on, to Brünnlitz in Slovakia, to Oscar Schindler's enamel factory. To get on Schindler's list was a wish that had to be paid for in gold, except for those who had worked at Schindler's before. For us, it was an impossible dream, for in Płaszów we had neither money, nor jewelry, nor any particular value to anyone except ourselves. The offices directly involved with the administration of the camp, and a handful of people from the essential services, were the only ones who could count on staying in Płaszów. In any case, the barracks were already partly dismantled. Mama's *Kommando* had been dissolved and was on the list for transport, as was Genia's. How could I let them go alone? I begged Büttner to add my name to the same list. He sighed, nodded his head, and went into the *Kommandatur*. He returned, and to my inquiring glance, grunted, "*Ja, ja dort sind schon die drei Nelken zusammen;* yes, yes, all three Nelkens are there together."

I thanked him. He stared at me in silence and I began to feel uneasy.

"For when is this transport scheduled?" I asked.

"Two or three days."

"And where to?"

"*Auschwitz.*"

The women's transport from Płaszów to Auschwitz on 21 October 1944 left relatively calmly. In the camp, which often held tens of thousands of people, hardly six hundred prisoners were left, most of them men, including forty German Kapos and a handful of Poles.

We stood for the roll call in fives, somewhere around two thousand of us, including the fortunate "Schindler Juden" from the enamel factory who were going to a special camp in Czechoslovakia. We walked out to the boxcars on the siding, each one of us with a rucksack.

When we moved from home into the ghetto, a truck had carried our furniture; from Traugutta 13 to Janowa Wola, a farm wagon; from there to Ghetto A, a pushcart, and from the ghetto to Płaszów, suitcases. And now we had only a rucksack in which were a comb, a toothbrush, a change of underwear, bread, a bowl, a small knife, and a spoon! The spoon was sacred, the last token that we belonged to civilization. Bread could be broken into pieces even without a knife and dipped into marmalade, or eaten with whatever they gave us. But to lap a soup straight from canteen or a bowl! Like a dog? No one ever parted with a spoon to the end of one's life.

We parted with Felek and Mama's friends, Bronia Feld and Regina Weiss, who worked in the KL Płaszów administration office and were needed there until the camp was liquidated. We stood in a group of five together: "those three Nelkens," Lola Wellner and Tiny, my friend from the *Fliegerhorst*. Her father, a musician, had worked with my mother and had been sent to Mauthaussen in the summer. The Germans had killed her youngest sister during the liquidation action in their small town of Słomniki; her mother and her other sister had been taken from Płaszów to a munition factory in Skarżysko. Tiny was left all alone and so she moved into our barracks and under my mother's protection.

The long procession of women moved through the gate toward the freight train on the siding without being goaded to move fast. Büttner walked alongside at the edge of the road, stopping now and then by the reddish boxcars. Ours was comparatively roomy. Before climbing in, I turned around to look once more at Kraków. After they had loaded us on for some time, we waited, for the locomotive, perhaps, because the train was standing at the siding. Büttner appeared at the open doors, followed by a youth carrying a box of cans of powdered milk. Nothing of this had reached us in the camp when Amon Göth had been the Kommandant. Now, too, it would not be of use to us for long. Büttner distributed this sweet ration the length of the entire train and suddenly clambered into our car. He stood far back inside it and bade us farewell in a hushed voice. He was truly moved.

"Someday the war will be over. Take care! Things will be well again, you will return home! I wish you *Alles Gute.* Chins up! *Lebewohl!*"

As the doors were being closed and bolted he waved to us.

I stood at the small barred window; the train picked up speed as it moved along the tracks out of the station. We sat dejectedly in the half-light of the boxcar. When the sky grew dim and the watchtowers of Płaszów flashed in the sunset, I left the little window and sat down next to Mama. The train traveled endlessly into the night.

And then someone standing near the window shouted that barracks could be seen. We got up to look. Indeed, low, even rows of barracks and vividly illuminated wires loomed in the twilight of the autumn evening. Human shadows flitted between the barracks.

At last, the train came to a halt. A barking of dogs and German screams reached us. "*Los! Raus Los!* Out, Out!"

A screeching rasp of doors. Head first, feet first, we jump out onto the ramp. Just don't get lost in the crowd. Mama! Genia! Lolusia, where are you? Where are you going to, Tiny? We were pushed from the ramp onto the road that lay between the barbed wire and barracks in the direction of the forest which was hidden from view by the train. My heart froze. On the horizon, against a background of dark trees, flames shot up to the sky.

"So it is true . . . One has to see for oneself to believe it . . . they burn people here," I whispered. There had been pyres in Płaszów, too, but here there are chimneys!

"Don't look over there, look at your feet or you will trip up. Here, take some sugar cubes. We have to eat them to give us energy and before they take them away," whispered Mama.

The road turned again into a *Lagerstrasse.* From the barracks we could hear broken questions in various languages about where this transport was from.

The weird, low building of the bathhouse—the famous sauna. We stand and we stand, we wait, not knowing for what because nothing is happening. Among us, float young men in stripes looking clean and healthy. It is impossible to communicate with them because they are Dutchmen from a *Sonderkommando*. Someone asks them in German for water. It is forbidden. Finally, it becomes clear that only tomorrow will the authorities come to take us away. We sit down wherever we are standing, right on the cement, and lean one against the other. Psychologically rather than physically tired from the long journey and the march, we lapse into a broken, feverish sleep.

That one night under the open sky has its effect. It is hard to recognize ourselves on the following day. Yellowish gray, crumpled, and aching, we sit dejected in mind and in body. There is nowhere to wash or anything with which to wash ourselves. There is nothing with which to slake our thirst. Nothing happens. The little birch forest, enveloped in gray smoke, is so sad.

Then a small, elderly German appears with a thick cane in his hand. He has a jutting jaw and protruding teeth like a shark, or like someone from the film, "Wolf-man." With his cane he herds us into the large hall of the sauna. Leave your things in the corner. Strip and wait! We will get our things back after we bathe.

Nudity is a natural condition; one figure against a natural background is beautiful, even if it doesn't have classical proportions. But thousands of naked people? Thousands of tightly crammed together naked people?

Nakedness could not be avoided in the camp, in the showers, during delousing, and on the bunks while undressing or dressing. My mother was a handsome woman with a beautiful, healthy body, but she was embarrassed to strip in public. I respected this and climbed onto our bunk only after she was in her nightgown, and in the morning I dressed first. So now, out of respect for her, I looked only at her face, as though the rest of her did not exist. When we arranged ourselves for the selection, we agreed that Mama would go first, Genia after her, and I would be at the end. If one of us were to be taken aside, I would join that group without waiting for the selection, so that none of us would have to face the worst alone. There wasn't much time to talk, but it was clear that the rejected women were to stay in this hall, while the others were sent through to the next one. Dr. Mengele stood in the doorway and wagged his finger toward death or toward life.

My mother passed the selection. Genia passed it. I passed it. Now we jostled against each other in an enormous tunnel. Out of the corner of our eyes we watched to see who was coming through behind us, and we nearly burst out laughing. It was Lolusia Wellner. Still young, very tall, and moving with the grace of a dancer, she held under each arm a large loaf of bread. "*Was hast du da*, What do you have there?" the startled doctor-criminal asked.

"*Brot zum essen*, bread to eat," answered Lolusia matter of factly, and she calmly walked past Mengele.

An illustrated magazine printed his photograph taken in Peru some thirty years older, bareheaded and with a mustache. I covered his forehead and mustache with strips of paper, and there was Mengele, staring up at me from beneath his peaked cap, with the same terrifying expression in his eyes. Looking up sideways with a lowered head . . . the pose itself makes my blood grow cold.

Suddenly, in our overcrowded tunnel teeming with naked women, men in stripes appeared and took to shaving all of us everywhere. Some women had their heads shaved completely bare. Lusia was unrecognizable and she wept. Erna Neiger tried to comfort her—"Don't worry. Where there's a head, there'll be hair!"

The women were directed from the other end of the tunnel into an adjoining hall. We all found ourselves in a vast, enclosed, windowless space. When the door to the tunnel was locked, an eerie silence descended. All at once, a shower poured down from above. "WATER!" we shouted, letting it flow freely over our parched, thirsty lips. So this really was a bath and not a gas chamber!

At the exit from the showers down a different corridor, clothes were thrown at us randomly. I got two men's pajama tops, a pair of men's socks, and a small crocheted tablecloth. Mama and Genia put on some bizarre looking dresses, as did Jeannette Suchestow, whom I hardly recognized in a tattered dress. Erna Neiger wailed at the top of her voice: "Look what they've given me, the blouse hardly reaches my bellybutton! How can I walk around with a bare ass? Tiny, your dress is far too big, you are dragging it on the floor, let's switch!" We were also issued clogs, heavy wooden shoes made out of unseasoned wood; and then they herded us off to the barracks.

We threaded our way in a long line along a road separated from the barracks by a triple row of electrified barbed wire. A gate. A road with barracks on each side. Another gate. The *Aufseherinnen* urge us on, the prisoner-guards urge us on, shouting in Slovakian. I am cold. I put the socks on my hands and wrap the tablecloth around my shoulders. The wooden clogs are huge and chafe my feet. Finally, we reach the barracks and line up for roll call. We looked at each other, not knowing whether to laugh at our clothing or to cry over our misery. We are in Lager B-IIb; in other words in Brzezinka, in Birkenau.

After we have been counted, we enter the barracks. It is dark. It takes a few moments for us to notice the contours of a stove that runs the length of the entire barracks and on either side triple-tiered bunks. Barefoot, we climb up to the top tier—the clogs must be left on the floor. There are so many of us that the Block elders make us double up on the bunks. Threadbare, thin, stinking straw mattresses. Two gray blankets for eight women. We lie down like sardines, each one on her right side, me between my mother and Tiny. I am revolted by the straw mattress, by this blanket that bites my skin. Actually, it's the lice embedded in the rough blanket that bite. I repulse myself, dressed in someone else's filthy pajamas. In the faint light German proverbs can be seen inscribed on the beams under the roof: "Speech is Silver, Silence is Gold"; "Work Ennobles"; "Cleanliness is Health."

"The sons of bitches! They have taken everything away from us—toothbrushes, soap, towels, and now they are telling us that cleanliness is health! Drop dead, you bastards!" Tiny snaps in utter fury. The vulgarities she is mouthing are at odds with her sweet, cherubic face. But this time, Mama raises no objections to her language. We lie side by side in silence. They switch off the lights. The depths of despair. I fall into a deep sleep.

Every night, I dreamed I was home in Kraków. Every morning, the terrifying reality returned. After the few first days in Birkenau, the boundaries became blurred: reality was a macabre nightmare, and the dream of freedom became "real life."

"Raus! Los! Kaffee holen! Raus, Out, take the coffee, you Kraków princesses!" The Slovakian prisoner-guards bang on the bunks with their sticks, routing us out and beating us blindly with their fists. Two of them had been in Płaszów and were now taking vengeance on the women, some of whom had treated them with contempt there. In Płaszów they had been the new arrivals to be mistreated; now our turn had come. I grope under the bunk because usually I am left with only one clog, or else two for the same foot. Today, even the one I could have used to stand on for the roll call has disappeared. I drag myself along on my bare feet, sinking up to my ankles in thick, muddy clay. Even worse is the return from the kitchen. We are all dragging a kettle of coffee—or rather a warm, brownish liquid. There won't be enough tin bowls, or equally battered mugs, for all of us. We manage to get one.

After the roll call, Mama and I go to the *Waschraum* to wash. Bedraggled women stand in line for a few drops of the muddy water that drips from a pipe in the middle of the barracks. As soon as we reach it—*Lagersperre*—we have to run back at top speed, because except for brief, specified time, it is forbidden to be out of the *Lagerstrasse.* My mother has managed to catch a bit of this dirty water into our mug. It is hard for us to figure out which is our barracks, because they are all alike. Ah! Kraków is over there, Block 20 or 22. Out of breath, we reach it the moment before the Slovakians close the gate.

A miracle! And now a second one! "Madam Nelken! I don't believe it!

Halinka! Do you remember me? Rózinka from Długosza Street 5!" She grabs us and we crowd into a tiny space separated from the rest of the barracks and from the Block elder's room.

Rózinka had lived with her mother in a ground floor apartment next door to our house in Kraków. In the evenings, they used to stand at a window filled with potted plants and gossip with the neighbors gathered by the gate. From time to time, Rózinka used to come to us for a few days to repair our linen, sew new dresses for us, or alter the old ones. For a few months now, she had been the Block elder's seamstress—a wonderful position.

Rózinka pushed us behind a curtain in the corner so that we could wash ourselves properly while she stood guard at the door. We took a bottleful of water back with us for Genia. We were supposed to come back at noon for soup. Fate had sent us a mighty protector—the little seamstress from Długosza Street.

We sneaked away furtively past the door of the Block elder's room, where a group of Hungarian women stood jabbering. All at once, one of them grabbed me by the hand—my "philosopher" friend from Płaszów! I could not understand what she was saying as she gesticulated in the Block elder's direction. Rózinka ordered us back to our bunk. After the evening roll call, the "philosopher" showed up with treasures: half a head of raw cabbage, a piece of regulation sausage, shoes and a skirt! She pulled out these marvels from beneath her jacket, explaining in German that these were gifts from the group of Hungarian girls with whom we had scrubbed the sauna in Płaszów.

"*Wir haben dich nicht vergessen*, we haven't forgotten you. From the moment we heard about the arrivals from Kraków, we searched for you. Don't cry, you shared things with us, too. Tomorrow we will bring you some bread, perhaps a sweater and an onion!"

In the camps, onion was the most desirable delicacy and a medicine more effective than other raw vegetables.

Rózinka helped my mother exchange these provisions for shoes for Genia, although she recommended eating cabbage for our health.

"I will 'organize' a pair of clogs for you somehow. The most important thing is for you to get a number. You're safer with a tattoo. Go outside now."

Our barracks filed out for the roll call. Whoever saw us now would have felt revulsion at first and only after that, perhaps, compassion. An icy rain fell, mixed with snow, even though this was the end of October. From the other barracks, screaming inmate-guards and the Kapo dragged out the remains of humans, the "Musselmen." They did not react to the beatings or the screaming, they staggered and then fell to the ground with blank expressions in their sunken eyes. We passed them on the way to the latrine. One of us asked where they were from. Nothing got through to them anymore. The following day a *Blocksperre* was announced. In the short interval before we left our rows after the roll call and reached the barracks, Mama pushed Genia and me toward a side wall where a bit of snow lay on the ground.

"Wash yourselves, quick!"

"With this dirty snow?" asked Genia in surprise.

"We won't be really clean, but you have to wash every day. One day without washing and you're lost. Like the 'Musselmen'."

I remembered her words, not only to the end of the war, but forever. My wise mother was concerned with maintaining an inner discipline, without which a human being, whether free or in bondage, is inevitably lost.

"Musselmann," "Schmuckstück": where did these terms come from? All of us whispered these words with horror, while the SS officials, the Kapos, and the inmates in charge pronounced them with inhumane and opprobrious contempt and repulsion. Physical and psychological resistance cooperate and keep a man in balance. Who inflicted the last blow of the whip to these tortured skeletons? Who screamed at them, snatched from them the miserable morsel of claylike bread? Who pushed them down, kicked them with booted foot, trampled and crushed their human dignity? When was the moment that their will to live broke down? These people, starved to skin and bones, and deadly ill, did not react anymore to yelling or beating. Unable to stand, they fell slowly down to the ground and with dull expressions in their empty, deeply sunken eyes lay in mud and excrement. The utterly destroyed, tortured human fragments, the guiltless victims of Hitler till now cry out to high heaven for vengeance.

The *"Schindler-Juden,"* Schindler's Jews, soon left for the enamel factory which their boss had moved from Kraków to Brünnlitz in Slovakia. Some women were also taken for other transports, although no one knew whether it was better to stay or to go into the unknown. It was not up to us, in any case. Rózinka delivered real shoes to us, worn out and not exactly our size, but a luxury in comparison with the wooden clogs. She also kept up her urgent reminders that it was not safe to be without a number, a file card, and an assigned job. Except for hauling kettles of coffee or soup and eternally standing at roll calls, there was nothing for us to do in the camp. Birkenau and Auschwitz were not like Płaszów with its many workshops producing goods for the Germans. This was an extermination camp, a *Vernichtungslager*, with no use for workers aside from those who carried out the daily, routine management of the camp. These staff workers were also put to death, though, and were easily replaced by new arrivals.

One day, the chief *Kommandant* of *Lager Auschwitz*, Franz Hoessler himself, appeared in our barracks with his retinue of SS officials. Clerks, typists, seamstresses, women with practical occupations were to step forward, and if they were accepted by the *Aufseherin* they were to cross over to the other side of the barracks beyond the long stove. Mama stepped forward and was accepted, and after her Genia and Tiny; I was, too, although strangely enough, I was assigned to the group of menial workers. They led us out to another, empty barracks in order to register us. I searched for my people. Tiny was there, and Genia, too, but where was Mama? Had the *Aufseherin* rejected her, after all?

Black spots danced before my eyes. Close to fainting, I forced my way through the crowd toward the exit, where the Slovakian clerks were registering and tattooing women. Hoessler stood in front of the barracks explaining something to the *Oberaufseherin*. As she turned away, I walked straight up to him and whispered, "*Herr Kommandant, bitte!*" He turned around in surprise. "*Was denn?* What?"

"You have here an excellent secretary from the Płaszów administration office, my mother. You chose her yourself. But by mistake she was left in that other barracks."

"*Płaszów Kommandantur?* Give her name and number to the *Schreiberin*, and then she will be brought to *Auschwitz I,*" he advised matter-of-factly and got into his chauffeured car.

The Slovakian functionaries standing at the door to the barracks looked at me in utter stupefaction. "Don't you know that it is forbidden to talk to the SS officials? And you were speaking to the *Kommandant* himself! You are lucky that he did not kill you right there on the spot! What did he tell you?"

"To bring the best secretary from Płaszów here at once!" I blurted out without thinking, and before they could stop me, I dashed across the empty space to our old barracks, as fast as I could go in those heavy shoes.

The gate was locked, and the German guards in the watchtowers shot anyone who was outside during the *Blocksperre*. I pulled at the doors, breaking the latch, and burst like a fury into the almost empty barracks. Only a few older women were left there, although not one of them was really old. My mother sat hunched over by the long stove. When she saw me she froze.

"For God's sake, why have you come back?"

"Nothing, never mind, come along!" I grabbed her by the hand and ran with her toward the exit. Trying to keep out of sight of the guards in the watchtowers, we ran as fast as we could to the other barracks. I thumped on the doors with my fists; the Slovakian opened it a crack and I flew inside, pulling my mother behind me. In a second, we mingled with the other women from Płaszów lined up to be registered.

Our names were inscribed onto the index cards, and we presented our left forearms for the tattoo. Still tense, my heart pounding wildly, I did not feel pain when the needle went in. One after another, all three Nelkens received their official numbers for life. Mine reads the same from left and right: A-26462.

It was quite simply a miracle that saved my mother. Everything threatened death: every word, motion, and gesture. If I had stopped to think for just one moment, I would not have dared to do anything. A true miracle. As if I had been a pawn in the hands of some other, mighty power. With thought switched off, blind instinct and immediate action took over.

Taken to the showers and given different rags from delousing, the freshly tattooed new arrivals set out on a several-mile-long march to the main camp, Auschwitz I. The road led between several parts of Lager Birkenau "A" and "B," which were themselves divided into other smaller squares all of which were separated by barbed wire. There was no escape from here. Even if one could have sneaked out through the electrified wire of one camp, there was still a second, a third, a tenth camp, as in a nightmarish labyrinth.

Again a bath, again other bizarre rags, although there aren't even enough for everyone. We will receive more in our barracks. An evening rain is starting as we walk half-naked through a gate bearing the sign "*ARBEIT MACHT FREI*" and into the men's camp. There are no wooden barracks here, but two-storey red-brick blocks instead. The first two on the left, one behind the other, have been sealed off for us with barbed wire.

Washrooms and toilets. Stairs! For more than two years I have not walked up stairs. On the second floor there are very large halls and bunks. Windows! We congratulate ourselves on getting here, though the Slovakians in charge harass us here as well. We receive blankets and some ragged clothing so that we have something to wear at the roll call in front of the block. The following day, an old *Oberscharführer*, Sell, arrives for roll call and inspects us carefully. He walks between the rows and looks attentively. I stand in the last row of five, but because of my height, I always tower above the others. He looks at me and I look straight at him, but I am relieved when he moves away. Here and there, he inquires about people's occupation. Slowly, he turns back, stops in front of our group, and pointing at me, asks an unbelievable question:

"What are you doing among these Jews?" He uses the polite form, "*Sie.*"

"I am one of them."

"Profession?"

"Laboratory assistant and draftsman," I reply, because that had been on my *Kennkarte.*

"Where did you work in Płaszów?" he asks, using the informal "*du*" now.

"In *SS Krankenrevier*, for Dr. Blanke, M.D."

"Blanke? I know him well. So, how was life there? Good?"

"Better than here!" I say without thinking, and almost squeal because my mother pinches me for talking so stupidly.

In the afternoon, a large group from our block was ordered to go to the bath again. As we were waiting for our clothes to come back from delousing, the *Aufseherin* and some SS men came to select people to work. We were standing in groups, naked: clerks, seamstresses, nurses, and maids. I and four others were with a group of painters and decorators.

Sell arrived at the door and shouted, "Laboratory assistants step out!" "There aren't any here, *Herr Arbeitseinsatzführer*," the *Aufseherin* respectfully reported. Sell did not give up. "There is one quite exceptional one who also knows drafting."

"Could he be looking for me?" I thought, and I curled myself up because I was naked. "The painters are here," said the *Aufseherin*, pointing to our group. "Good," said Sell, and he assigned three girls to an SS man from the printing office.

Standing by myself, I started to worry, because not too many of us were left. When Sell came close to my corner again, I whispered that I really could draw well. "How about typing?" "Yes, I can type, though not with great speed," I admitted honestly. "*Gut, Diese kommt zu mir*, this one's coming with me." He turned to the *Aufseherin*. "Please take down her name and number for the *Arbeitseinsatz-Kartei*."

The Slovakian clerk glanced at me with a jaundiced eye. "Well, did you ever luck out! A 'Prominent'!"

My mother had been ordered to sweep the block, and she had not been with us in the showers. We were happy about my good assignment, but my mood changed when it turned out that all of us who had work assignments were immediately moving to the women's camp in Auschwitz I. That *Frauenlager* was on the other side of the *Lagerstrasse*, not far away, but segregated behind the many rows of electrified barbed wire.

I had worried needlessly, though, because when the clerk read off the list of numbers of those who had to march out of the block, my number was not on the list. Neither were those of many others who had received good assignments. The clerk had written the numbers of her friends instead, or those of other prisoners who had paid her with cigarettes, or with delicacies from their parcels, in exchange for good placements.

We returned to our bunks, and they all marched out to the women's camp.

Nobody foresaw that Sell himself would be there to receive that transport. The number of women in the transport agreed with the list of numbers, but because *his* office worker was missing, he realized that the list had been forged. He sent the whole transport back, ordering the *Aufseherin* to punish the clerks and to deliver to the *Frauenlager* by dawn the women from the original list that he had signed. And so, at dawn, the Slovakian in charge pulled me out of our bunk and marched me off.

The office workers reported to Block elder Maria, a German Communist who had been imprisoned in Dachau in 1933. Including her time in Auschwitz, she had spent eleven years in concentration camps. She was as straight and as flat as a board. She always wore a black dress, and her short dark hair was always smoothly combed around her pale face. Her expression was always severe, as if no smile had ever graced it. She was a woman of few words, and these were always short and to the point and said in a quiet voice. Screaming was a sign of authority in the camp, but on Maria's block you never heard a loud word. In spite of being intimidated, I was not afraid of her. She was an honest, fair person, although somewhat cold and always serious, after the German fashion.

Maria glanced at me and ordered her Slovakian subordinate to issue me clothes. And so, I threw off my poor rags and put on clean, silk lingerie and stockings, comfortable shoes, and a beautiful navy blue dress with thin white stripes and a white collar. The dress was simple, but nicely cut from warm, lightweight wool. "Made in Paris," the label said. What young French girl had brought this elegant creation with her to Auschwitz? In addition, I received a coat—less spectacular than the dress—and a Turkish scarf which still carried a slight fragrance of perfume. In this elegant attire, I reported back to Maria, and then the Slovakian led me over to my new *Kommando* which was about to march out to work escorted by *Aufseherin* and German shepherds.

The office of the *Arbeitseinsatz-Kartei*, the central files of Auschwitz and its subordinate camps, was situated in a barracks opposite the main guardhouse and diagonally across from the entrance gate with the *ARBEIT MACHT FREI* sign. Sell's office was immediately on the right. Our office, consisting of two large rooms containing the registry and files, was to the right in the middle of the barracks. In the first room were two German inmates in charge of the papers and their Jewish typist, Judith, a classically beautiful Viennese girl with a Greek profile. Her sister, Lily, worked with us on the files in the second of the rooms.

We were typical of the Auschwitz community: ten young girls and three women; Catholic, Protestant, and Jewish; Austrian, Hungarian, Slovakian, and German; a Yugoslav partisan, a Czech Communist, and me, Polish.

Two rows of file cabinets stood in the middle of the room, their deep drawers full of folders and index cards for all inmates in Auschwitz-Birkenau and the subcamps: Buna, Monowitz, and the others. Each one of us worked on different letters of the alphabet. According to daily reports we received from the *Schreibstube*, the camp clerk's office, we kept track of transfers from block to block, work assignments, and the deaths of inmates. Jewish transports from all over Europe went to the gas chambers with only general remarks from the administration of the crematorium: *Verwaltung des Krematoriums gibt bekannt*—on such and such a day, so many thousand from such and such a country were gassed in Birkenau. Just that—GASSED.

In case of the death of a registered inmate, regardless of the cause—beating, "selection," starvation, exhaustion—we wrote "heart attack" or "pneumonia" on the index card, removed it from the files, and placed it into the *Totenkartei*, the death register.

On my first day, I was told to straighten up these *Totenkartei* in the next room. Index cards tied with string were stacked up to the ceiling, but a pile of them from the last few months had fallen out and was lying in a disorderly heap. I began to arrange them on the shelf when some writing in red pencil on one of the packages caught my eye: transport from Płaszów-Kraków *vergast* in May, along with the Hungarian transport. Gassed!

Shaking, I went through these index cards. He was there: Edmund Emanuel Nelken. My father.

I handled the daily reports from the *Verwaltung des Krematoriums*. There was always a long list of the names and tattoo numbers of gassed inmates. I remembered the flames blazing from the chimneys in Birkenau when I saw in what a frighteningly meticulous bookkeeping system the thousands of Auschwitz inmates were recorded, those of us still living or already on the *Totenkartei*. I did not believe that the Germans would allow even one witness to such documentation remain alive.

I pity my life,
the empty days passing
with tears—instead of laughter

I am sorry, very sorry
there is no hope for me,
it died long ago . . .

The storm seized me and carried me away
like a dry leaf.

I do not know what for, or where to go
on this terribly rocky road.
I do not know for whom or for what I wait.

I am so sorry
that fate pushed me into the mud
and drove me to the *unknown.*

How to live with so much yearning?
How to consent to such ignominy?

How can one die—when the world calls?
I am not yet twenty years old,
I am young!
     young!
       just *young!*
I am sorry for my life, so very sorry . . .

Auschwitz 1944

I got lost in the world.
I cannot find myself
and blindly tap
along a road I do not know.

I call for help, but
nobody listens.
I am so very tired.
How I long for serenity!

Auschwitz 1944

In the meantime, I was an office clerk, while my poor mother worked on road construction, and just behind our office barracks at that. I could see her every day, but I could not run out to her or give her a sign out of the window. It was torture to see her breaking rocks with a heavy hammer. Alis Bala advised me to ask the *Schreiberin,* the clerk, to have my mother transferred to our *Frauenlager.* Nothing came of it. A "Prominent" or not, I simply did not know how to demand or to bribe, and besides, I had nothing to bribe with.

Alis was a Czech Communist who worked next to me on the files. We were a friendly group without any division by rank in our daily duties. Vera, a pretty slender girl from Yugoslavia, was our *Kapo.* One day, she burst into our room in a state of high excitement. "Stop smoking! *Malchemuves* is in the corridor!" That Jewish expression, which means "Angel of Death," was our code name for Sell. And, indeed, very shortly afterwards he stood at the door and then walked around the file cabinets, asking Vera if everything was all right and how was *diese neue Polin,* the new Polish girl? *"Ja, gut,"* then he left.

I waited a few minutes, then ran to the bathroom window to see if Mama was at work. She was not there. Worried, I went back and almost collided with Sell in the corridor. Vera stood in the open door to our room and turned pale with terror. Suddenly, I heard myself whispering politely, *"Herr Arbeitseinsatzführer, bitte, bitte, darf ich Sie sprechen,* Please, please, may I speak to you?"

Surprised, Sell pointed his short leather whip toward his office: *"Da warten!* Wait there!"

I waited by the door until he had finished inspecting all the rooms and walked in behind him. Paralyzed with fear by now, I stood humbly at his desk. He said, "Well, am I worse than Dr. Blanke, *polnische Gräfin?"* Finally, I understood. He had taken me for Madame Suchestow, although she was not a *Gräfin,* a princess, either.

"I am not a *Gräfin!* Please, please, hear me out! My mother is an excellent office executive, but she is left in the *Männerlager.* You can do everything. Please, please, allow us to be together again!"

Sell turned toward the window. The uniform did not mask his deformed figure with its humped back and lowered left shoulder. He, himself, would most certainly not have passed Dr. Mengele's selection.

After a while he sat down at the desk and, playing with the whip, pierced me with his gaze.

"No one has close family here. You have your mother and you still complain? Of course I can transfer her to *Frauenlager,* but then someone else has to take her place at the road construction. Is this fair?"

"No, it is not."

He went on, "If you want to be *mit deiner Mutter* so much, I can send you back to the *Männerlager* and then both of you can break rocks together! Or I can send both of you to Birkenau where there are big ovens! Well then?"

"Herr Arbeitseinsatzführer will do as he wishes. I had to do what is my responsibility toward a parent. *Bitte um Verzeihung,* you can certainly understand my situation. If you were in my place, you would do the same."

"Geh weg zur Arbeit! Go back to work!"

I returned to our room, heartbroken. My colleagues wrung their hands. Heavens, that girl has lost her mother and herself! Sell will send them both to Birkenau! Alis and Lily treated me to a piece of bread with bacon, but I could not swallow it. Every bit tasted like bitter herbs. In the evening, terribly grieved, I marched with my group to our block to fall on my bunk to be able to weep freely at last. And there on the bunk sat Mama and Genia!

The *Aufseherin* had come for one Nelken, and not knowing which was the right one, had brought them both. Maria designated my Mama to work on the block and Genia to help her. All three Nelkens were together again.

The Polish word "kochany," darling, found its way into all the languages of multinational Auschwitz. Poles were the first inmates at this originally all-male camp. Women transports followed later, and the Poles, already somewhat accustomed to the inhuman Auschwitz routine, secretly helped the women. Hence every male who actively cared, regardless of his nationality, was simply a *"kochany."* He was often some unknown fellow sufferer who sent bread, soap, clothing, and letters through various channels. The letters were, perhaps, more important than the food. Men worked in our office, or came there every day with reports from the *Schreibstube,* men like Erwin or George, for example, both from Silesia. George was the real "kochany" of Ibi, my neighbor at the office. After the war they got married. Ibi did not return to Slovakia, but stayed with George in Auschwitz. George, Erwin, and a handful of other former inmates saved the camp from destruction after the war and turned it into a museum of multinational martyrdom and of the annihilation of European Jewry.

Erwin gave me a notebook bound in red leather. I wrote my poems in it. It was small enough to hide in a shoe or under my arm through all the camps I was in, and I still have it today. Erwin brought me a large slice of bread with bacon, saying it was from his Poznań friend, Zygmunt, who regularly sent food and letters to me through Erwin. I never met him, and I never knew what he looked like, but our correspondence and exchange of thoughts in Auschwitz brought the warmth of friendship and personal worth into our barren lives. I don't know if he survived Mauthausen, and if he did, where fate took him.

Our Yugoslavian Vera kept telling us with tears in her eyes how beautiful Split was, but after the war she married a young former inmate of Auschwitz and stayed in Poland. Her "kochany," however, was Adam Kopycinski from Kraków, the music director of the Auschwitz Symphony Orchestra. Just before Christmas 1944, the "Prominents"—the girls from our office—got permission to attend the concert and revue at the *Männerlager.* Among the inmates there were world-famous actors, comedians, opera singers, and musicians, most of whom did not survive the liquidation of Auschwitz and Mauthausen concentration camp in Austria. But then, standing on a podium, they bowed to the SS murderers and SS women wardens in the first few rows. Behind them, the male inmates stood in a dense crowd, and at the side of the podium, we, the few "Prominent" women inmates.

At the first few bars of Schubert's Unfinished Symphony, which my father had loved as much as he loved Beethoven's Fifth, I leaned against the wall and closed my eyes, unable to look at the SS-men or the rest of us in our striped clothes. Each note broke my heart. I remembered the concert hall in Kraków and my father listening intently. He is gone, gone, and, instead of him, here were his murderers, and they were listening to this heavenly music—what a sacrilege!

The film *The Green Meadow* was another bizarre entertainment. It was a torture to look at the scenery, at the fields and woods, and at the normal bustle of the everyday world in which tables were overloaded with food and people laughed and danced. What did we care about such a saccharine idyll with its happy ending? Even if this film had not been so stupid, each one of us had acquired once and for all time a different perspective on life. What we did appreciate were our own productions, sung or read aloud on the bunks.

Wann sagt man uns wieder "Gnädige Frau"
anstatt "Mistvieh"! und "blöde Sau"!
Wann zahlen wir wieder mit Marken und Franken
anstatt ein Stückchen Brot und ein bisschen zu zanken!

The anonymous German lyrics to the popular "Heimat Lied" gives me shivers even now with its contrast between the sweet melody and the frightening content:

Zwischen Weichsel und der Sola schon vertaucht
zwischen Sümpfen, Postenketten, Drahtverhau,
liegt das KL-Auschwitz, das verfluchte Nest
das der Häftling hasset wie die böse Pest.

Wo Malaria, Fieber, so viel Böses ist
und wo Herzenssehnsucht uns die Seele frisst
wo so viele sterben, ach, so kümmerlich
fern von ihrer Heimat, fern von Weib und Kind.

Posten stehen auf den Türmen Tag und Nacht
stehen schussbereit und halten scharfe Wacht.
Sie begleiten mich auf jedem Schritt und Ort
und sogar im Traume, wenn ich möchte fort!

Soll ich meine Heimat nicht mehr wiedersehen
und wie die Millionen durch den Schornstein gehen,
seid gegrüsst ihr Lieben, vom unbekannten Ort
und gedenket meiner, weil ich musste fort . . .

[Between the Vistula and the Sola, hidden among bogs, watchtowers, and entanglements of barbed wire, lies Auschwitz camp, a cursed place, hated by its prisoners like a plague. // Where malaria, typhus, and much evil reigns, and heartfelt longing devours our souls. Where so many perish in misery, far from their family homes, their wives, their children. // Guards stand on the towers day and night, armed, ready to shoot, and keeping strict watch, they accompany me everywhere, at every step, even in dreams, when I want to distance myself from here. // And if I never see my native parts again, and leave through the chimney, as millions of others have done, accept my best wishes from nowhere—and think about me, who was forced to depart.]

In 1976, when I was invited by the Alexander von Humboldt Foundation to lecture in Bonn and Berlin on "Humboldtiana at Harvard," I was also invited by the German alumni of Harvard University to attend their celebration of the bicentennial of the United States of America—a festive roasting of a wild boar in Rollandseck on the Rhein. It was "the summer of the century"—six weeks of non-stop sun and a heat wave in usually gloomy Bonn. Even the ever-so-proper Germans walked around without their jackets. We all met on the Rhein, at the foot of a hill, above which stood the grand villa and wildlife park of Baron Ferdinand von Lüdinghausen.

The view of the majestic river and the Siebengebirge was enchanting; one could see a castle, or the ruins of one, on every mountaintop. No wonder the Brothers Grimm wrote their fairy tales here!

I was about to reproach myself for daring to feel so good in Germany, when I realized that I had never been in the Rheinland before and hence I did not have any memories, good or bad. Besides, I thought, it was time to detach myself from past memories. I turned around to join the others—and suddenly I tensed up, as I had done THEN.

An enormous man with a "Raubritter's" or robber baron's, face—sharply cut features, piercing blue eyes, and "noble" dueling scars on his cheeks, our host was greeting his guests. Though dressed casually in shirt and shorts, he seemed to me to be wearing the uniform of a high SS officer. An American friend introduced us. The baron extended his left hand—I noticed that his right sleeve was empty—and invited me to join him in leading the way up the hill, where, in front of his "eagle's nest," the boars were roasting on an open fire.

We walked slowly at the head of a happy, noisy crowd, making small talk. "Frau Professor, shall we speak French, English, or Spanish?" he asked. "I am sorry, I do not speak Polish."

"We can speak in your language," I answered in German. "It is nice of you to host the bicentennial celebration. Have you been to America?"

"Yes, but not in the North. I was in Paraguay after the war." Aha!

"And what did you do that you had to escape to Paraguay?" I asked casually.

Slightly grinning, he answered in the same matter-of-fact tone, "It wasn't me. It was my father-in-law. I was in the army and lost my right arm in Russia."

"Good!" I whispered. He did not notice and kept on asking how I liked Germany? Was this my first visit to his country? Oh, not the first? Let's talk about it. Would I please like to sit at his table tonight? He introduced me to the baroness and one of his grown-up sons.

The torches were lit in the evening around the tables with food, wine, and beer. The guests ate, drank, and sang; we did, too, at our table with the baroness. She was a handsome, nice woman. It was not her fault that her father, a rich industrialist, had been sentenced at the Nuremberg trials to five years in prison. Hers was a marriage of big money and an aristocratic title: Herr Baron of Prussia.

It was an unreal evening! A big moon shone over the Siebengebirge *and the palace where Hitler met Chamberlain in preparation for the infamous Munich pact of 1938 that precipitated World War II. And here I was, singing along with the cream of German intellectual society.*

"How amazing!" said the baroness, "you know so many German Lieder! You must come and visit us again to see our wildlife park."

I did shortly thereafter. The baron showed me around the woods and clearings. It was pleasantly cool, and everywhere there were picturesque views of this idyllic landscape. All the time I wondered, had he noticed my Auschwitz tattoo?

The baron attended my lecture and invited me to a farewell party the next day, just before my departure for America. He drove me to Rolandseck and the wildlife park in his open jeep. Keeping his eyes on the narrow dirt road over the ravine, he said, "I am curious about your impressions of Germany today, as compared to your earlier stay here. Do you like the changes? Is it better?"

I almost burst out laughing, but instead gave a politely composed answer. "Of course! I am very happy with the change!"

"Meaning what, in particular?"

"Meaning, that for the first time I am in Germany as a free human being, and not as an inmate of your extermination camps."

His tanned face turned gray. The jeep braked rapidly, jolting dangerously over the tree roots. Was he going to throw me into a ravine? "What? I did not know . . . ," his voice trembled.

"I wear a sleeveless shirt all the time and you haven't noticed the Auschwitz tattoo on my forearm? It is not my telephone number!" It was an awkward joke.

"Auschwitz . . . but why?"

"Hitler knew why. I am Jewish."

His left hand on the steering wheel was shaking. Hardly audible, he whispered, "I should not have asked. I am sorry."

"You should ask. You should know now, if you really did not know then, what was going on in Hitler's Germany."

For a long while neither of us said a word. Then he turned to me. "Thank you for coming here, in spite of it all."

His wife greeted us at the front door of the villa with a guest book in her hand. "Please, sign your name here, Frau Professor, and do join us on the terrace."

The baron did not have a chance to tell her anything. He paced back and forth while I wrote:

"On the occasion of my first pleasant memories of Germany and the Wild Life Park in Rolandseck,

> *Halina Nelken*
>
> *Kraków-Poland*
>
> *K.L. Auschwitz A-26462*
>
> *Cambridge, Massachusetts, U.S.A."*

When I handed him the guest book, he read it, lifted his piercing, now deeply troubled eyes, and whispered, "Do I dare?" and kissed my hand.

On the terrace the guests—the "von" and the "zu" all German aristocrats—were seated around a large round table. The baron sat silently at my right, his eyes glued to the numbers on my left arm.

I enjoyed the elegant party, the rose garden around the terrace, the Drachenfels, the "dragon rock" across the Rhein with ships and barges, and our lively conversation, which inevitably switched to the war recollections of the older men. One of them complained how terrible it was in the Russian POW camp, having not enough meat, only half a loaf of bread, and cabbage with potatoes daily.

I looked sideways at the baron; his mouth in a crooked sarcastic grin said without words: "You are not going to impress her, you idiot." There was a silent alliance between us two, because no one else knew.

After coffee, everybody began to sing. The Germans are a musical people. We sang waltzes and operettas, tangos, and of course, Lieder. And then, suddenly, the "Heimat Lied." Oh, no!

"Why don't you join us in the singing? Don't you know the text?"

"I do, but a different one."

"Is there a second text to 'Heimat Lied'? Please, sing it to us!"

"I am not sure that you would want to hear it!"

"Please, please! Do sing it, please!"

"Well, remember, it was you who insisted!"

And I sang our Auschwitz version of their "Heimat Lied." The villa, the idyllic landscape, all of it disappeared, and I was again on our block in Auschwitz, singing in a sad, quiet voice. After I finished, there was silence.

The baron sat motionless with clenched lips, tears rolling down over his dueling scars. The baroness got up and embraced me.

What an unexpected switch! It was supposed to be a jolly farewell party, and it had turned into a confrontation with the past! Never before had they met a "Häftling," alive or dead. The sudden realization of the war crimes of their own nation left these people so shaken that it seemed as if I—I!—had to calm them down.

"Who wrote this song?"

"An anonymous German. All of us other nationals identified with it. This song, however, belongs to your German heritage." The baron remained silent for the rest of the evening.

Early the following morning, just before my departure, he telephoned to wish me a good trip and then asked, "Please, would you write down the text of the Auschwitz song for me? It will be a most important legacy for my sons and their children."

In the *Männerlager* of Auschwitz I, to the left of the main entrance gate with the cynical sign, *"Arbeit macht frei,"* stood two women's blocks. I could see them from our office, but only twice did I manage to go there to deliver some papers for the Block elder. I met a few girls I knew, and I brought warm underwear for Tiny. We laughed, because they were much too long for her and came down to the middle of her calves. During this visit, the entire camp suddenly disappeared in an artificial fog—a daytime air raid! The Russian "kukuruźniks" sometimes flew over the camp at night and they lighted up the sky with reflectors which the Germans called "Stalin's Christmas trees." There was a rumor that for protection against the air raids the SS-men would move into the inmates' blocks.

"To hell with this, including all of us!" Tiny spat out in a surly voice. "What good is it that the Russians are closing in? The Germans will finish us off at the last minute. Nothing can help us!"

But an event that had happened before we arrived in Auschwitz saved our transport from immediate immolation: the October 1944 revolt of the inmates from the *Sonderkommando*. They threw the chief of the crematorium into the flames alive, blew up the building with dynamite, cut the electric barbed wire, and ran away in all directions. It was not known at this time whether anyone had succeeded in escaping, or whether all of them had been caught and killed. The Auschwitz and Birkenau crematoria could hardly keep up with turning the gassed people into ashes, and there the largest crematorium had been destroyed in the revolt.

The death machine began to stumble, killing on a much smaller scale. Instead of high technological death, we were left to starvation, exhaustion, and disease. On the way to our office, we passed by the experimental block, and once we saw the unlucky "guinea pigs" of Dr. Mengele being loaded onto a covered truck. Our office received an official statement from the crematorium listing their numbers for recording in the death files. The German bureaucracy was always deadly serious and strict to the point of absurdity. But sometimes it served a useful purpose.

Toward the end of November, a German entered our office together with Büttner! Something had gotten mixed up in the records of our transport out of Płaszów, and he had to check them personally. Flabbergasted as I was, I tried hard not to show that I knew him. Büttner searched the files systematically, walking around our large inmates' register. Finally, he approached me and pulled out the lower file draw. Before I could reach for the folders, he tugged at the cuff of his coat, and out into the Files fell letters, folded into little squares. Büttner went on perusing the papers as though nothing had happened. He scribbled a few notes, asked me to prepare the answers by tomorrow, looked again into the register at Lily's side of the table, and left. It had been a strictly official visit.

My head was spinning; was this a coincidence, or did he know where to find me? "Prepare the answers by tomorrow" could mean preparing the files or answering the correspondence he had carried from Płaszów. But communication between the camps was unheard of—and particularly from such a mail carrier!

Erwin promised to smuggle the letters to Birkenau provided that some of the women from our transport were still there. I hid the rest of the letters in the corner of my kerchief and delivered them to our block. The addressees were overjoyed!

Felek had written that only a few inmates were left in Płaszów. They were all to be transferred soon to the camps in Częstochowa or Gross-Rosen. If the end was indeed near, Felek could escape. In time, I would discover how difficult an escape could be.

Next day, with the answers from my block wrapped in my handkerchief, I waited for the "mailman." Büttner arrived in the afternoon. I handed him a large folder, and underneath it, the small bundle of letters. He blew his nose nonchalantly on a corner of this handkerchief. Then he put the hanky under the cuff of his coat and perused the files.

Just as he was returning the folder to me, we heard heavy boot steps in the hallway. Vera hissed, *"Malchemuves,"* and there in the doorway stood Sell.

My heart froze. Before Sell had noticed him, Büttner said "Heil Hitler" and lifted his arm in Nazi greeting. His face turned chalky pale.

"*Was wollen Sie hier?* What do you want here?"—Sell was surprised.

"I am looking for you, *Herr Arbeitseinsatzführer!*"

"Here? Among the inmates?!"

"I just asked where your office was."

"Well, follow me, *Oberscharführer*," and a reconciled Sell invited the intruder into his room. Büttner's postman mission could have cost him his life.

In December, Auschwitz was covered by snow. The barbed wire resembled fluffy puffs of cotton. After the evening roll call, we had to shake off our shoes thoroughly in order not to mess up Maria's sparkling model block. All the bunks were made up with neatly folded blankets, the floors were shined, and not a speck of dust could be seen. Since our blocks were used exclusively for sleeping, such tidiness was relatively easy to maintain. Right after the morning roll call, we went to work, while the orderlies urged their own, less prominent slave girls to clean the block. There was only one free hour after the evening roll call for our errands, to visit the bunks for gossip, or to run to the always overcrowded washroom. My mother wrapped me in our blanket and sent me outside to air the bedding. Soon, others followed my example, slipping on the snow around the block. Mama also had discovered that early in the morning the washroom was empty, so that we could wash without hurrying, do our laundry, and even sleep a little afterwards before getting dressed. There was not enough time in the evening. We had to be in bed under the covers before the Block elder's nightly inspection. Every evening Maria walked through the whole hall and along all the bunks and opened the windows to let in fresh air. In the deep silence, her footsteps clattered on the floor. Then, in a calm voice, like the principal in a boarding school, she would finish her rounds, "*Gute Nacht!*"

Christmas. In the evening I heard the sound of a Polish carol played on a violin. I followed the sound to the cellars of the block and joined a group of Polish girls. Rumors were circulating about the tragedy of the Warsaw uprising. We stood between the bare walls of the cellar and quietly sang a traditional lullaby about the Christ Child. The fingers of the violinist were blue because it was freezing in the cellar. When we got to the part about the baby crying and shivering without a shirt we looked at each other because we knew how he felt. We stamped our feet for warmth and sang "They Came to Bethlehem" in a lively fashion, and then it was time to go back to our hall. Maria walked around in silence, as usual. "Merry Christmas. Sleep well!" She turned off the light as we answered in unison, "Good night, Frau Maria!"

At the beginning of January 1945, the air-raid alarms went off twice during the day. How did the Germans make that artificial fog which covered the entire camp like thick cotton? We did not go to the shelter but tended to our files as if nothing had happened.

Once, however, something out of the ordinary did happen. We saw out of the barracks window that gallows were being brought into the *Frauenlager*. Two gallows!

George and Erwin knew because the bunkers for the condemned convicts were in the *Männerlager*, and news filters through the walls. I had heard rumors as well. Four girls who had worked in the munitions factory, one of whom was named Róża Robota, had systematically smuggled dynamite in loaves of bread to the *Sonderkommando*, making it possible to blow up the crematorium.

On that frosty evening, all the *Kommandos* returned from work early and assembled directly in between the blocks for roll call. In front of us, the two scaffolds loomed dark against the brightly lit barbed wire.

The four condemned girls were brought up amid a funereal silence. The hundreds of women held their breath. Camp *Kommandant* Hoessler started to read out the sentence of death which had been decreed by the authorities in Berlin. Two bodies were hanging from the scaffold when suddenly the sky lightened—Stalin's Christmas trees, a Russian air raid! The female wardens panicked and drove us into the blocks.

We stood in the darkness of the basement in terrified silence, listening to the heavy drone of the airplanes, desperately praying for the bombs to drop on the camp and for everything to end once and for all. If the two other victims had to die, then let us die with them. Suddenly, one of the girls broke the deadly silence by reciting under her breath Julian Tuwim's poem, "The Germans in Paris."

The bowed heads rose slowly. If Tuwim only knew how his poetry lifted our spirits in that horrible hour.

The air-raid alarm was called off, and once again we stood between the blocks. The *Kommandant* read out the next part of the death sentence from Berlin, and the next two victims climbed up onto the scaffold. From one of them, a loud, clear scream in Polish shook us: "*Zemsta!* Vengeance!" And then the knot strangled her, and now four bodies, their heads twisted to the side, swung from the gallows.

The absolute silence was pierced by the shouts of the female wardens herding us back into the blocks. A few days later, the evacuation of Auschwitz began.

In the middle of January 1945, there was a commotion in the office barracks and a frantic packing of papers and files. Someone whispered that we should destroy the current files, because if the evacuation were to actually happen and people were to escape, it would be better to cover the traces. Hans, an Austrian political inmate, pointed out quite correctly that that was absurd, because each one of us, living or dead, had his own accurate file in Berlin. We agreed that it would be better to preserve these files for the future, although probably not our own future.

On 18 January, Erwin let me know that the last of Płaszów concentration camp had apparently arrived and were in Birkenau. And, indeed, Büttner appeared, and in the general confusion handed out letters, almost in full view. Our Felek had not escaped along the road. He was close to us now, and yet out of reach behind the hundreds of rows of electrified wire. Genia naively thought that we would all meet in Gross-Rosen. Here, the whole camp was preparing to march out. I received a pair of soft leather shoes which laced over the ankles and were three sizes too large. I looked like "Puss in Boots," but I walked around in them for two years after the war. We were each given two loaves of bread, and, arranged in rows of five, awaited the march out.

Auschwitz was to be razed to the ground, together with those who could not withstand the transport. It is not easy to evacuate over sixty thousand people. The head of the marching columns was already far to the west of Auschwitz, and all roads in the camp were blocked with masses of prisoners. "Los! Los! Move! Move!" shouted the SS guards, their officers nowhere to be seen because they had fled in cars. We did not know that on 18 January, when the evacuation of Auschwitz began, Kraków was already free of Germans. It was two days before we finally left behind the accursed barbed wire of the death camp and started out on the road.

The unbroken chain of inmates shuffles on wooden shoes over bumpy frozen roads across white fields and snow-covered forests. Severe frost. An enormous moon sends down its dazzling rays, as cold as steel. A starry winter sky and a mercilessly cold moon will always be associated in my mind with this terrible march. Our feet move mechanically. Our shoulders are bowed by the weight of our rucksacks and our little bundles of things. At dawn, the corpses of those who have been shot lie along both sides of the road, like rags on snow which is red with blood. Unneeded weight is tossed on the road, even those regulation loaves of bread.

I ignore Mama's warning that snow won't quench thirst, and I eat it by the handful. We wind through pristine villages, more bare fields, more forests. The guards goad us on with rifles. There are some sixty thousand of us—so many more of us than guards—yet so few of us escape. But at what point, and to where, could these thousands of people escape? Whosoever dares to accuse the Jews of marching in a cowardly, obedient fashion to their deaths would do well to recall the international masses of Auschwitz inmates—

Catholics, Protestants, agnostics—marching to Mauthausen, Gross-Rosen, and Ravensbrück.

On the third night, we were given a rest stop at a little village near Wodzisław. A veritable invasion upon snow-covered farm buildings. We found ourselves on straw in a stable, so exhausted that we were incapable even of chewing our frozen bread.

"I don't think I'll be able to move out of here. I have no energy left," Mama whispered, defeated for the first time by inhuman misery.

"Why should we move? Let's stay here," I whispered back. "It's dark, no one will notice if we burrow down into the straw."

"No, no! They'll kill us. I am going with the transport to Gross-Rosen," Genia wept. "You can stay, but I'm scared, I'm not going to escape!"

It was still dark when I woke up from a short sleep. My whole body ached. Mama and Genia were still asleep. Carefully avoiding the sleeping women, I went out of the stable. A lantern blinked in the cow barn across the courtyard. I stood at the door. The cows chewed hay; two women were getting ready to start milking. "Blessed be our Lord," I greeted them in the traditional way. Foamy streams of milk filled the pails. The warm barn and the black and white cows grazing mildly seemed a paradise.

"Do you want some milk?" asked the peasant woman, dipping a mug into the warm milk.

"Thank you. I'll take it to Mama," I whispered. "My mother isn't going to be able to withstand this torture." I did not have the courage to say, "For God's sake, give her a shelter!" because I knew that they would be risking their lives to do so, and I didn't have the right to expect anything. I looked at them with tears in my eyes, and without saying a word, I begged for help. They stood there with their full pails, embarrassed. Finally, they went out into the barnyard and into their cottage. Going back to the stable with my mug of milk, I noticed a small door to a basement hidden between the farm buildings. Dawn arrived. The guards began to yell, and from all sides, tired women came out and formed themselves into fives along the road.

In vain, I tried to persuade Genia. No. Absolutely not! She was not going to endanger herself by escaping. And now we were going to leave her by herself, because I had gone crazy in the head! Her small yellowish gray tear-stained face was swollen. That idiot was my brother's wife, and because of him I felt responsible for her. She would die if we abandoned her. But my mother could not survive any more marching.

Behind the backs of the half-conscious, sleepy Auschwitz women, I spirited my mother to the half-open little basement door; when suddenly, from her row of five standing ready on the road, Genia screamed, "Hala! Where have you run off to? You've left me all alone!" I remembered the *Fliegerhorst*, where Inga's scream had cut off my road to freedom. I did not have the heart to save myself, while that passive Genia dragged herself along with her last might. I kissed my mother's pale and cold cheek, gave her my bread, and closed the door to the basement. I was certain that she was safe now, that the farmers would hide her, but the simple fact of parting with her caused me physical pain. Gritting my teeth, I dragged myself out onto the road and joined a group of five near the moaning Genia. "Stop your screaming! I'm coming with you!" And so we walked together, through the hardest months, up to the end of the war and until our return to Kraków.

A sizable group of prisoners escaped during this rest stop. They happened on good farmers and were home by February. My mother, unfortunately, fared otherwise, as she told me when we finally found each other again in Kraków after the war. After a few hours in the basement, she had to go outside. Had our transport not passed through the village earlier, the farmers might have taken her for a witch bundled up in a blanket. To be fair to them, they did feed her and give her provisions for the road—but then they threw her out. Their farm was at the edge of the village, at a distance from other houses. My poor mother had no idea which direction to go in, or where. She waded through snowdrifts until she heard the shuffling of thousands of feet somewhere along the road. Ironically, a transport seemed her only hope of salvation. It was better to be with Auschwitz inmates than to freeze to death alone in an open field. Climbing out of the bushes by the side of the road, she stood in confusion. It was a transport of men, probably the last one to leave the camp. My mother explained to the guards that she had lost her daughter, and she gave her number and her name. At that, one of the men asked, "Halina's mother?" They were inmates from the clerk's office and from mine!

On that same day, they loaded the men's transport to Mauthausen. In a corner of the boxcar, the men made my mother a shelter with a little roof out of empty cartons. They looked after the handful of stray women during the whole journey and up to the moment when the women were sent to an outcamp in Ebensee and the men to the stone quarries of Mauthausen.

There was the Auschwitz of Mengele, of gas chambers and crematoria. There was the Auschwitz of fighting and of conspiracy. These Auschwitzes have their biographies. Where is the book about the noble, humane Auschwitz? After all, such an Auschwitz existed too! Its title is a single Polish word—Kochany!

3   BOTTOMLESS PIT

The small railroad station in Wodzisław had surely never before been host to several thousand such passengers. On all the main and branch lines, endless rows of freight and cattle cars crammed with prisoners rolled slowly on their way toward Gross-Rosen in the west or Mauthausen in the south.

Our train consisted of open coal wagons, some with a sheltered booth on one side. Nobody counted how many corpses were left on the roads anymore, but the German mania for *abzählen*, counting, survived everything, and we had to move forward five abreast in an orderly fashion. In a short time, we were divided off every few rows into groups and loaded into various wagons. When the wagons were added to a different train, our separation from one another was final.

We sat on the dirty floor, shivering with cold. Genia had lost her blanket, I had given mine to my mother. Felek was certainly here somewhere, but how were we to find him? I jumped down to stretch my legs. Another transport was moving down the length of the train, prodded on by guards with dogs. A beautiful German shepherd ran next to the wagon and the guard sicced him on me! I had nowhere to retreat, so I stood looking calmly into the dog's eyes. His naked fangs disappeared, and his angry snout changed into a dog's usual, honest expression. The guard pulled on the leash and charged at me, screaming. The dog positioned himself between us, leapt up at the guard's shoulders, and threw him to the ground. Just like our dog at home, who always attacked Felek, instead of me whenever Felek tried to turn him on me for the fun of it! In the confusion, I slipped into the next coal car to wait out the storm. The guard got up and furiously beat the poor animal, who was more compassionate than he was. He would have killed the dog had he not had to salute a few SS officers passing by. Then, together with his dog, he climbed into the sheltered sentry booth in our car. I waited awhile until I was certain that he would not recognize me, then dragged myself back toward our wagon. And suddenly—Büttner.

Unshaven and as disheveled as we were, he whispered, "Run away, escape while you are on Polish soil! Felek was sent to Gross-Rosen. Where is your mother?"

I burst into tears. At least I did not have to worry about her; I didn't know that she had been turned away from the farm and was also in some wagon in Wodzisław. But I was exhausted to the limits of my physical endurance and tortured by a sudden feeling of abandonment and loneliness. I cried help-lessly, unashamed of my tears. With my obligations, how could I escape? Mama is not here, Felek is not here, and I am with good-for-nothing Genia who lost our bread and her blanket . . . In my rucksack we had only a spoon, a mug, a comb, and a toothbrush: that was our whole treasure. In my despair I wept only, as never before.

"Wait here, I will bring you something for the road."

"You won't find us, but thanks just the same. Besides, nothing can help us now, we are lost."

"Not you, my brave girl, not you!" He smiled sadly. "I will be right back. *Kopf hoch!* Chin up!"

I waited and waited. The guards were already bolting the coal wagons when I noticed Büttner. He tossed three cans of meat and bread wrapped in a blan-ket up into the wagon. The train set off slowly. Büttner stood there with a nice smile on his unshaven face, gesturing: "Chin up! *Kopf hoch!*"

That was my last encounter with that decent man, who, thanks to testi-monies on his behalf from the former prisoners of Płaszów, was released after only a few months in a penitentiary for members of the SS. His colleagues were sentenced to many years of imprisonment, some of them for life.

I lost track of time. A gloomy sky above us, eternally gray by day, black by night. It drizzles with rain or snows on the tightly packed beggars lying side by side on the filthy floor of the coal wagon. In vain, we try to pull kerchiefs or blankets over our heads, but nothing protects us against the windy rain or icy snow. We sleep. It is as though our whole being has fallen into winter hiberna-tion. Even the "calls of nature" operate at a slowed speed. The huge German shepherd lies near me, with his head and his paws on my legs. I can't move because he immediately starts to growl or bares his teeth. After a few days, he lets me stroke him and sprawls all over us. We have gone numb beneath his weight, but we are warm.

The train drags on endlessly, stopping now and then. The guards jump down to fetch their rations, but only once do they distribute bread to us. At last, Gross-Rosen. We can't even pull into the station because the camp that was supposed to receive us is also being evacuated. We travel on through

Hitler's Germany, which has become a single camp surrounded by barbed wire. I get up with great effort and notice that as far as the eye can see there are barracks and wire: work camps; internment camps; POW camps; civilian camps; concentration camps: Sachsenhausen, Oranienburg, Ravensbrück. We arrive at this last one after two weeks, stupefied with anguish. They unload us onto the ramp, and I am immediately placed in the group that has the task of taking the corpses out of the wagons. Even these starved and emaciated corpses are too heavy for me. I faint from the effort. Tiny is standing over me; she happened to be in the wagon where I fainted, and she drags me back to our transport.

Some of the women arriving from Auschwitz are put in tents pitched in the mud. We get an empty barracks with a cement floor which had probably once been a warehouse. They have stuffed so many of us in here that we can't sit down except one on top of another. The faint light from the dim bulbs stays on all night.

At the crack of dawn—Oh, miracle!—they announced that kettles of soup had arrived! The entire barracks jumped up and stampeded to the exit where two kettles were standing. As the human wave carried me to the vicinity of the blessed kettle, someone grabbed at my coat: "I am dying! They are trampling me to death! Help!" The woman's eyes were almost popping out of their sockets. I don't know with what superhuman strength I leaned back, trying to stop the stampede. I screamed even though no one could hear me above the crowd. I don't know what miracle enabled me to squeeze through the mass of humanity changed into wild beasts by hunger. I pulled the half-dead woman through with me to the exit and leaned against the wall of the barracks, breathing heavily myself. My heart was in my throat, I had spots in front of my eyes, and I was soaked with sweat.

"Thank you, Miss. They would have trampled me to death, small as I am. Thank you for saving my life." She looked at me with a normal expression on her haggard face, and then added in a different tone of voice, "Heavens, we're going to miss out on soup, Miss! Let's go back in the barracks!"

In my mind, I waved my hand in resignation, because I did not have the energy to make a real gesture. Best sit down here, mud or no mud, and not move. At that moment I realized with horror that I was turning into a "Muselmann." With enormous effort, I bent down slowly, picked up a handful of snow, and wiped my face. The little woman had disappeared, and I, too, went back to the barracks. They had distributed almost all the soup already; I received some watery dregs and a piece of bread to share with Genia.

The following day I volunteered for work because they promised additional soup in exchange for carrying wooden planks. I didn't really have the strength, but sitting scrunched up in the stinking barracks was worse. I breathed easier walking in the pine woods. We received a mug of thick kale soup for our work. I ate half of it, carrying the rest for Genia. When I reached our barracks, I was burning with fever and only half-conscious. Typhus. Genia ate my soup, but she had not saved my place. I collapsed in a faint on top of some women who were lying on the floor and regained consciousness to find myself between Neska G. and Genia, with my head on Tiny's lap. In my moments of consciousness, I wrote a poem down in Erwin's small notebook.

Reality was worse than the hallucinations of typhus. I remember fragments: women on all sides holding me up in standing position during roll call or dragging me by the shoulders on the road to the main camp in Ravensbrück. I don't know by what miracle I ended up with the Kraków women being transported to Malchow, and in the compartment of a passenger train at that! Somehow, here, I started to get better almost immediately. Dark forests, windmills with large arms like those in Holland flashed past the windows. The small stations had names that sounded and looked Polish from the times when the area had belonged to Poland. Malchow. They unloaded us here. Outside the little town we passed a camp for French civilian workers. Not far from that, in the same woods, stood the barracks of our camp. The Kommandant was an *Aufseherin* from Płaszów, that thin stick Danz with the barking voice. We were assigned to Block 5 in a barracks divided into smaller rooms. There were more of us than there were bunks, so we had to double up.

In Malchow concentration camp, we were simply dying of starvation. No one went to work except for a few administration clerks and the privileged kitchen workers. Our only activity was to drag ourselves to the hours-long roll calls at dawn and in the afternoons. We were able to stay outside in the fresh air only for a short time after the roll call before they shoved us back into the barracks. They distributed soup once at six in the morning, and then again at ten at night on the following day, leaving us effectively without food for two days. The piece of bread which was originally divided between four people was gradually divided between ten. In every group, one trustworthy person measured this mud-and-sawdust loaf with a piece of string and sliced it into even portions. For whole days at a time, we talked about food; each night we listened with delight to the unbroken roar of heavy bombers flying toward Berlin. When the planes flew back in the opposite direction at dawn, we sent them our best wishes, imploring all the gods for their safe return to their base.

There was no longer any question which side would lose this war, nor that it would not last much longer. As our will to live grew ever stronger, so each one of us deteriorated further. The group in our room managed to stay alive only by sheer force of will. Klara B. from Drohobycz brought political news from the civilian French laborers on the other side of the barbed wire. The news was always good, the more so because it was reported to us after the distribution of our soup, which inclined us to view the world in an optimistic light. Mrs. B. (Blumenkranz?), whose translations had introduced Polish readers to the beauty of foreign literature, continued to do so with the living word; she narrated "Amok" by Stefan Zweig as smoothly as if she were reading it out loud: "Large Southern Cross moved toward the horizon . . ." Ada P. from Będzin sang Jewish folksongs as well as the lyrical repertoires of Ordonówna and Vera Grant. Pani Preger, who for all of our misery never lost the bearing of an elegant lady, sang Grieg's "Solvejg's Song" in her clear, well-trained voice. By now she had managed to forgive me that the bullet that had been intended for me had bruised her calf during the August "Action" in Płaszów.

I did not have the strength to sing, so I whistled symphonies and sonatas or the lighter music of operettas. I recited classics of Polish poetry and—even though it is embarrassing to mention them in the same breath—my own poems. It was precisely these poems that immediately resonated for all the listeners because they reflected a reality known to all of us.

The Nobel Prize does not have greater value to the winners than the extra bowl of soup offered to the "artists" with the unanimous approval of the entire room. From our bunks we watched the kettle in which, in the interests of fairness, the soup had been stirred with a plank taken from the bunk in order to prevent anything from sinking to the bottom. Had we not done this, some of us would have had only water, while others would have had potato peels or a piece of turnip. After we had all been served, the leftovers were offered to our artists and poets.

Pani Preger shared a bunk with Tiny opposite me and Genia, while on the other side slept Sala R. from the *Fliegerhorst* and always ready-to-laugh Lúska. There were two of us to a bunk. It was uncomfortable sleeping like sardines, head to foot on the narrow bunk, but we soon lost so much weight that there was enough space. Our top bunks, at least, had enough light, useful for hunting for lice. Over time, though, it became increasingly difficult to climb up and down because we were fainting from weakness.

An obsession with food. Every morning began with the question: "What are you cooking today?" From every bunk we heard delicious recipes: the Ukrainian girls near the window were cooking pierogi. Klara suggested Russian knishes made with grated potatoes. The two kosher homemakers next to Ada P. had just returned from the butcher, skimmed their chicken soup, and prepared dough for noodles. Pani Preger whipped coffee cream for her walnut pastry. Someone by the door recommended vegetable pudding and shouted, "Just a second! I have to check on my pot roast! On Wednesday I always cook a pot roast with dumplings and beets on the side."

On Wednesday. We had lost track of dates; there were only the days of the week. I made a mark every day in my little notebook, like Robinson Crusoe. If this notebook had had one more page, I would have written down the recipes for all these magnificent meals. Apart from Pani Preger, the girls on our bunks did not have much to say on the subject of cooking—only Genia knew how to make schnitzels. Lúska tortured us with visions of a crisp roll with sliced cold cuts. Sala dreamt of scrambled eggs. I was tormented by a craving for breaded veal liver with fried potatoes—once hated and now so desired—carrots sauted in butter and lemon, crowned by a desert of applesauce. Soon I became more modest: let it be a pork chop with sauerkraut. And finally, my unreachable dream was a boiled potato and bread like in that poem of mine which I had to recite over and over again to my roommates.

At the request of the other rooms in Block 5, we organized a show entitled, "In Two Weeks," because every change for the better in international politics or in our own little world was supposed to happen in this magical period of time. Hence my opening song:

> Hey, forward march, you who are healthy,
> We're off on our way to Kraków!
> Bread under our arms, forward through the forest!
> Two weeks and they'll liberate us.

My Kraków song and poem opened and closed our artistic performances. Ada performed romantic tangos; our songwriters prepared cheerful folksongs; I recited a satire about our room and drew our caricatures on the wall over our bunks because we had no paper. I also wrote my poems on a wooden plank taken from the bottom of our bunk. Janka W. copied them on a piece of wrapping paper. She had saved them for over forty years, and in 1987 she mailed copies of them to me from Australia, where fate had taken her after the war.

Malchow is situated on the Mecklenburg plain among evergreen forests totally lacking in undergrowth. The naked stems of widely spaced trees exude sadness like cypresses. Such a forest, bare from one end to the other, is not friendly to people or animals; no one can find shelter in it. Was it on purpose that they had thinned it, so that no one could escape from the neighboring camps? This black forest, lifeless even in the sunlight of spring, stood beyond the barbed wire keeping ominous watch.

Waiting for the soup, we dragged ourselves outside, greeting acquaintances from the other barracks. The sun cruelly revealed our gaunt faces. Exhausted and starved, we could hardly stand on our feet. Lena S. lay on the ground, her head on her mother's lap. What a gorgeous girl Lena had once been, with the refined beauty of a China doll! All those of Felek's friends who admired fiery brunettes with slanted dark eyes had been after her. Now, bluish-gray and yellow, Lena struggled to whisper a few words. She did not perk up even when Klara bought unbelievable news from the French laborers. Nothing came for free, so we in Room 4 resolved to take even smaller rations, so that Klara could exchange a quarter of a loaf of bread for a page of newspaper. Klara could hardly control her excitement, rushing toward us from the corner behind the latrine. A conference in Crimea! Yalta! The war would be over at any moment!

The news electrified the entire camp even though we still had no had soup. We stood on unsteady legs during the roll call, but we had joyful hope in our hearts. Danz, in her full authority as *Kommandant,* walked stiffly in her high boots among the rows of inmates, seeking the weakest victims to prey on during the hours-long roll call. More and more of us did not give her this satisfaction. We sank lifeless to the ground on our own.

That very same evening, Lena died. Cruel fate had killed the only child, but allowed her mother and father to survive the war.

Standing on this roll call, I composed a poem in my head. It was a long one, so I wrote it out later on the wooden plank. That same evening I read it aloud, but the effort proved too much for my starved body. I fainted and woke when Klara pushed a piece of bread crust into my mouth. "Only a few days more!" she said. "Hang on! You have to survive!"

Easter came. We continued our imaginary cooking. The Catholics baked ham and traditional pastries to be blessed in the church, the Jews cooked gefilte fish with aromatic spices for the Seder. By now, the same loaf of bread was being divided among eight, and very soon among ten, people. Our group of six, Pani Preger, Tiny, Genia, Sala, Lúska, and I joined up with four neighbors, so I cut the rectangular brick of muddy bread into five portions, and each couple then divided their piece in two. Genia received her half-portion in silent disapproval, so I left the privilege of cutting our portion to her. She had first choice as well, so there could be no suspicion in her mind that my piece was larger by two crumbs than hers. Our own knife made the ritual of cutting bread easier; Tiny had devised it ingeniously from a spoon handle she hammered with a rock, as in the Stone Age.

Even this minuscule ration was suspended by Danz as a punishment for the escape of two Russian girls who worked in the kitchen and suddenly disappeared. Without any food for almost two days, we fainted and fell over like dominos during the eight-hour-long roll call.

"We too *skoro pajdiom damoj*, we too will go home soon," our Ukrainian girls said. They had been deported from the Ukraine in 1942 as civilian laborers for a munitions factory. In the spring they got homesick and decided to walk back home. Just like that! From Hitler's Germany! They walked *damoj*, home, but the police caught them near Wrocław and deported them to Auschwitz. Now, in our Room 4, they sang melancholy folksongs. From the top bunk across from ours, Masza kept telling us, mixing Polish and Ukrainian words, "Corn grows at home high and gold, there is no dry sand like in Malchow. The soil there is shiny, *oczyn*, fertile, and as black as," she looked around, searching for a simile and then shouted happily, "as my dirty feet!" The whole room laughed.

At the beginning of April 1945, it was obvious that we were to go on a transport again. I borrowed a needle and from a piece of our blanket I sewed a haversack in which to keep our provisions. Mama would have been proud of my rediscovered practical talent. But it had almost similar results as my alteration of the striped inmate garb in the *Nachrichtengerätelager*, the haversack was useless, because the day before departure Danz deprived us of food. At roll call she ordered us in her high-pitched bark to leave behind blankets, bowls, mugs, and everything else—all our miserable possessions. There had been no time to evacuate the Auschwitz warehouses before the liquidation of the camp, so the Germans had made us wear as much clothing as possible. This clothing was taken away in Ravensbrück and exchanged for tattered rags. Now Danz was robbing us of the little we had been able to salvage. Whoever had decent-looking shoes had to give them up for sandals made of a wooden sole tied to the foot with a piece of string.

I stood barefoot during the roll call. For once, being skinny came in handy. I hid my little notebook, comb, and spoon in my shoes and hung them over my shoulder. They were not visible under my dress and jacket. I saved my shoes, and I threw away the "sandals" which were impossible to walk in.

Our "Room-Elder" was not so lucky. She carried a bottle of water. Danz grabbed this treasure and splashed it into her eyes. When the girl lifted her hands to cover her face, Danz noticed a blanket which she had wrapped around herself under her jacket. Like a fury, Danz tore up the jacket and blanket and hit the poor girl over the head with the bottle until the glass broke and she bled profusely.

I testified to this particular incident as a witness in the trial of the Auf-seherin in the court in Kraków toward the end of 1947. From the defendant's bench, Danz yelled in her high-pitched bark: "Der Häftling lügt! The prisoner is lying!"

The judge had to remind Danz who was the prisoner now.

Again the open cattle cars. In the sentry booth, guards and an *Aufseherin*. At least, there was enough space to sit comfortably with our backs against the walls of the wagon. A raw, damp cold. I covered my legs with the empty haversack. Danz had deprived us of any food rations the day before departure and for the two days' transport. The train traveled fast through most of the stations, but at one it was stopped by a signal. The women in the wagons shouted, "*Brot!* Bread!" Someone threw a few parsnips in the second wagon, but ours was standing in too full view in the middle of the station for anyone to dare to feed us. Night fell, the clear night of early spring. Our "sextet" sat huddled together, with Klara in the middle. We fell asleep and woke up hallucinating from hunger. Which transport was this? Still the one from Kraków, or perhaps the one from Auschwitz? The train skidded on the switches, rolled with a screech into the blacked-out station in Magdeburg, stopped, and, as it did so, we heard the ear-splitting howling of the sirens. An air raid. Not only could it be heard, but fleets of heavy bombers were also visible in the clear sky. Anti-aircraft artillery began to rumble; the women wardens and the guards jumped out of the train and ran for cover. Machine guns were positioned all around the platform and aimed straight at our train—the only long train at the station—to prevent anyone from taking the opportunity of escaping during the confusion. The next moment, all hell broke loose. The searchlights criss-crossed the sky, the bombs were dropping—straight on us, it seemed! Some women jumped up and waved their striped jackets, as if the pilots could see us and change their aim! Shots rang out at the station; the Germans thought the girls were giving secret signals to the pilots, like spies! A deafening explosion shook the ground; on all sides there were oceans of fire. I grabbed Genia's hand, hid my head on Klara's lap, and covered myself with the empty knapsack, so as not to see us perishing in flames, though not the flames of Auschwitz. Klara looked quietly at the blazing sky. "If one has to perish, then better at friendly hands," she said.

Finally, the air raid was over. The city was burning around the station. Flames shot high into the sky. Our train moved on to Leipzig, where the camp at the Hasag munitions factory, once in Skarżysko Kamienna in Poland, took us up. Hundreds of people from Kraków were producing hand grenades with the chemicals *pikryn* and *trotyl*, which changed people into "canaries," turning their clothing, hair, and skin yellow. Tiny was reunited here with her mother and sister, after two years. There were also French and Russian female prisoners, as well as Polish women who had arrived after the defeat of the Warsaw uprising.

In the barracks we received the first food after four days of our involuntary fast—a thick soup, exquisite if compared to the murky unsalted water we got at Malchow. The Block elder, a young Varsovian, called us to carry water and clean latrines. "Let's go, Jews. Learn hard work!"

We had to take out buckets full of human waste. Someone had to do it, but why did these Polish girls, who were slaves just as we were, ridicule the "lazy Jewish work" of women who could hardly stand on their feet with exhaustion? One room-orderly pushed me and squealed with pleasure when I fell down and excrement poured all over me. I managed to get up and looked straight into their eyes: "It is good luck, a sign that I will survive, go back to Kraków, and become president!"

The embarrassed Block elder took me back to the barracks and gave me a bucket of hot water to wash myself in and some clothes to change into. When I returned the bucket to her room with thanks, some Polish girls were discussing a literary program being organized in celebration of the national holiday commemorating the Constitution of Third of May 1764.

"You don't know anything about it!" said one of them.

"Oh, really?" I said, and I recited the fragment of "Pan Tadeusz" by Mickiewicz, "Jankiel's Concert," and sang the song that every child in Poland knew by heart.

"Would you like to participate in our program, Miss?" (it was "Miss," now!) the Block elder asked. "We're organizing this among ourselves, unofficially, but every talent counts!" What a change! I had suddenly become one of them, I thought with bitter irony as I returned to my bunk, where the bread ration was being distributed—one loaf of bread for five people! Twice as much as in Malchow, and the ration for the factory workers was even larger.

On the following day, we could sign up for work in the factory or in these latrines. Given the choice, I preferred not to dirty my hands producing grenades which could kill our liberators, and so I went back to the latrines. The Block elder, apparently regretting that first incident in the latrines, called me in shortly for a pleasant chat in her room.

Two years later, the Block elder and I met accidently on the street in Kraków. Warsaw was in ruins, and like many others she had resettled there. She still had not forgotten that incident in the latrines. She admitted that she had never before known a Jew personally, face to face, and she apologized again.

The next day we were transferred to a tall brick building in the environs of the factory proper. In a tall room upstairs there were eight-story bunks—Genia and I climbed to the very top. In the general confusion of the camp, we lost some of our friends. None of us was ordered to work anymore. We did not even have roll calls unless there was an air raid during the day or at night, and then we had to go to the shelter in the basement. We enjoyed this "vacation": the soup and adequate rations of bread, cheese, or a piece of sausage were distributed regularly. These few days in Leipzig gave us the strength to survive the next three weeks until the end of the war. One morning, when we had lain down again to sleep after breakfast, the sirens woke us up. I turned over on my side, but I did not feel like getting up. All of a sudden there was a terrifying bang, an ear-splitting boom, and I was thrown out of bed. When the dust settled, I realized that where there had been a wall there was now nothing. The bunks had collapsed when a fragment of the bomb shook the building. The bomb had ripped through the wall and crashed into the cellar, badly wounding many women who were hiding there.

We were ordered to return to the Polish Block elder's barracks. Some of our friends were still there, including Klara. Genia and I were given a few days' rations in advance, which meant two loaves of bread for both of us! In triumph, we took our treasures to our bunk.

Seeing how badly scratched and bruised I was, Klara sent me to the infirmary. The beds in the corridor were full of victims of the air raid, some no more badly injured than I was, and among them I saw Inga and her mother! It was our first meeting since the *Fliegerhorst* in Rakowice two years earlier, when I had procured false papers for them. But they did not have time for me now, because Inga's mother was trying to convince the doctor that both of them had to stay in the hospital if the camp were evacuated. They had made themselves at home here, and there was no way they were going on the transport! Neither of them asked where I had been during this time, or whether I needed anything; they scarcely noticed me! And for people like this I had renounced my own freedom when they had been unable to escape with me.

I left them without a word and returned to Genia, disgusted and depressed. And now came the final blow. As though she didn't know that one never parts with bread, Genia had placed our loaves on the bunk and gone off to gossip with some girls. Of course, our bread was stolen.

There was no crime worse than stealing bread. It amounted to murder. Genia suspected Pani L. from the lower bunk, whose daughter was our friend. Pani L. also knew my parents. After the war when she came to visit my mother, I could not shake hands with her, but turned away and left the room. Embarrassed, Pani L. left shortly afterwards. My mother was incensed by my lack of manners. When I explained what had happened in Leipzig, my mother, to my astonishment, justified their behavior.

"What do you want from them? They were hungry."

"And how about Genia and me, weren't we starving? And you? Would you steal bread from someone else when you knew it would hurt them, in order to save us?"

My mother thought for a moment. "I don't know. Perhaps not. But luckily you all survived. Forget how vile and ungrateful people who had once been close to you became at that time. We have to use different moral standards to judge people who lived under those conditions."

Flabbergasted and angry, I raised my voice: "But I lived under those conditions too. I didn't steal! I didn't betray anyone's trust! No one suffered because of me!"

"You are my daughter," my mother smiled. "Don't torture yourself. Forget Inga and forget Pani L."

We left Leipzig on the hunger march through Saxony without a crumb of bread. Klara gave us a carrot—our only provision. Day and night we trudged along roads strewn with the corpses of spent women, falling over during the short rest stops right where we were standing. Genia complained endlessly that she had blisters on her feet. During the shooting, a tiny splinter of bullet went through her shoe and pierced her heel. Now she really could hardly crawl. She leaned against me, and although she was terribly emaciated, she weighed heavily on my arm.

The roads were jammed with German refugees, soldiers, prisoners, and foreign laborers from the now defunct munitions factories. Behind us, a blaze—the western front. Near Dresden, a blaze in front of us—at last—the eastern front! We turned around and went back through the same towns and villages we had just come through—Riesa; Nossen; Oschatz. Like a dog chasing its own tail, we were going around in a circle running away from the front, because, according to Himmler's order, "under no circumstances, may a prisoner fall into the hands of the enemy alive." Our guards, old men from the *Volksturm*, had no idea where we were going, but they still tormented us. The front surrounded us on all sides. It was hard to believe that the powerful allied armies with their airplanes, armored cars, and tanks could not manage to catch up with, and free, five thousand women stumbling along at a snail's pace with the last ounce of strength in their bodies.

Now April warms us with its sun, now it sprays us with icy rain and snow. We hide in cement pipes by the road and immediately fall asleep. The transport, in the meantime, walks on, and no one notices our absence. Linka, a young married woman, decides that we can stay here until the end of the war, but Genia, her cheeks bright with fever, opposes it right away. She is afraid. They will shoot us. She isn't going to risk it; she is going to search for our transport and will tell everyone where we escapees are hiding. We have hardly gone a few paces when she feels faint and we have to drag her along the road by her arms. In the ditch by the side of the road, the first verdure of spring—sorrel! dandelions!

Chewing the sour leaves, we catch up with the transport. We make our way through a village. Here and there small groups of German farmers watch us from afar. The children laugh: *Hexenparade!* A procession of witches! Of course we all looked like old witches. The German prisoners among us beg their countrymen for bread, for water—but nobody moves. Perhaps they are afraid of our guards, of one another, of their neighbors; perhaps they simply do not care. At the well beyond the village, we fill our empty can with water. If someone makes a fire later, we'll put grass in it for "tea."

A rest stop. In the field before us, mounds, and in them, potatoes. The more energetic girls run ahead and return with the life-giving spoil. I don't have the strength to move and just look on sorrowfully as the mounds blacken with the starved women. Then a German peasant woman runs screaming out of the village: *"Herr Gott nocheinmal! Diebstahl! Verfluchte Schweine!* Dear God! Thieves! Damned Swine!"

A rattle of machine guns from the guards standing in a row on the road and shooting. The field turns into a battlefield, dead bodies everywhere. Our translator of German literature perishes here, together with her young niece. The girl had almost reached the road. She is lying potato in hand, eyes turned upward, mouth open, bare teeth grinning.

"Los! Los! Aufstehen! Los! Weiter marschieren! Get Up! Get Up! March On!" The guards drive us on with the butts of their rifles. We leave the German farmer to her potatoes and her field strewn with corpses and move on. Hunger hallucinations during the march at night. Could this be a street in Kraków? The royal Castle Wawel to the left? No, it is a grove by the road. Dear Lord, I am losing my mind. I sleep marching. A white tablecloth, a plate full of savory steaming potatoes and a loaf of bread. One can cut big slices along the length of bread and eat, eat to satiation . . .

Our macabre procession moves on in pouring rain. A rest stop. We lie in a ditch by the road, all eight of us covered with Linka's damp and heavy blanket. German tanks rumble down the center of the road. The first, the second, the third rolls by, the next one drives straight into the women sleeping on the road. Terrible screams. Henka and Ila Karmel, the young poets from Kraków, are left with broken legs. Their mother is dead.

"Los! Los! Raus von hier! Move! Move!" The table in my dreams disappears, there is only a Great Hunger clawing at my guts. The women mechan-

ically form themselves into fives. The front of the march moves on and is soon lost in the morning fog. From the rear there are shots and screams; someone has been killed again.

I drag Genia along. Even I am marching in a stupor. The morning is cold and clear. In the rising sun, the dew sparkles on the flowers of roadside apple and pink-cherry trees. The words of a song, "we have to gather happiness like fresh cherries . . . ," whirls in my head senselessly. Happiness!

White starched curtains are drawn into the windows of identical little houses. The eyes of the shadow-women look with hate at these sleepy, white windows. Behind them, people sleep in clean beds. No one is forcing them to march on swollen feet all over Saxony. They do not know the meaning of so many years of suffering and humiliation, of reaching the brink of exhaustion, the limit of which is this three-week-long Gehenna of starvation and lack of rest. The aroma of coffee and freshly baked bread wafts from the houses. The columns disperse. The *Aufseherin* scream; the guard does not, because right at that moment he's gorging himself on sausage. The very sight of it makes my ears ring, and black spots dance in front of my eyes. I hold on to Linka.

"I can't, I can't go on any longer," Genia moans. Her thin and sharp-featured face looks gray and old; tears flow down her hollow dirty cheeks and a louse wanders slowly across her temple.

Again Oschatz, Riesa, Nossen—how many more times are we going to cross the same towns? Leipzig to Dresden, Dresden to Leipzig, and back again.

Our procession moves into a night illuminated by a fiery glow from the fronts. At one point, I go down to the side of the road on trembling legs and fall into the ditch like a rag. Enough. If they shoot me, they shoot me. Genia's muffled moans reach me. She is standing over me and complaining, but this time to no effect. I do not have the strength to talk, to reason with her, to move. Linka and her blanket join me in the ditch.

"*Was ist los! Was macht ihr da, verfluchte Scheisse!* What's the matter? What are you doing there, you pieces of damn shit?"

"That's exactly it! We're shitting!" answers Linka and lifts her skirt. Genia also squats down under a bush. Slowly, the transport moves ahead. The voices of the guards at the rear subside. We crawl out of the ditch. Behind us twinkle the lights of a village; in front of us, through the rain, the transport shuffles, the wooden shoes hitting against the cement road. We are alone. Alone!

I suddenly feel a surge of energy. We have to vanish off this road! We reach the forest across the meadow and huddle together beneath a huge tree, covering ourselves with the blanket. I am too hungry and agitated to sleep. A thousand thoughts whirl through my aching brain, but despite every conceivable doubt, each tired beating of the heart in my emaciated chest rings out freedom! *Freedom!*

My sensitive ear catches the soft echo of footsteps. An animal of some kind? We hold our breath. The footsteps draw closer, and we hear men's quiet voices.

"*Du, da liegt doch jemand.* Someone is lying there."

"*Aber wo! Komm schnell, weg davon!* Who! Come quickly, let's get out of here!"

Before dawn, 24 April 1945. This ought to be the date of my birthday. As the sky grew light I noticed a path on the other side of our tree and on the path two military uniforms, helmets, and two rifles! If anyone were to find us here, perhaps we would be suspected of having aided two deserters! As fast as we could, we pushed deeper into the forest. Linka tore her striped jacket into pieces, we ripped the bands with our numbers off our shabby clothes, and we buried them all in the bushes. We made up a story about being civilian laborers from a factory near Magdeburg which had been evacuated after the bombardment. Our belongings were lost, and we wanted to wash and relax and search for our transport. With this fairy story on our lips, we went to the village before sunrise. At the well, we splashed water on our faces and combed our dirty hair. A farm hand from the village walked by. "Guten Morgen!" I said to him in perfect German and told him our phony story.

"I don't understand. I am a peasant from Oleszyce." he said in Polish.

"A compatriot!" we squealed happily, but did not change our little story. He led us to a small house where some Polish-Ukrainian families, deported here forcibly, lived. How kindly they welcomed us, dirty, stinking strangers that we were! They had to go to work, so they left us in the cottage with a large kettle of hot water to wash in, bread, coffee, and—a bed with a big feather comforter! I looked in a mirror and did not recognize my own face. The three of us got into bed, fell asleep immediately—and dreamt about the transport!

In the evening, the Polish farm laborers gathered to discuss what we all should do. The French and Dutch forced laborers had already escaped to the Americans. But the Germans had reinforced their sentries, and it was now hard to get out of the village. It was better to wait it out. If we wanted to go to work, the German farmers would gladly take us because there was no one left to work the fields.

During all six years of war, Genia had not lifted a finger, but now she decided to work as a maid. So did Linka and I. The farmers I worked for lived at the edge of the village of Nossen. Theirs was the last house, surrounded by open fields.

A small hallway divided the kitchen and the *gute Stube,* the living room, from the cowshed. The immaculately clean black and white Holstein cows turned around to look at me and went back to chewing hay. Fluffy white chickens walked around the neat courtyard. In a separate enclosure stood a bull. The old farmer was changing his bedding and told me to fetch fresh straw. Before I managed to return, the bull, being a bull, messed on the floor. The old farmer mumbled angrily, "What kind of work do you call this?" So I had to clean it up again. This time I waited for his inspection with a shovel under the bull's tail, just in case. "*Na, schon gut.* OK Go get breakfast."

I sat with them in the kitchen, eating bread and drinking coffee. The farmer's wife, Hannelore, with her gray hair tucked neatly under the kerchief, asked me my qualifications. "I am a housemaid," I answered, without blinking an eye; considering how many windows I had cleaned and floors I has scrubbed, it was not a lie. She pointed out to me where I should pick up the freshly laid eggs. I could not resist, and drank a few raw in the corner of the chicken shed. Hannelore counted the eggs and shook her head because there were only fifteen! She went with me down to the cool basement. At the sight of shanks of smoked ham, rolls of sausage, pails of cream, and tubs of butter, I almost fainted. Had I been able to get at that stuff, I would not have come out of that basement alive. Many of us did die right after the war, because a depleted body could not absorb food right away. Hannelore climbed up the stairs to the attic to show me the small neat room where their farm hand once had slept, "the ungrateful Dutchman who left us with no one to work the fields." If things quieted down, she would paint the walls nicely. She brought me fresh linens, a stiffly starched tablecloth, brushed nonexistent dust from the mirror, and asked where my suitcase was? I repeated my story.

"*Lieber Gott!* Dear Lord! I will give you a skirt and blouse at once."

"But, *bitte,* with long sleeves." I could not reveal my Auschwitz tattoo and was about to tell her another white lie, but Hannelore just shook her gray head with approval at the modesty of Polish girls; others would gladly parade around half-naked.

The shutters of that clean little room, cut in the shape of a heart, opened onto a cheerful spring world. For the first time in six years of war, I had my own place again, and my own bed with a big fat feather comforter. The wall over the bed was covered with numbers: logarithms, geometrical figures, fractions. Hannelore told me that the Dutchman constantly worked on numbers and calculations; they had even suspected him of being a spy, but he was just a student of mathematics. Obviously, like me in Malchow, he also had no paper on which to write. In the evenings, I went to the nearby farms to meet Linka and Genia, who had already managed to fry her chopped cutlets.

A queen never slept better than I did on this first night in my own bed. Next morning, however, the unrest and commotion in the village reached us, too.

The farmer mumbled something into his mustache and put clothes, blankets, pillows, and a lot of trunks on the large wagon pulled by two strong horses. Hannelore moaned, why, oh, why did they have to leave everything and go to relatives in Leipzig? She begged me to take care of the farm until their return. An hour later, I became the lady in charge of a house, a flower garden, a vegetable garden, an orchard, twenty chickens and a rooster, a bull, and six cows which I did not know how to milk. At noon, the cows were bellowing in pain. I ran over to the neighbors across the large meadow. Only a very old woman was left there, but she took pity on my cows and milked them. After feeding the chickens, I sat on my bed, unable to get over the reversal of my fortune. Genia arrived to visit, and practical as she had suddenly become, she checked the wardrobe in my room which was full of the farmer's and his son's suits. Then she turned her attentions to the large trunk under the bed. We opened it—an SS uniform with the emblems of a Gestapo officer! Perhaps he had once tormented my father in the ghetto? Tortured my father in Płaszów? Furious, I slammed the trunk shut and kicked it under the bed. The war was still not over.

My farmers returned home in the evening. There was such enormous traffic on the bridge that they had waited all day long and lost all inclination to escape. Whatever happened, it was better to stay in one's own place. At night, officers from the Wehrmacht requisitioned the house for their quarters. In the morning they ordered us all to run away or to hide in the cellar, because there was to be military action here. Indeed, heavy howitzers stood at the edge of the fields next to nests of machine guns. Tanks rolled behind the house in preparation for the battle. I wanted to go to Genia, but Hannelore told me to help her carry blankets and pillows down to the cellar. And so, during the last battle of the Second World War, I sat in a cellar with the parents of a Gestapo criminal. The house shook from the thunder of artillery. Each time, old Hannelore sank into her down comforter with loudly wailing, "Du lieber Gott! Jesus, Maria, um Gotteswillen!" The old man grunted something beneath wreaths of sausages in the corner.

What a horrendous irony of fate! If the little house were hit, I would perish a second or two before noon, sharing a common grave with the Germans! Finally, the explosions and the shooting quieted down, as did the mad running of the officers over our heads. The farmer sneaked carefully upstairs and came back right away. How clever! He had hung a sheet out of the window on the side of the meadow, so the villagers would not notice his white flag. We could hear the rumbling of tanks outside, isolated shots, and the sound of steps in the kitchen:

"Zind gier deutsche Zoldaten! Hände hoch! Are there any German soldiers here? Hands above your heads!"

No German speaks like this. In a second, I rushed out of the cellar and up to the hallways. I was standing face to face with my victorious *Nike,* with my *Freedom*—a tired, dust-covered Russian soldier with a smoking rifle in hand.

I threw myself on him in tears, wanting to press my lips to his hard, chapped hands. I squeezed them with all my might. He stepped back, astounded: "*Szto wy, germanskaja zenszczyna!* What are you doing, German woman?"

"No! I am not German, I am from Poland!" I tore my left sleeve to reveal the Auschwitz tattoo. Now it was he who reached for my hand, "*Ja znaju . . . Znaju . . .* I know, I understand."

The farmers came out of the cellar, and the Russian soldier blocked their way with his rifle. "*Byili dobri!* Were they good? If not, I will kill them," and he told them to go out into the yard where there stood a group of disarmed German soldiers.

I looked at the Germans, who only yesterday had been so sure of themselves, and in their eyes, in their slouched postures, in the uncertain gestures of their hands—I saw fear. Now they were experiencing what we had felt facing the merciless gaze and contempt of our German tormentors. How many times during the roundups, roll calls, and "selections" had I seen this tensed expression of terror etched on the faces of people around me! Now I could see it in Hannelore's trembling chin, in the servile bow of the farmer who tried to explain something and turned to me with a humble request. What did I care about them? How did I know whether they were cruel or honest people during the six years of war? But perhaps this son was a renegade, his Gestapo affinity not their fault? The farmer grabbed my hands begging for mercy as a hundred questions raced through my mind. Finally I nodded yes, they were good to me—after all, it was true—and the Russian let them go back home. The farmer could not hide a triumphant grin. I turned away with revulsion and contempt.

Military trucks stopped at the gate for the German POWs. A tank with a Red Star rumbled along to pick up my liberator. We shook hands: "*Do swidania, dziewuszka.* Good-bye, girl!" "Good-bye! I will never, ever, forget you. Return home soon in good health!"

As if nothing had happened, Hannelore called us to come *Kaffee trinken!* I became angry with myself. Thousands of times we had dreamed of revenge for all the enormous evils the Germans had committed, and I had been unable to avenge anything. I suddenly realized that no vengeance would be adequate, even a death for a death. I could not do it, I could not! I did not want to be their judge. Let them live with their guilty conscience—I had had enough of blood, corpses, and hatred.

I looked at the wide landscape, bathed in the rays of the setting sun, emerald green with new vegetation, and redolent of spring. Fragrant petals were falling soundlessly from the fruit trees. Suddenly I was overcome by unbounded, intoxicating joy. I ran across the meadow "full of gold dandelions" like in my poem to Freedom, calling aloud: "I survived the war! I survived Hitler! Today, I am born again! I am young! I am free! Before me, the whole world!"

My colleagues in misery from our transport were liberated a few days later in nearby villages. The guards had locked them in barns ready to burn them all, but the Russians were faster and put out the fire. The women were safe. We all discussed what to do next.

To me, the answer was clear. Kraków was my world. My home was there and my mother; whoever of my family was alive would return to Kraków. Genia, always practical, collected linen, tablecloths, plates, and pots for her future housekeeping, reasoning that she was just taking back a little of what had been robbed from her. I just took a change of lingerie, a dress, and a towel. If our house still existed in Kraków, everything I needed would be there. I didn't want German rags! Linka agreed with Genia and packed her trunk full, and both of them loaded a pushcart with their spoils. Early in the morning on 9 May 1945, the day marking the end of the Second World War in Europe, we set out in the direction of Dresden, on the road toward home.

The roads were crowded with people whose sole possessions consisted of a small bundle under their arm. On one side of the road, the Poles, Russians, Ukrainians, Czechs, and Hungarians moved east; on the other, the French, Italians, Belgians, and Dutch moved west. Leaving the hated German soil at last, everyone in this joyful crowd clutched their most cherished possession— the flag of their own country.

Saxony charmed us in the end with the beauty of its landscape and its neat villages, blooming lilacs, sunny fields and woods. Singing aloud together, we pushed our cart, the white and red Polish flag waving high, and entered Dresden in triumph. We were welcomed by the statue of Bismarck towering with ridiculously pompous pride over the ruins of the dead city.

At the station stood a long freight train decorated with green branches and filled with people. It was practically teeming with concentration camp stripes. We pushed the cart, and from all sides heard greetings:

"Servus *Häftling!* Hello, prisoners! Here is Auschwitz! Buchenwald! Ravensbrück! Oranienburg! Dachau! Who is from Prague? Here is Warsaw!"

We were helped into an open car, where the men "organized" some seats taken from a bombed-out first-class train. With its steps, roof, and buffers tightly packed, swarms of people liberated from cruelest slavery were now returning home singing merrily. Toward evening, the train, detached from its engine, sat in an open field, while the locomotive was rolled onto another track and sent back for the next transport. The company from the wagons moved into the fields to "organize" potatoes, water, and wood to make a fire. As in a Gypsy encampment, campfires blazed the length of the wagons; the air carried the haze of smoke and the smell of potatoes cooked with onion. As a joke, we arranged a roll call before distributing the delicious supper and some portions of bread. The head of each wagon had the task of writing down how many people lived in his car and of distributing the rations from the "Kommandantur" of the Red Army. We gorged ourselves on soup with our Auschwitz group of young people from Warsaw, with tall Mietek, with the veterinarian Danek, and with "underaged" Henek, so-called because he had arrived at the camp in a transport of children. There was laughter and singing in the wagons. From the military train standing nearby came the sounds of an accordion and a choir of Russian soldiers singing a melancholy tune. The dark blue transparent sky glistened with the light of a full moon; there was a fragrance of earth and fresh verdure. The world was beautiful, but most beautiful of all was the sense of untrammeled freedom.

Never before had any of us ever felt—nor would any of us ever feel afterwards—so absolutely, intensely, happy and free as we did during this unique "vacation from life" between liberation and homecoming—and the normal duties of adult human beings.

After a few days, we arrived at Rawicz in Silesia, where our piratical camp train successfully "organized" wagons filled with sugar for Berlin.

"Sugar for the German bastards! Let them swallow their coffee bitter," rose the shout from the wagons, as the stripes swooped down like locusts.

Linka found some rhubarb and cooked a compote, so thick that you could stand a spoon in it. Stuffed, we went to sign up with the Red Cross, because there were already Polish offices in Rawicz. We hardly managed to catch our train, which moved unexpectedly, only to stop again at a bridge in disrepair. The journey was happy, but endless.

In Częstochowa we decided to change to a passenger train. Linka and Genia could not be parted from their cart, but how were we to get into a crowded train with so much luggage? I was taking their suitcases from them through an open window when the train started moving, and they were left behind on the platform with their cart full of bundles. No parting was dangerous anymore. Genia would be able to find her way to Długosza 7.

At last, through the window, flickered the panorama of my native city, the dearest city in the whole world—Kraków. Only now was I really home, even though I did not know whether that home existed or whom I should find there. Trembling with emotion, I got off the train, and through my tears I looked at the well-known streets, green Planty, and a blue streetcar. I got onto it as in a dream, though I did not have a single groszy for the ticket. The conductor noticed my Auschwitz tattoo, waved his hand, and let me ride for free.

On the corner of the Main Market Square I rushed for the exit, jostling people as I went. The suitcase fell out of my hands with a bang and landed on the street. Above the city floated the silvery sound of the trumpet from the tower of St. Mary's Church, the same *hejnał* that had been played every hour since the thirteenth century. I drank in the sight of the market with its cobblestones, the slender towers of the Gothic church piercing the deep azure sky, the Renaissance building of Sukiennice. Everything was as it had been, the horse-driven carriages and the flower sellers and the *hejnał* welcomed me home!

"Take this junk out of the way!" grumbled an older passenger trying to get off the streetcar. "No one can get by! What is going on here?"

I tore my eyes away from the view, and I grabbed the irritated man with both hands and shouted loudly and happily:

"What do you mean, what's going on? Dear sir, I'm free, I'm home! I'm beginning my life!"

Our home on 7 Długosza Street was there, but my mother was not. Our apartment on the top floor was occupied by strangers who would not even let me in over the threshold to look at my own room. Our old tenants welcomed me with open arms and I wandered around, staying with one and then with another of them for the first few days and nights. Genia stayed with a girl friend in Kazimierz, the old Jewish part of the city of Kraków where she had lived before the war. We received a hundred złoty each from the Association of the Former Inmates of German Concentration Camps. We also registered at the Jewish Committee where there was a kitchen, an infirmary, and a center for the recording and researching of Hitler's crimes. At the committee one met other survivors and learned the fate of one's families and friends. It was here that I met Erna N., who was about to leave for Silesia to be reunited with her father, a survivor of Gross-Rosen. Cordial as always, she invited me to her flat on the fourth floor of Starowiślna 78. There were two rooms, a small windowless study, a bath, and a kitchen together with the essential furniture: a bed, a sofa, and two chairs. Erna asked me to take care of the apartment and to stay in it if she did not return in a week. It was thus that I inherited a new home on the Old Vistula Street, now renamed "Heroes of Stalingrad." For fun, I put a card on the front door saying, "Halina Nelken, Professional Globetrotter," not even suspecting what voyages awaited me in the future.

Glad to have my own place, I ran to fetch Genia. Looking sick and yellow, she was scrubbing the kitchen floor. Was this the "friendly care" she had counted on? "Heavens," I said, "all through the war you did not dirty your hands with work if at all possible—so why now? Come with me, immediately!" This time she came without an argument to the infirmary. She had jaundice. We were given medicine and oatmeal, sugar and a jar of honey. After a few days in our own place, she got much better, and now I could set out on the search for my mother. No one knew her whereabouts—the only trace was in the small village near Wodzisław where I had hidden her in a cellar.

The always overcrowded freight train moved irregularly, and the trip was endless. After two sleepless nights, I reached the small railroad station in Silesia. I had forgotten the name of the village, but hoped for help from the local Red Cross or from the militia, which shared offices in the same building. Everybody remembered that terrible Auschwitz transport. The commandant, an elderly man, listened to me with compassion and ordered one of his men to give me a ride on a motorcycle through the surrounding villages—not one of which resembled the village I remembered. The commandant, deciding that it must be further from the town, ordered a horse and carriage and rode with me.

At last! A path on the side of the road and familiar farm buildings: the barns to the left, the house with the basement across the courtyard. The maids looked at us anxiously. I explained to them about my mother, they grew uneasy and nodded, yes, there had been a woman. They would gladly have hidden her, but she didn't want to stay, she wanted to go to her daughter. And the Germans shot people if they found someone in the barn. They gave her food and she left through the fields.

"That's not true!" I exclaimed in despair. "It's not true at all! A lot of people were saved by the farmers in this area, and now they pay them in gold for having hidden them for a few days! My mother didn't have the strength to walk and she stayed here with my knowledge. Why did you chase her away to a certain death?"

Pale at first, the maids now turned red with shame. "It wasn't us, it was the farmer, but we were all afraid."

The commandant stepped forward. "If her mother doesn't return home, you'll pay for it. I'll find all of you and let you rot in prison for what you did! Shame on you!" and he spat at their feet. He saw me back to the train to Kraków. "You let me know, child, and I will pay them back. But the war has only just ended, people are slowly returning home, and, God willing, your mother will, too."

How different, how hopelessly sad was my second return to Kraków. I climbed up to my apartment on the fourth floor and heard the happy sound of many voices. Two sisters, Giza and Lola, a motorcyclist named Lolek and his girl friend had moved into my flat. Kraków, untouched by air raids, was crowded beyond capacity by people who had come there after the Warsaw uprising, by POWs, and by prisoners back home from the concentration camps. Every apartment was bursting at the seams, and it was normal to take strangers, or people who had shared the same misery, in under one's roof. But Genia had allowed herself to be removed from the rooms into the small windowless pantry!

"What do you want? You should have stayed here and protected the place.

Besides, it is only temporary, they will soon leave to go abroad and so will I, as soon as Felek returns." She joined the crowded party celebrating freedom in my two rooms. Instead of being amused, I was annoyed, and tried to relax on a cot in the kitchen. Early in the morning, they were all still asleep when I left for an aimless walk in the direction of Market Square. Nothing mattered anymore. I had survived the war, but for what? For whom? Who cared about me? Who was there to advise me? Who would be happy if I should eventually succeed in life? Who would understand and encourage me if I failed? Genia? I almost laughed. Where were my parents; Felek; my aunts; uncles; my cousins? I turned into Planty. Even the flowering chestnut trees covered with morning dew could not cheer me up. The avenues were still empty, but on the benches people in striped uniforms slept with bundles under their heads. My comrades in bondage slept here on their way home, and who knew if they would ever find their families?

We stand in life like naked stems of a leafless tree with cut-off branches. Our survival does not make sense.

I typed the first poem I wrote after the war in the office of the AFIGKZ (The Association of Former Inmates of German KZ). The president urged me to see the editor of the chief newspaper in Kraków, who read it and shook his head sadly. "It is terribly pessimistic," he said. "We are entering the period of joyfully rebuilding Poland and creating socialism. I'm sorry, I cannot publish such disillusioned and depressing work."

Not willing to return to a home where there was no place for me, I again walked slowly along Planty. The passersby walked briskly past me, preoccupied with their own business. Only I was in limbo. Suddenly, a young man gave me a bear hug. "Halina Nelken! You are taking a promenade on Planty, while in Mauthausen your mother is crying her eyes out over you and Felek!"

I could not believe it. Mauthausen was a camp for men only. How could my mother be there? Where from?

"I talked with her a week ago," he said. "If I had known your whereabouts, I would have taken her with us, because the Americans gave us a truck to search for our families. I found my sister here, and we are returning to Austria tonight. All my family perished, no one is left, so we will settle in Palestine. Your brother was seen in Dachau. People search and travel everywhere, as long as it is possible."

"It will always be possible!" I exclaimed. "We are living in a different world now. Soon there will be a united Europe!" Little did I know that the impenetrable Iron Curtain was already being prepared for us. "Thanks for your consolation. Perhaps by some miracle, we all will be together again!" I sighed. If I believed in such a miracle, I would have gone with him at once. But as it was, I wrote a few words on the reverse side of my poem. Should I join my mother in

Austria? Or should I wait for her in Kraków at my new address? Either way, I now had a slight ray of hope.

Three weeks later, a frail and tired woman knocked at my door. I let her into the dim hallway; surely, I thought, it must be someone for Lola. "Pardon me, but is this the apartment of . . . ?" I recognized the voice! "MAMA!"

Only then, in July 1945, on the day of our reunion, was the Second World War over for us.

The next day, my mother looked around our temporary "kolchoz" and shook her head. I knew that saying of hers, "nothing lasts as long as 'in the meantime.'" Indeed, we stayed for over ten years in this temporary apartment on the fourth floor, although without Genia and the girls.

"It is time to start a normal life," said Mama. "No more counting on financial help from some welfare committees. Tomorrow I am going to work. Hala, you are to go back to school! Genia, what would you like to do?"

Genia would not like to do anything except wait for Felek. We had no idea that he had been in the hospital in Dachau for a few months, or that as soon as he could walk again, he had enrolled at the university in Munich to study medicine. In November he would arrive in Kraków for one day only to take us all with him to Germany, although at that time only Genia left with him. This would happen in the autumn, but now it was July. My mother began to work at the Historical Commission which prepared the documents for the trials of the German war criminals. But how could she alone work for all three of us? Schools were overcrowded with students all day long, and my classes were held in the afternoon; in order to help, I was ready to wait on tables in a café before school. It was a popular job among the young intelligentsia. A waitress? Oh, no, Mama would have nothing to do with that. She approved, however, of my working as a typist for a literary journal because it was a "cultural environment." And so, for half a day I would hear, "Miss Nelken, would you type my essay, please?" And for the other half I would hear, "Nelken, you are late again. Translate Horace, please."

Every day, my mother went to her office, and I went to the offices of *Kultura* and to school. Genia waited for Felek. Normal life had begun.

Normal? . . .

The invasion of Poland on 1 September 1939 began the Second World War which ended 9 May 1945. In the meantime, there were 2077 days which had to be lived through.

No one in the world was, or could have been, prepared for the art of existence and the art of dying under German occupation—not even Jews, persecuted for thousands of years. For us, a familiar known world turned into the darkest void, where ghettos, labor camps, concentration and death camps emerged, like isolated planets united by a common goal hitherto unknown to us—extermination.

The uprising in the Warsaw Ghetto—the heroic struggle not for life, but for death with dignity—was the proudest moment in the martyrology of Polish Jews. The uprising overshadowed somewhat another, very long struggle, equally heroic, albeit one without arms and without open battle.

On those strange planets of our surreal existence, an everyday struggle for life—human life—went on according to individual cultural and religious tradition. It manifested itself in attempts to bring some order, compassion, some culture, and the satisfying of needs for education, for the arts, for poetry readings, and for concerts. It was evident in the organizing of clandestine schools, hospitals, and orphanages, and in voluntary care for the destitute as long as it was officially permissible to be sick, old, or just a small child, all of which soon became crimes punishable by death; shortly after, the strong and healthy also went by the millions to the gas chambers.

During 1942–45, the years of the Final Solution, of the *Endlösung*, this struggle still did not cease, it just took different forms.

While recalling the horror of destruction, the countercurrent of unselfish instinctive solidarity of victimized people should *never* be forgotten. It is totally wrong to imagine Auschwitz, Dachau, Ravensbrück, all concentration camps, cursed and wretched as they were, as places where everybody was on his own. If they were—no one would have survived; or perhaps it would not have been worth surviving, if indeed all men were evil.

But people helped one another: obviously families did, then members of the same community, city, or village. Later, as our world shrank, people from the same camp, the same barracks, the same bunk—just human to human, Jews or non-Jews from different nations, speaking different languages. It is enough to look through the papers of the trial of Amon Göth, the *Kommandant* of the camp in Kraków-Płaszów, and the testimonies of the witnesses talking of the *mutual* help of the Jewish and Polish prisoners. The same applies to Auschwitz under the cruel rule of Rudolf Höss.

Confronted constantly with life and death situations we had to respond at once without "maybe," "perhaps," or Hamlet-like deliberation about what should, or could, be done. To join the "O.D." ghetto police for privileges—or to stay away from identifying oneself with oppressors? To drag one's feet at forced labor so that others would have to work twice as hard? To smuggle food under the jacket, although if caught it meant the shooting of the entire *Kommando,* always punished collectively and always by death? And during the endless roll calls, the *Appel*'s, to protect a sick inmate from the hawk-eye of inspecting SS officers by moving to the front row—while all we wished then was to be invisible? Still, this is how people saved me during my typhoid fever in Ravensbrück.

And during the deportation, to go to the right with mother, or to the left with a lover? This question did not exist for parents. I do not know one example of a parent's escaping alone, but I know of many parents who could have been rescued, yet went to death with their children, small or grown, who could not.

In this stark black and white world without nuances, we faced decisions— moral choices, in fact—all the time. Although the circumstances might have excused negative behavior, I like to stress that the choices were mostly ethical. The inhuman environment intensified character traits: a bad person tended to become evil, a good one—almost a saint. Such people could be found in every group of five or ten prisoners who chose the "one just" person to cut a loaf of bread into even daily portions. Such people mobilized others to be considerate and sharing. Inner strength and moral attitude were contagious.

And people helped others, if possible, with direct action, if not, with an encouraging word, song and poem, a friendly smile or kindly gesture, a reassuring glance—all equally important for not giving up hope!

Except for the fact that the war was finally won by the Allies, there is no rational explanation why and how anyone, Jews or non-Jews, survived Hitler's concentration camps. And we, the Jewish survivors of the Holocaust.... Because millions perished—and we did not—we have the awesome responsibility to speak for all of us. We have to give the true testimony against the image often distorted by the shallow theories put forward by some "experts on the Holocaust." Their deliberations often tarnish the legacy of the twentieth century Holocaust.

I would like to recall each of us, one by one, as we were in our instinctive constant struggle for our—and others'—humanity and moral and physical survival. Striving so hard to stand upright and live a "normal life" in absurd condition and on the brink of total annihilation, we clung to the traditional values trying to retain basic human decency. Such a struggle continued during the terrible moments of our persecution and amid our constant everyday hardships. For so many of us this "everyday" was the last day of our life.

What is the legacy of the Holocaust?

To me—it is the prevalence of human integrity and goodness of heart, indestructible even in an ocean of cruelty and evil, which gave me courage, hope, and strength to survive, and to live free of bitterness and hatred.

GLOSSARY

Appel, roll call

Appelplatz, roll call grounds

Arbeiterviertel, workers' quarter

Arbeitsamt, employment office

Arbeitseinsatzfuhrer, head of work detail

Arbeitseinsatz-Kartei, card file

Arbeitsgelande, work area

Arbeitslager, labor camp

Aufenthaltsraum, recreation room

Aufseherin, female guard

Ausgesiedelte, innocent expression for re-
    located persons (in fact, deportees to the
    camps or death)

Aussiedlung, innocent expression for re-
    location (in fact, deportation to the
    camps or death)

Baudienst, construction detail

Bauhof, construction depot

Bauleitung, German construction firm

Blocksperre, curfew in the concentration
    camp

Block Alteste, block-elder

Fliegerhorst, air-force base

Fliegerkaserne, air-force barracks

Frauenlager, women's camp

Gerätelager, tool depot

Häftling, prisoner, inmate

Hauptman, captain

Hauptscharführer, SS commander-in-chief

Judenvernichtungskompanie, command
    to annihilate the Jews

Judenfresser, Jew-hater

Judenrat, Jewish committee in the ghetto

Judenrein, clean of Jews, free of Jews

Kapo, inmate, head of work detail in the
    camps

Kaserne, barracks

Kennkarte, identity card

Kinderheim, children's home

Kohlenlager, coal depot

Kommandant, commander

Kommandantur, commander's office

Kommando, work detail

Konzentrationslager, concentration camp

Krankenhaus, hospital

Krankenrevier, infirmary

Lagerführer, camp commander

Lagerstrasse, main camp road

Lagersperre, barracks lock-up

Landwirtschaft, agriculture

Lebensraum, living space

Liebesgeschichte, love story

Luftwaffe, air force

"Muselmann," starved inmate close to
    death

Männerlager, men's camp

Nachrichtengerätelager, communication
    device depot

Oberarzt, physician-in-chief

Oberaufseherin, chief female guard

Oberfeldwebel, sergeant

Oberscharfuhrer, head commander of SS
    unit

Ordnungsdienst, O.D., Jewish police in
    the ghettos

Pflichtgefühl, sense of duty

Rassenschände, racial miscegenation

Richthofenkaserne, barracks named after Richthofen, the "Red Baron," WWI air force ace

Scharführer, SS unit commander

"Schmuckstück," jewel (see "Muselmann")

Schreiberin, female clerk

Schreibstube, administrative office

Siebengebirge, mountain range in Rheinland

Sonderkommando, special commando

Strassenreinigung, street cleaning

Totenkartei, death register

Totenkopf, skull—Gestapo emblem

Unterkunft, lodging

Unteroffizier, petty officer

Vernichtungslager, extermination camp

Verwaltung des Krematoriums, crematorium administration

Volksdeutsch, ethnic German

Volksturm, "people's" militia

Vorarbeiter, foreman

Waschraum, washroom

Wehrmacht, armed forces

Zwangsarbeitslager, forced labor camp

BIOGRAPHICAL NOTE

Halina Nelken was born in Kraków, Poland. World War II interrupted her schooling; she was resettled into the ghetto and later deported to the German concentration camps. She survived eight of them, including Płaszów, Auschwitz, and Ravensbrück.

After returning to Kraków in 1945, she finished high school and studied at the Jagiellonian University, where she earned her degree in the history of art and philosophy. She worked at the National Museum in Kraków as one of the curators in the gallery of paintings, until she left Poland in 1958. Following a year at the Academy of Fine Arts in Vienna, she moved to the United States in 1959. A year later she began working at the Fogg Art Museum, Harvard University.

Nelken is the author of several scholarly books and papers on art and culture, written in Polish, English, and German. Her bicentennial exhibition and its catalog "Humboldtiana at Harvard" were awarded a prize by the Alexander von Humboldt Foundation in Bonn, Germany. She also taught classes in art history and introduced the only course in the Boston area on Polish art and history. Her long-standing research on Jewish motifs in Polish art resulted in the first ever show on this subject at Brandeis University in 1986. Her book *Images of a Lost World*, published by the Institute for Polish-Jewish Studies at Oxford University, served as the primary source for the first exhibition in Poland on this topic at the National Museum in Kraków.

At the invitation of the International Executives Service Corps, she went to Africa in 1989 and 1994 to help protect Shona art and Malawian painting—the great cultural heritage of Zimbabwe and Malawi—against dispersion in the world without a trace. She taught the community of sculptors in Harare, Zimbabwe, and painters in Blantyre, Malawi, how to catalog and record their works according to accepted museum practices.

Halina Nelken continues to write and give guest lectures. She lives in Cambridge, Massachusetts.

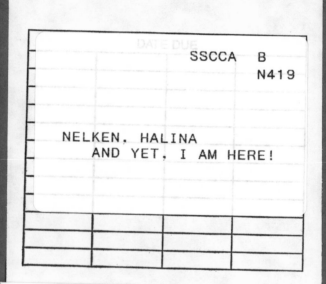